HR Analytics

The Future of HR

HR Analytics
The Future of HR

DEEPA GUPTA
Professor and Dean
G.L. Bajaj Institute of Management
Greater Noida

MUKUL GUPTA
Principal
G.L. Bajaj Institute of Management
Greater Noida

PARTH MUKUL GUPTA
Director
Zarthcorp Tech Pvt. Ltd.
Greater Noida

PHI Learning Private Limited
Delhi-110092
2025

In fond memory of ***Shri Asoke K. Ghosh*** *(October 1942 – February 2024), Founder Chairman and Managing Director of PHI Learning, whose vision endlessly inspires.*

The Legacy Continues....

Published by Pushpita Ghosh, PHI Learning Private Limited, Rimjhim House, 111, Patparganj Industrial Estate, Delhi-110092 and Printed by Syndicate Binders, A-20, Hosiery Complex, Noida, Phase-II Extension, Noida-201305 (N.C.R. Delhi).

₹795.00

HR ANALYTICS: THE FUTURE OF HR
Deepa Gupta, Mukul Gupta and Parth Mukul Gupta

ISBN-978-81-19364-90-9 (Print Book)
ISBN-978-81-19364-56-5 (e-Book)

The export rights of the book are vested solely with the publisher.

Dedicated to
our loving
SAI

&

(Late) Smt. Meena Gupta

Contents

Preface

Welcome to the world of HR Analytics, a realm where the power of data is changing the way Human Resources operates. In this book, "HR Analytics: The Future of HR," brought to you by PHI Publications, we are on an exciting voyage to uncover the vast landscape of HR analytics. This book is your trusty guide, carefully crafted to assist HR professionals, data enthusiasts, and decision-makers in unlocking the potential of HR data analytics.

In today's rapidly changing business world, HR professionals have a unique opportunity to use data and analytics to tackle complex workforce challenges and make strategic HR decisions. To do this successfully, it is crucial to grasp the core concepts, best practices, and emerging trends that underpin HR analytics.

It gives us great pleasure to introduce this book on HR Analytics, which aims to provide a comprehensive understanding of the unique challenges and opportunities associated with HR Analytics in the present era.

The book is structured in a way that it provides a theoretical framework for HR Analytics and also offers practical insights into the field. The book is divided into 15 chapters, each offering insights into different aspects of HR analytics, from the basics to advanced applications, ethics, and what lies ahead. Here's a quick overview of what awaits you:

Chapter 1: Introduction to HR Analytics lays the groundwork by defining HR analytics, explaining its importance, benefits, challenges, and what the future holds.

Chapter 2: Data Collection and Management in HR Analytics delves into collecting, handling, and analysing HR data, with a focus on various techniques.

Chapter 3: Recruitment Analytics explores how analytics can streamline the entire hiring process, from sourcing candidates to making smart hiring decisions.

Chapter 4: Performance Management Analytics looks at measuring and boosting employee performance, complete with key metrics and best practices.

Chapter 5: Employee Engagement Analytics dives into the world of employee engagement, showing you how to measure it, enhance it, and overcome challenges.

Chapter 6: Diversity, Equity, and Inclusion (DEI) Analytics reveals how analytics can drive diversity and inclusion efforts, set benchmarks, and address disparities.

Chapter 7: Ethical Considerations in HR Analytics spotlights the ethical side of HR analytics, including privacy, bias, transparency, and ethical decision-making.

Chapter 8: Implementation of HR Analytics outlines the practical steps for deploying HR analytics, covering objectives, tool selection, integration, challenges, and best practices for a successful implementation.

Chapter 9: Workforce Planning and Succession Planning highlights the importance of strategic planning and talent management in ensuring an organization's resilience.

Chapter 10: Employee Wellness and Well-being discusses HR's role in promoting employee well-being, work-life balance, mental health, and flexible work arrangements.

Chapter 11: Monitoring the Impact of Interventions explores how HR professionals assess the effectiveness of HR initiatives, focusing on tracking and evaluating outcomes to improve employee performance, engagement, and satisfaction.

Chapter 12: Ethical and Legal Considerations in HR Analytics covers the legal and ethical aspects, including data privacy, responsible data use, and data security.

Chapter 13: Future of HR Analytics takes you on a journey through the evolution of HR analytics and its integration with emerging technologies like AI and blockchain. It continues this exploration, focusing on building a data culture, leadership, technology selection, and best practices.

Chapter 14: Emerging Trends in HR Analytics explores the ever-changing landscape, with a focus on agile HR analytics and the need for continuous learning.

Chapter 15: Data Visualization and Reporting in HR Analytics highlights the importance of clear and actionable data presentation, covering effective visualization principles, tools, and techniques for creating impactful reports and dashboards, and offering guidance on selecting appropriate visuals, ensuring accessibility, storytelling with data, and developing a reporting strategy that supports data-driven HR decision-making.

In the Annexure, you will find useful tools, templates, and surveys to help you on your HR analytics journey, making sure you are well-prepared to collect and analyse data effectively.

In writing this book, our aim has been to provide a comprehensive and practical guide for students, researchers, and practitioners of HR Analytics. We have drawn upon our experiences as researchers and consultants in the field, as well as the insights and experiences of other experts in the field. We have also tried to ensure that the book is accessible and engaging, with a focus on practical applications and real-life examples. Overall, our hope is that this book will serve as a valuable resource for students, academics, researchers and practitioners, who are interested in understanding the intricacies of HR Analytics. We believe that by increasing our understanding of this important field, we can unlock the full potential of Human Resource and ensure a brighter future for all.

For students, in particular, and the faculty fraternity

For the convenience of the students, engaging case studies, practice questions, objective-type questions, and sample question papers have been added to assist them in revising the material covered in the chapters.

Teachers can access additional study materials online in the form of PowerPoint presentations organised chapter-wise, which can be accessed upon request. Visit: https://www.phindia.com/HR_analytics_deepa_mukul_partha

Regarding the challenges our students and faculty members faced while studying HR Analytics, we have gained a great deal of knowledge. In order to benefit everyone involved in HR analytics, this book is the result of the feedback we have received from them over the years and is provided to the readers.

As you navigate through this book, you will gain the knowledge and tools to transform HR management with data-driven insights. Whether you are new to HR analytics or a seasoned pro keeping up with the latest trends, this book will give you a comprehensive understanding of HR analytics, empowering you to have a positive impact on your organization and its employees. The authors with rich experience in the teaching HR have pooled their knowledge and experience to create this valuable resource. We hope it becomes your guiding light as you navigate the exciting, challenging, and transformative world of HR analytics.

Thank you for your interest in this book. We hope that you find it informative and insightful. So Get ready for a transformative journey through HR analytics. Let's explore the data-driven future of HR together!

Deepa Gupta
Mukul Gupta
Parth Mukul Gupta

Acknowledgements

Curiosity leads to research, and human beings are curious by nature. To satisfy their hunger for knowledge, they go on enquiring about more and more facts. But without the help and cooperation of other individuals, it is not possible for a researcher to reach any conclusion. To acknowledge a debt is not to pay it but merely to admit that you owe it. And so, we owe all praise to the Almighty God, under whose blessing we have been able to accomplish this task of bringing out this book successfully. Equal credit goes to our parents, Late Smt. Meena Gupta and Shri R.S. Gupta and Smt. Sudha Gupta and Shri S.K. Gupta, who made us what we are today through their hard work, devotion, support, care, love, and prayer.

Each and every work needs support and guidance for the successful achievement of its aims and objectives. This book also had support from many hands, and above all, the blessings of our godfathers, Dr. R.K. Agrawal (Chairman, R.K. Group of Educational Institutions) and (late) Maj. Gen. K.K. Ohri—AVSM who inspired us to go higher and higher in the field of education. It was their guidance, direction, and support that kept us working to make them feel proud of us.

It gives us immense pleasure to extend our most sincere thanks and deep sense of gratitude to Smt. and Shri Pankaj Agrawal, Vice Chairman, GL Bajaj Educational Institutions, Greater Noida, for their blessings, advice, and support from day one till the completion of this work.

We express our sincere thanks and gratitude to Dr. Anil Sahasrabudhe, Hon'ble Chairman, National Educational Technology Forum (NETF); Prof. T. G. Sitharam, Hon'ble Chairman AICTE; Dr. Buddha Chandra Shekhar, COO, AICTE; Dr. Ravindra Kumar Soni, Adviser II AICTE,; Prof. K.K. Agarwal, Ex-Chairman, NBA; Prof. Sangeeta Shukla, Hon'ble VC, CCS, Meerut; Shri Kunwar Shekhar Vijendra, Hon'ble Chancellor—Shobit University; Dr. VM Bansal, Chairman, NDIM, Delhi; Dr. Sandeep Pachpande, Chairman, ASM Group of Institutions; Shri Dev Murti, Chairman—SRMSCET; Prof. (Dr.) V. Ramgopal Rao, Hon'ble VC, BITS Pilani; Prof. (Dr.) Gurinder Singh, Hon'ble Group VC, Amity Universities; Prof. J.P. Pandey, Hon'ble VC, AKTU, Lucknow; Dr. Prabhat Ranjan, Hon'ble VC, DY Patil International University; Dr. Raj Nehru, Hon'ble VC, SV Skill University, Dr. Raj Singh, Hon'ble VC, Jain University, Bengluru; Dr. Madhu Chitkara, Hon'ble Pro. VC, Chitkara University, Punjab; Dr. P.B. Sharma, Hon'ble VC Amity University Gurgram; Dr. Vikas Singh, Hon'ble VC, Geeta University, Dr. Sadeep Sancheti, Hon'ble VC, Marwadi University, Prof. Vinay Pathak, Hon'ble VC, CSJM, Kanpur; Dr. Justin Paul, Professor, University of Puerto Rico, San Juan, PR, USA, Dr. Pawan Budhwar, Hon'ble Asso. Dy. VC International, Aston Business School; Jim Westerman, Director of Sustainable Business, Appalachian State University;

Dr. Rajat Panwar, Associate Professor, Oregon State University; Dr. Bhimaraya Metri, Director, IIM, Nagpur; Dr. Ram Kr. Kakni, Director, IIM Raipur, for their blessings, benevolent support and guidance.

We render our special thanks to Dr. Bilal Mustafa, AMU; Dr. Yogesh Diwedi, Swansea University, UK; Dr. Ajay Rana, VC Amity University, Gr. Noida; Dr. Rajiv Thakur, Group Director, Japuria Shool of Business; Dr. Manas Mishra, Director GLBITM; Dr. Sapna Rakesh, Director GLBIMR; Prof. (Dr.) Daviender Narang, Director, Japuria Shool of Business; Dr. H.C. Gurunani; Dr. D.S. Raghav; Dr. Rakesh Yadav, IFTM Uni.; Dr. Sandeep Chandel, DAMS; Dr. Ashwani Varshney, Japuria Institute; Dr. Monika Agarwal, Sharda University; Dr. Savita Mohan, GIMS; Dr. Shakti Prakash, IEC.

We must not forget to place on record our sincere appreciation and gratitude to our learned professors and authors of a number of excellent books on the subject whose work made us learn and understand the subject.

We express our sincere thanks and gratitude to PHI Learning and its wonderful editorial team. We express our sincere thanks and gratitude to the Founder Chairman and Managing Director (Late) Mr. Asoke K. Ghosh, and Ms. Pushpita Ghosh, Managing Director, PHI Learning Private Limited, for this opportunity. The entire team of editors, composers, and designers has contributed enormously to making the book what it is in the hands of the reader.

Our heartfelt gratitude and loads of thanks go to our children, Saideep Gupta and Junior, who were put through a lot of inconvenience while writing this book. We do express our gratitude and thanks to our entire Gupta family, friends, colleagues, and students for providing constructive and valuable suggestions.

Last but not least, our warmest appreciation goes to everyone whom we could not mention here but who has directly or indirectly supported and helped us to face this challenge of giving a present form to this book.

Deepa Gupta
Mukul Gupta
Parth Mukul Gupta

CHAPTER

1

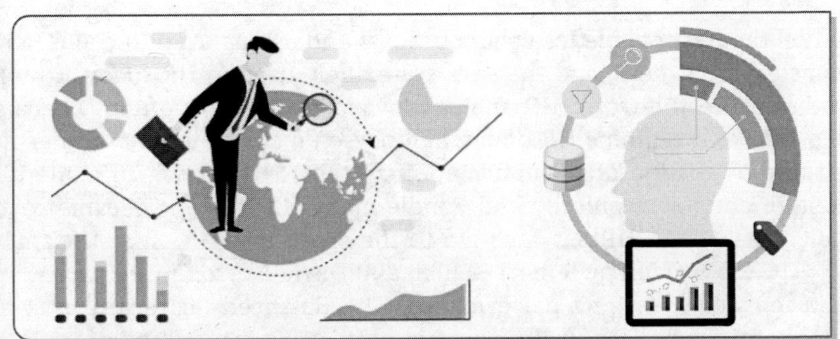

Introduction to HR Analytics

HR analytics, which is also called people analytics or talent analytics, is a new area that uses data analysis to help managers make better choices about how to manage their employees. Data has been used in HR for a long time, but it's only been in the last few years that advanced analytics methods have been used to get more information about how HR processes work.

People first started using computers to handle salary and employee records in the 1950s and 1960s. This was the start of HR analytics. But companies didn't start using data to learn more about their employees until the late 1990s and early 2000s.

Google's Chief HR Officer, Laszlo Bock, came up with the word "people analytics" in 2010. He did this because he saw how data analysis could help HR make better decisions. HR analytics is now used by companies of all sizes and in all kinds of businesses to learn more about their employees. The field has grown very quickly since then.

People who work for a company collect and analyse HR data to make their employees more productive. This is called human resource analytics. As a result, companies need to use it to make choices about hiring, training, managing performance, and keeping employees based on data. There has been a big rise in the use of HR analytics in recent years, but the practise has its roots in the early 1900s.

History of HR analytics in the past A mechanical engineer named Frederick Winslow Taylor came up with the idea of "scientific management" in the early 1900s. This is where HR analytics got its start. Taylor thought that work processes could be made more productive by looking at them and breaking them down into smaller, easier jobs. Through watching, analysis, and measurement, he also thought that workers could be taught to do these jobs more quickly and accurately. Time and motion studies were created from Taylor's ideas and were used to look at work processes and find ways to make them better.

In the early 1900s, industrial psychology also became popular. This field looked at how to use psychological concepts to make workplaces more productive and efficient. Hugo Munsterberg's work had a big impact on this area. He thought that psychology could be used to find the best people for each job. Tests and exams used to choose employees were based on Munsterberg's ideas, and they are still widely used in HR today. How HR analytics came to be in the 1980s, the word "HR analytics" wasn't used very often. It became easier for companies to gather and examine HR data when personal computers and other new apps came out. This led to the creation of HR information systems (HRIS), which made it possible for businesses to store data electronically and handle many HR tasks. It became easier to make reports and look at data with HRIS, which led to the creation of the first HR analytics tools.

It was created by Robert Kaplan and David Norton in the 1990s and became very popular as a tool for managing performance. The Balanced Scorecard uses a group of performance factors to check how well an organisation is doing and give a full picture of what it does. Many businesses used this tool, which gave them a way to figure out how HR actions affected the business's overall success.

The area of HR statistics started to change quickly in the early 2000s. This happened because technology got better, big data grew, and HR became more important in improving the performance of an organisation. Social media and other digital outlets have also made it easier for companies to gather information about how their employees behave and how engaged they are with their work.

In recent years, HR data has become an important tool for businesses that want to stay ahead of the competition. Using advanced tools like predictive analytics and machine learning lets you look at a lot of HR data and find patterns and trends that were hidden before.

People analytics, which aims to make employees more engaged and keep them on the job, is at the heart of HR analytics right now. This method uses data to understand how employees behave, what they like, and what drives them. This lets programmes and solutions be adjusted to the specific needs of each employee.

Using artificial intelligence (AI) and machine learning to handle HR tasks and improve decision-making is another important trend in HR analytics. AI tools that look at HR data in real time give organisations insights and suggestions that help them make better decisions.

These days, HR data is an important part of many companies' HR plans. It means getting information about the workforce from a lot of different sources, such as employee polls, performance data, and even social media posts. Its goal is to find patterns, trends, and connections that will help with talent management, keeping employees, and getting them involved in their work.

People analytics is another name for HR analytics. It is the study and analysis of human resources data to help businesses make better choices. This includes collecting and analysing data about the performance, engagement, and other HR measures of the staff.

Statistical and data analysis tools are used on HR data as part of this process to learn more about the workforce and make better decisions. As part of HR, it includes collecting, organising, and analysing data about things like hiring, performance, pay, training, growth, and involvement.

At its core, HR analytics tries to use data to make smart choices and improve HR practises. By looking at HR data, companies can predict their future staffing needs, come up with good ways to find, keep, and grow people, and find trends that help them make decisions.

HR analytics uses many different tools and methods, such as data visualisation, machine learning, predictive modelling, and artificial intelligence, to help improve HR processes, make employees happier and more productive, and eventually improve business results.

This analytical method helps companies learn more about their employees, improve their work, and make choices based on data, which increases total productivity and the effectiveness of the company. By looking at employee data, you can make smart choices about how to hire, train, and keep employees.

How do you do HR analytics? HR analytics includes gathering, analysing, and making sense of data about employees. This includes surveys about staff involvement, performance, recruitment, training, pay, perks, and demographics. Its goal is to find trends, patterns, and ideas that can be used to make HR choices based on data.

It uses many different tools and methods, such as statistical analysis, machine learning, data visualisation, and prediction analytics. The goal is still to give HR workers information about their employees that will help them improve their HR practises, get their employees more involved, and get better business results.

Why is HR analytics important for people who work in HR? There are several reasons why HR workers should care about HR analytics. First, it lets you make decisions based on data, which shows you where HR practises can be improved. For example, finding teams with high change rates lets you make special plans to keep those people.

Second, it tracks how well HR practises are working, which helps make changes that make things run more smoothly. Third, it improves employee involvement by figuring out what makes them care, like how training and development programmes work.

Finally, HR Analytics connects HR actions with business results by using data analysis to show how those actions affect the success of the organisation. How can HR Analytics be used to improve HR practices? HR analytics involves collecting, analysing, and interpreting human resource data for informed business decisions. In today's data-driven workplace, its importance has surged, and here's why:

1. **Recruitment and Talent Management:** By analysing recruitment data, HR professionals can identify effective sources and predict employee performance, optimizing resource allocation for attracting top talent.
2. **Employee Engagement and Retention:** Data analysis on satisfaction, turnover rates, and performance aids in recognizing areas for improvement, thus enhancing employee satisfaction and retention strategies.
3. **Training and Development:** Analysing performance data helps spot skill gaps and training needs, leading to improved employee performance and job satisfaction.
4. **Performance Management:** Assessment of performance data enables adjustments in performance management processes, aligning them better with organizational goals and employee needs.
5. **Diversity and Inclusion:** HR analytics highlights areas for improvement in diversity and inclusion efforts through the analysis of demographic and performance data.
6. **Compensation and Benefits:** By leveraging HR analytics, organizations ensure competitive compensation packages in line with industry standards while evaluating the return on investment for these programs.

HR analytics can help organizations make more informed decisions about their HR practices, leading to improved employee satisfaction, retention, and overall organizational performance.

TABLE 1.1 Uses of HR analytics in HR practices

How can HR Analytics be used to improve HR practices?					
Recruitment and Talent Management	Employee Engagement and Retention	Training and Development	Performance Management	Diversity and Inclusion	Compensation and Benefits

HR ANALYTICS VERSUS TRADITIONAL HR

Human resources (HR) is an important part of any business because it manages the people who work there, who are its most valuable asset. In the past, HR has been a people-focused role that made choices based on experience, gut feelings, and personal connections. However, HR analytics has become a new way to manage human resources in the last few years. HR analytics is the process of making choices about HR by using data, statistics, and machine learning methods.

Traditional HR

Traditional HR is a people-driven function that focuses on managing employees and their needs. In the old way of doing things, HR was all about handling workers and their needs. This method requires a lot of face-to-face communication. Human Resources (HR) workers spend a lot of time meeting with employees, interviewing them, and getting to know them as people. The old way of doing HR is reactive, which means that HR workers only get involved with an employee when there is a problem that needs to be fixed. People often say that the old way of doing HR is biased, slow, and reactive. For instance, when hiring people, HR workers might make choices based on gut feelings and personal connections instead of objective data. It can also take a while for standard HR to adapt to changes in the workforce, which can cause waste and missed chances.

HR Analytics

HR analytics is a way of handling people that is based on data. Using data and statistical analysis to make better choices about hiring, keeping employees, and other HR-related tasks is what HR analytics is all about. Machine learning algorithms are also used in HR analytics to find trends and make guesses about what will happen in the future with HR. Large and small businesses alike are using HR statistics more and more. Organisations can make better decisions, cut costs, and work more efficiently with the help of HR data. For instance, HR analytics can be used to find trends in the number of employees who leave, which can help companies come up with ways to keep employees and save money.

TABLE 1.2 HR Analytics Vs Traditional HR

Aspect	*HR Analytics*	*Traditional HR*
Data collection	Uses data-driven approach	Relies on manual methods
Decision-making process	Data-driven decisions	Intuition-based decisions
Focus	Predictive	Reactive
Objective	Proactive	Reactive
Metrics	Quantitative	Qualitative
Scope	Enterprise-wide	Departmental
Reporting	Real-time	Periodic
Analysis	In-depth	Surface-level
Efficiency	High	Low

HR Analytics refers to the practice of collecting and analysing data to make informed decisions in HR. Traditional HR, on the other hand, relies on manual methods and intuition-based decisions. HR Analytics uses a data-driven approach, while traditional HR is reactive and focuses on qualitative metrics. HR Analytics is proactive and enterprise-wide, while traditional HR is departmental and periodic in reporting. HR Analytics provides in-depth analysis in real-time, while traditional HR provides surface-level analysis. The efficiency of HR Analytics is high, while traditional HR's efficiency is low.

BENEFITS OF HR ANALYTICS

Utilizing HR analytics in organizations offers numerous advantages. The following outlines some of the key benefits:

1. **Improved Decision-making:** HR analytics equips HR professionals with unbiased data for more informed decision-making. This data aids in identifying areas for improvement, devising effective strategies, and assessing the impact of HR-related activities.
2. **Increased Efficiency:** HR analytics enables organizations to pinpoint inefficiencies and streamline HR processes. Automation of repetitive tasks, such as data entry, frees up HR professionals to focus on strategic activities.
3. **Cost Savings:** HR analytics identifies areas of resource wastage, reducing costs. For instance, it helps pinpoint the most effective recruiting channels, minimizing the need for expensive job postings or recruitment agencies.
4. **Better Talent Management:** By analysing data on employee performance and engagement, HR analytics assists in identifying and retaining top talent. It enables HR professionals to develop strategies for employee improvement, engagement, and motivation.
5. **Predictive Analytics:** HR analytics predicts future HR-related outcomes, such as identifying employees likely to leave. This proactive approach helps HR professionals take steps to retain valuable employees.

CHALLENGES OF IMPLEMENTING HR ANALYTICS

Implementing HR analytics, aimed at improving HR decision-making through data and analytics, poses several challenges:

1. **Data Quality:** HR analytics relies on high-quality data, which may not always be available due to incompleteness, inconsistency, or inaccuracy in HR systems.
2. **Data Integration:** Integrating HR data stored in multiple systems, especially in different formats, can be challenging, hindering the creation of a comprehensive workforce view.
3. **Lack of Analytics Skills:** HR professionals may lack the necessary skills for effective data analysis. Training in statistical analysis, data visualization, and machine learning is essential for proficient use of HR analytics.
4. **Resistance to Change:** Some employees may resist HR analytics implementation, fearing job losses or privacy reduction. Proactive communication about the benefits and addressing concerns is crucial.
5. **Cost:** Implementing HR analytics may necessitate significant investment in technology, training, and analytics tools. Assessing the return on investment (ROI) is crucial before implementation.
6. **Ethical Considerations:** HR analytics involves personal data, requiring compliance with data privacy regulations and ethical considerations during data collection and analysis.

Addressing these challenges demands careful planning, effective communication, and continuous evaluation to ensure the HR analytics program delivers value.

THE PROCESS OF HR ANALYTICS

The HR analytics process involves the following steps:

1. **Identifying HR Metrics:** Determine data to collect and analyse, such as turnover rates, recruitment costs, training expenses, and employee engagement scores.
2. **Gathering Data:** Collect relevant data from HR databases, surveys, performance reviews, and social media.
3. **Cleaning and Preparing Data:** Clean and transform data to ensure accuracy and usability.
4. **Analysing Data:** Use statistical methods and tools to identify patterns, trends, and insights.
5. **Communicating Findings:** Present insights and recommendations to relevant stakeholders clearly and concisely.

KEY BENEFITS OF HR ANALYTICS

1. **Improved Decision-making:** HR analytics provides data-driven insights for informed decisions.
2. **Increased Efficiency:** Analysis of HR data helps identify areas for process improvement and increased efficiency.

3. **Enhanced Employee Engagement:** HR analytics identifies factors contributing to employee engagement, facilitating improvement strategies.
4. **Reduced Turnover:** Analysis of employee data helps identify factors influencing turnover, enabling retention strategies.

HR analytics empowers organizations to gain workforce insights, enhance employee performance, and make data-driven decisions, ultimately boosting overall productivity and effectiveness.

THE FUTURE OF HR ANALYTICS

HR analytics has gained popularity as organizations recognize the value of data-driven decision-making in workforce management. The future of HR analytics includes the following trends:

1. **Increased use of Predictive Analytics:** Predictive analytics identifies future outcomes based on historical data, aiding in employee retention, recruitment, and training effectiveness.
2. **Integration with Artificial Intelligence (AI):** AI applications in HR analytics, such as chatbots for recruitment and sentiment analysis for employee engagement, will advance with more sophisticated machine learning algorithms.
3. **Increased use of People Analytics Platforms:** HR professionals will adopt people analytics platforms to streamline data analysis, track performance, identify skill gaps, and enhance retention rates.
4. **Focus on Employee Experience:** HR analytics will measure and improve employee experience, addressing factors like physical workspace, company culture, and growth opportunities.
5. **Increased use of Real-Time Data:** Real-time data analytics tools will become more prevalent in HR decision-making, enabling monitoring of employee engagement, performance, and early issue identification.

CHALLENGES IN HR ANALYTICS

1. **Data Quality:** Ensuring accurate, complete, and relevant data poses a challenge, requiring a deep understanding of data and adherence to data privacy concerns.
2. **Lack of Standardization:** HR data scattered across different systems and formats complicates comparison and analysis, necessitating standardization efforts.
3. **Skills Gap:** The technical and analytical skills required for HR analytics may be lacking among HR professionals, requiring training and development programs.
4. **Ethical Concerns:** Ethical considerations around privacy, fairness, and transparency in using employee data require attention and transparency from HR professionals.

KEY METRICS IN HR ANALYTICS

Overview of the key metrics that HR analytics can help track and improve, such as employee engagement, retention, productivity, and performance.

There are various metrics that HR analytics can help track and improve, including:

1. **Employee Engagement:** Employee engagement is a key statistic that shows how emotionally connected a worker is to their job, their co-workers, and the company. HR data can help you keep track of and examine how engaged your employees are, figure out what affects engagement, and come up with ways to get your employees more involved. Surveys, focus groups, or conversations can be used to find out how engaged people are.

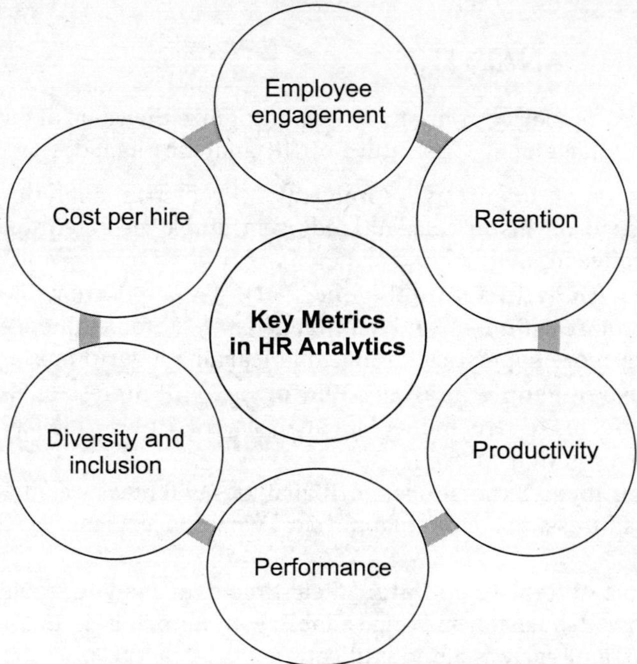

FIGURE 1.1 Key metrics in HR analytics.

2. **Retention:** Retention rate is the percentage of employees who stay with an organization over a specific period. High retention rates indicate a healthy work environment and good management practices. HR analytics can help identify the reasons for high or low retention rates, such as job satisfaction, compensation, or management practices, and develop strategies to improve retention.
3. **Productivity:** Productivity measures an employee's output in a specific period. HR analytics can help identify the factors that impact employee productivity, such as workload, work environment, and technology, and develop strategies to improve productivity. Key performance indicators (KPIs) like sales income, output per hour, or customer happiness can be used to measure productivity.
4. **Performance:** Performance metrics measure an employee's performance against specific goals and objectives. HR analytics can help track and analyse employee performance, identify areas for improvement, and develop strategies to improve performance. Performance can be measured using KPIs such as revenue growth, customer satisfaction, or quality metrics.

5. **Diversity and Inclusion:** Metrics related to diversity and inclusion gauge an organization's initiatives in fostering a diverse and inclusive workplace. Utilizing HR analytics aids in monitoring and evaluating these metrics, pinpointing areas needing enhancement, and formulating strategies for advancing diversity and inclusion. Metrics might encompass employee demographics, the diversity of job roles, and employee perceptions of the work environment.
6. **Cost per Hire:** This metric assesses the overall expenses incurred in recruiting and on boarding a new employee. Leveraging HR analytics allows for the monitoring and analysis of the cost per hire, identification of areas ripe for improvement, and the development of strategies aimed at reducing these expenses. Calculating the cost per hire involves tallying expenses such as job postings, recruitment events, travel costs, and other pertinent expenditures linked to hiring a new employee.

HR analytics provides organizations with the ability to track and analyse key metrics that impact employee engagement, retention, productivity, performance, diversity, and inclusion. By using HR analytics, organizations can identify areas for improvement and develop strategies to improve the overall health of the workplace.

INTUITION VERSUS ANALYTICAL THINKING

The human mind is a complex and multifaceted instrument, capable of remarkable feats of cognition and decision-making. Intuition and analytical thinking are two distinct cognitive processes that play a pivotal role in human decision-making, problem-solving, and creativity. These two modes of thought have been the subject of considerable debate and exploration, with some advocating the supremacy of one over the other. Exploring the dynamics of intuition versus analytical thinking can shed light on the strengths and limitations of each, and how they complement one another.

Intuition: The Silent Whisper of Wisdom

Intuition, which people sometimes call a gut feeling or an instinct, is the unconscious way that people come to decisions without using clear, step-by-step thinking. It's how quickly, easily, and often for no reason the mind makes a choice or judgement. Your intuition is based on a lot of your own feelings, events, and learned habits from the past. The inner voice tells us what to do when we least expect it and gives us a sense of certainty even when there isn't any proof.

Intuition works quickly and often gets things right. It's an adaptation that evolved over time to help our ancestors deal with situations that were unknown and could be risky. It still helps us in modern times, especially when we need to make quick choices or when we need to look at complicated problems as a whole and find patterns. Trusting their well-honed feelings, experts in many fields often make important choices based on intuition.

But instincts can also be wrong at times. It can be affected by cognitive flaws and mental states, which can cause people to make bad decisions. People often see patterns where there aren't any (apophenia) and are prone to overconfidence bias, which can sometimes lead perception wrong. It's important to find a balance between intuition and logical thought so that rash choices are tempered by careful consideration.

Analytical Thinking: The Rational Sentry

Analytical thinking involves a purposeful and systematic method of addressing problems consciously. It includes breaking down intricate problems into more manageable parts and subjecting them to logical examination. It relies on reason, evidence, and structured processes to reach conclusions. Analytical thinking is methodical, precise, and objective, and it is the cornerstone of the scientific method and critical thinking.

Analytical thinking allows us to critically evaluate arguments, solve intricate problems, and make well-informed decisions based on a rational foundation. It is particularly useful in fields that demand precision, like mathematics, engineering, and the physical sciences. When applied correctly, analytical thinking mitigates the biases and emotional influences that can affect intuitive judgments.

Nevertheless, the downside of analytical thinking is its inherent demand for time and cognitive resources. It may be cumbersome in situations that require immediate responses or when confronted with incomplete or ambiguous information. Additionally, excessive reliance on analytical thinking alone can lead to decision paralysis, as individuals may become bogged down in endless analysis without ever reaching a conclusion.

Harmonizing the Two Modes

The interplay between intuition and analytical thinking is often presented as a dynamic balancing act. The key to effective decision-making and problem-solving lies in knowing when to rely on each mode and when to integrate them harmoniously. This integration involves using intuition to form initial hypotheses or gut feelings and then subjecting these to analytical scrutiny. It means acknowledging the strengths of both processes and leveraging them in tandem.

In practice, this could mean using intuition to brainstorm creative ideas and analytical thinking to evaluate their feasibility and merit. It could also involve consulting one's intuitive sense of right and wrong before applying analytical ethical principles to a moral dilemma.

The art of integrating these two modes of thought becomes especially crucial in complex and multifaceted scenarios where both rapid insights and rational scrutiny are essential. Decision-makers who can harness the strengths of both intuition and analytical thinking stand a better chance of achieving optimal outcomes.

So, the tension between intuition and analytical thinking represents a fascinating and valuable aspect of human cognition. These dual modes of thought offer complementary tools for navigating the challenges of everyday life, from routine decisions to profound philosophical inquiries. Recognizing their individual strengths and limitations, and learning to harmonize them, is the hallmark of a truly agile and effective thinker.

HUMAN RESOURCE MANAGEMENT SYSTEM AND HUMAN RESOURCE INFORMATION SYSTEM

Human Resource Management System (HRMS) and Human Resource Information System (HRIS) are integral components of modern business management. They have revolutionized the way organizations handle their human resources, from recruitment and employee onboarding to performance management and payroll processing.

Understanding HRMS and HRIS

HRMS and HRIS are often used interchangeably, but they do have distinct roles within the human resources function. Both systems are technology-based solutions designed to streamline HR operations, increase efficiency, and provide valuable insights for decision-making.

1. *HRIS (Human Resource Information System)*

HRIS is primarily focused on managing and processing employee data. It serves as a centralized database that stores information related to employees, such as personal details, work history, performance evaluations, and benefits. This system allows HR professionals to access, analyse, and generate reports based on this data, thus facilitating better personnel management.

2. *HRMS (Human Resource Management System)*

HRMS is a broader system encompassing HRIS. It not only handles employee data but also includes modules for functions like recruitment, applicant tracking, training and development, workforce planning, payroll, and time and attendance. HRMS integrates all these functions, providing a holistic approach to human resource management.

Components of HRMS and HRIS

To fully appreciate the functionalities of HRMS and HRIS, it's essential to understand their key components:

1. **Employee Data Management:** Both systems have a database to store essential employee information, ranging from basic personal details to more complex data like performance metrics and disciplinary records.
2. **Recruitment and Applicant Tracking:** HRMS often includes modules for posting job openings, managing applications, and tracking the recruitment process. HRIS may have limited functionality in this area.
3. **Training and Development:** HRMS typically provides tools for employee training and development, allowing HR to monitor employee progress and allocate resources efficiently.
4. **Payroll and Compensation:** HRMS is equipped to handle payroll processing, ensuring accuracy and compliance with tax laws. HRIS may provide limited payroll support or integrate with external payroll systems.
5. **Performance Management:** Both systems can facilitate performance appraisals, feedback, and goal setting, but HRMS typically offers more comprehensive solutions for performance management.
6. **Benefits Administration:** HRMS generally includes features for benefits management, including enrolment, tracking, and reporting. HRIS may have this functionality to a lesser extent.

Data Sources in HRMS/HRIS

How well HRMS and HRIS work depends a lot on the quality and number of data sources they use. There are two main types of these sources:

1. ***Internal Data Sources***

- **Employee Records**: The HR department's employee records, which include personal information, work experience, and achievement data, are the main source of internal data.
- **Time and Attendance Systems**: These systems track employee attendance and working hours, supplying critical data for payroll and scheduling.

2. ***External Data Sources***

- **Job Boards and Career Websites**: For recruitment, HRMS may extract data from job boards and career websites to source potential candidates.
- **Training Institutions**: Data from universities, training institutions, and external learning platforms can inform the training and development components of HRMS.
- **Government Databases**: HRIS and HRMS may pull data from government sources for tax-related information and employment verifications.

Human Resource Management Systems (HRMS) and Human Resource Information Systems (HRIS) stand as pivotal tools for contemporary HR departments. They offer comprehensive solutions tailored to manage the workforce, adapting their functionalities to the specific organizational needs. The efficacy of these systems heavily relies on the acquisition of precise, dependable data from diverse sources, both internal and external. Empowering HR professionals, these systems facilitate informed decision-making, enabling them to optimize the organization's most valuable asset: its people.

BUSINESS INTELLIGENCE

Business Intelligence (BI) serves as an integral element in modern business functionality, equipping organizations with the necessary tools and insights crucial for informed decision-making and achieving success. Essentially, BI involves the collection, analysis, and presentation of data to bolster business decision-making. This comprehensive overview will focus on two fundamental facets of BI: summarization and reporting.

Summarizing in Business Intelligence

Summarizing is the initial stage of the BI process and involves the extraction and consolidation of data from various sources. This data may include transaction records, customer data, market trends, and more. The purpose of summarizing is to distil large volumes of raw data into a more manageable and meaningful format. This process encompasses:

1. **Data Collection:** BI systems gather data from a multitude of sources, which may include databases, spreadsheets, web services, and more. Data can be structured (such as sales figures) or unstructured (like social media comments).
2. **Data Integration:** Diverse data sources often require integration to form a unified dataset. This step is crucial for ensuring data consistency and reliability.

3. **Data Transformation:** Data transformation includes cleaning, enriching, and structuring data. It might involve removing duplicates, filling in missing values, or standardizing data formats.
4. **Data Aggregation:** Summarizing data often means aggregating it to higher levels, such as weekly or monthly summaries, to enable easier analysis and reporting.
5. **Data Modelling:** Developing data models helps in organizing data in a way that is conducive to analysis. This can involve the creation of data cubes, relational databases, or other structures.

Once data is successfully summarized, it can be used for various purposes, including reporting and analysis.

Reporting in Business Intelligence

Reporting is the subsequent step in the BI process. After data has been summarized, it is transformed into valuable information through the creation of reports and dashboards. Reporting in BI serves several important functions:

1. **Information Dissemination:** Reports convey essential information to various stakeholders within an organization. These stakeholders could be executives, managers, or front-line employees, each with their specific information needs.
2. **Performance Monitoring:** BI reporting allows organizations to track key performance indicators (KPIs) and gauge the success of their strategies. This can include metrics related to sales, marketing, finance, and operations.
3. **Decision Support:** Informed decision-making is at the core of BI reporting. By presenting data in a clear and comprehensible format, reports empower decision-makers to make choices that drive the business forward.
4. **Trend Analysis:** BI reports enable the analysis of historical data and trends, helping organizations identify patterns and plan for the future.
5. **Ad Hoc Reporting:** Many BI systems offer ad hoc reporting capabilities, allowing users to generate custom reports on the fly, which is valuable for addressing specific questions or scenarios.
6. **Data Visualization:** Effective visualization of data through charts, graphs, and dashboards is an integral part of reporting, making it easier for users to grasp insights at a glance.

In modern BI, reporting has evolved significantly with the advent of self-service BI tools that empower non-technical users to create their reports and dashboards. These tools often come with user-friendly interfaces, drag-and-drop features, and interactive visualizations.

So, Business Intelligence is a broad field that includes more than just reporting and summarising data. Summarising turns raw data into a shape that can be used, and sharing makes this information easy for stakeholders to find. All of these parts of BI work together to help businesses make choices based on data, improve performance, and stay ahead of the competition in today's data-driven business world. The addition of cutting edge technologies like AI and machine learning keeps pushing the limits of what is possible in BI, creating fresh ways to look at data and come up with new insights.

THE MODEL OF PREDICAMENT MANAGEMENT

Predicament management is a crucial process employed by individuals, organizations, and governments to address and navigate challenging situations. These situations, often unforeseen and disruptive, can range from natural disasters and economic crises to complex social and political issues. Managing predicaments effectively is essential for maintaining stability, minimizing negative impacts, and fostering resilience.

Understanding the Model of Predicament Management

The Model of Predicament Management is a comprehensive framework designed to guide decision-makers through the complexities of managing predicaments. This model is adaptable and can be applied in various contexts, including business, emergency response, public policy, and personal life. It typically consists of several interconnected phases, each of which plays a crucial role in managing a predicament:

1. **Preparation and Planning:**
    - The first step in predicament management involves proactively identifying potential predicaments and developing strategies to address them. This phase includes risk assessments, contingency planning, and resource allocation.
    - It is essential to establish clear communication channels, define roles and responsibilities, and create response protocols in this stage.
2. **Identification and Early Warning:**
    - Promptly recognizing the emergence of a predicament is critical to mitigate its impact. Early warning systems and situational awareness tools are essential for timely detection.
    - Effective information gathering and analysis are key components during this phase to assess the nature and severity of the predicament.
3. **Response and Crisis Management:**
    - Once a predicament is confirmed, swift and coordinated action is required. The response phase involves activating pre-established plans and mobilizing resources.
    - Effective crisis management may involve decision-making under pressure, resource allocation, and public communication. Leadership and adaptability are crucial during this phase.
4. **Recovery and Resilience:**
    - After the initial response, the focus shifts to recovery and rebuilding. This phase involves addressing the consequences of the predicament, restoring normalcy, and fostering resilience.
    - Long-term recovery efforts may include psychological support, infrastructure repair, and economic revitalization.
5. **Learning and Adaptation:**
    - Continuous improvement is central to predicament management. After every predicament, it is essential to evaluate the response and identify lessons learned.
    - Adaptation involves updating plans and procedures to better prepare for future predicaments based on the knowledge gained from previous experiences.

6. **Prevention and Mitigation:**
   - The final phase of the model emphasizes proactive measures to prevent or reduce the impact of future predicaments. This includes policy changes, risk reduction strategies, and public awareness campaigns.
   - Prevention and mitigation efforts are closely linked to the planning phase, as they inform the development of preparedness strategies.

Key Principles of the Model

1. **Adaptability:** The model emphasizes the importance of adaptability in the face of evolving predicaments. It acknowledges that no two predicaments are identical and that the approach should be flexible and responsive.
2. **Communication:** Effective communication is a thread that runs through every phase of predicament management. Timely and accurate information exchange is critical for decision-makers and the public.
3. **Resource Management:** Proper allocation of resources, including personnel, finances, and technology, is vital for an effective response and recovery.
4. **Resilience and Learning:** The model encourages a culture of resilience and continuous learning. By incorporating feedback and experience into planning and response, organizations and individuals can become better prepared for future predicaments.

Benefits of the Model of Predicament Management

1. **Proactive Approach:** The model promotes a proactive approach to predicaments, reducing the likelihood and severity of crises.
2. **Resource Optimization:** It helps organizations allocate resources effectively, preventing waste during crises.
3. **Resilience Building:** Over time, organizations that follow this model become more resilient and better equipped to handle future predicaments.
4. **Improved Stakeholder Relations:** Effective communication and transparency foster trust and improve relations with stakeholders.
5. **Continuous Improvement:** The learning and adaptation component ensures that organizations continually refine their predicament management processes.

The Model of Predicament Management is a comprehensive and adaptable framework that offers a structured approach to handling challenging situations. Whether it's a natural disaster, a business crisis, or a global pandemic, this model provides a roadmap for decision-makers to prepare, respond, recover, and learn from predicaments. By understanding and applying its principles, individuals, organizations, and governments can better navigate the unpredictable challenges that life presents.

HUMAN CAPITAL MEASUREMENT AND STRATEGY IMPLEMENTATION

In today's dynamic and competitive business landscape, organizations are increasingly recognizing the importance of measuring what truly matters, especially when it comes to their most valuable asset—human capital. The traditional approach of business analysis, which mainly focuses on financial metrics and operational efficiency, is evolving into a more comprehensive and nuanced process known as rational analysis. This shift underscores the need to measure not just tangible assets but also the intangible and often overlooked aspects of human capital, aligning them with an organization's strategic objectives.

Human Capital Measurement

Human capital, often referred to as the knowledge, skills, and abilities of an organization's workforce, is a critical driver of sustainable competitive advantage. As businesses evolve, it becomes essential to quantify and assess this intangible asset to make informed decisions about talent management, employee development, and strategic planning. Human capital measurement involves the systematic collection and analysis of data related to an organization's workforce, covering aspects like:

1. **Skills and Competencies:** Evaluating the skill sets and competencies of employees to identify gaps and opportunities for growth.
2. **Engagement and Satisfaction:** Measuring employee engagement and job satisfaction to gauge their commitment to the organization.
3. **Productivity and Performance:** Assessing individual and team performance to link it to organizational outcomes.
4. **Succession Planning:** Identifying potential leaders within the organization to ensure a seamless transition in key positions.
5. **Diversity and Inclusion:** Monitoring diversity metrics and fostering an inclusive work environment for a more diverse and innovative workforce.

Implementing Strategy

To stay competitive, organizations must bridge the gap between strategy formulation and execution. Implementing strategy involves aligning an organization's resources, including human capital, to its strategic goals. Rational analysis is essential in this context as it ensures that human capital is not merely a cost centre but a strategic asset. Human capital measurement informs strategy implementation in the following ways:

1. **Strategic Alignment:** Human capital data allows organizations to match their talent pool with strategic objectives. This ensures that employees possess the necessary skills and competencies to execute the strategy effectively.
2. **Resource Allocation:** Rational analysis helps in allocating resources efficiently, including budgets for talent acquisition, training, and development, in line with the strategic priorities.
3. **Performance Management:** Continuous measurement of human capital performance ensures that individuals and teams are contributing to the strategic goals. This can lead to timely interventions or adjustments if necessary.
4. **Feedback Loops:** Through data analysis, organizations can create feedback loops that enable them to adapt their strategies in real-time based on the performance and feedback from the workforce.
5. **Risk Mitigation:** By identifying potential skill gaps or attrition risks, organizations can proactively address challenges that might hinder strategy execution.

From Business Analysis to Rational Analysis

The shift from traditional business analysis to rational analysis signifies a more holistic approach to decision-making. While business analysis mainly focuses on financial indicators and operational efficiency, rational analysis integrates quantitative and qualitative data to provide a more comprehensive understanding of the organization's human capital and how it impacts strategic execution.

Rational analysis considers not only the "what" but also the "why" and "how" behind human capital metrics. It employs data analytics, surveys, feedback mechanisms, and qualitative assessments to provide a deeper insight into the workforce. This approach acknowledges that a well-rounded understanding of human capital is essential for long-term success and adaptability in an ever-changing business environment.

Thus, measuring what is important, particularly human capital, and implementing strategies based on rational analysis is becoming increasingly critical in the modern business landscape. By recognizing the value of human capital and embracing a rational approach to its measurement and analysis, organizations can make more informed decisions, improve their strategic execution, and ultimately achieve sustained success in a competitive world.

HUMAN REVENUE VERSUS HUMAN CAPITAL PLANNING

Human revenue and human capital planning are two essential aspects of an organization's strategic management and development. They both play a crucial role in ensuring a company's long-term success, but they focus on different elements of the workforce.

Human Revenue

Human revenue refers to the direct financial returns generated by an organization's employees. It's often associated with short-term gains, such as sales, revenue from services, or immediate cost-cutting measures. Human revenue measures the immediate contributions of employees to the organization's bottom line. Following are some key points related to human revenue:

1. **Short-term Focus:** Human revenue primarily concerns itself with the here and now. It's about maximizing the productivity of the existing workforce to generate immediate financial returns.
2. **Measurable and Tangible:** It is relatively easy to measure human revenue. Metrics like sales figures, cost savings, and revenue per employee can provide a clear picture of the financial impact of employees on the organization.
3. **Operational Efficiency:** Improving human revenue often involves streamlining processes, enhancing sales efforts, and optimizing operations to boost short-term profits.
4. **Limited Investment in Employee Development:** Organizations that solely focus on human revenue may be reluctant to invest in employee training, development, or long-term talent retention strategies.

Human Capital Planning

Human capital planning, on the other hand, takes a more strategic and long-term approach to managing an organization's workforce. It focuses on developing, retaining, and leveraging the skills and capabilities of employees to achieve sustained growth and competitiveness. Following are some key points related to human capital planning:

1. **Long-term Strategy:** Human capital planning looks beyond immediate financial gains and aims to create a sustainable, competitive advantage for the organization. It takes a holistic approach to talent management.
2. **Intangible Assets:** Unlike human revenue, the benefits of human capital planning are often intangible and not immediately quantifiable. It involves investing in training, development, and creating a positive work environment to foster employee growth and loyalty.
3. **Talent Acquisition and Retention:** Human capital planning involves recruiting and retaining top talent, which requires a strong employer brand, comprehensive onboarding processes, and a focus on employee engagement and development.
4. **Innovation and Adaptability:** Organizations that prioritize human capital planning are better positioned to adapt to changing market conditions, foster innovation, and maintain a competitive edge in the long run.

Significance for Businesses

Both human revenue and human capital planning have their roles within an organization, and they are not mutually exclusive. However, finding the right balance between the two is critical for overall success. They both are significant because of:

1. **Balance and Synergy:** Organizations that balance human revenue and human capital planning can reap both short-term financial gains and long-term strategic advantages. A strong workforce can contribute to immediate results while being groomed for future challenges.
2. **Competitive Advantage:** Human capital planning ensures that a company's workforce remains adaptable, innovative, and loyal, giving it a competitive edge in the market.
3. **Risk Mitigation:** Overreliance on human revenue without investing in human capital planning can leave a company vulnerable to market fluctuations, talent shortages, and a lack of innovation.
4. **Sustainability:** Human capital planning is essential for the long-term sustainability of an organization, ensuring it can navigate evolving market dynamics and challenges.

So, human revenue and human capital planning are both vital aspects of managing a workforce. Organizations should recognize the importance of balancing these two approaches to achieve short-term financial goals and long-term sustainability. By doing so, businesses can maximize the value of their human resources while securing their position in a competitive marketplace.

HCM: 21 MODEL—THE BIG PICTURE

Human Capital Management (HCM) is a strategic approach to managing an organization's workforce to maximize performance and achieve business goals. The "HCM: 21 model" is an innovative and contemporary framework that synthesizes 21st-century best practices in managing human capital. This model is designed to provide organizations with a holistic view of how to optimize their human resources and adapt to the rapidly evolving world of work.

HCM: 21 Model Components

1. **Talent Acquisition and Recruitment**: The first pillar of HCM: 21 involves finding and attracting top talent. It focuses on strategies for identifying, recruiting, and onboarding individuals who align with the organization's values and goals.
2. **Learning and Development**: This aspect centres on continuous learning and skill development for employees. It includes training programs, mentorship, and opportunities for growth and advancement.
3. **Performance Management**: Performance management in the HCM: 21 model is not just an annual review but an ongoing process. It emphasizes regular feedback, goal setting, and the alignment of individual performance with organizational objectives.
4. **Diversity, Equity, and Inclusion**: Promoting diversity, equity, and inclusion is a critical part of the 21st-century workforce. The HCM: 21 model emphasizes creating an inclusive environment that leverages the diverse perspectives and talents of employees.
5. **Workforce Well-being**: Employee well-being is a top priority in the HCM: 21 model. It includes physical, mental, and emotional health, as well as work-life balance.
6. **Data-driven Decision-making**: Data analytics plays a significant role in HCM: 21. Organizations use data to make informed decisions about their workforce, from identifying trends to predicting future needs.
7. **Technology Integration**: Technology is leveraged to streamline HR processes, improve communication, and enhance the employee experience. The model promotes the integration of cutting-edge HR technologies.
8. **Agile Workforce**: The concept of an agile workforce is key to adapting to rapidly changing markets. It involves flexibility in roles, cross-functional teams, and the ability to pivot quickly in response to new challenges.
9. **Leadership and Culture**: Effective leadership and a positive organizational culture are critical. The HCM: 21 model encourages leaders to set the tone for the workplace and foster a culture of continuous improvement.

Benefits of HCM: 21 Model

1. **Competitive Advantage**: Organizations that implement the HCM: 21 model gain a competitive advantage by having a highly engaged and skilled workforce that can adapt to changing market conditions.
2. **Increased Employee Satisfaction**: By focusing on well-being, development, and inclusion, employee satisfaction and retention rates are likely to increase.

3. **Improved Productivity**: A well-managed workforce is a productive workforce. The HCM: 21 model enhances productivity by aligning individual goals with the organization's objectives.
4. **Future-Proofing**: The model equips organizations to adapt to the future of work, which may involve automation, remote work, and other transformative changes.

The HCM: 21 model represents a comprehensive approach to managing human capital in the 21st century. It integrates talent acquisition, learning and development, performance management, diversity, equity, inclusion, well-being, data-driven decision-making, technology, agility, leadership, and culture to create a high-performing and adaptable workforce. By adopting this model, organizations can position themselves for success in an ever-evolving business landscape where people are the most critical asset.

HR METRICS AND HR ANALYTICS

Human Resources (HR) plays a critical role in any organization, ensuring that the workforce is effectively managed, developed, and motivated to achieve the company's goals. To improve HR decision-making and align HR practices with organizational objectives, HR professionals rely on two essential tools: HR metrics and HR analytics. These tools provide valuable insights into workforce performance, employee engagement, and overall HR effectiveness.

HR Metrics: Measuring What Matters

HR metrics are quantifiable measurements that provide a snapshot of various aspects of the workforce. They help HR professionals track, evaluate, and report on specific HR-related activities and outcomes. HR metrics focus on assessing the current state of HR processes, workforce demographics, and the effectiveness of HR initiatives.

HR Metrics

- **Definition:** HR metrics are quantifiable measurements or key performance indicators (KPIs) that provide insights into various aspects of the HR function. These measurements are used to assess the efficiency, effectiveness, and overall performance of HR processes and initiatives.
- **Purpose:** HR metrics are primarily used to monitor and evaluate HR activities, such as recruitment, employee engagement, training, and retention. They help HR professionals track progress, identify trends, and pinpoint areas for improvement within their department.
- **Examples:** Common HR metrics include turnover rate, time to hire, absenteeism rate, employee satisfaction scores, training hours per employee, and diversity metrics. These metrics offer a snapshot of the HR function's performance and can be used to assess the impact of HR strategies on the organization.
- **Use Cases:** HR metrics are essential for HR managers to gauge the effectiveness of their day-to-day operations and long-term strategies. For example, they can use turnover rate data to understand employee retention issues and take corrective actions.

Common HR metrics include:

1. **Turnover Rate:** The percentage of workers who depart the company during a certain time period is measured by this indicator. Elevated rates of employee attrition may suggest possible problems with staff retention and job satisfaction.
2. **Employee Engagement:** Employee engagement surveys and metrics assess how involved, committed, and satisfied employees are with their work and the organization. High engagement levels are often associated with better performance and reduced turnover.
3. **Recruitment Metrics:** These metrics track the efficiency and effectiveness of the recruitment process, such as time-to-fill, cost-per-hire, and the quality of candidates sourced.
4. **Training and Development Metrics:** These metrics measure the effectiveness of training programs and the impact of professional development on employee performance.
5. **Absenteeism Rate:** It quantifies the frequency and duration of employee absences, which can indicate morale and workplace issues.

HR metrics provide a clear picture of HR operations and can help HR departments identify areas that need improvement. They are often considered "lagging indicators" as they report on past performance.

HR Analytics: Turning Data into Actionable Insights

HR analytics takes HR metrics to the next level by using data and statistical analysis to gain deeper insights into the workforce and predict future trends. HR analytics focuses on answering critical business questions and making data-driven recommendations to drive strategic decision-making. It is about using data to understand the past, predict the future, and optimize HR processes.

- **Definition:** HR analytics, often referred to as people analytics, is a more advanced and data-driven approach to HR. It involves the collection, analysis, and interpretation of HR-related data to make predictive and prescriptive insights. HR analytics goes beyond mere measurement and delves into the exploration of causation and prediction.
- **Purpose:** The primary purpose of HR analytics is to help organizations make informed, strategic decisions related to their workforce. It aims to identify patterns, correlations, and causal relationships between HR factors and business outcomes.
- **Examples:** HR analytics can involve predicting employee turnover, assessing the impact of specific training programs on productivity, identifying the drivers of employee engagement, and forecasting future talent needs based on business growth projections.
- **Use Cases:** HR analytics can provide invaluable insights to HR leaders and organizational executives. For instance, by analysing data on employee turnover and its causes, HR analytics can offer recommendations on how to reduce turnover and its associated costs, ultimately contributing to the organization's bottom line.

Key components of HR analytics include:

1. **Data Collection and Integration:** Gathering data from various HR systems, including HRIS (Human Resource Information Systems), performance management software, and time and attendance systems.
2. **Data Analysis:** Employing statistical and analytical tools to identify patterns and trends in HR data, such as predicting turnover or understanding the factors influencing employee performance.
3. **Predictive Analytics:** Using historical data to make predictions about future workforce trends, such as identifying which factors are likely to contribute to high employee turnover in the next year.
4. **Prescriptive Analytics:** Offering recommendations on how to address HR challenges and improve outcomes based on data analysis. For example, providing insights on which benefits package would likely boost employee retention.

HR analytics can drive strategic HR decisions, such as improving talent acquisition strategies, enhancing employee engagement initiatives, and optimizing workforce planning. It's considered a "leading indicator" as it focuses on future trends and helps organizations proactively address HR challenges.

Key Differences

1. **Focus:** HR Metrics focus on measuring specific HR-related data to assess the current state and performance of HR processes, while HR Analytics delve deeper into data analysis to derive actionable insights and predictions.
2. **Purpose:** HR Metrics are primarily used for monitoring and reporting, while HR Analytics is more strategic and is used for decision-making and planning.
3. **Data Complexity:** HR Metrics typically involve straightforward data collection and reporting, while HR Analytics requires advanced data analysis techniques, including statistical modelling and machine learning.
4. **Predictive Capability:** HR Analytics has a strong predictive component, allowing organizations to anticipate future trends and make proactive decisions, whereas HR Metrics are generally more historical and descriptive.

HR Metrics provide the foundational data for HR management, offering a snapshot of HR activities, while HR Analytics takes this data to a higher level, providing valuable insights and predictions that guide strategic decision-making, ultimately contributing to the overall success of the organization. Both metrics and analytics have a crucial role to play in modern HR management, with each serving distinct but complementary purposes.

ANALYTICS FRAMEWORKS—LAMP, HR SCORECARD AND WORKFORCE SCORECARD

Analytic frameworks play a crucial role in various domains, helping organizations make data-driven decisions and gain insights into their operations. Three notable analytic frameworks that have been widely adopted are LAMP, HR Scorecard, and Workforce Scorecard.

LAMP (Linux, Apache, MySQL, PHP/Perl/Python)

LAMP is an open-source software stack that combines several key technologies to create a robust web application development environment. Each component of the LAMP stack serves a specific purpose:

1. **Linux:** This is the operating system that forms the foundation of the LAMP stack. It is known for its stability, security, and flexibility. Linux provides a solid platform for hosting web applications.
2. **Apache:** Apache is one of the most widely used web server software. It handles incoming HTTP requests, processes them, and serves web pages to clients. Apache is highly configurable, allowing developers to customize their web server environment.
3. **MySQL:** As an open-source relational database management system (RDBMS), MySQL is utilized for storing and handling data necessary for web applications. It has garnered recognition for its speed, scalability, and reliability.
4. **PHP/Perl/Python:** These are server-side scripting languages used to build the dynamic components of web applications. They enable developers to create interactive and data-driven web pages. PHP is the most commonly used in the LAMP stack, but Perl and Python are also options.

LAMP is a versatile framework that underpins countless websites and web applications. It is particularly popular for its cost-effectiveness, robustness, and the extensive community of developers and resources available. This framework is used across various industries and applications, making it an essential tool for web development.

HR Scorecard

The HR Scorecard is a strategic framework designed to help HR professionals and organizations measure and improve the effectiveness of their human resources management practices. It focuses on aligning HR functions with overall business objectives, thereby ensuring that HR activities contribute to the achievement of organizational goals. The HR Scorecard typically includes the following key elements:

- **Alignment with Business Strategy:** The HR Scorecard first seeks to understand the overarching business strategy and then identifies HR initiatives that can support and enhance that strategy.
- **Key Performance Indicators (KPIs):** KPIs are defined to measure HR performance and effectiveness. These may include metrics related to recruitment, employee retention, training and development, and more.
- **Cause-and-Effect Relationships:** The HR Scorecard often employs a cause-and-effect approach to demonstrate how HR practices impact organizational performance. It shows how improving HR metrics can lead to improved business outcomes.
- **Continuous Improvement:** The HR Scorecard is not a one-time assessment but an ongoing process of monitoring, measuring, and improving HR performance.

The HR Scorecard is valuable for organizations looking to optimize their human resources management, align HR activities with the company's strategic goals, and demonstrate the value of HR initiatives to top management.

Workforce Scorecard

The Workforce Scorecard is a framework that extends beyond traditional HR metrics to focus on a broader set of workforce-related metrics, encompassing not just HR activities but also the strategic management of talent and human capital. It includes the following components:

- **Talent Acquisition and Retention:** The Workforce Scorecard measures how well an organization attracts, hires, and retains talented employees.
- **Employee Engagement:** It assesses the level of employee commitment, job satisfaction, and motivation within the organization.
- **Leadership and Succession Planning:** This aspect evaluates the organization's ability to develop and nurture leadership talent and plan for future leadership needs.
- **Learning and Development:** It measures the effectiveness of training and development programs and their impact on workforce capabilities.
- **Workforce Diversity and Inclusion:** The Workforce Scorecard also examines how diverse and inclusive the workforce is, which is crucial for modern organizations.

The Workforce Scorecard is a valuable tool for organizations seeking to gain a holistic view of their workforce and how it contributes to overall business success. It emphasizes the need for strategic workforce management beyond traditional HR functions.

So, LAMP, HR Scorecard, and Workforce Scorecard are three distinct analytic frameworks with unique applications. LAMP serves as a foundation for web development, HR Scorecard enhances human resources management, and Workforce Scorecard provides a comprehensive view of talent and workforce management. Organizations can leverage these frameworks to make informed decisions and drive performance improvements in their respective domains.

Questions for Discussion

Short Questions

1. What is HR Analytics?
2. When did the term "people analytics" originate?
3. What are some early roots of HR analytics?
4. What are the main goals of HR analytics?
5. How does HR analytics use data to improve HR practices?
6. What are some challenges in implementing HR analytics?
7. What are the key benefits of using HR analytics?
8. What is predictive analytics in HR?
9. How can HR analytics help improve employee engagement?
10. What are the trends in HR analytics for the future?

Long Questions

1. Can you explain the historical perspective of HR analytics, from its inception to the present day?
2. What are the key differences between traditional HR and HR analytics, and how does HR analytics address the limitations of traditional HR?
3. Can you outline the steps involved in the HR analytics process?
4. What are some challenges organizations may face when implementing HR analytics, and how can they overcome these challenges?
5. Could you provide an overview of the key metrics that HR analytics can help track and improve, such as employee engagement, retention, productivity, and performance?

CHAPTER

2

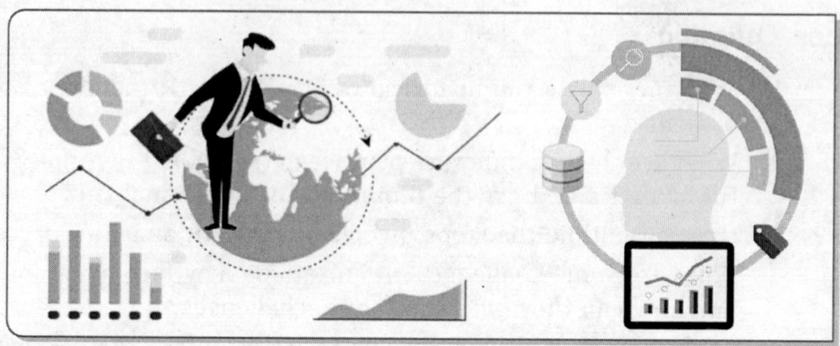

Data Collection and Management in HR Analytics

An essential component of HR analytics is data management and collecting. The process of using data to obtain insights into many areas of human resource management, such as workforce planning, hiring, employee engagement, and retention, is known as HR analytics.

HR practises and decision-making are improved by the use of data and analytics approaches, or HR Analytics. HR Analytics draws its data from a variety of sources, including performance reviews, personnel records, and surveys. In HR Analytics, gathering and managing data is essential since it lays the foundation for making decisions based on data.

Compiling information from many sources, including employee records, questionnaires, and performance reviews, is a component of the data gathering process. Structured and unstructured data are the two primary categories into which the gathered data may be divided. Unstructured data, such employee input from surveys, is difficult to organise. In contrast, structured data, like employment records, is readily organised into databases or spreadsheets.

The process of organising, storing and maintaining gathered data in a way that is safe and easily accessible is known as data management. This guarantees the validity, correctness, and completeness of the data as well as the elimination of any mistakes or discrepancies. After the data has been cleansed and arranged, it may be analysed to produce insights that will help in decision-making.

Organisations may discover patterns, make wise decisions, and improve HR procedures with the help of efficient data collection and administration via HR analytics. Assuring the pertinent nature and ethical origin of the gathered data is crucial, nevertheless. Moreover, compliance with data privacy laws like the CCPA and GDPR as well as data security are critical factors. To collect and manage data effectively in HR analytics, organizations need to follow a few key steps:

1. **Defining the Scope:** The first step in data collection is to define the scope of the analysis, including the type of data needed, the sources of data, and the analysis goals. This helps to ensure that the data collected is relevant and useful for the analysis.

2. **Collecting Data:** HR professionals use various methods to collect data, including surveys, assessments, interviews, and performance metrics. Surveys are commonly used to collect data on employee engagement, job satisfaction, and work-related issues. Assessments are used to evaluate employee skills and competencies, while interviews provide insights into employee behaviour and attitudes. Performance metrics, such as productivity, absenteeism, and turnover rates, are used to evaluate employee performance.
3. **Cleaning and Processing Data**: Once the data is collected, it needs to be cleaned and processed to remove errors, inconsistencies, and irrelevant data. This is done to ensure that the data is accurate, complete, and relevant for analysis.
4. **Storing Data:** HR professionals use various tools and platforms to store and manage employee data, including HR information systems (HRIS), data warehouses, and cloud-based platforms. These platforms provide a centralized repository for employee data, making it easier to manage and analyse.
5. **Analysing Data**: Human Resource (HR) professionals employ diverse methodologies for scrutinizing employee data, encompassing descriptive, predictive, and prescriptive analytics. Descriptive analytics serve to summarize and portray employee data, whereas predictive analytics anticipate forthcoming trends and potential outcomes. In contrast, prescriptive analytics offer data-driven insights for decision-making and provide recommendations based on analysis.
6. **Reporting and Communicating Results**: The final step in data collection and management is to report and communicate the results of the analysis to stakeholders, including HR managers, business leaders, and employees. This helps to ensure that the insights gained from the analysis are translated into actionable recommendations that can improve organizational performance and employee engagement.

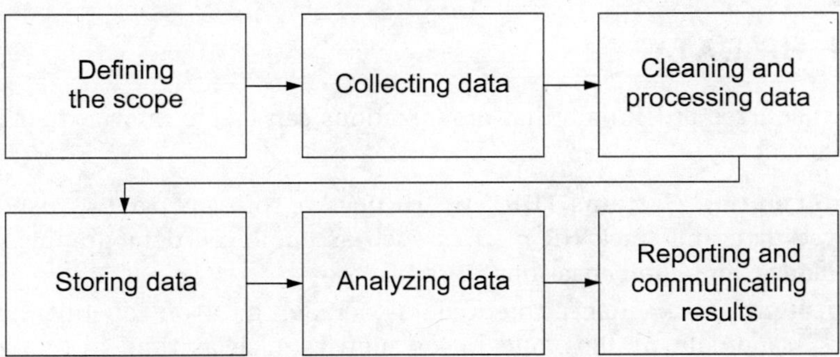

FIGURE 2.1 Steps to collect and manage data.

Overall, effective data collection and management are critical to the success of HR analytics. By following these steps, organizations can use data to gain insights into their workforce and make data-driven decisions to improve their HR practices.

How to collect and manage HR data, including best practices for data privacy and security Collecting and managing HR data is an important aspect of HR analytics. It is crucial to follow best practices for data privacy and security to protect sensitive information. Following are some steps to consider:

1. **Identify the Data You Need:** Determine the data that you need to collect for HR analytics. This may include employee demographics, performance metrics, compensation data, and other relevant information.
2. **Collect Data Ethically:** Ensure that you are collecting data ethically, which means that you are obtaining data with informed consent and following privacy regulations. Data should only be collected for legitimate business purposes and should not be used for discriminatory purposes.
3. **Use Secure Storage and Management Systems:** Use secure storage and management systems to keep data safe. This may include firewalls, password-protected systems, encryption, and other security measures.
4. **Train Employees on Data Privacy:** Train employees on data privacy best practices and security measures. This includes how to handle sensitive information, how to store and share data securely, and how to report data breaches.
5. **Develop a Privacy Policy:** Develop a privacy policy that outlines how HR data will be collected, stored, and used. This policy should also include information on data retention and disposal.
6. **Conduct Regular Security Audits:** Conduct regular security audits to ensure that your data management practices are up to date and effective. This can help identify vulnerabilities and ensure that your systems are secure.
7. **Stay up-to-date on Privacy Laws and Regulations:** Stay up-to-date on privacy laws and regulations to ensure that your data management practices comply with current regulations.

By following these best practices, one can collect and manage HR data safely and effectively for HR analytics.

SOURCES OF HR DATA

There are various sources of HR data that organizations can use to inform their HR analytics, some of which include:

1. **HR Information Systems (HRIS):** HRIS is a software that is used to manage employee data and track HR metrics such as employee demographics, attendance, performance, and compensation.
2. **Recruitment Data**: Recruitment data includes data on job postings, applicant tracking, candidate profiles, and hiring metrics such as time to fill, cost per hire, and source of hire.
3. **Employee Surveys:** Employee surveys are a way to collect employee feedback on various aspects of the workplace, such as engagement, satisfaction, and culture.
4. **Performance Data:** Performance data includes information on employee goals, objectives, feedback, and ratings.
5. **Payroll Data:** Payroll data includes information on employee salaries, wages, bonuses, and benefits.
6. **Time and Attendance Data:** Time and attendance data includes information on employee work hours, absences, and time-off requests.

7. **Exit Interview Data:** Exit interview data includes information on why employees are leaving the organization and can provide insights into areas that may need improvement.
8. **Training and Development Data**: Training and development data can include information on the number of employees trained, training completion rates, and the effectiveness of training programs.
9. **Social Media:** Social media data can provide insights into employee sentiment and brand reputation.
10. **Publicly Available Data:** Publicly available data such as industry benchmarks, demographic data, and economic data can also provide insights into HR metrics.
11. **Health and Safety Data:** Health and safety data can include information on workplace accidents, injuries, and illnesses.
12. **Diversity and Inclusion Data:** Diversity and inclusion data can include information on the representation of different groups within the organization, such as gender, race, and ethnicity.

HR professionals utilize diverse methodologies to analyse employee data, employing descriptive analytics to summarize and depict employee information, predictive analytics to forecast future trends, and prescriptive analytics to make data-informed decisions and suggestions. Organizations harness these data sources to derive valuable insights about their workforce, pinpoint areas for enhancement, and implement data-centric strategies to refine their HR practices.

TYPES OF HR DATA

Organizations can gather and scrutinize various types of HR data to gain deeper insights into their human resources practices. Following are some common types of HR data:

1. **Demographic Data:** This encompasses details like age, gender, ethnicity, educational background, and work history. Such data aids in comprehending the workforce composition and identifying spots where diversity and inclusion initiatives may be necessary.
2. **Performance Data:** This category includes metrics related to employee performance such as productivity, sales figures, customer satisfaction ratings, and other relevant performance indicators. This information assists organizations in gauging employee performance and identifying avenues for enhancement.
3. **Engagement Data:** This category consists of data concerning employee engagement, including feedback from satisfaction surveys, turnover rates, and retention figures. These insights help organizations gauge employee engagement levels and pinpoint areas where HR practices can be improved.
4. **Compensation Data:** Details regarding employee salaries, bonuses, and benefits fall into this category. This data allows organizations to compare their compensation practices against industry benchmarks and make adjustments where necessary.
5. **Recruitment Data:** Information encompassing applicant numbers, recruitment sources, time-to-hire metrics, and cost-per-hire fall under this category. These

metrics offer insights into the effectiveness of recruitment strategies and areas where adjustments might be needed.

6. **Training and Development Data:** This involves statistics related to employee training initiatives, including completion rates, training costs, and the efficacy of training programs. This data enables organization to evaluate the effectiveness of their training initiatives and identify areas for improvement."

By collecting and analysing these various types of HR data, organizations can gain valuable insights into their HR practices and make data-driven decisions to improve employee performance, engagement, and retention.

TABLE 2.1 Different types of HR data

Types of HR Data	*Description*
Employee Data	Personal and professional information about employees, such as age, gender, education, performance metrics, and compensation data.
Recruitment Data	Information related to recruitment processes, such as the number of applicants, recruitment sources, time-to-hire, and cost-per-hire.
Employee Engagement Surveys	Surveys used to measure employee satisfaction, motivation, and commitment to the organization.
Exit Interviews	Interviews conducted with departing employees to identify reasons for leaving and areas for improvement in HR practices.
Training and Development Data	Information on the number of employees trained, training completion rates, and the effectiveness of training programs.
Performance Data	Information on employee productivity, quality of work, and customer satisfaction.
Time and Attendance Data	Information on employee attendance, leave requests, and overtime.
Health and Safety Data	Information on workplace accidents, injuries, and illnesses.
Diversity and Inclusion Data	Information on the representation of different groups within the organization, such as gender, race, and ethnicity.

OVERVIEW OF THE DIFFERENT DATA ANALYSIS TECHNIQUES USED IN HR ANALYTICS

HR analytics is the application of data analysis techniques to people-related data in order to gain insights and make informed decisions about human resources management. There are a variety of data analysis techniques used in HR analytics, each with its own strengths and limitations. Following are the some of the most common data analysis techniques used in HR analytics:

1. **Descriptive Analytics:** Descriptive analytics is used to describe and summarize HR data. It involves the use of charts, graphs, tables, and other visualizations to

show trends and patterns in HR data. Descriptive analytics can help HR managers understand the current state of their workforce, identify areas of strength and weakness, and make decisions based on that information.

2. **Predictive Analytics:** Predictive analytics involves using historical HR data to forecast future trends and outcomes. It employs statistical models and algorithms to recognize patterns and relationships within HR data, aiding in predictions about forthcoming events. HR managers leverage predictive analytics to anticipate workforce changes, spot potential issues, and make data-informed decisions to tackle them.
3. **Prescriptive Analytics:** Prescriptive analytics revolves around recommending actions derived from HR data analysis. It utilizes algorithms and models to determine the best strategies for achieving desired outcomes. This form of analytics assists HR managers in making informed decisions regarding talent management, recruitment, employee engagement, and other HR functions.
4. **Text Analytics:** Text analytics focuses on analysing unstructured HR data, such as employee feedback, surveys, and social media content. By utilizing natural language processing (NLP) and machine learning techniques, text analytics extracts insights from textual data. HR managers benefit from text analytics by identifying prevalent themes and sentiments in employee feedback, comprehending the drivers of employee engagement, and pinpointing areas for improvement.
5. **Machine Learning:** Machine learning, a subset of artificial intelligence, employs algorithms and statistical models to identify patterns and relationships in HR data. Its applications in HR encompass recruitment, talent management, employee engagement, and performance management. Machine learning aids HR managers in making more precise predictions, uncovering concealed patterns and relationships, and automating routine HR tasks.
6. **Network Analysis:** Network analysis is used to analyse relationships between employees and other entities in the organization. It involves the use of graph theory and other mathematical techniques to identify patterns and relationships in HR data. Network analysis can help HR managers identify key influencers in the organization, understand the flow of information and communication, and identify potential bottlenecks in decision-making processes.

HR analytics is a powerful tool for HR managers to gain insights and make informed decisions about their workforce. By using a combination of these data analysis techniques, HR managers can identify patterns and relationships in HR data, make predictions about future outcomes, and make data-driven decisions to improve the performance and engagement of their workforce.

DESCRIPTIVE ANALYTICS FOR HR DATA

Descriptive analytics is the process of analysing data to understand what has happened in the past. In the context of HR data, descriptive analytics can help you gain insights into employee demographics, workforce trends, and HR metrics such as turnover rates and employee engagement scores.

Stated are some examples of descriptive analytics for HR data:

1. **Demographic Analysis:** You can analyse HR data to understand the composition of your workforce in terms of age, gender, race/ethnicity, educational level, and other relevant factors. This can help you identify diversity and inclusion gaps and tailor your recruitment and retention strategies accordingly.
2. **Turnover Analysis:** By analysing historical data on employee turnover, you can identify patterns and trends in the reasons for employee exits. This can help you identify problem areas and take corrective action, such as improving employee engagement, compensation and benefits packages, and career development opportunities.
3. **Performance Analysis:** You can analyse HR data to understand employee performance trends, such as average performance ratings, performance distribution across departments, and top performers by job role. This can help you identify performance gaps and take corrective action, such as providing training and development opportunities or revising job descriptions.
4. **Recruitment Analysis:** Through the examination of recruitment data, valuable insights into the efficiency of recruitment processes emerge, including metrics like time to fill, cost per hire, and source of hire. Analysing this data optimizes recruitment strategies and resource allocation.
5. **HR Metric Analysis:** Evaluation of HR metrics such as employee engagement scores, absenteeism rates, and overtime hours uncovers workforce trends and highlights areas for enhancement. This analysis aids in boosting employee satisfaction, productivity, cost reduction, and revenue increase.

Descriptive analytics is a valuable tool for gaining insights from HR data, facilitating data-driven decisions, and enhancing workforce management practices.

PREDICTIVE HR ANALYTICS

Predictive HR analytics involves leveraging data, statistical algorithms, and machine learning to forecast future outcomes in HR processes such as hiring, performance management, and employee retention. By scrutinizing past and present data, predictions about future HR events become feasible, such as identifying potential high-performing candidates or employees at risk of leaving the organization.

Predictive HR analytics provides significant advantages for HR professionals, enabling proactive measures to retain valuable employees and make more informed hiring decisions. This technology has the potential to optimize resources, enhance the workforce, and reduce turnover. However, ethical use is essential to prevent discrimination against specific groups.

Understanding Predictive Analytics in HR

Predictive analytics utilizes data, statistical algorithms, and machine learning to predict future outcomes based on historical data. In HR, predictive analytics enhances HR practices by foreseeing workforce trends, behaviours, and outcomes.

Some of the common applications of predictive analytics in HR include:

1. **Recruitment and Selection:** Utilizing historical data to identify suitable candidates and predict their likelihood of accepting a job offer.
2. **Employee Retention:** Identifying turnover factors and predicting employees at risk of leaving, aiding in the development of retention strategies.
3. **Performance Management:** Identifying factors influencing employee performance and predicting future performance levels.
4. **Succession Planning**: Predictive analytics can help in identifying employees with high potential for leadership roles and predicting their readiness for future roles.
5. **Diversity and Inclusion**: Predictive analytics can help in identifying areas of the organization that may be lacking diversity and predicting the impact of diversity initiatives.

To use predictive analytics in HR, organizations need to have access to relevant data, such as employee data, performance data, and recruitment data. They also need to have the right technology and analytical tools to analyse the data and generate insights.

It's important to note that predictive analytics is not a magic bullet and should be used in conjunction with other HR practices and strategies. It's also important to ensure that the use of predictive analytics is ethical and transparent, and that employees' privacy is protected.

Predictive Modelling

A statistical method called predictive modelling is used to forecast future events using past data. It entails analysing previous data and finding patterns using mathematical and computational techniques, which are then utilised to forecast upcoming occurrences or behaviours.

Numerous industries, including marketing, finance, healthcare, and engineering, frequently employ predictive modelling. Large datasets are frequently analysed for patterns, which are then utilised to forecast future trends, consumer behaviour, and other crucial business KPIs.

Machine learning, which includes teaching algorithms to find patterns in data and generate predictions based on those patterns, is one of the most widely used approaches in predictive modelling. Neural networks, decision trees, and statistical regression analysis are other methods utilised in predictive modelling.

In data science, predictive modelling is a method for forecasting future occurrences that are not yet known. In order to forecast potential future events, it entails examining past data and spotting patterns and trends. Many different businesses, such as banking, healthcare, marketing, and insurance, utilise predictive modelling extensively to estimate results, identify opportunities and dangers, and make data-driven choices.

The following steps are commonly involved in the predictive modelling process:

1. **Data Collection and Cleaning:** The first step is to gather pertinent/relevant data and cleaning it to make sure it is correct, accurate, and comprehensive.
2. **Data Exploration and Visualization:** The next step is to find patterns and correlations, examine and visualise the data.
3. **Feature Engineering:** Feature engineering involves selecting and transforming the relevant features or variables that will be used in the model.
4. **Model Selection:** The next step is to select the appropriate predictive modelling algorithm based on the problem at hand and the type of data available.

5. **Model Training:** The selected model is then trained on the historical data to learn the patterns and relationships.
6. **Model Evaluation:** The trained model is evaluated using a validation dataset to assess its performance and determine where the trained model needs to be improved.
7. **Model Deployment:** Once the model is evaluated and meets the desired performance criteria, it is deployed to make predictions on new data.

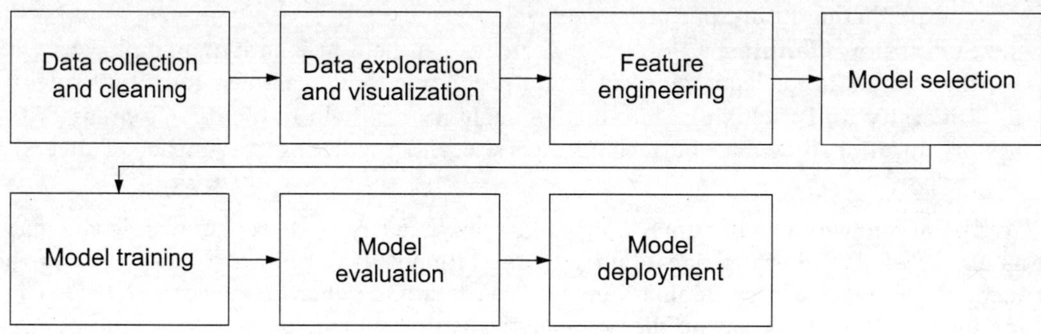

FIGURE 2.2 The predictive modelling process.

There are various techniques and algorithms used in predictive modelling, including regression analysis, decision trees, random forests, neural networks, and support vector machines. The choice of algorithm depends on the nature of the problem, the type of data available, and the desired level of accuracy.

Applications for predictive modelling include anticipating equipment failure, detecting fraud, predicting disease outbreaks, projecting revenue, and predicting customer attrition. The choice of algorithm, the calibre of the model-building process, and the quantity and quality of data utilised all affect how accurate predictive models are.

In short, predictive modelling is a powerful tool used in data science to make predictions about future events. It involves a structured process of collecting, cleaning, exploring, and visualizing data, selecting the appropriate algorithm, training and evaluating the model, and deploying it to make predictions.

PRESCRIPTIVE ANALYTICS FOR HR DATA

Prescriptive analytics uses data, statistical tools, and machine learning to figure out what the best thing to do is in a certain scenario. In the context of HR data, prescriptive analytics can be used to identify the best strategies for managing employee performance, improving retention rates, and optimizing hiring processes.

Following are some examples of how prescriptive analytics can be applied to HR data:

1. **Performance Management:** By analysing data on employee performance, such as productivity, quality of work, and customer satisfaction, prescriptive analytics can identify the best strategies for improving performance. For example, the analysis might suggest providing additional training, changing work assignments, or adjusting performance metrics to better align with business goals.

2. **Retention Management:** By analysing data on employee turnover, prescriptive analytics can identify the factors that contribute to high turnover rates and provide recommendations for improving retention. For example, the analysis might suggest increasing compensation, improving work-life balance, or enhancing employee engagement programs.
3. **Hiring Optimization:** By analysing data on job applicants and current employees, prescriptive analytics can identify the best strategies for hiring and retaining top talent. For example, the analysis might suggest adjusting job descriptions, targeting specific recruiting channels, or offering more competitive compensation packages.

Prescriptive analytics can help HR departments make more informed decisions and optimize their processes to achieve better outcomes for the organization and its employees. However, it's important to note that prescriptive analytics should be used in conjunction with human judgment and expertise, rather than replacing them entirely.

TEXT ANALYTICS FOR HR DATA

Text analytics is a powerful tool for HR data analysis. It can help HR professionals to extract meaningful insights from large volumes of unstructured data, such as employee feedback, resumes, and performance reviews.

Following are some ways that text analytics can be applied to HR data:

1. **Employee Sentiment Analysis:** Text analytics can be used to analyse employee feedback and identify common themes and sentiment. This can help HR professionals to understand how employees feel about the company, their job, and their colleagues.
2. **Resume Screening:** Text analytics can be used to screen resumes and identify candidates with the desired skills and experience. This can save HR professionals a lot of time and help them to identify the most qualified candidates more quickly.
3. **Performance Review Analysis:** Text analytics can be used to analyse performance reviews and identify patterns and trends in employee performance. This can help HR professionals to identify areas where additional training or support may be needed.
4. **Diversity and Inclusion Analysis:** Text analytics can be used to analyse job postings and identify language that may be biased or exclusionary. This can help HR professionals to create more inclusive job descriptions and attract a more diverse candidate pool.

To sum up, text analytics can help HR professionals to make data-driven decisions and improve their HR practices. However, it's important to ensure that the data used in text analytics is anonymized and that privacy regulations are followed.

MACHINE LEARNING FOR HR DATA

Machine learning (ML) can be applied to various types of data, including HR data. ML algorithms can help automate tasks related to hiring, employee retention, performance management, and employee engagement.

Following are some examples of how machine learning can be used in HR:

1. **Resume Screening:** ML algorithms can be used to screen resumes and identify the best candidates based on skills, experience, and education.
2. **Predicting Employee Turnover:** By analysing past employee data, machine learning can help predict which employees are at a higher risk of leaving the company, allowing HR teams to take proactive measures to retain them.
3. **Performance Management:** Machine learning can be used to identify patterns in employee performance data and make recommendations for improvement.
4. **Employee Engagement:** ML can be used to analyse employee engagement survey data and identify factors that are most important for employee satisfaction, allowing HR teams to take targeted actions to improve employee engagement.
5. **Diversity and Inclusion:** Machine learning can be used to identify and eliminate biases in the hiring process and ensure that the hiring process is fair and inclusive.

Machine learning can help HR teams make data-driven decisions that improve the efficiency and effectiveness of HR processes. However, it is important to ensure that the data used to train these algorithms is representative and unbiased to avoid perpetuating existing biases in HR practices.

NETWORK ANALYSIS IN HR ANALYTICS

Network analysis is a useful tool in HR analytics because it lets companies look at how workers connect and relate to each other and find patterns of behaviour that can affect performance and productivity.

Social network analysis is a popular use of network analysis in HR analytics. This includes mapping and analysing the social relationships between workers, such as who talks to whom, who has the most power, and who has the best connections within the company. This knowledge can help you figure out who the important people are and how to communicate with them most effectively.

Team network analysis is another use of network analysis in HR analytics. This includes looking at the web of connections within a team to find its strengths and weaknesses and come up with ways to make it work better together and be more productive.

One can also use network analysis to find out how engaged your employees are by looking at how they talk to each other and work together. This lets you see which employees are really involved and which ones may not be.

Network analysis can tell us a lot about the connections and relationships that make an organisation work. It can also help human resources workers make choices based on data to boost the company's productivity, engagement, and teamwork.

STATISTICAL MODELLING TECHNIQUES FOR HR DATA

There are several statistical modelling techniques that can be applied to HR data to gain insights and make data-driven decisions. Few examples are as follows:

1. **Regression Analysis:** Regression analysis can be used to understand the relationship between one or more independent variables (e.g., age, education, experience) and a dependent variable (e.g., job performance, salary). This can help HR teams identify factors that contribute to employee success and inform decisions related to hiring, promotion, and compensation.
2. **Cluster Analysis:** Cluster analysis is a technique used to group similar data points together based on their characteristics. In HR, this could involve grouping employees based on their skills, job roles, or other factors. This can help HR teams identify patterns and develop targeted interventions to improve employee engagement, retention, and performance.
3. **Time Series Analysis:** Time series analysis involves analysing data over time to identify trends and patterns. In HR, this could involve analysing data on employee turnover or absenteeism to identify patterns and develop strategies to reduce these metrics.
4. **Decision Trees:** Decision trees are a type of machine learning model that can be used to predict outcomes based on a set of input variables. In HR, decision trees could be used to predict which candidates are most likely to succeed in a particular job or which employees are most likely to leave the organization.
5. **Neural Networks:** Neural networks are a type of machine learning model that can be used to analyse complex data sets. In HR, neural networks could be used to analyse data on employee performance and identify patterns that predict success or failure in a particular job.

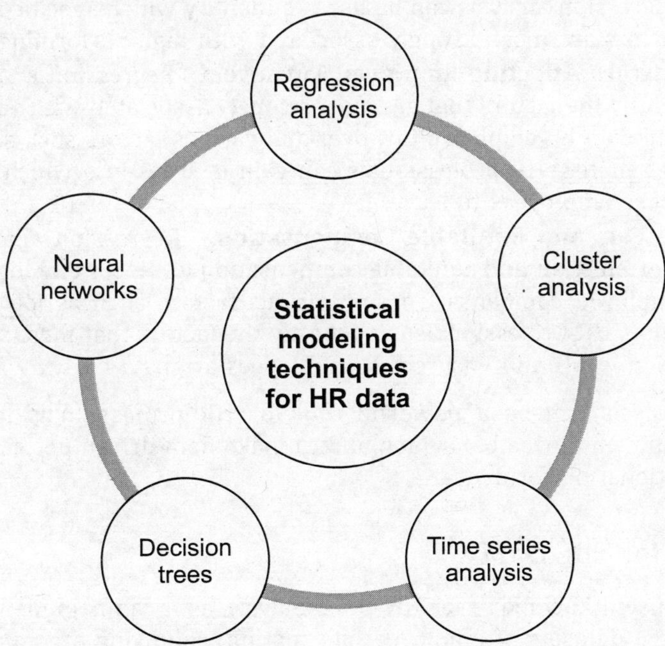

FIGURE 2.3 Statistical modelling techniques for HR data.

Overall, statistical modelling techniques can help HR teams make data-driven decisions that improve employee engagement, retention, and performance.

Regression Analysis in HR Analytics

A statistics method called regression analysis is used to look at the connection between a dependent variable (also called the result or response variable) and one or more independent variables (also called predictor or explanatory variables). The purpose of regression analysis is to discover how changes in the dependent variable are connected to changes in the independent factors.

By fitting a statistical model to the data, we can guess what the dependent variable is based on the numbers of the independent variables. This method is known as regression analysis. Most of the time, simple linear regression is used to look at regression. It is thought that the dependent variable and the independent variable(s) are linked in a straight line.

Regression analysis comes in many forms, such as multiple regression, logistic regression, polynomial regression, and more. A lot of different areas use regression analysis. Some examples are economics, banking, engineering, and the social sciences.

Regression analysis is a commonly used statistical method in HR Analytics. It is used to understand the relationship between two or more variables and to predict future outcomes. In HR Analytics, regression analysis can be used to:

1. **Predict Employee Performance:** Regression analysis can be used to identify the key factors that are most strongly associated with employee performance. For example, regression analysis can be used to identify which specific skills, experience, or other factors are most strongly associated with high-performing employees.
2. **Identify Factors Affecting Employee Turnover:** Regression analysis can also be used to identify the factors that are most strongly associated with employee turnover. By analysing data on employee turnover and various factors such as job satisfaction, salary, and benefits, HR professionals can gain insights into which factors are most likely to cause employees to leave.
3. **Determine Fair and Equitable Compensation:** Regression analysis can also be used to determine fair and equitable compensation levels for employees. By analysing data on employee compensation and various factors such as job title, experience, and education, HR professionals can identify the factors that most strongly influence compensation levels and ensure that employees are paid fairly.

Regression analysis can be a powerful tool for HR professionals looking to better understand and predict employee behaviour, and to make data-driven decisions that can help to improve organizational performance.

Cluster Analysis for HR Data

Cluster analysis is a useful technique for HR data analysis, as it can help identify patterns and groupings within large datasets of employee information. Following are some steps you can take to conduct a cluster analysis on HR data:

1. **Identify the Variables:** The first step is to identify the variables you want to include in your analysis. These may include demographic information (such as age,

gender, or education level), job-related information (such as job title, department, or tenure), and performance metrics (such as productivity or customer satisfaction ratings).

2. **Choose a Clustering Method:** There are several different methods for clustering data, including hierarchical clustering and k-means clustering. Choose the method that best fits your data and research question.
3. **Pre-process the Data:** Before running the cluster analysis, you may need to pre-process the data to ensure that it is in a suitable format. This may include transforming categorical variables into numerical values, standardizing the data, or removing outliers.
4. **Run the Cluster Analysis:** Once the data is prepared, run the cluster analysis using your chosen method. This will group employees together based on the similarities between their data points.
5. **Interpret the Results:** Finally, interpret the results of the cluster analysis to gain insights into the data. This may include identifying clusters of employees with similar characteristics, examining differences between clusters, and exploring how different variables contribute to the clustering.

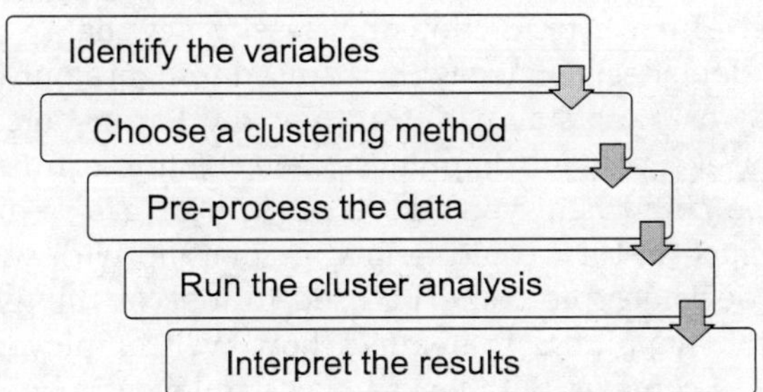

FIGURE 2.4 Steps involved in conducting a cluster analysis on HR data.

Cluster analysis can be a powerful tool for HR professionals looking to gain a deeper understanding of employee data and make more informed decisions about workforce management.

Time Series Analysis

Time series analysis is a powerful technique for analysing and forecasting data that varies over time. When applied to HR data, time series analysis can help identify patterns, trends, and anomalies in employee-related metrics such as turnover rates, performance metrics, and employee engagement scores.

To do time series analysis on HR data, you must first gather the data and set it up in a way that makes sense as a time series. Usually, this means collecting data points on a regular basis (like once a month, three times a year, or yearly) and putting them in order of when they happened.

You can use a number of statistical methods and software tools to look at the data once it is in a time series format. Moving averages, exponential smoothing, and ARIMA models are all common ways to look at time data.

Finding the average of a certain set of data points over a period of time is what moving averages are all about. This can help even out short-term changes in the data and show longer-term patterns.

In a way that is similar to moving averages, exponential smoothing gives more weight to data points that are more recent. There may be times when this is helpful, like when the data changes with the seasons or the year.

Autoregressive Integrated Moving Average (ARIMA) models are a more advanced method that can find intricate trends in data. A lot of people use ARIMA models to make predictions, and they can help you guess what HR measures, like turnover rates or employee involvement scores, will be in the future.

To sum up, time series analysis can provide valuable insights into the behaviour of HR data over time and help organizations make data-driven decisions about their workforce.

Decision Trees

Decision trees can be an effective tool for analysing HR data. Decision trees are a type of algorithmic model that can be used for both classification and regression analysis. They work by recursively splitting the data based on the most important features, creating a tree-like structure that can be used to make predictions or classify new data.

When looking at HR data, decision trees can be used to figure out what makes employees perform well, be happy at work, and stay with the company. For instance, a decision tree could be used to look at things like pay, job happiness, and commute time that affect employee turnover. The decision tree could help you figure out which factors are the most important for predicting turnover, which in turn could help you come up with ways to lower turnover.

In the same way, a decision tree could be used to look at things like training chances, management style, and job happiness that affect how well employees do their jobs. This information could be used to come up with ways to get employees to work harder and produce more. In general, decision trees can help you look at HR data and find patterns and trends that can help you make decisions and plan your HR strategy.

Neural Networks in HR Analytics

Neural networks are very useful for HR analytics because they can help find trends and connections in very large and complicated datasets. Neural networks are a type of machine learning programme that is based on how the brain is built and how it works. They are made up of layers of nodes, or neurons, that are linked together and process information to make forecasts.

In HR analytics, neural networks can be used for a variety of tasks, including:

1. **Predictive Analytics**: Neural networks can be used to predict employee turnover, performance, and engagement based on data such as demographics, job history, and performance metrics.
2. **Sentiment Analysis**: Neural networks can be used to analyse employee feedback and sentiment in surveys, social media, and other sources to identify patterns and trends in employee satisfaction and engagement.

3. **Talent Management:** Neural networks can be used to identify high-potential employees and to recommend training and development opportunities based on their skills and performance.
4. **Diversity and Inclusion:** Neural networks can be used to identify patterns and trends in hiring and promotion practices to help organizations identify and address biases and promote diversity and inclusion.
5. **Employee Engagement:** Neural networks can be used to analyse data on employee behaviour and interactions to identify factors that contribute to engagement and to recommend strategies for improving engagement.

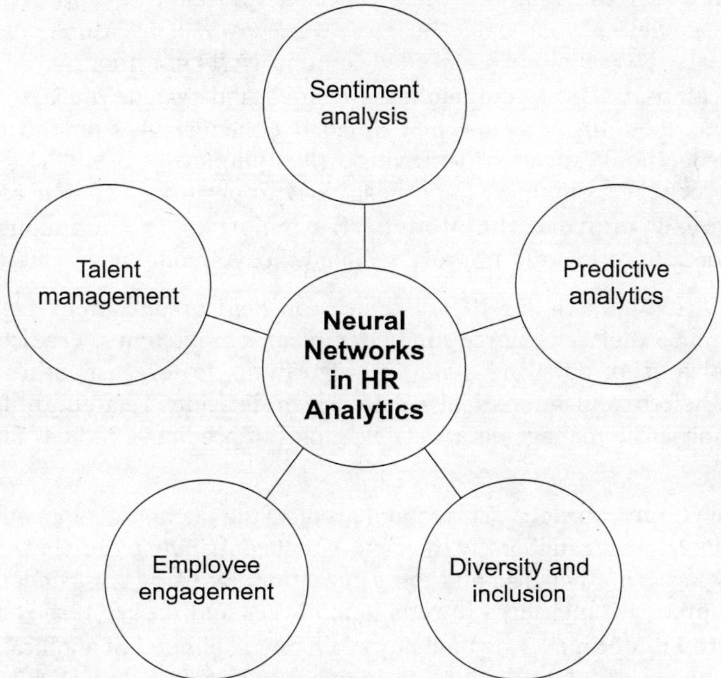

FIGURE 2.5 Tasks of neural networks in HR analytics.

Neural networks can help organizations to make better decisions about talent management, employee engagement, and diversity and inclusion by providing insights into complex data sets that would be difficult to analyse using traditional methods.

BUILDING PREDICTIVE MODELS FOR HR OUTCOMES

Building predictive models for HR outcomes can be a valuable tool for organizations to make informed decisions regarding their workforce. Following are some general steps you can follow to build predictive models for HR outcomes:

1. **Define the Outcome:** The first step is to define the HR outcome you want to predict. This could be anything from employee turnover, employee performance, or employee engagement.

2. **Gather Data:** The next step is to gather data on your employees, such as demographics, job history, performance data, and any other relevant information that can help predict the outcome you defined.
3. **Identify Predictors:** Once you have your data, you need to identify the predictors that are most relevant to the outcome you want to predict. This could include factors like job tenure, job performance, salary, and other employee attributes.
4. **Choose a Modelling Approach:** There are many different modelling approaches you can use, including regression analysis, decision trees, random forests, and neural networks. Choose the approach that is best suited for your data and outcome.
5. **Train and Test the Model:** Once you have chosen your approach, you need to train the model on your data and test its accuracy using a holdout dataset. Make adjustments to your model as needed to improve its accuracy.
6. **Use the Model:** Once your model is trained and tested, you can use it to make predictions about the outcome you defined. Use the insights from the model to inform your HR decisions, such as identifying which employees are at risk of leaving the company or which employees are most likely to perform well in a new role.
7. **Continuously Improve the Model:** It's important to continuously collect and analyse data to refine and improve your predictive model over time.

Building predictive models for HR outcomes can help organizations make data-driven decisions and optimize their workforce for better business outcomes. Predictive models for HR outcomes involve using data and statistical algorithms to forecast future HR outcomes. These models can help organizations make data-driven decisions related to hiring, employee retention, and performance management. Few examples of predictive models for HR outcomes are:

1. **Employee Churn Model:** This model predicts the likelihood of an employee leaving the organization. It can identify the factors that contribute to employee turnover, such as salary, work-life balance, and job satisfaction. By using this model, organizations can take proactive measures to retain employees and reduce turnover.
2. **Candidate Fit Model:** This model predicts the likelihood of a job candidate being a good fit for a particular position. It can analyse candidate data such as their resume, work experience, and skills, and compare it to the requirements of the job. By using this model, organizations can make more informed hiring decisions and improve their recruitment process.
3. **Performance Prediction Model:** This model predicts an employee's future job performance based on their past performance data. It can analyse factors such as productivity, attendance, and customer satisfaction ratings. By using this model, organizations can identify high-performing employees and provide targeted training and development opportunities to help them reach their full potential.
4. **Absenteeism Prediction Model:** This model uses historical data on employee absenteeism to forecast the likelihood of an employee missing work. The model considers factors such as the employee's job role, work schedule, and personal characteristics to predict absenteeism risk.
5. **Succession Planning Model:** This model uses historical data on employee performance and career development to identify potential successors for key

positions within the organization. The model considers factors such as job-related skills, leadership potential, and career aspirations to identify high-potential employees who could be groomed for future leadership roles.

6. **Diversity and Inclusion Prediction Model:** This model uses historical data on employee demographics and diversity and inclusion metrics to forecast the organization's future diversity and inclusion outcomes. The model considers factors such as recruitment strategies, retention initiatives, and employee engagement to predict the organization's future diversity and inclusion performance.

Overall, predictive models for HR outcomes can help organizations make more informed decisions related to their workforce, leading to improved employee satisfaction, retention, and productivity.

TABLE 2.2 Representation of predictive models for HR outcomes

Model	*Description*	*Outcome*
Logistic Regression	A statistical model that use a collection of input variables to forecast a binary result	Employee retention, employee turnover, employee engagement
Decision Trees	An method for machine learning that makes use of a tree-like representation of decisions and their potential outcomes	Employee turnover, employee satisfaction, employee performance
Random Forest	A technique for group learning that builds a large number of decision trees and outputs the class that is the average of the classes	Employee retention, employee turnover, employee engagement
Neural Networks	A collection of algorithms that may be used to learn and generate predictions based on incoming data and that simulate how the human brain works	Employee retention, employee turnover, employee engagement, employee performance
Support Vector Machines	An approach for machine learning that uses a hyperplane to divide data into classes and maximises the gap between the classes	Employee turnover, employee satisfaction, employee performance
Gradient Boosting	A method of machine learning that iteratively adds new models to a group of weak learners to produce a strong learner	Employee retention, employee turnover, employee engagement

Note: These are just a few examples of predictive models that can be used in HR. The specific outcomes that each model can predict may vary depending on the input variables and the organization's specific needs.

Questions for Discussion

Short Questions

1. What is HR Analytics, and why is data collection important in this field?
2. What are some best practices for ensuring data privacy and security in HR data collection?
3. List some common sources of HR data.
4. What are the key steps in effective data collection and management in HR Analytics?
5. How can cluster analysis be beneficial for HR professionals?
6. What types of patterns can time series analysis reveal in HR data?
7. How do decision trees help in HR data analysis?
8. What are neural networks, and how can they be applied in HR analytics?
9. Can you provide examples of HR outcomes that can be predicted using predictive models?
10. What is logistic regression, and how is it used in HR analytics?
11. How does random forest differ from decision trees in HR data analysis?
12. What are some key benefits of using support vector machines in HR analytics?

Long Questions

1. Explain the significance of data collection and management in HR Analytics. How do they contribute to improving HR practices?
2. Describe the steps involved in effective data collection and management for HR Analytics. How can organizations ensure data accuracy and relevance?
3. Discuss the importance of ethical data collection in HR Analytics. How can organizations collect data ethically and comply with privacy regulations?
4. Explain the different types of HR data and their significance in improving HR practices and decision-making.
5. Provide an overview of the data analysis techniques used in HR Analytics, including descriptive analytics, predictive analytics, prescriptive analytics, text analytics, machine learning, and network analysis. How can each technique benefit HR professionals?
6. What is predictive modelling, and how is it applied in HR Analytics? What are some common applications of predictive analytics in HR?
7. Describe prescriptive analytics in HR. Provide examples of how it can help HR professionals make informed decisions.
8. Explain the role of machine learning in HR Analytics. What are some applications of machine learning in HR data analysis?
9. Describe network analysis in HR Analytics. How can organizations use network analysis to improve collaboration and productivity among employees?

10. Explain the concept of regression analysis in HR analytics. Provide examples of HR-related variables that can be analysed using regression analysis, and discuss how this technique can inform HR decisions.
11. Describe the steps involved in conducting a cluster analysis on HR data. How can HR professionals benefit from identifying clusters within their employee data?
12. How does time series analysis work in the context of HR data, and what are the key methods used in time series analysis for HR metrics? Provide examples of HR metrics that can be analysed using time series analysis.
13. Discuss the role of decision trees in HR data analysis. Provide examples of HR scenarios where decision trees can be applied to gain insights and make informed decisions.
14. Explain the concept of neural networks in HR analytics. How can neural networks be used for predictive analytics, sentiment analysis, talent management, diversity and inclusion, and employee engagement in HR?
15. Explore various predictive models for HR outcomes, such as employee churn, candidate fit, performance prediction, absenteeism prediction, succession planning, and diversity and inclusion prediction. How can these models benefit HR departments in different ways, and what are the typical input variables for each model?
16. Compare and contrast different modelling techniques commonly used in HR analytics, including logistic regression, decision trees, random forests, neural networks, support vector machines, and gradient boosting. When and why might one technique be preferred over others in specific HR scenarios?

CHAPTER

3

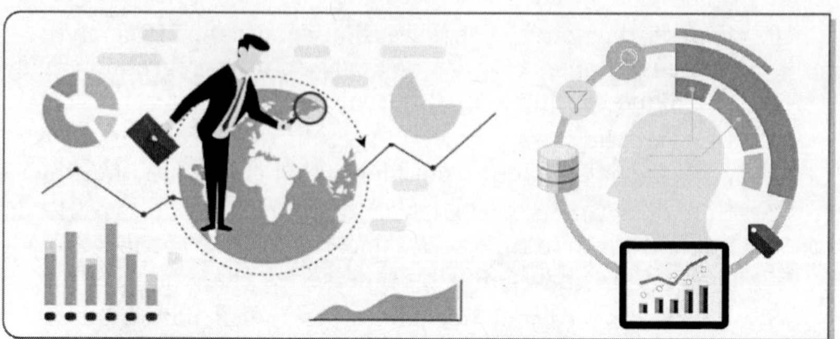

Recruitment Analytics

Recruitment analytics is the process of using data and statistical analysis to make better decisions in the recruitment process. It involves collecting, analysing, and interpreting data related to recruiting efforts to gain insights into the effectiveness of recruitment strategies and to improve decision-making.

Recruitment analytics can help organizations to identify the best sources of candidates, optimize job postings, and evaluate the performance of recruiting teams. It can also be used to analyse candidate behaviour, such as the factors that influence candidate acceptance rates and the reasons why candidates drop out of the recruitment process.

Recruitment analytics can be used to answer a wide range of questions related to recruitment, such as:

- Which recruiting sources are most effective in attracting candidates?
- What is the average time it takes to fill a job vacancy?
- What is the cost per hire for each recruiting source?
- What are the most common reasons for candidate dropouts?
- What are the key factors that influence candidate acceptance rates?

By leveraging recruitment analytics, organizations can make data-driven decisions that result in more efficient and effective recruiting processes, leading to better hiring outcomes and a more productive workforce.

Recruitment analytics refers to the use of data analysis and metrics to improve the recruitment process, make informed decisions, and optimize hiring strategies. It is a critical component of talent acquisition, enabling organizations to make data-driven decisions to attract, retain, and develop top talent.

Recruitment analytics involves collecting and analysing data at every stage of the hiring process, from sourcing candidates to on-boarding. Some of the metrics used in recruitment analytics include time to hire, cost per hire, quality of hire, candidate conversion rates, source of hire, and retention rates.

One of the primary goals of recruitment analytics is to improve the quality of hire. By analysing data on candidate performance, turnover, and other key metrics, organizations can identify the most effective hiring strategies and make data-driven decisions to attract and retain the best talent.

Another key benefit of recruitment analytics is that it helps organizations to optimize their recruitment budget. By analysing the cost per hire, organizations can determine which recruitment channels are the most effective and allocate their resources accordingly.

Recruitment analytics can also provide insights into diversity and inclusion in the recruitment process. By analysing data on candidate demographics, organizations can identify areas where they may be falling short in terms of diversity and take steps to address any biases or gaps in their recruitment strategies.

Recruitment analytics provides valuable insights into the hiring process, allowing organizations to identify areas for improvement, predict future recruitment needs, and make data-driven decisions. With the help of recruitment analytics, companies can measure the effectiveness of their recruitment strategies and make necessary changes to optimize their process.

There are several key metrics that companies can use to measure the success of their recruitment efforts, including:

1. **Time to Hire:** This metric measures the time it takes to fill a position from the point of posting the job ad to the time a candidate accepts an offer. Reducing the time to hire can help organizations fill positions faster and reduce the cost per hire.
2. **Cost per Hire:** This metric measures the total cost of recruiting a new employee, including advertising, job postings, recruitment events, and other expenses. Reducing the cost per hire can help organizations optimize their recruitment budget.
3. **Candidate Experience:** This metric measures the satisfaction of candidates during the recruitment process, including the application process, interview experience, and communication with recruiters. Providing a positive candidate experience can help organizations attract and retain top talent.
4. **Quality of Hire:** This metric measures the performance and retention rates of new hires. Analysing the quality of hire can help organizations identify successful recruitment strategies and improve their hiring process.

Recruitment analytics can be used to optimize recruitment strategies in several ways, including:

1. **Identifying the Most Effective Sourcing Channels:** By analysing data on where successful candidates come from, organizations can identify the most effective sourcing channels and allocate their recruitment budget accordingly.
2. **Improving the Screening Process:** By analysing data on candidate qualifications and interview performance, organizations can identify the most effective screening criteria and improve their screening process.
3. **Optimizing the Interview Process:** By analysing data on interview performance and candidate feedback, organizations can identify areas for improvement in their interview process and make necessary changes.
4. **Predicting Future Recruitment Needs:** By analysing data on recruitment trends, organizations can predict future recruitment needs and proactively plan for hiring.

So, recruitment analytics is an essential tool for optimizing the hiring process and improving the effectiveness of recruitment strategies. By collecting and analysing data on key recruitment metrics, organizations can make data-driven decisions and improve their recruitment process to attract and retain top talent.

IMPORTANCE OF USING ANALYTICS IN RECRUITMENT

Using analytics in recruitment can be crucial for making informed decisions, optimizing hiring processes, and improving the overall quality of hiring. Following are some of the key reasons why analytics are important in recruitment:

1. **Data-driven Decision Making:** Recruitment analytics can provide valuable data that can help organizations make informed decisions about their recruitment strategies. By analysing data related to the job market, applicant pool, and hiring outcomes, organizations can optimize their recruitment processes and make more effective hiring decisions.
2. **Improved Candidate Selection:** Analytics can help identify the most qualified and suitable candidates for a given position by analysing data on candidate skills, experience, and job fit. This can help organizations avoid bias and ensure they are making the best possible hiring decisions.
3. **Streamlined Recruitment Processes:** By using analytics to track key recruitment metrics such as time-to-hire, cost-per-hire, and applicant sources, organizations can identify areas for improvement and optimize their recruitment processes to save time and resources.
4. **Better Retention and Employee Satisfaction:** Recruitment analytics can help organizations identify the factors that contribute to employee turnover and dissatisfaction. By analysing data related to employee engagement, job satisfaction, and performance, organizations can take proactive measures to improve retention and ensure their employees are happy and productive.
5. **Identifying the Best Sources of Hire:** Analytics can help you determine which recruitment sources are most effective in attracting top-quality candidates, such as job boards, social media, or employee referrals.
6. **Predicting Candidate Success:** By analysing data on previous hires, you can develop models to predict the likelihood of a candidate's success based on factors such as their experience, education, and skills.
7. **Improving Diversity and Inclusion:** Analytics can help identify gaps in diversity and inclusion efforts in recruitment by tracking demographic data on applicants and new hires, allowing companies to make more data-driven decisions to promote diversity and inclusion.

Thus, using analytics in recruitment can help companies make better, data-driven decisions, optimize their hiring processes, and ultimately attract and retain top-quality talent.

BENEFITS OF RECRUITMENT ANALYTICS

Recruitment analytics involves the use of data to measure and analyse recruitment processes and outcomes. Some of the benefits of recruitment analytics include:

1. **Improved Hiring Outcomes:** Recruitment analytics helps organizations identify the most effective recruitment strategies, channels, and sources, enabling them to make data-driven decisions that improve the quality of their hires and reduce turnover rates.
2. **Cost Savings:** By identifying the most effective recruitment channels and sources, organizations can save money by focusing their recruitment efforts on those channels that deliver the best results.
3. **Time Savings:** Recruitment analytics can help organizations streamline their recruitment processes, reducing the time it takes to fill open positions and enabling recruiters to focus on higher-value activities.
4. **Diversity and Inclusion:** Recruitment analytics can help organizations identify and address bias in their recruitment processes, leading to a more diverse and inclusive workforce.
5. **Talent Pipeline Management:** Recruitment analytics can help organizations build and manage a talent pipeline, identifying high-potential candidates for future roles and reducing the time and cost of filling open positions.
6. **Continuous Improvement:** Recruitment analytics provides ongoing feedback on recruitment processes and outcomes, enabling organizations to continuously improve their recruitment strategies and tactics.

Recruitment analytics can help organizations make more informed and effective recruitment decisions, leading to better hiring outcomes, cost savings, and a more diverse and inclusive workforce.

SOURCING ANALYTICS

Overview of Sourcing Analytics

Sourcing analytics refers to the use of data analysis and reporting techniques to gain insights into the procurement and sourcing processes of a business. This can include analysing spend data, supplier performance, and contract compliance, among other areas.

Sourcing analytics refers to the use of data and analytical techniques to gain insights into the effectiveness and efficiency of sourcing activities. This involves collecting and analysing data on various aspects of the sourcing process, such as supplier performance, cost of goods, lead times, and quality control, among others.

The primary goal of sourcing analytics is to help organizations make better-informed decisions related to their procurement and sourcing strategies. By analysing the data, organizations can identify areas of improvement, such as identifying cost savings opportunities, improving supplier relationships, and reducing risk, in their sourcing process and take steps to optimize it, leading to cost savings, improved supplier performance, and better outcomes.

The following are some key components of sourcing analytics:

1. **Data Collection:** This involves gathering data from various sources, including internal and external data sources such as ERP systems, supplier databases, and market data.
2. **Data Analysis:** This involves using analytical tools and techniques such as data visualization, statistical analysis, and predictive modelling to identify patterns and trends in the data.
3. **Supplier Performance Monitoring:** Sourcing analytics can help organizations track the performance of their suppliers and identify areas where they can improve. This can include tracking delivery times, product quality, and compliance with regulations.
4. **Cost Analysis:** Sourcing analytics can help organizations identify cost-saving opportunities by analysing data on the cost of goods, transportation costs, and supplier pricing.
5. **Risk Analysis:** Sourcing analytics can help organizations identify and mitigate supply chain risks, such as disruptions in the supply chain or issues with supplier compliance.
6. **Forecasting:** Sourcing analytics can help organizations forecast demand and plan for future sourcing needs, ensuring they have the right suppliers and resources in place to meet demand.

Thus, sourcing analytics is a powerful tool for organizations looking to optimize their sourcing and procurement processes. By leveraging data and analytics, organizations can gain insights into their sourcing activities and make data-driven decisions that lead to improved supplier performance, cost savings, and better outcomes.

Sourcing analytics can involve the use of various tools and techniques, such as data visualization, machine learning, and predictive analytics. These tools can help businesses to identify patterns and trends in their sourcing data and make more informed decisions.

Some common metrics and KPIs (key performance indicators) used in sourcing analytics include:

- Total spends
- Cost savings
- Supplier performance metrics (e.g. on-time delivery, quality)
- Contract compliance
- Supplier diversity metrics
- Risk management metrics

Overall, sourcing analytics can help businesses to optimize their sourcing processes, reduce costs, and improve supplier relationships, leading to increased efficiency and profitability.

Measuring the Effectiveness of Sourcing Channels

Measuring the effectiveness of sourcing channels is crucial for any organization, as it helps them to allocate resources and optimize their recruitment strategy. Following are some ways one can measure the effectiveness of their sourcing channels:

1. **Track Candidate Sources:** Start by tracking where your candidates are coming from. This could be through your website, job boards, social media, employee referrals, etc. Keep a record of how many candidates each source generates.
2. **Conversion Rate:** Measure the conversion rate of each candidate source. This is the percentage of candidates who applied or were contacted through a specific source and went on to the next stage of the recruitment process. For example, if 100 candidates applied through a job board and 10 were invited for an interview, the conversion rate would be 10%.
3. **Time-to-Hire:** Measure the time it takes to fill a position through each source. This will help you identify which sources are generating candidates who are a good fit for the role and are more likely to be hired quickly.
4. **Cost-per-Hire:** Measure the cost of recruiting through each source. This includes the cost of job postings, advertising, and any fees associated with the source. Divide this cost by the number of hires made through that source to get the cost-per-hire.
5. **Quality of Hire:** Measure the quality of candidates hired through each source. This can be done by tracking their performance, retention rate, and other relevant metrics.
6. **Retention Rate:** This metric measures the percentage of hires who remain with the organization for a certain period. By tracking the retention rate for each sourcing channel, you can identify which channels are producing hires who are likely to stay with the organization for a longer time.

By measuring the effectiveness of sourcing channels, you can identify which sources are generating the most qualified candidates, which sources are most cost-effective, and which sources are taking longer to generate qualified candidates. This will help to optimize your recruitment strategy and allocate resources where they will have the greatest impact.

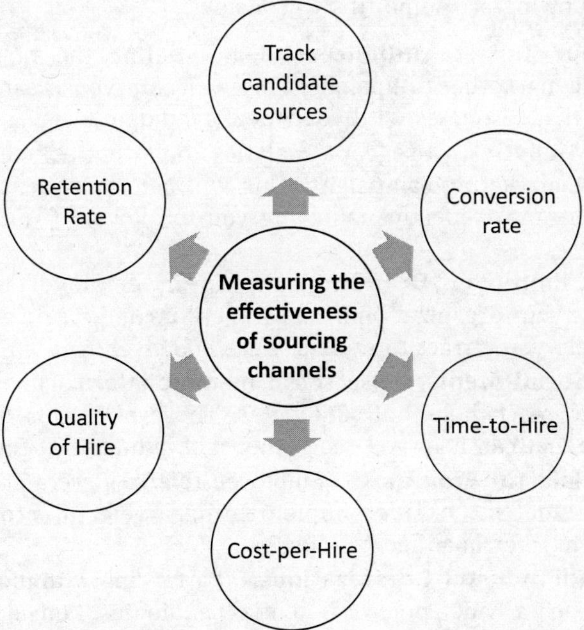

FIGURE 3.1 Measuring the effectiveness of sourcing channels.

Identifying Top-performing Sources

To identify top-performing sources, the following steps should be considered:

1. Determine your criteria for what makes a source "top-performing." For example, is it the number of views, the level of engagement, or the accuracy of the information provided?
2. Use analytics tools to track metrics such as page views, time on site, bounce rate, social media shares, and backlinks.
3. Conduct surveys or gather feedback from your audience to find out which sources they find most valuable.
4. Keep track of the sources that consistently provide high-quality content and engage with your audience.
5. Look for sources that have a strong reputation in your industry or niche.
6. Monitor your competitors and see which sources they are using to stay ahead in the game.
7. Use tools such as Google Trends to identify sources that are currently trending and attracting a lot of attention.

By following these steps, you should be able to identify the top-performing sources for specific needs and goals. Remember to regularly review and update your sources to ensure you are providing your audience with the most relevant and valuable information.

Optimizing Recruitment Marketing Spend

Optimizing recruitment marketing spend can help companies attract top talent while also controlling costs. Following are some tips to consider:

1. **Define Your Target Audience:** Clearly define the target audience for your recruitment marketing campaigns. This will help you create relevant and effective messaging that resonates with your ideal candidates.
2. **Use Data Analytics:** Use data analytics tools to track the performance of your recruitment marketing campaigns. This will help you identify which channels and messages are most effective, allowing you to allocate your marketing spend more efficiently.
3. **Prioritize Employer Branding:** Invest in employer branding initiatives to differentiate your organization from competitors and create a strong employer brand. This can help you attract top talent more effectively and efficiently.
4. **Leverage Social Media:** Use social media platforms like LinkedIn, Twitter, and Facebook to reach potential candidates. These platforms offer powerful targeting capabilities that can help you reach the right audience at the right time.
5. **Consider Referral Programs:** Employee referrals are a great way to source high-quality candidates. Consider implementing a referral program that incentivizes employees to refer qualified candidates.
6. **Partner with Industry Organizations:** Partnering with industry organizations can help you reach a wider pool of potential candidates. Consider sponsoring events or hosting webinars that target your ideal audience.

By following these tips, you can optimize your recruitment marketing spend and attract the right candidates more efficiently.

TABLE 3.1 Steps involved in optimizing recruitment marketing spend

Step	*Description*
Step 1: Define recruitment goals	Set clear recruitment goals and targets for your marketing strategy. For example, do you want to fill a certain amount of open positions, raise knowledge of your brand, or get better applicants?
Step 2: Identify target audience	Figure out exactly who you want to reach with your recruitment marketing strategy. For example, you could target job hunters with certain skills, experience, or demographics.
Step 3: Choose recruitment channels	Pick the ways to hire people that will help you reach your ideal candidates the best, like job boards, search engines, email marketing, employee recommendations, and social media.
Step 4: Allocate recruitment budget	Figure out how much money you want to spend on each recruitment channel based on how well it works and how much it costs, and then make a budget plan that will get you the best return on your investment (ROI).
Step 5: Create compelling content	Make interesting employment content that shows off your job brand, talks about the culture of your company, and grabs the attention of the people you want to hire.
Step 6: Monitor campaign performance	Use measures like clicks, views, conversions, and cost per hire to track how well your job marketing effort is doing and make changes to your plan as needed to improve ROI.
Step 7: Measure and optimize results	Look at the results of your recruitment marketing effort to see what worked and what could be done better. Then, change your approach to get the most out of the money you spent on recruitment marketing.

SCREENING ANALYTICS

Screening analytics refers to the use of statistical and analytical methods to identify potential risks and opportunities in large datasets. It is a process that involves analysing large amounts of data to identify patterns, trends, and anomalies that could be indicative of underlying issues or opportunities.

Screening analytics is used in various industries, including finance, healthcare, and marketing, to detect fraudulent activities, identify potential health risks, and uncover insights about consumer behaviour.

The process of screening analytics typically involves data collection, cleaning, and preparation, followed by statistical analysis and data visualization. Advanced techniques, such as machine learning and artificial intelligence, are also used to develop predictive models that can help identify future trends and patterns.

The goal of screening analytics is to identify patterns and trends in large datasets that would be difficult to detect using traditional methods. This can help organizations make data-driven decisions and identify areas for improvement, ultimately leading to better outcomes and increased efficiency.

Measuring the Effectiveness of Screening Criteria

Checking how well screening criteria work at finding or excluding a certain group of people is part of figuring out how effective they are. Metrics like sensitivity, specificity, positive predictive value (PPV), negative predictive value (NPV), and accuracy are often used to measure how well screening factors work.

Sensitivity is the share of people who really have the condition that are true results. Specificity is the percentage of people who are actually not sick who do not have the disease. The proportion of true positives among all people who test positive for the condition is called PPV. The proportion of true negatives among all people who test negative for the condition is called NPV. Accuracy is the percentage of right ratings out of all the people who were checked.

To find out how well screening criteria work, you must first describe the group you want to look at and the criteria themselves. The screening criteria are the things that are used to find or leave out people from the target population, which is the group of people who are at risk for the condition of interest.

You can use data from a validation study or a real-world screening programme to figure out the sensitivity, specificity, PPV, NPV, and accuracy of the screening criteria once you know the target group and screening criteria. You can use these measures to see how well the screening criteria worked generally and to see how different screening methods worked.

It is important to remember that screening criteria may or may not work based on how common the condition is, how sensitive and specific the screening test is, and how common false positives and false negatives are. Because of this, it is important to think about these things when figuring out what the results of screening criteria ratings mean.

Identifying Top-performing Screening Methods

Recruitment analytics is an essential component of the recruitment process as it helps organizations make data-driven decisions in their hiring process. Screening methods are an important part of recruitment analytics, and some of the top-performing screening methods are:

1. **Resume Screening:** Resume screening is a traditional method of screening candidates. It involves reviewing the candidate's resume and assessing their qualifications and experience against the job requirements.
2. **Behavioural Assessments:** Behavioural assessments help employers evaluate a candidate's personality traits, values, and work style. These assessments can be conducted using various tools, such as personality tests, situational judgment tests, and cognitive ability tests.
3. **Video Interviews:** Video interviews are an increasingly popular screening method, especially in remote hiring. They allow employers to assess a candidate's communication skills, body language, and overall presentation.
4. **Skills Assessments:** Skills assessments evaluate a candidate's technical skills, such as coding, writing, or design. These assessments can be conducted through online tests or by providing a sample project to complete.

5. **Reference Checks:** Reference checks involve contacting the candidate's previous employers or colleagues to verify their employment history, performance, and character.
6. **Pre-employment Tests:** Pre-employment tests measure a candidate's cognitive abilities, such as critical thinking, problem-solving, and attention to detail.
7. **Background Checks:** Background checks verify a candidate's education, employment history, criminal record, and other relevant information.

It's essential to note that no single screening method can provide a complete picture of a candidate's suitability for a role. Therefore, organizations should use a combination of screening methods to make informed hiring decisions.

TABLE 3.2 Top-performing screening methods of recruitment analytics

Screening method	*Description*	*Advantages*	*Disadvantages*
Resume screening	Reviewing resumes of job applicants to determine if they meet the minimum qualifications for the job.	Quick and easy to implement.	Limited information and potential for bias.
Behavioural Assessments	Evaluating an applicant's personality traits and behavioural tendencies to determine how well they fit with the job and the company culture.	Helps identify candidates with the right personality and work style for the job.	Can be time-consuming and expensive.
Cognitive ability tests	Assessing an applicant's mental ability and aptitude to determine their potential for success in the job.	Provides objective information about a candidate's abilities.	Can be challenging to administer and interpret.
Skills Assessments	Testing an applicant's knowledge and skills related to the job requirements.	Helps identify candidates with the necessary skills for the job.	May not be suitable for all types of jobs.
Job auditions	Allowing job candidates to perform actual job tasks or simulations to assess their skills and abilities.	Provides a realistic preview of the job and how well a candidate can perform it.	May not be feasible for all types of jobs.
Reference checks	Contacting the candidate's previous employers or references to verify their work history and performance.	Provides additional information about a candidate's work history and character.	Can be time-consuming and may not provide objective information.

Note: There are many other screening methods and techniques available to recruiters, and the effectiveness of each will depend on the specific needs and requirements of the job and the company.

Optimizing the Candidate Experience during Screening

Optimizing the candidate experience during screening is an important aspect of recruitment analytics. Following are some tips to improve the candidate experience during screening:

1. **Be Clear about the Screening Process:** Candidates should have a clear understanding of the screening process and what they can expect at each stage. This includes the type of screening assessments they will be required to complete, the timeline for the screening process, and who they can contact for questions or support.
2. **Make the Screening Process as Efficient as Possible:** The screening process should be designed to be as efficient as possible. This means using technology to automate certain parts of the process, such as resume screening or pre-screening questions, so that candidates can move through the process quickly.
3. **Provide Feedback to Candidates:** Candidates appreciate feedback, even if it's negative. Providing feedback to candidates can help them improve their chances of success in the future and also improve their perception of your company. Automated feedback can be generated using pre-defined response templates.
4. **Communicate Effectively with Candidates:** Communication is key during the screening process. Candidates should be kept informed at each stage of the process, and communication should be prompt and professional. Automated messaging can help streamline the process.
5. **Ensure a Positive Candidate Experience:** The candidate experience during the screening process should be positive. Candidates should feel that they are being treated fairly and with respect. They should also have a positive impression of the company and its values, even if they are not selected for the position.

Thus, optimizing the candidate experience during screening requires a combination of technology, communication, and empathy. By prioritizing the candidate experience, you can improve your recruitment analytics and attract top talent to your organization.

HIRING ANALYTICS

Hiring analytics is the practice of using data analysis and statistical models to make better hiring decisions. It involves collecting and analysing data about job applicants, including their qualifications, skills, experience, and performance during the recruitment process.

The main objective of hiring analytics is to improve the efficiency and effectiveness of the recruitment process by providing insights that can help organizations make better hiring decisions. It can also help companies to identify areas for improvement in their recruitment process, such as where they are losing good candidates or where there are bottlenecks that slow down the hiring process.

Some common metrics used in hiring analytics include time-to-fill (how long it takes to fill a job opening), cost-per-hire (how much it costs to fill a job opening), and quality-of-hire (how well the new hire performs on the job).

Hiring analytics can be used by both large and small companies, and it can be applied to various stages of the recruitment process, such as sourcing, screening, interviewing, and on-boarding. It can also be used to evaluate the effectiveness of different recruitment channels and to identify the best sources for attracting top talent.

Hiring analytics can help organizations make better hiring decisions, reduce recruitment costs, and improve the quality of their workforce.

Measuring the Effectiveness of Hiring Decisions

Measuring the effectiveness of hiring decisions involves assessing the success of the recruitment and selection process in terms of hiring the right people for the right job. Measuring the effectiveness of hiring decisions is important for organizations to ensure that they are making the right hiring choices and investing their resources wisely. Following are some ways to measure the effectiveness of hiring decisions:

1. **Employee Performance:** One of the most effective ways to measure the effectiveness of hiring decisions is to evaluate the performance of the new employee. This can be done by setting clear performance goals and tracking progress over time. If the employee is meeting or exceeding expectations, it is a good indication that the hiring decision was effective.
2. **Retention Rate:** Another way to measure the effectiveness of hiring decisions is to track the retention rate of new employees. If a high percentage of new hires stay with the organization for an extended period of time, it suggests that the hiring decision was effective.
3. **Time-to-Hire:** The time it takes to fill a position can also be an indicator of the effectiveness of hiring decisions. If it takes a long time to fill a position, it could suggest that the hiring process is not efficient or effective.
4. **Cost-per-Hire:** Measuring the cost of the hiring process can also provide insight into the effectiveness of hiring decisions. If the cost-per-hire is high, it may indicate that the organization is not getting the best return on their investment.
5. **Hiring Manager Satisfaction:** It's also important to gather feedback from hiring managers on their satisfaction with the new hire. If they are satisfied with the new employee's performance and fit within the organization, it suggests that the hiring decision was effective.

So, measuring the effectiveness of hiring decisions requires a combination of quantitative and qualitative data. By using a variety of metrics, organizations can get a comprehensive understanding of how well their hiring process is working and make adjustments as necessary.

Identifying Top-performing Hiring Sources

Identifying top-performing hiring sources is an essential step in optimizing a company's recruitment process. Following are some steps to follow to identify top-performing hiring sources:

1. **Define and Track Metrics:** Identify the key metrics that you want to track to evaluate your hiring sources' performance. This could include the number of applicants, quality of applicants, time to hire, cost per hire, and retention rate. Make sure to track these metrics consistently across all hiring sources.
2. **Analyse Data:** Collect data on each hiring source and analyse it to determine which sources are performing well and which ones are not. You can use various data analysis

tools and software to extract and analyse data from your recruitment software or applicant tracking system.

3. **Compare Results:** Compare the results of different hiring sources based on the metrics you identified in step one. This will help you determine which sources are most effective in delivering quality candidates.
4. **Evaluate ROI:** Calculate the return on investment (ROI) for each hiring source. This involves looking at the cost of the source and the quality of the candidates it delivers. Determine which sources provide the best ROI.
5. **Adjust Your Strategy:** Based on the results of your analysis, adjust your hiring strategy to focus on the top-performing hiring sources. Consider investing more resources in these sources and optimizing your recruitment process to better leverage their strengths.

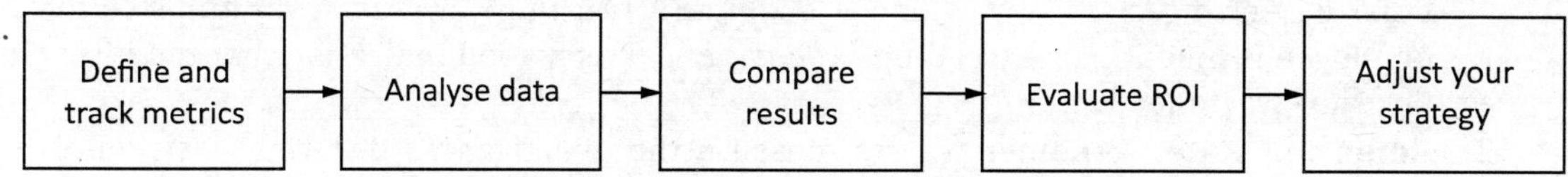

FIGURE 3.2 Steps to Identify top-performing hiring sources.

Thus, identifying top-performing hiring sources requires a data-driven approach that involves analysing metrics and evaluating ROI. By following these steps, you can improve your recruitment process and attract better-quality candidates while minimizing costs.

Optimizing the On-boarding Process

Optimizing the on-boarding process involves improving the experience for new hires during their initial days, weeks, and months on the job. Following are some steps you can take to optimize the on boarding process:

1. **Develop a Clear On-boarding Plan:** Create a comprehensive on-boarding plan that includes all the necessary steps and information new hires need to be successful in their role. This plan should outline everything from completing HR paperwork to training, and should be communicated to new hires before they start.
2. **Automate Paperwork:** Use technology to automate the paperwork process as much as possible. This will allow new hires to complete necessary paperwork before they arrive, minimizing delays and reducing the time spent on administrative tasks during on-boarding.
3. **Provide Training:** Provide new hires with the training they need to be successful in their roles. This may include job-specific training, as well as training on company policies and procedures.
4. **Assign a Mentor:** Assign a mentor or buddy to new hires to help them navigate their new environment and answer any questions they may have. This will help new hires feel more comfortable and supported during their first few weeks.
5. **Gather Feedback:** Regularly gather feedback from new hires on their on-boarding experience. This will help you identify areas for improvement and make adjustments as necessary.

6. **Use Technology:** Utilize technology to streamline the on-boarding process, such as using an online platform for training or providing new hires with access to a company intranet where they can find information and resources.

By optimizing the on-boarding process, you can help new hires feel more comfortable and confident in their roles, leading to higher retention rates and greater success for both the employee and the company.

BEST PRACTICES FOR RECRUITMENT ANALYTICS

Recruitment analytics can help companies make informed decisions about their hiring processes, but it's important to use best practices to ensure that the data is accurate and actionable. Following are some best practices for recruitment analytics:

1. **Define Clear Metrics:** Identify the metrics that matter most to your company and define them clearly. Common metrics include time-to-fill, cost-per-hire, quality-of-hire, and applicant-to-interview ratio.
2. **Collect Clean Data:** Ensure that your data is accurate, consistent, and complete. Use standardized job descriptions and application forms, and regularly review and clean your data to remove duplicates and errors.
3. **Use a Data-driven Approach:** Use data to identify patterns and trends in your hiring process, and use that information to make informed decisions about how to improve your recruitment efforts.
4. **Create a Dashboard:** Develop a dashboard that provides real-time visibility into your recruitment metrics. This can help you identify trends and issues as they arise, and take corrective action as needed.
5. **Integrate Your Data:** Connect your recruitment data with other HR systems, such as your applicant tracking system, to gain a holistic view of your hiring process.
6. **Invest in Technology:** Use technology to automate your recruitment analytics and make it easier to collect, analyse, and report on your data. There are many tools available that can help you streamline your recruitment analytics efforts.
7. **Use Benchmarks:** Compare your recruitment metrics to industry benchmarks to identify areas where you may be falling short or excelling. This can help you set realistic goals and track your progress over time.

By following these best practices, you can ensure that your recruitment analytics are accurate, actionable, and valuable for your organization's talent acquisition strategy.

Tips for Implementing a Successful Recruitment Analytics Strategy

Implementing a successful recruitment analytics strategy requires a thoughtful and strategic approach. Following are some tips to consider:

1. **Define Your Goals:** Start by defining what you want to achieve through your recruitment analytics strategy. For example, do you want to improve your recruitment efficiency, reduce time to fill, or enhance candidate experience? By defining your goals, you can tailor your analytics strategy to meet your specific needs.

2. **Identify Relevant Data Sources:** To gain insights into your recruitment process, you'll need to collect data from various sources. This might include applicant tracking systems (ATS), social media platforms, job boards, and employee referral programs. Identify which data sources are most relevant to your goals and ensure that the data is accurate and consistent.
3. **Choose the Right Metrics:** Selecting the right metrics is critical to measuring the success of your recruitment analytics strategy. Identify key performance indicators (KPIs) that align with your goals, such as time-to-fill, cost-per-hire, and candidate quality.
4. **Utilize Data Visualization Tools**: Analysing and interpreting large volumes of data can be challenging. Data visualization tools such as dashboards and reports can help to simplify complex data and provide insights into recruitment trends and patterns.
5. **Involve Stakeholders:** Recruitment analytics should involve stakeholders across the organization, including HR teams, recruiters, hiring managers, and executives. Engage with these stakeholders throughout the recruitment analytics process to ensure that the data is meaningful and actionable.
6. **Continuously Evaluate and Refine:** Recruitment analytics is an ongoing process, and it's essential to continuously evaluate and refine your strategy to optimize recruitment outcomes. Regularly review your KPIs, assess your recruitment data sources, and adjust your strategy as needed to ensure that you're meeting your recruitment goals.

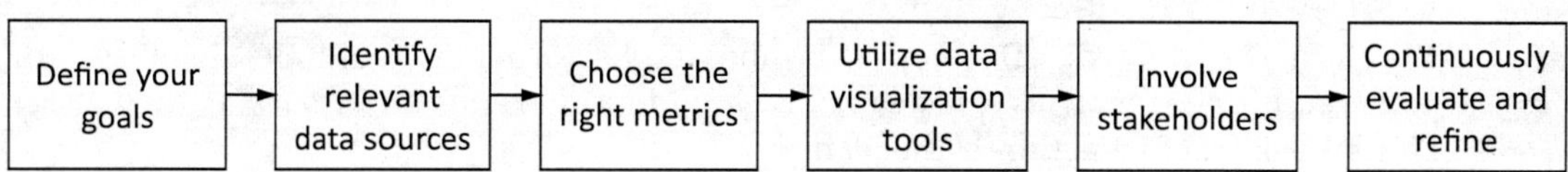

FIGURE 3.3 Tips for implementing a successful recruitment analytics strategy.

By following these tips, you can implement a successful recruitment analytics strategy that helps you make informed recruitment decisions and optimize your hiring outcomes.

Common Pitfalls to Avoid when using Recruitment Analytics

Recruitment analytics is the use of data and statistical methods to improve recruitment processes and make better hiring decisions. However, there are several common pitfalls that organizations should avoid when using recruitment analytics. Following are some of them:

1. **Over-reliance on Data:** Data can provide valuable insights, but it should not be the only factor in making hiring decisions. It's important to balance data with other considerations, such as a candidate's cultural fit, soft skills, and work experience.
2. **Biased Data:** Recruitment analytics can be biased if the data used is biased. This can happen if the data is collected from a biased sample or if there are inherent biases in the data collection methods. Organizations should ensure that their data is representative and unbiased.

3. **Lack of Context:** Recruitment analytics can provide insights, but it's important to consider the context of the data. For example, a low retention rate for a certain position could be due to poor hiring practices or a high turnover rate in the industry.
4. **Ignoring Qualitative Data:** Recruitment analytics often focuses on quantitative data, such as applicant tracking system data or interview scores. However, qualitative data, such as candidate feedback or hiring manager feedback, can provide valuable insights into the recruitment process.
5. **Failure to Adjust Strategies:** Recruitment analytics should be used to improve recruitment processes and make better hiring decisions. However, organizations may fail to adjust their strategies based on the insights gained from the data. It's important to take action based on the data and continuously evaluate and adjust strategies as needed.

Emerging Trends in Recruitment Analytics

Recruitment analytics is an increasingly important area for organizations looking to optimize their hiring processes and make data-driven decisions. Following are some emerging trends in recruitment analytics:

1. **Predictive Analytics:** Using data to forecast future events is known as predictive analytics. When it comes to hiring, this may entail reviewing historical hiring data to determine which applicants have the best chance of succeeding in a certain position. Recruiters may focus their outreach efforts by using predictive analytics to determine which prospects are more likely to accept a job offer.
2. **Diversity Analytics:** As organizations increasingly recognize the importance of diversity and inclusion, recruitment analytics is also starting to focus more on measuring and analysing diversity-related metrics. This might include analysing the diversity of candidate pools, tracking the demographics of candidates at various stages of the hiring process, and assessing the impact of diversity initiatives on hiring outcomes.
3. **Candidate Experience Analytics:** The candidate experience has become an increasingly important factor in recruitment, with organizations recognizing that a positive candidate experience can help attract and retain top talent. Recruitment analytics can be used to track and analyse candidate feedback and engagement metrics, allowing recruiters to identify areas where they can improve the candidate experience.
4. **Talent Analytics:** Recruitment analytics can also be used to analyse broader talent trends, such as identifying which skills are in high demand, tracking talent mobility between different roles and industries, and forecasting future talent needs. This type of analysis can help organizations stay ahead of the curve when it comes to identifying and attracting top talent.
5. **Artificial Intelligence and Machine Learning:** As with many areas of business, AI and machine learning are starting to play an increasingly important role in recruitment analytics. This might involve using machine learning algorithms to analyse resumes and identify top candidates, or using Chabot's to streamline the initial stages of the hiring process. As these technologies continue to evolve, we can expect to see even more innovation in the recruitment analytics space.

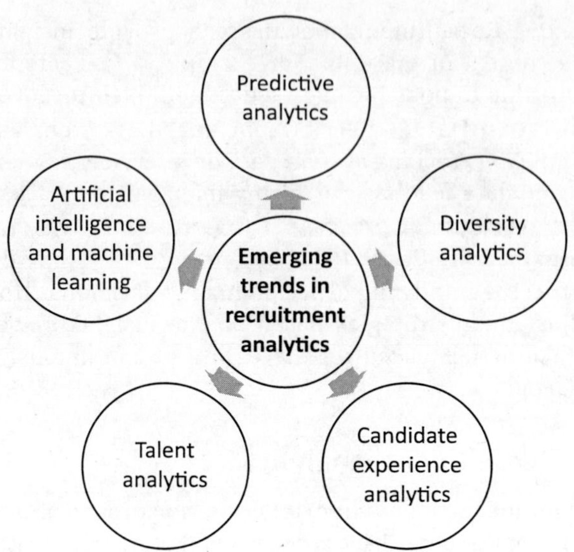

FIGURE 3.4 Emerging trends in recruitment analytics.

Cases/Examples of Companies that have Successfully used Recruitment Analytics to Optimize their Recruitment Processes

Recruitment analytics refers to the use of data analysis to make data-driven decisions and optimize recruitment processes. Recruitment analytics has become an essential tool for many companies to optimize their recruitment processes, improve hiring outcomes, and reduce costs. Following are some examples of companies that have successfully used recruitment analytics:

1. **Hilton Worldwide:** Hilton Worldwide uses recruitment analytics to improve its candidate sourcing and hiring practices. By analysing data on the performance of past hires, Hilton is able to identify the most successful sources of candidates and adjust its recruitment strategies accordingly. For example, if the data shows that candidates from a particular job board perform better than those from other sources, Hilton will focus more heavily on that job board in its recruiting efforts.
   Lessons learned: Recruitment analytics can provide valuable insights into the effectiveness of different recruitment strategies, allowing companies to optimize their hiring processes and improve the quality of their hires.
2. **Google:** Google uses recruitment analytics to improve its candidate selection process. By analysing data on past hiring decisions, Google is able to identify the traits and qualifications that are most predictive of success at the company. For example, if the data shows that candidates with certain educational backgrounds or work experience perform better at Google, the company will focus more heavily on those qualifications in its hiring process.
   Lessons learned: Recruitment analytics can help companies identify the characteristics that are most important for success in a particular role or at a particular company, allowing them to make more informed hiring decisions.

3. **IBM:** IBM uses recruitment analytics to improve its diversity and inclusion initiatives. By analysing data on the demographic makeup of its candidate pool and hiring decisions, IBM is able to identify areas where it needs to improve its diversity efforts. For example, if the data shows that the company is not attracting enough candidates from underrepresented groups, IBM will adjust its recruitment strategies to reach a more diverse pool of candidates.
   Lessons learned: Recruitment analytics can help companies identify areas where they need to improve their diversity and inclusion efforts, allowing them to create more equitable and inclusive workplaces.
4. **Xerox:** Xerox, a global document management company, used recruitment analytics to improve their retention rates. By analysing data from their recruitment process, they were able to identify the characteristics of successful employees and the factors that contribute to turnover. This information allowed them to optimize their recruitment process to target candidates who were more likely to stay with the company and be successful in their roles.
5. **Unilever:** Unilever, a multinational consumer goods company, used recruitment analytics to improve their diversity and inclusion efforts. By analysing data from their recruitment process, they were able to identify areas where bias was present and take steps to eliminate it. They also used analytics to track the diversity of their candidate pool and to monitor the success of their diversity and inclusion initiatives.
6. **Humana:** Humana, a health insurance company, used recruitment analytics to reduce their time-to-fill and improve their quality of hire. By analysing data from their recruitment process, they were able to identify bottlenecks and inefficiencies in their process and implement changes that streamlined their hiring process. They also used analytics to identify the best sources of talent for different job categories and to measure the success of their recruitment marketing campaigns.
7. **Marriott:** Marriott has implemented an analytics-driven recruitment process that allows the company to identify top-performing candidates and develop targeted recruitment strategies to attract them. The company also uses data to track the success of its recruitment campaigns and adjust them as needed.
8. **Procter & Gamble:** Procter & Gamble uses data analytics to improve its recruitment process in several ways, such as predicting which candidates are most likely to accept a job offer, identifying the best recruitment channels to use, and tracking the performance of its recruiters.

These are just a few examples of companies that have successfully used recruitment analytics to optimize their recruitment processes and achieve better hiring outcomes. As the use of data analysis continues to grow in the recruitment industry, more companies are likely to follow their lead and leverage the power of analytics to improve their recruitment efforts. Companies that use recruitment analytics effectively are able to make data-driven decisions about their hiring processes, resulting in better quality hires and more efficient recruitment practices. However, it's important to note that recruitment analytics are only as useful as the data they are based on, so it's important for companies to collect and analyse high-quality data in order to get the most value from their analytics efforts.

FUTURE OUTLOOK FOR RECRUITMENT ANALYTICS

Recruitment analytics is the use of data to inform and improve recruitment processes. It involves collecting and analysing data to gain insights into factors such as candidate sourcing, applicant tracking, selection criteria, and employee retention. Recruitment analytics is becoming increasingly important for organizations as they seek to optimize their hiring processes and attract the best talent. The future outlook for recruitment analytics is promising, as organizations increasingly recognize the value of data-driven decision making in their recruitment strategies. With advancements in technology, there are a few trends and future outlooks that are emerging for recruitment analytics:

1. **Use of Artificial Intelligence (AI) and Machine Learning (ML):** AI and ML are already being used in recruitment analytics to identify patterns in resumes, assess candidate fit and predict job performance. In the future, this technology will continue to evolve and become more sophisticated, enabling recruiters to make more informed hiring decisions.
2. **Greater Focus on Diversity, Equity, and Inclusion (DE&I):** Organizations are recognizing the importance of diversity and inclusion in the workplace and are using recruitment analytics to measure the effectiveness of their DE&I initiatives. In the future, we can expect to see more advanced analytics tools that will help companies to identify and address any potential biases in their hiring processes.
3. **Real-time Analytics:** Real-time analytics will enable recruiters to make decisions on the fly based on up-to-the-minute data, helping them to respond quickly to changing circumstances.
4. **Predictive Analytics:** Predictive analytics will become more sophisticated, allowing organizations to predict which candidates are most likely to be successful in a role based on a range of data points, including past job performance, education, and experience.
5. **Emphasis on Candidate Experience:** With the rise of social media and review sites like Glassdoor, candidate experience is becoming increasingly important. In the future, organizations will use recruitment analytics to measure candidate satisfaction and identify areas where they can improve the recruitment process to enhance the candidate experience.

TABLE 3.3 Future outlook for recruitment analytics

Trends/Aspects	*Description*
Increased Demand	There will be an increased demand for recruitment analytics as companies realize the importance of data-driven hiring decisions. Recruitment analytics will be used to assess the effectiveness of recruitment campaigns, identify gaps in the recruitment process, and make informed decisions about hiring strategies.
Artificial Intelligence	The use of artificial intelligence (AI) in recruitment analytics will continue to grow. AI-powered tools will be used to analyse job descriptions, resumes, and candidate profiles to identify the best candidates for a given role. AI algorithms will also help in predicting candidate success, which will help in reducing hiring bias.

Trends/Aspects	*Description*
Predictive Analytics	Predictive analytics will become more sophisticated, enabling recruiters to predict the likelihood of a candidate accepting an offer, their performance, and potential retention. Predictive analytics will help recruiters to make better hiring decisions by providing insights into candidate behaviour and characteristics.
Candidate Experience	Recruitment analytics will increasingly focus on candidate experience, including areas such as candidate engagement, feedback, and satisfaction. Candidate feedback and sentiment analysis will be used to improve the recruitment process, enhance employer branding, and reduce candidate dropouts.
Diversity and Inclusion	Recruitment analytics will play a critical role in promoting diversity and inclusion in the workplace. Analytics will be used to identify hiring biases, track diversity metrics, and develop strategies to improve diversity and inclusion in the recruitment process.
Employer Branding	Recruitment analytics will be used to track and analyse the effectiveness of employer branding initiatives. Analytics will help companies to understand the impact of employer branding on candidate attraction and retention, and to make informed decisions about employer branding strategies.
Mobile Recruiting	With the rise of mobile technology, recruitment analytics will also focus on mobile recruiting. Analytics will be used to track candidate engagement through mobile devices, optimize the mobile application process, and improve the overall candidate experience.
Skills Gap Analysis	Recruitment analytics will be used to identify skills gaps within the organization and develop strategies to address these gaps. Analytics will help companies to identify the skills they need to acquire, the skills that are in high demand, and the skills that are becoming obsolete.
Employee Referrals	Employee referrals will continue to be an important source of candidates, and recruitment analytics will help companies to optimize their referral programs. Analytics will be used to track the effectiveness of referral programs, identify top-performing referral sources, and reward employees for successful referrals.
Talent Pool Management	Recruitment analytics will be used to manage talent pools, allowing companies to quickly identify and engage with potential candidates when positions become available. Talent pool analytics will help companies to develop targeted recruiting strategies and reduce time-to-hire.

Overall, the future outlook for recruitment analytics is positive, with continued advancements in technology and an increasing focus on data-driven decision making, we can expect to see more sophisticated and effective recruitment analytics tools emerging in the coming years.

Questions for Discussion

Short Questions

1. What is recruitment analytics? How does recruitment analytics benefit organizations?
2. What are some key metrics used in recruitment analytics?
3. Why is the quality of hire an important metric in recruitment analytics?
4. What are the primary goals of sourcing analytics?
5. What metrics can be used to measure the effectiveness of sourcing channels?
6. What is the role of screening analytics in the recruitment process?
7. How can organizations measure the effectiveness of screening criteria?
8. Why is it important to optimize the candidate experience during screening in recruitment analytics?
9. What is hiring analytics? What are some common metrics used in hiring analytics?
10. How can hiring analytics benefit both large and small companies?
11. What are some key metrics for measuring the effectiveness of hiring decisions?
12. What are some common pitfalls to avoid when using recruitment analytics?

Long Questions

1. Can you explain the importance of recruitment analytics in detail and provide examples of how it can impact an organization's hiring process?
2. What are the key benefits of using recruitment analytics, and how can it help organizations improve their recruitment strategies and outcomes?
3. Describe the various components and steps involved in sourcing analytics and how organizations can use it to enhance their procurement and sourcing processes.
4. Explain the process of measuring the effectiveness of screening criteria in recruitment analytics, including the metrics used and their significance.
5. How can organizations optimize their recruitment marketing spend using data analytics, and what steps are involved in achieving this optimization?
6. Discuss the role of technology and automation in improving the candidate experience during screening, and provide recommendations for creating a positive candidate experience.
7. Explain how recruitment analytics can contribute to improving diversity and inclusion in the hiring process and why it is important for organizations to focus on these aspects.
8. What are the key steps involved in measuring the effectiveness of hiring decisions, and why is this important for organizations?
9. What are the best practices for implementing a successful recruitment analytics strategy, and how can organizations define their goals effectively?
10. What are the emerging trends in recruitment analytics, and how are they shaping the future of talent acquisition?
11. Can you provide specific examples of companies that have successfully used recruitment analytics to achieve better hiring outcomes?
12. What is the future outlook for recruitment analytics, and how do you envision it evolving in the coming years?

CHAPTER

4

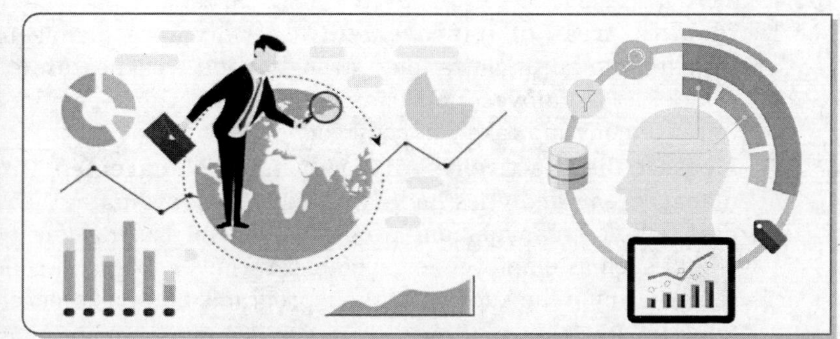

Performance Management Analytics

Performance Management Analytics is a process that involves the use of data and analytics to measure, monitor, and improve organizational performance. It is a critical component of performance management, which involves setting goals, tracking progress, and making data-driven decisions to improve performance.

Performance Management Analytics uses various data sources such as financial data, operational data, and customer data to provide insights into organizational performance. It involves analysing data to identify trends, patterns, and outliers, and then using that information to make informed decisions that can lead to improved performance.

The main goal of Performance Management Analytics is to provide decision-makers with accurate and relevant information to make informed decisions. It allows organizations to track progress towards their goals, identify areas of improvement, and develop strategies to address performance issues.

Some common metrics used in Performance Management Analytics include revenue growth, customer retention rates, employee turnover, and profitability. These metrics can be tracked over time and compared to industry benchmarks to assess organizational performance.

Performance Management Analytics is a critical process that helps organizations to improve their performance and achieve their strategic objectives. By leveraging data and analytics, organizations can make informed decisions that lead to improved performance, increased efficiency, and better outcomes.

IMPORTANCE OF PERFORMANCE MANAGEMENT ANALYTICS

Performance management analytics play a crucial role in helping organizations make data-driven decisions related to employee performance and organizational effectiveness. Following are some of the key reasons why performance management analytics are important:

1. **Identify Areas of Improvement:** Performance management analytics provide insights into an organization's strengths and weaknesses. By analysing key metrics related to employee performance, organizations can identify areas that need improvement and take corrective action.
2. **Measure the Effectiveness of Performance Management Programs:** Performance management analytics help organizations evaluate the effectiveness of their performance management programs. By measuring key performance indicators (KPIs) such as employee engagement, turnover rate, and productivity, organizations can determine the success of their programs and make necessary adjustments.
3. **Support Decision-making:** Performance management analytics provide data that can be used to inform key decision-making processes. For example, data on employee performance can be used to inform decisions related to promotions, bonuses, and training programs.
4. **Improve Employee Engagement:** Performance management analytics can help organizations identify the factors that contribute to employee engagement and satisfaction. By analysing data related to employee engagement, organizations can identify the areas that need improvement and take action to improve employee satisfaction and retention.
5. **Align Performance with Business Objectives:** Performance management analytics can help organizations align individual performance with business objectives. By measuring employee performance against key business metrics, organizations can ensure that individual performance is contributing to overall organizational success.

TABLE 4.1 Importance of performance management analytics

Importance of performance management analytics	*Description*
Data-driven decision making	Performance management analytics allows organizations to make decisions based on data, rather than assumptions or gut feelings. This leads to more informed and accurate decision making, which can result in improved performance and outcomes.
Identify strengths and weaknesses	Performance management analytics can help identify areas of an organization that are performing well and areas that need improvement. This information can be used to allocate resources, set goals, and develop strategies for improvement.
Continuous improvement	By monitoring performance metrics over time, organizations can identify trends and make continuous improvements to their operations. This can result in increased efficiency, productivity, and profitability.
Employee engagement	Performance management analytics can provide valuable insights into employee engagement and satisfaction. This information can be used to develop strategies to improve employee retention, productivity, and morale.

(*Contd.*)

Importance of performance management analytics	*Description*
Goal setting and tracking	Performance management analytics allows organizations to set goals and track progress towards those goals. This helps ensure that everyone in the organization is working towards a common objective, and can lead to better performance and outcomes.
Identify training needs	Performance management analytics can help identify areas where employees may need additional training or development. This can help improve employee skills and knowledge, resulting in improved performance and outcomes.
Benchmarking	Performance management analytics can provide organizations with benchmarks to compare their performance against similar organizations. This can help identify areas where the organization is lagging behind, as well as areas where it is outperforming its peers.

Performance management analytics are crucial for organizations to make data-driven decisions related to employee performance and organizational effectiveness. By analysing key metrics related to employee performance, organizations can identify areas for improvement, measure the effectiveness of performance management programs, support decision-making, improve employee engagement, and align performance with business objectives.

BENEFITS OF PERFORMANCE MANAGEMENT ANALYTICS

Performance management analytics is the process of using data to measure, analyse, and improve employee performance. It involves collecting and analysing data on employee performance, identifying trends and patterns, and using that information to make data-driven decisions that improve the effectiveness of the organization.

Following are some benefits of using performance management analytics:

1. **Improved Decision-making:** Performance management analytics enables organizations to make informed decisions based on data-driven insights. By analysing data on employee performance, organizations can identify areas of improvement and make data-driven decisions to optimize their workforce.
2. **Enhanced Employee Engagement:** Employees are more likely to be engaged and motivated when they have a clear understanding of their performance and how it impacts the organization. Performance management analytics can provide employees with regular feedback on their performance, which can help them improve and feel more engaged.
3. **Increased Productivity:** By analysing data on employee performance, organizations can identify inefficiencies and areas of improvement in their workforce. This can help them optimize their processes, reduce costs, and increase productivity.
4. **Better Talent Management:** Performance management analytics can help organizations identify high-performing employees and those who may need

additional support or training. This information can be used to develop targeted talent management strategies, such as succession planning and career development programs.

5. **Improved Organizational Performance:** By using performance management analytics, organizations can improve the overall performance of their workforce, which can lead to increased revenue, profitability, and customer satisfaction.

Hence, performance management analytics can help organizations make data-driven decisions, enhance employee engagement, increase productivity, better manage talent, and improve organizational performance.

KEY METRICS IN PERFORMANCE MANAGEMENT ANALYTICS

Performance management analytics involves measuring and analysing employee performance data to improve productivity and achieve organizational goals. Key metrics that are commonly used in performance management analytics include:

1. **Key Performance Indicators (KPIs):** KPIs are metrics that are used to evaluate how well an organization is meeting its goals and objectives. These can include financial metrics such as revenue, profit margins, and return on investment, as well as operational metrics such as customer satisfaction, employee productivity, and quality of products or services.
2. **Employee Turnover Rate:** This metric measures the percentage of employees who leave an organization within a given period. High turnover rates can indicate problems with leadership, workplace culture, or compensation.
3. **Absenteeism Rate:** This metric measures the percentage of scheduled work hours that employees miss due to illness, personal reasons, or other factors. High absenteeism rates can indicate low employee engagement or poor workplace morale.
4. **Time-to-Fill:** This metric measures the time it takes to fill a job vacancy from the moment it is identified to the time the position is filled. A long time-to-fill can indicate recruitment and hiring challenges.
5. **Performance Ratings:** These are ratings assigned to employees based on their performance in various areas, such as productivity, quality of work, teamwork, and communication skills. Performance ratings can help identify areas where employees need additional training or support.
6. **Goal Attainment:** This metric measures the extent to which employees or teams achieve their individual or collective goals. Tracking goal attainment can help identify areas where performance improvements are needed.
7. **Training and Development**: This metric measures the amount of training and development opportunities offered to employees, as well as their participation rates. Investing in training and development can lead to higher employee engagement and improved performance.
8. **Balanced Scorecard:** The balanced scorecard comprises a collection of metrics spanning four distinct perspectives—financial, customer, internal processes, and learning and growth—and functions as a framework. The primary objective of

its design is to furnish a comprehensive perspective on the performance of the organisation and guarantee that strategic objectives are congruent with routine activities.

9. **Employee Engagement:** An indicator of employee commitment and motivation, employee engagement is a metric. This can be assessed via feedback mechanisms such as surveys, focus groups, or other techniques, and it can facilitate the identification of areas that require enhancement in order to boost employee satisfaction and productivity.
10. **Customer Satisfaction:** Customer satisfaction is a metric utilised to quantify the degree to which consumers are content with a particular service or product. It can be assessed via feedback forms, surveys, and other methodologies, and can facilitate the identification of areas that require enhancement in order to bolster consumer loyalty and retention.
11. **Cost of Goods Sold (COGS):** The direct expenses incurred in the manufacturing and distribution of a service or product are quantified by COGS. In conjunction with revenue metrics, this can include materials, labour, and administrative expenses, and is frequently used to assess profitability.
12. **Return on Investment (ROI):** ROI is a metric that measures the return on a specific investment, such as a marketing campaign or new product launch. It is calculated by dividing the net profit from the investment by the cost of the investment, and is often used to evaluate the effectiveness of different initiatives.
13. **Time to Market:** Time to market is a metric that measures the time it takes to bring a new product or service to market. This can include product development, testing, and marketing efforts, and is often used to evaluate the efficiency of different processes and identify areas where improvements can be made.
14. **Revenue:** This is the total amount of money generated by the organization. Revenue is an important metric for measuring the financial health of the organization.
15. **Profit:** This is the amount of money the organization makes after subtracting its expenses. Profit is an important metric for measuring the financial success of the organization.
16. **Productivity:** This is the measure of how efficiently the organization is using its resources to achieve its goals. Productivity is an important metric for measuring the success of the organization in achieving its objectives.

By tracking these and other performance management analytics metrics, organizations can gain insights into their employees' performance, identify areas where improvements are needed, and take action to address issues before they become significant problems.

Key Performance Indicators (KPIs)

Key Performance Indicators (KPIs) are critical metrics that can be used to track and measure an organization's progress towards achieving its strategic goals. The steps to use KPIs effectively in performance management analytics:

1. **Define your KPIs:** Start by defining the KPIs that are most relevant to your organization's goals. These should be metrics that are directly linked to the success

of your business objectives. For example, if your objective is to increase customer satisfaction, then you might choose KPIs such as customer retention rate or net promoter score.

2. **Collect the Necessary Data:** Once you have identified your KPIs, you need to gather the necessary data to measure them. This may involve collecting data from different sources such as CRM systems, financial systems, or customer feedback surveys.
3. **Establish Baselines and Targets:** Establish a baseline for each KPI to measure your current performance level. Then, set targets for where you want to be in the future. These targets should be specific, measurable, achievable, relevant, and time-bound (SMART).
4. **Monitor and Analyse KPIs:** Monitor your KPIs regularly to track progress and identify areas where performance needs to be improved. Use analytics tools to analyse KPI data to gain insights into performance trends and identify patterns or anomalies.
5. **Take Action:** Use the insights gained from KPI analysis to take corrective actions where necessary. Identify areas where performance is lagging, and take steps to address the root cause of the problem.
6. **Communicate Results:** Communicate performance results to key stakeholders regularly, using visualizations and reports that are easy to understand. This will help stakeholders to understand the organization's progress towards achieving its goals and identify areas for improvement.

TABLE 4.2 Key Performance indicators as metrics in performance management analytics

Step	*Description*
1	Define the objectives and goals of the organization, department, or individual.
2	Identify the Key Performance Indicators (KPIs) that align with the objectives and goals.
3	Determine the appropriate metrics for each KPI.
4	Collect and analyse data on a regular basis to track performance against the KPIs.
5	Use data visualization tools to create dashboards and reports that provide insights into performance.
6	Use the insights gained to make informed decisions and take actions to improve performance.
7	Monitor progress and adjust strategies as needed to ensure that performance remains on track.
8	Communicate results and progress to stakeholders on a regular basis to ensure transparency and accountability.
9	Continuously review and refine the KPIs and metrics to ensure they remain relevant and aligned with organizational goals.

By following these steps, you can use KPIs effectively as metrics in performance management analytics, enabling you to track progress towards your business objectives, identify areas for improvement, and take corrective actions to achieve your goals.

Employee Turnover

Employee turnover is an important metric in performance management analytics because it can have a significant impact on an organization's bottom line. High employee turnover can result in increased recruitment and training costs, reduced productivity, decreased morale, and a negative impact on an organization's reputation.

Organisations are able to discover areas in which they need to enhance their management practises and employee engagement initiatives by monitoring and studying the rates of employee turnover. For instance, if a specific department has a greater turnover rate than other departments, this may be an indication that there are problems with the leadership or the culture of the workplace that need to be addressed.

In addition to monitoring employee turnover rates, businesses should also investigate the factors that lead to people leaving their positions. As a result, this can give significant insights on areas in which the organisation needs to improve, such as compensation and benefits, possibilities for career growth, or work-life balance.

As an additional benefit, performance management analytics may assist organisations in locating and retaining individuals who perform exceptionally well. The identification of top performers and the development of measures to maintain their motivation and engagement may be accomplished by organisations through the tracking of performance metrics such as productivity, quality of work, and employee engagement.

Employee turnover is an important metric to track in performance management analytics, as it can provide valuable insights into the effectiveness of an organization's recruitment, retention, and talent management strategies. Following are some steps to use employee turnover as a metric in performance management analytics:

1. **Define the Turnover Rate:** Determine the proportion of personnel who have departed from the organisation within a specified timeframe, commonly one year. Multiplying the result by 100 after dividing the quantity of departing employees by the mean number of personnel during the corresponding time frame.
2. **Analyse the Turnover Rate:** Look at the turnover rate for the organization as a whole and for different departments or job categories. This can help identify areas where turnover is higher than average and where retention strategies may be needed.
3. **Identify the Reasons for Turnover**: Conduct exit interviews with departing employees to understand why they are leaving the organization. This can help identify trends and issues that may be contributing to turnover.
4. **Benchmark the Turnover Rate:** Compare the organization's turnover rate to industry averages and to the turnover rates of other companies in the same geographic region. This can help identify whether the organization is experiencing high turnover compared to its peers.
5. **Develop Retention Strategies:** Use the insights gained from analysing turnover to develop retention strategies that address the root causes of turnover. This could include improving employee engagement, offering competitive compensation and

benefits, providing opportunities for career development, and creating a positive work culture.

6. **Monitor Progress:** Track the turnover rate over time to determine whether retention strategies are having an impact. If the turnover rate is decreasing, this may indicate that retention strategies are effective.

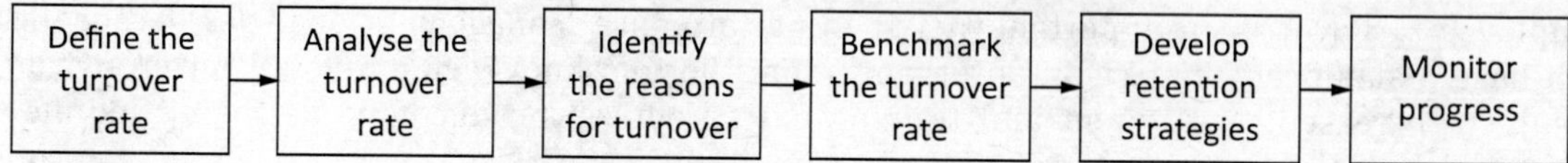

FIGURE 4.1 Steps to use employee turnover as a metric in performance management analytics.

Employee turnover is a critical metric in performance management analytics because it can provide valuable insights into an organization's management practices, employee engagement strategies, and overall health. By tracking and analysing turnover rates and reasons for turnover, organizations can develop strategies to improve retention, reduce costs, and increase productivity.

TABLE 4.3 Employee turnover in performance management analytics

Metric	*Description*	*Calculation*
Employee turnover rate	the proportion of workers who quit their jobs within a specific time frame.	Number of departing workers throughout the time ÷ Average of all employees during the period × 100
Voluntary turnover rate	the proportion of workers who, over a specific time period, departed the company willingly.	Number of voluntary terminations throughout the period ÷ average number of employees overall × 100
Involuntary turnover rate	the proportion of workers who, over a specific time period, departed the company without their consent.	Number of involuntary terminations during the course of the period ÷ average number of employees overall × 100
Turnover cost	The price incurred by the company to replace a departing employee.	Expense of recruiting and onboarding ÷ The quantity of workers that quit at that time
Time-to-fill	The duration of time it takes to fill a position following an employee's departure from the company.	The total number of days needed to fill vacancies within that time ÷ The quantity of vacancies that were filled

These metrics can be used to assess the impact of employee turnover on the organization's performance. High turnover rates can indicate issues with employee engagement, satisfaction, and retention, while high turnover costs can negatively affect the organization's financial performance. Time-to-fill can also provide insights into the efficiency of the organization's hiring processes. By tracking these metrics over time, organizations can identify trends and make data-driven decisions to improve their performance management strategies.

Employee Engagement

The involvement of employees is a critical component of performance management analytics. Employee motivation pertains to the degree of dedication, engagement, and interest that individuals place in their occupation and the institution. There is a positive correlation between employee engagement and productivity, innovation, and organisational loyalty. Measuring employee engagement is, therefore, an essential metric for any organisation seeking to enhance its performance management strategy.

An assortment of methodologies exists for assessing employee engagement, encompassing individual interviews, focus groups, and employee surveys. These approaches may assist organisations in identifying areas for development and the factors that contribute to employee engagement. The following are frequent contributors to employee engagement:

1. **Autonomy and Empowerment:** Employees who have a sense of control over their work and feel empowered to make decisions are more likely to be engaged.
2. **Recognition and Rewards:** Employees who feel appreciated and recognized for their contributions are more likely to be engaged.
3. **Clear Goals and Expectations:** Employees who understand their role and have clear goals and expectations are more likely to be engaged.
4. **Supportive Management:** Employees who have supportive managers who provide guidance and feedback are more likely to be engaged.
5. **Opportunities for Growth and Development**: Employees who have opportunities for growth and development are more likely to be engaged.

By measuring employee engagement, organizations can identify areas for improvement and develop strategies to improve employee engagement. This can lead to better performance management and ultimately, better organizational performance.

It can be used as a valuable metric in performance management analytics as it can provide insight into how satisfied and motivated employees are, and how likely they are to stay with the company. Following are some steps to use employee engagement as a metric in performance management analytics:

1. **Define what Employee Engagement means for your Organization:** Employee engagement can mean different things to different organizations. It is important to define what employee engagement means for your organization and how you will measure it. This could include conducting surveys, analysing employee turnover rates, or tracking attendance and punctuality.
2. **Collect Data on Employee Engagement:** Once you have defined what employee engagement means for your organization, you can collect data on it. This could include surveys, focus groups, one-on-one interviews, or data from employee performance reviews.
3. **Analyse the Data:** Once you have collected data on employee engagement, you can analyse it to identify trends, patterns, and areas for improvement. You can use data visualization tools to create charts, graphs, and dashboards that will help you visualize the data and make informed decisions.
4. **Use Employee Engagement Data in Performance Management Analytics:** You can use employee engagement data as a key performance indicator (KPI) in performance

management analytics. For example, you could use employee engagement scores to measure the effectiveness of your performance management program. You could also use employee engagement data to identify high-performing employees and develop retention strategies to keep them engaged and motivated.

5. **Continuously Monitor and Improve Employee Engagement**: Employee engagement is not a one-time event but an ongoing process. It is important to continuously monitor and improve employee engagement by regularly collecting data, analysing it, and taking action based on the insights gained. This could include implementing employee engagement initiatives, providing training and development opportunities, or improving communication and collaboration within the organization.

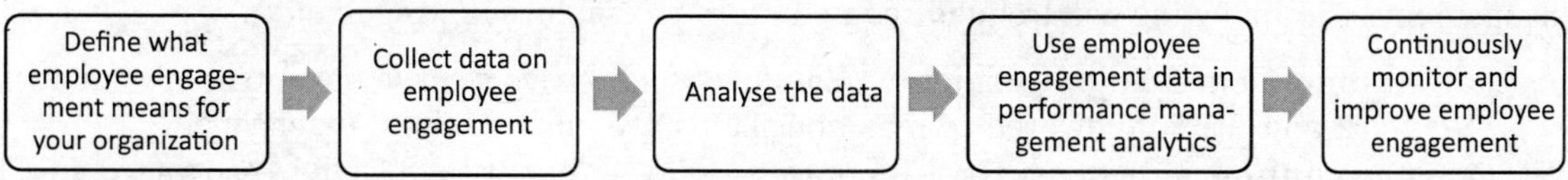

FIGURE 4.2 Steps to use employee engagement as a metric in performance management analytics.

Following table outlines how to use employee engagement as a metric in performance management analytics:

TABLE 4.4 How to metric use in performance management analytics

Metric	*Description*	*How to use in performance management analytics*
Employee Engagement	A measure of the degree to which employees feel connected to and invested in their work and the organization.	Use employee engagement surveys to gather data on employee attitudes and perceptions, and track changes in engagement over time. Combine this information with other measures of performance, like sales, productivity, and customer happiness, to find links between involvement and performance. Use these ideas to come up with ways to get people more involved and boost performance.

In addition to the above, here are some specific examples of how to use employee engagement as a metric in performance management analytics:

- Use employee engagement scores as a leading indicator of future performance. Research has shown that highly engaged employees are more productive, more likely to stay with the organization, and more likely to deliver better customer service. By tracking changes in engagement over time, you can identify potential performance issues before they become serious problems.
- Identify key drivers of engagement by analysing survey data. Employee engagement surveys typically ask questions about factors such as leadership, communication, career development, and work-life balance. By analysing the data, you can identify which of these factors have the strongest impact on engagement, and focus your efforts on addressing those areas.

- Use engagement data to evaluate the effectiveness of performance management processes. If engagement scores are consistently low among employees who have been through the performance management process, it may be a sign that the process needs to be redesigned. For example, if employees feel that performance goals are not clearly communicated or that feedback is not constructive, these issues can be addressed through changes to the performance management process.
- Use engagement data to track the impact of interventions aimed at improving engagement. For example, if you implement a new recognition program or introduce flexible work arrangements, you can track changes in engagement scores to evaluate the effectiveness of these interventions. If engagement scores improve, you can continue to invest in these initiatives. If not, you may need to explore other solutions.

Absenteeism

Absenteeism can certainly be an important metric to track in Performance Management Analytics. Absenteeism refers to the frequency and duration of employee absences from work. It can have a significant impact on productivity and overall organizational performance, as well as employee morale and engagement.

Tracking absenteeism can help organizations identify trends and patterns, such as certain days of the week or times of year when absenteeism tends to be higher. This information can then be used to develop strategies to reduce absenteeism, such as offering flexible schedules or improving employee wellness programs.

Additionally, tracking absenteeism can help managers identify individual employees who may be struggling with attendance issues. This can allow them to provide support and resources to help those employees improve their attendance and overall performance.

It is important to note, however, that absenteeism should not be the only metric used in Performance Management Analytics. Other metrics, such as employee engagement, job satisfaction, and productivity, should also be taken into consideration to gain a more comprehensive understanding of overall performance.

Absenteeism can be used as a metric in Performance Management Analytics by following these steps:

1. **Define Absenteeism:** The first step is to define what absenteeism means for your organization. This could be the number of days an employee has missed work, the percentage of days missed, or the number of instances an employee has been absent.
2. **Set Baseline:** Establish a baseline for absenteeism by looking at historical data to determine the average rate of absenteeism. This will help you identify trends and outliers in the data.
3. **Identify Causes:** Analyse the causes of absenteeism by looking at patterns and trends in the data. For example, is absenteeism higher in certain departments or during certain times of the year? This will help you identify areas where you can target interventions to reduce absenteeism.
4. **Develop Interventions:** Once you have identified the causes of absenteeism, develop interventions to address the root causes. For example, if absenteeism is higher in certain departments, you may need to address issues related to workload, job satisfaction, or employee engagement.

5. **Monitor Progress:** Track the impact of interventions over time by continuing to monitor absenteeism rates. This will help you determine if the interventions are having the desired effect and if additional interventions are needed.
6. **Link to Performance:** Finally, link absenteeism rates to overall performance by analysing the relationship between absenteeism and other performance metrics, such as productivity, quality, and customer satisfaction. This will help you understand the impact of absenteeism on overall performance and identify areas where improvements can be made.

TABLE 4.5 How to use absenteeism as metrics in performance management analytics

Metric	*Definition*	*Calculation*	*Interpretation*
Absenteeism rate	The percentage of scheduled work-days missed by employees.	(Total number of days missed by employees/Total number of scheduled work-days) × 100%	A low absenteeism rate generally indicates high employee engagement and job satisfaction, while a high rate may indicate issues with employee morale, job dissatisfaction, or other organizational problems.
Frequency rate	The average number of absences per employee.	Total number of absences/Total number of employees	A high frequency rate may suggest a pattern of absenteeism among specific employees or departments that requires investigation and intervention.
Duration rate	The average length of time an employee is absent per absence.	Total number of days missed by employees/Total number of absences	A high duration rate may indicate a need for more comprehensive measures to address the underlying causes of absenteeism, such as health or family issues.
Cost of absenteeism	The financial impact of employee absenteeism on the organization.	(Total cost of absenteeism/Total payroll expenses) × 100%	The cost of absenteeism can be significant, including direct costs such as lost productivity and indirect costs such as decreased morale and increased workload for other employees. Analysing the cost of absenteeism can help identify areas for improvement and guide the development of effective absence management strategies.
Absenteeism trend	The direction and magnitude of change in absenteeism over time.	Compare absenteeism rates or other metrics over multiple periods (e.g. months, quarters, years)	Analysing absenteeism trends can help identify patterns and factors that may be contributing to changes in employee behaviour and engagement, and guide efforts to improve employee retention and productivity.

By using absenteeism as a metric in Performance Management Analytics, organizations can identify areas where interventions are needed to improve employee engagement, reduce turnover, and increase overall productivity.

Performance Ratings

Performance ratings are often used as a key metric in performance management analytics, as they provide a way to measure and evaluate employee performance in a systematic and consistent manner. By analysing performance ratings, organizations can identify patterns and trends in employee performance, pinpoint areas for improvement, and make data-driven decisions about performance management practices.

Performance ratings can be based on a variety of factors, including job skills, job knowledge, productivity, teamwork, communication, leadership, and customer service. They can be measured using a variety of methods, such as self-assessments, peer evaluations, supervisor evaluations, and 360-degree feedback.

It is important to make sure that performance ratings are accurate, fair, and reliable when they are used as a key measure in performance management analytics. There shouldn't be any bias in the ratings, and they should be the same for all raters. The ratings should also not have any mercy or halo effects.

Companies might use employee involvement scores, absenteeism rates, and turnover rates along with performance grades to figure out how well their performance management is working. It is possible for companies to get a better picture of employee performance and the factors that affect it by looking at these measures along with performance scores.

The steps one need to take to use performance scores as a measure in HR analytics are:

1. **Define the Performance Rating System:** The first step is to define the performance rating system that will be used to measure employee performance. This may involve defining the different levels of performance and the criteria for each level.
2. **Collect Performance Data:** Once the performance rating system is defined, performance data must be collected for each employee. This can be done through various methods such as self-evaluations, manager evaluations, and feedback from colleagues.
3. **Analyse the Data:** Once the data is collected, it can be analysed to identify trends and patterns in employee performance. This analysis can be done using various statistical methods such as regression analysis or correlation analysis.
4. **Identify Areas for Improvement:** Based on the analysis, areas for improvement can be identified for each employee. These areas can be used to develop targeted training and development programs to help employees improve their performance.
5. **Set Performance Goals:** Performance ratings can also be used to set performance goals for employees. These goals can be based on the employee's current performance rating and the areas for improvement identified through analysis.
6. **Monitor Progress:** Once performance goals are set, progress can be monitored through regular performance evaluations. This can be done using the same performance rating system used to collect initial data.

TABLE 4.6 Using performance ratings as metrics in performance management analytics

Metric name	*Definition*	*Calculation*	*Interpretation*
Average performance rating	The average score given to employees based on their performance review.	Add up all performance ratings given and divide by the number of employees.	A high average performance rating indicates that employees are meeting or exceeding expectations, while a low average rating may indicate performance issues within the organization.
Distribution of performance ratings	The percentage of employees who received each performance rating.	Count the number of employees who received each performance rating and divide by the total number of employees.	A distribution that is heavily skewed towards high or low ratings may indicate issues with the performance review process or biases in the evaluation process.
Performance rating by department	The average performance rating for employees in each department.	Add up all performance ratings for employees in each department and divide by the number of employees in that department.	This metric can help identify which departments are performing well and which may need additional support or resources.
Performance rating by manager	The average performance rating for employees under each manager's supervision.	Add up all performance ratings for employees under each manager's supervision and divide by the number of employees.	This metric can help identify which managers are effective at developing and managing their employees and which may need additional support or training.
Performance rating vs. goals	The percentage of employees who met or exceeded their performance goals.	Count the number of employees who met or exceeded their goals and divide by the total number of employees.	This metric can help determine if employees are setting realistic goals and if they have the skills and resources necessary to achieve them.

It's important to note that Performance Ratings should not be the only metrics used in Performance Management Analytics, as they can be subjective and prone to bias. It's essential to combine them with other objective performance metrics and to use them as part of a larger, comprehensive approach to performance management.

Thus, using performance ratings as metrics in performance management analytics can help organizations identify areas for improvement and develop targeted training programs to improve employee performance. It can also help set performance goals and monitor progress towards those goals.

Time-to-Fill

Time-to-Fill is a critical metric in Performance Management Analytics that measures the time taken by an organization to fill a job opening from the point of requisition to the time of hiring. It is an essential key performance indicator (KPI) in talent acquisition and is used by organizations to assess their recruiting efficiency and the overall effectiveness of their recruitment processes.

Time-to-Fill is calculated by dividing the total number of days it takes to fill a job opening by the number of job openings. The formula is as follows:

Time-to-Fill = Total number of days taken to fill the job opening / Number of job openings

The importance of Time-to-Fill as a key metric in Performance Management Analytics lies in its ability to provide valuable insights into the efficiency and effectiveness of an organization's recruitment process. A high Time-to-Fill indicates that the organization's recruiting process is slow, which could negatively impact the organization's ability to attract top talent and compete in the market.

On the other hand, a low Time-to-Fill indicates that the recruiting process is efficient and effective and that job vacancies may be filled fast, preventing productivity loss from empty jobs. A reduced Time-to-Fill can also aid in lowering hiring-related expenses like advertising and agency fees.

As a result, Time-to-Fill is a crucial performance management analytics indicator that may assist firms in gauging the success of their hiring procedures, pinpointing areas in need of development, and guaranteeing that they draw in and keep top personnel.

The steps to utilise Time-to-Fill as a performance management analytics statistic are as follows:

1. **Define the Metric:** To use Time-to-Fill as a metric, you first need to define it clearly. Time-to-Fill is the number of days it takes to fill a job vacancy from the date the position was opened to the date the candidate accepts the job offer.
2. **Collect Data:** Collect data on the time it takes to fill each open position. This data can be obtained from recruitment systems or applicant tracking software. You may need to collect additional data such as the type of job vacancy, the recruitment source, and the hiring manager.
3. **Analyse the Data:** Analyse the data to identify trends and patterns in the Time-to-Fill metric. Look for areas of improvement such as long recruitment times or bottlenecks in the recruitment process.
4. **Set Targets:** Based on the data analysis, set targets for Time-to-Fill for each type of job vacancy. These targets should be realistic and achievable.
5. **Monitor Progress:** Monitor progress regularly by tracking the Time-to-Fill metric against the targets set. Identify any deviations from the targets and take corrective action as necessary.
6. **Use the Insights:** Use the insights gained from the analysis to improve the recruitment process. Make changes to the recruitment process or modify recruitment strategies to reduce the Time-to-Fill metric.

Time-to-Fill is a key performance metric used in Performance Management Analytics to measure the effectiveness of an organization's recruitment process. It is the number of days from the time a job requisition is opened to the time a candidate is offered and accepts the job. By collecting data, analysing trends, setting targets, monitoring progress, and making changes to the recruitment process, organizations can improve their hiring practices and reduce Time-to-Fill.

TABLE 4.7 Using Time-to-Fill as a metric in performance management analytics

Metric name	*Time-to-Fill*
Definition	The number of days from the time a job requisition is opened to the time a candidate is offered and accepts the job
Calculation	Total number of days to fill a job opening/Total number of job openings filled
Purpose	To measure the effectiveness of an organization's recruitment process
Target	Depends on the organization's specific recruitment goals and needs, but generally a shorter Time-to-Fill is desirable
Analysis	High Time-to-Fill can indicate inefficiencies in the recruitment process such as a lengthy screening process or a lack of qualified candidates. It can also result in increased costs and lost productivity. Low Time-to-Fill can indicate a streamlined and effective recruitment process, but can also indicate rushed decisions and potential mismatches between job requirements and candidate qualifications.
Action	If Time-to-Fill is high, the organization may need to review and improve their recruitment process, such as expanding the pool of potential candidates or streamlining the screening process. If Time-to-Fill is low, the organization may need to review and ensure that candidates are being thoroughly evaluated to ensure the right fit for the organization.

Time-to-Fill can provide valuable insights into an organization's recruitment process and help to identify areas for improvement.

DATA COLLECTION AND ANALYSIS

Performance management analytics involves collecting and analysing data to evaluate an organization's performance and make data-driven decisions. In this process, data collection and analysis play a crucial role. Following are some key steps involved in data collection and analysis in performance management analytics:

1. **Define the Data:** The first step in data collection is to define the data that needs to be collected. This may include financial data, customer satisfaction data, employee performance data, and other relevant metrics.
2. **Determine the Sources of Data**: Once the data is defined, the next step is to determine the sources of data. This may include internal sources such as databases and spreadsheets or external sources such as surveys and market research reports.

3. **Collect the Data:** Data can be collected in a variety of ways, including surveys, interviews, observations, and automated data collection methods such as sensors and tracking software.
4. **Clean and Prepare the Data:** Once the data is collected, it needs to be cleaned and prepared for analysis. This involves removing any irrelevant data, checking for errors and inconsistencies, and formatting the data into a usable format.
5. **Analyse the Data:** With the data cleaned and prepared, the next step is to analyse it. This may involve using statistical methods to identify patterns and trends in the data, creating charts and graphs to visualize the data, and conducting comparative analysis to identify areas of improvement.
6. **Interpret the Results:** The final step is to interpret the results of the analysis. This involves using the insights gained from the data to make informed decisions about performance management. It may also involve communicating the results to stakeholders and taking action based on the insights gained.

Data collection and analysis are critical steps in performance management analytics. By collecting and analysing data, organizations can gain insights into their performance and make data-driven decisions to improve their operations.

Sources of Performance Management Data

There are several sources of data that can be used for performance management analytics. Some of the key sources of performance management data are:

1. **Performance Reviews:** This is a common source of performance data that is collected through an evaluation of an employee's performance over a specific period. The data collected can include ratings on key performance indicators (KPIs), feedback from managers, peers and customers, and self-evaluation.
2. **Customer Feedback:** Performance management analytics can be enriched by customer feedback that provides insights into how well a business is meeting customer expectations. This feedback can come from sources such as surveys, social media, and online reviews.
3. **Sales Data:** Sales data can be used as a source of performance management data to measure how well a sales team is performing against targets. Sales data can be analysed to identify trends and patterns that can help identify areas for improvement.
4. **Financial Data:** Financial data such as revenue, profit, and return on investment can be used as performance management data to measure how well an organization is meeting its financial goals. This data can be analysed to identify areas for improvement and help guide strategic decision-making.
5. **Operational Data:** Operational data such as production output, quality metrics, and cycle time can be used as performance management data to measure how well an organization is performing in its operations. This data can be analysed to identify inefficiencies and areas for improvement.
6. **Employee Engagement Surveys:** Employee engagement surveys can be used as a source of performance management data to measure how engaged and committed employees are to their work. This data can be used to identify areas for improvement in employee motivation, training, and development.

Thus, a wide range of data sources can be used for performance management analytics, and organizations should carefully consider which sources of data are most relevant to their goals and objectives.

Data Collection Methods for Performance Management Analytics

Performance management analytics can be used to analyse employee performance, identify areas for improvement, and evaluate the effectiveness of training programs. To conduct effective performance management analytics, it is important to collect relevant data using appropriate methods. Following are some data collection methods for performance management analytics:

1. **Employee Surveys:** Employee surveys can be used to collect feedback on job satisfaction, work environment, workload, and other factors that may impact employee performance. Surveys can be conducted anonymously to encourage honest feedback and can be administered online or in-person.
2. **Performance Reviews:** Performance reviews can provide valuable data on employee performance, including strengths and weaknesses, areas for improvement, and specific examples of job-related achievements. Performance reviews can be conducted annually or more frequently, depending on organizational needs.
3. **Key Performance Indicators (KPIs):** KPIs are specific metrics that measure performance against predefined goals. KPIs can be used to track employee performance over time and identify areas where improvements can be made.
4. **Observations:** Observations can be used to gather data on employee performance in real-time. Managers can observe employees as they perform their duties and note areas where improvements can be made.
5. **Interviews:** Interviews are used to collect data from employees, managers, and other stakeholders about their experiences and perceptions. This method can be used to identify areas for improvement, assess employee engagement, and gather feedback on performance management processes.
6. **Focus Groups:** Focus groups can be used to gather feedback from employees on specific topics or issues related to performance management. Focus groups can be structured to encourage open and honest feedback and can provide valuable insights into employee perceptions and attitudes.
7. **Data Mining:** Data mining can be used to analyse large amounts of data to identify patterns and trends related to employee performance. Data mining can be used to identify factors that contribute to high-performing employees and to develop predictive models to identify potential performance issues.
8. **Social Media Monitoring:** Social media monitoring can be used to gather data on employee sentiment and perceptions. By monitoring social media channels, organizations can identify issues related to employee morale, job satisfaction, and other factors that may impact performance.

Performance management analytics can be a powerful tool for organizations looking to improve employee performance and optimize their workforce. By collecting relevant data using a combination of these methods, organizations can gain insights into employee performance and take steps to improve it.

Data Analysis Techniques

Performance management analytics is a data-driven approach to managing employee performance, with the goal of improving overall organizational effectiveness. In order to make sense of the data, there are various data analysis techniques that can be used in performance management analytics. Following are some of the techniques commonly used:

1. **Descriptive Analytics:** This technique involves analysing historical data to gain insights into past performance trends. Descriptive analytics is often used to identify patterns and trends in performance data that can be used to inform future decision making.
2. **Diagnostic Analytics:** This technique involves analysing data to identify the root cause of performance issues. Diagnostic analytics is often used to determine why certain performance metrics are not meeting expectations.
3. **Predictive Analytics:** This technique involves using statistical models to predict future performance trends based on historical data. Predictive analytics is often used to identify future performance issues before they occur.
4. **Prescriptive Analytics:** This technique involves using data analysis to identify specific actions that can be taken to improve performance. Prescriptive analytics is often used to inform decision making about how best to allocate resources to achieve desired outcomes.
5. **Benchmarking:** This technique involves comparing an organization's performance metrics to those of other organizations in the same industry or sector. Benchmarking can provide insights into areas where an organization is underperforming relative to its peers.
6. **Data Visualization:** This technique involves presenting data in a visual format that is easy to understand. Data visualization can help to identify patterns and trends in performance data that might not be immediately apparent when looking at raw data.
7. **Key Performance Indicators (KPIs):** KPIs are metrics that organizations use to measure their performance against specific goals. They help organizations to track progress towards their goals and identify areas where they need to improve.

Performance management analytics relies on a combination of these data analysis techniques to identify performance issues, inform decision making, and improve organizational effectiveness.

APPLICATIONS OF PERFORMANCE MANAGEMENT ANALYTICS

Performance management analytics is the use of data analysis tools and techniques to measure and evaluate the performance of an organization, department, team, or individual employees. Some of the applications of performance management analytics are:

1. **Identifying Performance Trends:** Performance management analytics can help identify trends in employee performance, such as areas where employees are excelling and areas where they may need additional support or training.

2. **Performance Reviews**: Performance management analytics can be used to inform performance reviews, allowing managers to provide more objective feedback based on data-driven insights.
3. **Goal Setting:** Performance management analytics can help managers set realistic and measurable goals for their employees, and track progress towards those goals over time.
4. **Employee Engagement**: Performance management analytics can be used to measure employee engagement and identify factors that contribute to high levels of engagement, such as recognition programs, work-life balance, and opportunities for growth and development.
5. **Resource Allocation:** Performance management analytics can help managers allocate resources more effectively, such as determining which departments or teams require additional resources to improve performance.
6. **Talent Management:** Performance management analytics can be used to identify high-performing employees and potential future leaders, and to develop targeted training and development programs to help those employees reach their full potential.
7. **Risk Management:** Performance management analytics can help organizations identify potential risks and vulnerabilities, such as high turnover rates or low employee engagement, and develop strategies to mitigate those risks.
8. **Benchmarking:** Performance management analytics can be used to benchmark an organization's performance against industry standards, identify areas for improvement, and measure progress over time.

Performance management analytics is the process of using data and analytical methods to monitor and optimize the performance of an organization or its employees. Some examples of applications of performance management analytics are:

1. **Employee Performance Evaluation**: Performance management analytics can be used to evaluate the performance of employees in an organization. This can include analysing employee data such as attendance, productivity, and customer feedback to identify areas of improvement.
2. **Talent Management:** Performance management analytics can help organizations identify high-performing employees and develop strategies to retain and develop their talent. This can include analysing employee data to identify areas where employees need training or development.
3. **Sales Performance Analysis:** Performance management analytics can help organizations track sales performance and identify areas where sales teams need improvement. This can include analysing sales data such as conversion rates, revenue per sale, and customer feedback.
4. **Customer Service Performance Analysis**: Performance management analytics can help organizations track customer service performance and identify areas where service teams need improvement. This can include analysing customer service data such as response times, customer satisfaction scores, and complaint resolution rates.

5. **Financial Performance Analysis**: Performance management analytics can help organizations track financial performance and identify areas where they need to improve. This can include analysing financial data such as revenue, expenses, and profit margins to identify areas where costs can be reduced or revenue increased.
6. **Operational Performance Analysis:** Performance management analytics can help organizations track operational performance and identify areas where processes can be optimized. This can include analysing operational data such as production rates, inventory levels, and supply chain performance.
7. **Supply Chain Performance Management:** Performance management analytics can be used to analyse supply chain performance metrics, such as inventory turnover, order fulfilment time, and delivery accuracy. This data can help supply chain managers optimize their operations, reduce costs, and improve customer satisfaction.

Performance management analytics can help organizations make data-driven decisions to improve performance, reduce costs, and increase efficiency.

Identifying High-Performing Employees

Identifying high-performing employees is a crucial task in performance management analytics. Following are some key steps that can help you identify top performers:

1. **Define What High Performance Means:** Before you can identify high-performing employees, you need to define what high performance means in your organization. This may involve setting specific goals and expectations for different roles, departments, or teams.
2. **Collect and Analyse Data:** Performance management analytics relies on data to identify high-performing employees. You may collect data from a variety of sources, including performance reviews, productivity metrics, sales reports, customer feedback, and more. Once you have collected the data, you can use analytics tools to analyse it and identify patterns and trends.
3. **Use Objective Criteria:** When identifying high-performing employees, it's important to use objective criteria that are based on data and measurable outcomes. This helps to ensure that the process is fair and transparent.
4. **Consider both Quantitative and Qualitative Data:** While quantitative data such as sales numbers or productivity metrics can be helpful in identifying high-performing employees, it's also important to consider qualitative data such as feedback from managers and peers, as well as observations of behaviour and work habits.
5. **Consider Potential for Growth:** While current performance is important, it's also important to consider an employee's potential for growth and development. High-performing employees may have the skills and qualities needed to take on more challenging roles or responsibilities in the future.
6. **Communicate Results and Provide Feedback:** Once you have identified high-performing employees, it's important to communicate the results to them and provide feedback on their performance. This helps to reinforce positive behaviours and encourage continued growth and development.

TABLE 4.8 Various metrics and indicators to identify high-performing employees

Metric	*Description*
Goal Attainment	Measures how well employees meet their individual goals and objectives.
Quality of work	Evaluates the quality of an employee's work, including accuracy, thoroughness, and attention to detail.
Timeliness	Measures how well an employee completes tasks and projects on time.
Initiative	Evaluates the extent to which an employee takes the initiative to identify and solve problems or improve processes.
Collaboration	Measures an employee's ability to work well with others and contribute positively to team dynamics.
Leadership	Evaluates an employee's ability to take charge, influence others, and drive results.
Customer satisfaction	Measures how well an employee meets the needs and expectations of customers.
Innovation	Evaluates an employee's ability to generate new ideas, approaches, and solutions to problems.
Learning and development	Measures an employee's willingness and ability to learn and develop new skills and knowledge.
Attendance and punctuality	Evaluates how well an employee adheres to work schedules and attendance policies.

It's important to note that the specific metrics used may vary depending on the organization's goals and values. Additionally, these metrics should be considered in conjunction with other factors, such as the employee's tenure, job responsibilities, and overall contribution to the organization.

Identifying Areas for Improvement

Performance management analytics can be a useful tool for identifying areas for improvement for high-performing employees. Following are some potential areas to consider:

1. **Skill Development:** High-performing employees may benefit from additional training or development opportunities to expand their skill sets. Analysing performance data can help identify specific areas where an employee could benefit from further development.
2. **Goal Setting:** While high-performing employees are often excellent at achieving goals, they may benefit from setting more challenging goals or from setting goals that align more closely with organizational objectives.

3. **Time Management:** Even high-performing employees can struggle with time management. Analysing performance data can help identify areas where an employee may be spending too much time on certain tasks or not enough time on others.
4. **Collaboration:** High-performing employees may benefit from additional opportunities to collaborate with others in the organization. Analysing performance data can help identify areas where an employee could benefit from working more closely with others.
5. **Innovation:** High-performing employees may benefit from being encouraged to think more creatively or to challenge the status quo. Analysing performance data can help identify areas where an employee may be able to contribute more to innovation within the organization.
6. **Leadership Development:** High-performing employees may benefit from additional leadership development opportunities, even if they are not in a formal leadership role. Analysing performance data can help identify areas where an employee may be able to improve their leadership skills.
7. **Communication:** High-performing employees may benefit from additional communication training or development. Analysing performance data can help identify areas where an employee could improve their communication skills, such as giving presentations or providing feedback.

It's important to note that while these areas may be relevant for high-performing employees, they may not be applicable to every employee. Each employee's performance data should be analysed on a case-by-case basis to identify areas for improvement that are specific to them.

Aligning Performance Goals with Business Objectives

Performance management analytics is a process of measuring and analysing employee performance in order to improve business outcomes. It involves collecting and analysing data on key performance indicators (KPIs) to determine how well employees are performing in relation to business objectives. One of the most important aspects of performance management analytics is aligning performance goals with business objectives.

Companies must provide precise, quantifiable, and well defined goals that are connected to the broader company plan in order to match performance goals with business objectives. This involves identifying the key performance indicators (KPIs) that are most important to the business and determining how they can be measured and tracked.

Once the KPIs have been identified, companies can use performance management analytics to monitor progress and identify areas where improvements can be made. This involves collecting data on employee performance and analysing it to identify trends and patterns. Companies can then use this information to develop strategies to improve performance and achieve their business objectives.

The actions that companies should take to successfully match performance goals with business objectives:

1. Define clear, measurable, and specific performance goals that are linked to the overall business strategy.

2. Identify the key performance indicators (KPIs) that are most important to the business.
3. Determine how the KPIs can be measured and tracked using performance management analytics.
4. Collect data on employee performance and use performance management analytics to monitor progress.
5. Analyse the data to identify trends and patterns, and develop strategies to improve performance and achieve business objectives.

By aligning performance goals with business objectives, companies can ensure that they are focusing on the right areas to achieve their goals. Performance management analytics can help companies to identify areas where improvements can be made and to develop strategies to improve employee performance and drive business success.

Improving Employee Retention

Improving employee retention in performance management analytics involves using data analysis to identify the factors that contribute to employee turnover and developing strategies to address them. Following are some steps you can take:

1. **Analyse Employee Turnover Data:** Use analytics tools to analyse employee turnover data and identify patterns or trends. Look for commonalities among employees who have left the company, such as job title, department, tenure, and performance ratings.
2. **Identify the Reasons for Turnover:** Once you've identified the patterns, investigate the reasons behind them. Conduct exit interviews or surveys to gather feedback from departing employees. This will help you to identify the root causes of turnover and develop strategies to address them.
3. **Evaluate Your Performance Management System:** Review your current performance management system to determine if it's contributing to turnover. Are performance expectations clear? Are employees receiving regular feedback and coaching? Are rewards and recognition aligned with performance?
4. **Develop Retention Strategies:** Use the insights gained from your analysis to develop strategies to improve employee retention. For example, if employees are leaving due to lack of career growth opportunities, you can create development plans and career paths for employees. If employees are leaving due to poor manager-employee relationships, you can provide training to managers on how to build better relationships with their employees.
5. **Monitor and Adjust Your Strategies:** Continuously monitor your retention strategies to evaluate their effectiveness. Use analytics to track key metrics such as employee engagement, turnover rates, and performance ratings. Adjust your strategies as needed to ensure that they're achieving their intended outcomes.

By using performance management analytics to improve employee retention, you can create a more engaged, motivated, and productive workforce that's better equipped to achieve your organization's goals.

TABLE 4.9 Strategies for improving employee retention

Strategy	*Description*
Competitive salary and benefits	Offer salaries and benefits that are competitive with other companies in your industry. Conduct regular market research to ensure that you are offering fair compensation packages.
Career development opportunities	Provide opportunities for career growth and development, such as training programs, job rotations, and mentorship programs. This can help employees feel valued and invested in their future with the company.
Work-life balance	Offer flexible work arrangements, such as telecommuting and flexible schedules, to help employees balance work and personal commitments. Encourage employees to take time off when needed and promote a healthy work-life balance culture.
Recognition and rewards	Recognize employees for their hard work and contributions through regular performance evaluations, bonuses, and awards. This can help employees feel appreciated and motivated to continue doing good work.
Positive workplace culture	Create a positive workplace culture that values open communication, respect, and collaboration. Foster a sense of community and encourage employees to build relationships with one another.
Employee feedback and involvement	Encourage employee feedback and involvement in company decision-making. This can help employees feel like their opinions matter and that they are part of the company's success.
Leadership and management	Train and support managers to be effective leaders who can inspire and motivate their teams. Provide regular feedback and coaching to ensure that managers are meeting the needs of their employees.
Health and wellness programs	Offer health and wellness programs, such as gym memberships, mental health resources, and healthy food options. This can help employees feel supported in their overall well-being.

These are just a few strategies that companies can use to improve employee retention. It's important to note that what works for one company may not work for another, so it's important to tailor retention strategies to the unique needs and culture of your organization.

Improving Employee Development

Employee development refers to the ongoing process of improving and enhancing the skills, knowledge, and abilities of employees within an organization. It involves providing training, education, and opportunities for professional growth and development to enable employees to perform their jobs effectively and advance in their careers.

Organisations engage in staff development for a number of reasons. Firstly, giving workers the chance to learn and develop makes them feel valued and appreciated, which boosts their morale and increases job satisfaction. Second, when workers pick up new abilities and information that they may use at work, performance and productivity may increase. Thirdly, since employees are more inclined to remain with a company that supports their professional growth, it can aid in attracting and keeping top talent.

Formal training programmes, job shadowing, work rotations, coaching and mentoring, and on-the-job learning are just a few of the several ways that employees may grow. It may also entail encouraging staff members to seek professional certifications or more education, as well as providing them with opportunity to attend conferences, seminars, and workshops.

Enhancing employee development is a continuous activity that calls for a blend of organisational commitment, resources, and methods. Few strategies to improve staff development are:

1. **Identify the Needs of Employees:** Conduct surveys, assessments, and evaluations to identify the skills, knowledge, and abilities that employees need to succeed in their roles. Use this information to tailor training and development programs to the specific needs of individual employees.
2. **Create a Learning Culture:** Promote a culture of continuous learning and development within the organization. Encourage employees to pursue their professional development goals and provide them with the necessary resources and support to do so.
3. **Provide Training and Development Opportunities:** Offer a variety of training and development programs, such as on-the-job training, mentoring, coaching, job shadowing, and workshops. Ensure that these opportunities align with the identified needs of employees and provide a clear path for career advancement.
4. **Recognize and Reward Employees:** Recognize and reward employees for their achievements and contributions to the organization. Celebrate milestones, such as completing training programs or achieving certifications, and provide incentives for employees to pursue their professional development goals.
5. **Evaluate the Effectiveness of Training and Development Programs:** Regularly evaluate the effectiveness of training and development programs to determine their impact on employee performance and business outcomes. Use this information to make necessary improvements and adjustments to the programs.

TABLE 4.10 Improving employee development

Strategies	*Description*
Regular feedback	Providing frequent and specific feedback on performance can help employees identify areas of improvement and provide a sense of direction to improve.
Personalized learning	Customizing employee training and development programs based on their individual needs and goals can help them acquire new skills and knowledge.
Career development plans	Creating a clear career development plan for each employee, outlining their career goals, and identifying training and development opportunities can help them feel more invested in their jobs and motivated to succeed.

(*Contd.*)

Strategies	*Description*
Coaching and mentoring	Pairing employees with coaches or mentors can provide them with support, guidance, and advice, leading to increased engagement and growth opportunities.
Encourage knowledge sharing	Encouraging employees to share their knowledge and skills with others can foster a culture of continuous learning, collaboration, and innovation.
Reward and recognition	Recognizing and rewarding employees for their achievements, milestones, and contributions can boost their morale, motivation, and job satisfaction.
Flexibility and work-life balance	Providing flexible work arrangements and promoting work-life balance can help employees feel more engaged, productive, and committed to their jobs.
Use of technology	Leveraging technology tools, such as e-learning platforms and gamification, can enhance employee learning experiences and make training more engaging and interactive.
Cross-functional Projects	Assigning employees to cross-functional projects can provide them with opportunities to learn new skills, collaborate with colleagues from different departments, and gain exposure to different aspects of the organization.
Continuous improvement	Adopting a continuous improvement mind-set and constantly seeking ways to improve training and development programs can help ensure that employees receive the most relevant and effective training possible.

By implementing these strategies, organizations can create a culture of continuous learning and development, increase employee engagement and retention, and improve overall organizational performance.

Challenges and Limitations of Performance Management Analytics

Performance management analytics, like any other form of data analysis, come with several challenges and limitations. Following are some of the common ones:

1. **Data Quality:** The accuracy and completeness of data are critical to the success of performance management analytics. If the data is inaccurate, incomplete, or outdated, the results of the analysis will be unreliable and may lead to wrong conclusions.
2. **Data Integration:** Performance management analytics often require data from various sources, such as HR systems, financial systems, and operational systems. Integrating these data sources can be a significant challenge, as each system may have its own data format and structure.
3. **Data Privacy and Security:** Performance management analytics may involve sensitive data, such as employee salaries and performance evaluations. Ensuring the

privacy and security of this data is critical to maintaining the trust of employees and stakeholders.

4. **Skillset:** Analysing performance data requires a specific skillset, such as data analysis, statistics, and business acumen. Organizations may need to invest in training or hiring individuals with these skills.
5. **Complexity:** Performance management analytics can be complex, requiring a deep understanding of the organization's strategy, goals, and objectives. This complexity can make it difficult to design and implement effective analytics programs.
6. **Implementation:** Even with accurate data and skilled analysts, implementing performance management analytics can be challenging. Organizations must ensure that the insights gained from the analysis are actionable and integrated into the decision-making process.

Thus, performance management analytics offer many benefits, but they also come with challenges and limitations. Organizations must be aware of these challenges and take steps to address them to ensure the success of their analytics programs.

Bias and Discrimination

Performance management analytics can be a powerful tool for organizations to measure employee productivity, identify areas for improvement, and make data-driven decisions about performance. However, if not designed and implemented carefully, performance management analytics can perpetuate bias and discrimination.

One common problem is that the data used for performance management analytics may be biased. For example, if certain groups of employees are given fewer opportunities for professional development or are disproportionately assigned to less challenging projects, their performance metrics may be lower than those of other employees. Using these biased metrics to evaluate performance can unfairly penalize certain groups and lead to further discrimination.

Another issue is that performance management analytics can be used to reinforce stereotypes and biases. For example, if a certain leadership style is consistently rewarded, employees who do not fit that mould may be unfairly penalized. Similarly, if a certain demographic group is consistently promoted, while others are not, this can lead to systemic discrimination.

To prevent bias and discrimination in performance management analytics, it is important to:

1. **Use Diverse Data Sources:** Make sure that the data used for performance management analytics is not biased and takes into account factors such as job responsibilities, tenure, and project complexity.
2. **Use Multiple Measures of Performance:** Instead of relying solely on a single metric, consider using a range of measures of performance, such as peer evaluations, customer feedback, and qualitative assessments.
3. **Regularly Review and Analyse the Data:** To ensure that performance management analytics are not reinforcing biases, it is important to regularly review and analyse the data, looking for patterns of discrimination or bias.

4. **Train Managers and Employees:** Train managers and employees on the importance of diversity and inclusion in performance management, and provide them with tools to recognize and address bias.

By being aware of the potential for bias and discrimination in performance management analytics and taking steps to prevent it, organizations can use data to make fair and objective decisions about performance.

Technological Limitations

Performance management analytics involves using technology to collect and analyse data about employee performance. However, there are several technological limitations that can impact the effectiveness of performance management analytics:

1. **Inaccurate Data:** Performance management analytics rely on accurate data, but there can be errors in data collection and entry that can lead to inaccurate results.
2. **Data Overload:** Organizations can collect vast amounts of data, but analysing and making sense of all that data can be a significant challenge, leading to information overload.
3. **Data Silos:** Performance data can be stored in multiple systems, making it difficult to access and analyse the data cohesively.
4. **Lack of Standardization:** Without a standard process for data collection, analysis, and reporting, it can be challenging to compare performance data across departments or job functions.
5. **Outdated Technology:** Legacy systems and outdated technology can limit the ability to collect and analyse performance data effectively.
6. **Cybersecurity Risks:** Collecting and storing employee performance data can increase the risk of cybersecurity breaches and data theft.
7. **Technology Infrastructure:** The technology infrastructure required to support performance management analytics can be costly. Organizations may need to invest in hardware, software, and data storage solutions to support the analytics.
8. **Analytical Skills:** The effective use of performance management analytics requires analytical skills that are not always present in an organization. Organizations may need to invest in training and development to build the necessary skills in-house or hire external experts.

To overcome these limitations, organizations should invest in modern technology platforms that are designed for performance management analytics, ensure data accuracy through regular data audits, establish data governance policies to manage data silos and ensure standardization, and regularly update their cybersecurity protocols.

Best Practices for Performance Management Analytics

Performance management analytics refers to the use of data and analytics to improve organizational performance. Following are some best practices for performance management analytics:

1. **Define Key Performance Indicators (KPIs):** KPIs are the metrics that an organization uses to measure its progress towards achieving its goals. Define KPIs that are relevant to your organization's goals and objectives.

2. **Collect Quality Qata:** Collecting quality data is critical to performance management analytics. Ensure that the data is accurate, relevant, timely, and complete.
3. **Use Data Visualization Tools:** Data visualization tools help you to analyse and present data in a way that is easy to understand. Use tools such as charts, graphs, and dashboards to visualize your data.
4. **Analyse Data Regularly**: Regular analysis of data helps you to identify trends and patterns that can help you to make better decisions. Set up a regular schedule for data analysis.
5. **Use Predictive Analytics:** Predictive analytics helps you to forecast future trends and identify potential issues before they occur. Use predictive analytics to make informed decisions about your organization's future.
6. **Share Insights:** Sharing insights with stakeholders helps to build a culture of data-driven decision-making. Use data to communicate insights with stakeholders and encourage them to use data in their decision-making processes.
7. **Continuously Improve:** Performance management analytics is an ongoing process. Continuously review and refine your KPIs, data collection methods, and analytics techniques to improve your organization's performance.

TABLE 4.11 Some best practices for performance management analytics

Best Practice	*Description*
Identify Key Performance Indicators (KPIs)	Define the metrics that align with your business goals and measure progress toward achieving those goals.
Establish data governance	Ensure the accuracy, consistency, and security of the data used in performance management analytics.
Use relevant data sources	Use data sources that are relevant to the KPIs being measured and ensure that the data is accurate, timely, and complete.
Analyse data regularly	Regularly analyse performance data to identify trends, patterns, and opportunities for improvement.
Use visualization tools	Use visualization tools to help identify trends and patterns more easily and quickly.
Collaborate across departments	Foster collaboration across departments to ensure that performance management analytics are aligned with overall business goals.
Develop action plans	Use the insights gained from performance management analytics to develop action plans that address areas of improvement.
Communicate results	Communicate performance management analytics results to stakeholders to ensure that everyone is aware of progress toward achieving business goals.
Continuously monitor and adjust	Continuously monitor performance management analytics to identify opportunities for improvement and adjust processes as necessary.

These best practices are not exhaustive, but they provide a good starting point for organizations looking to establish effective performance management analytics.

EXAMPLES OF SUCCESSFUL IMPLEMENTATION OF PERFORMANCE MANAGEMENT ANALYTICS AND LESSONS LEARNED FROM THEM

Performance management analytics can be a powerful tool to help organizations optimize their workforce and business processes. Following are some examples of successful implementation of performance management analytics and the lessons learned from them:

1. **General Electric (GE):** GE implemented a performance management system called "GE Workout," which involved teams of employees coming together to identify and solve problems in their business processes. The system included analytics to track progress and identify areas of improvement. The lessons learned from GE's implementation include the importance of involving employees in the process and using data to drive decision-making.
2. **Walmart:** Walmart used performance analytics to identify inefficiencies in its supply chain and reduce inventory levels. By using data to optimize inventory levels, Walmart was able to reduce costs and improve its bottom line. The lessons learned from Walmart's implementation include the importance of using data to identify opportunities for improvement and the need to continuously monitor and adjust performance management strategies.
3. **Ford Motor Company:** Ford used performance management analytics to improve its manufacturing processes and reduce costs. By using data to identify bottlenecks and inefficiencies in the production process, Ford was able to optimize its operations and improve quality. The lessons learned from Ford's implementation include the importance of involving all stakeholders in the process and using data to drive continuous improvement.
4. **Google:** Google uses performance analytics to track employee performance and identify areas of improvement. By using data to identify areas of strength and weakness, Google is able to provide targeted coaching and training to its employees. The lessons learned from Google's implementation include the importance of using data to personalize employee development and the need for ongoing communication and feedback.

Hence the key lessons learned from successful implementation of performance management analytics include the importance of involving employees in the process, using data to drive decision-making, continuously monitoring and adjusting performance management strategies, involving all stakeholders, and using data to personalize employee development.

FUTURE DIRECTIONS FOR PERFORMANCE MANAGEMENT ANALYTICS

Performance management analytics is an essential tool for organizations to track, analyse, and improve employee performance. In recent years, there have been significant advancements in technology and data analytics, which have revolutionized the way companies approach performance management.

Following are some future directions for performance management analytics:

1. **Incorporating Artificial Intelligence:** With the rise of artificial intelligence (AI) and machine learning, performance management analytics can now leverage predictive analytics and algorithms to provide insights into employee performance. AI can help identify patterns in employee behaviour and performance that are not immediately visible to human analysts.
2. **Integration with HR Analytics:** Performance management analytics can be integrated with other HR analytics to provide a more comprehensive view of employee performance. By combining data from different sources, such as employee engagement surveys, workforce demographics, and compensation data, organizations can gain a better understanding of how employee performance is affected by these factors.
3. **Real-Time Feedback:** Performance management analytics can provide real-time feedback to employees, helping them to adjust their behaviour and improve their performance quickly. This can be achieved through the use of automated feedback systems that provide immediate feedback based on data collected from various sources.
4. **Use of Gamification:** Gamification can be used to make performance management more engaging and fun. By incorporating game-like elements such as points, badges, and leader boards, organizations can encourage employees to improve their performance and compete with each other.
5. **Focus on Soft Skills:** Performance management analytics can be used to measure and improve soft skills such as communication, teamwork, and leadership. This can be achieved by collecting data on these skills from various sources such as employee surveys, feedback from managers, and peer evaluations.

The future of performance management analytics is exciting, with technology playing a critical role in transforming the way organizations approach employee performance. By leveraging AI, integrating with HR analytics, providing real-time feedback, using gamification, and focusing on soft skills, organizations can create a more effective and engaging performance management system that benefits both employees and the organization.

New Technologies and Tools for Performance Management Analytics

Performance management analytics involves collecting and analysing data to measure and improve the performance of an organization, department, or individual employee. There are several new technologies and tools that have emerged in recent years that are helping organizations to better manage and analyse performance data. Following are some examples:

1. **Artificial Intelligence (AI) and Machine Learning (ML):** AI and ML algorithms can analyse large volumes of data, identify patterns, and make predictions about future performance. They can also help automate data collection and analysis, freeing up time for managers to focus on strategic planning.
2. **Predictive Analytics:** Predictive analytics tools use statistical models to forecast future trends based on past data. This can help organizations make more informed decisions about resource allocation, staffing, and strategic planning.

3. **Dashboards:** Dashboards are interactive visual displays of performance data that can be customized to show key performance indicators (KPIs) and other metrics in real-time. They allow managers to quickly identify areas that need improvement and track progress over time.
4. **Cloud-based Performance Management Systems:** Cloud-based performance management systems allow organizations to store and access performance data from anywhere with an internet connection. They also offer features such as goal setting, performance tracking, and feedback tools.
5. **Gamification:** Gamification is the use of game design elements in non-game contexts. It can be used to engage employees in performance management activities such as goal setting, training, and feedback. By making these activities more enjoyable and interactive, gamification can increase participation and motivation.
6. **Mobile Apps:** Mobile apps allow employees to access performance data and complete performance management tasks on the go. They can also provide real-time feedback and coaching to help employees improve their performance.
7. **Social Recognition:** Social recognition tools allow employees to give and receive recognition for good performance in a public forum. This can help boost morale and increase engagement.

These are just a few examples of the new technologies and tools available for performance management analytics. By leveraging these tools, organizations can gain deeper insights into their performance data, make more informed decisions, and improve overall performance.

Emerging Trends in Performance Management

Performance management is an essential part of managing employees in any organization. Over the years, performance management has evolved, and new trends have emerged to improve the process. Following are some of the emerging trends in performance management:

1. **Continuous Performance Management:** Traditional performance management involved annual or bi-annual reviews, which often lacked specificity and left little room for improvement throughout the year. Continuous performance management involves frequent check-ins between managers and employees to provide feedback, set goals, and track progress regularly. This approach allows for timely feedback and encourages a continuous improvement mind-set.
2. **Focus on Employee Development:** Performance management is no longer just about rating an employee's past performance. Instead, it has become a tool for developing employee skills and abilities. Organizations are increasingly using performance management to identify skill gaps and provide training and development opportunities to bridge those gaps.
3. **Incorporating Technology:** Technology has transformed many aspects of our lives, and performance management is no exception. Emerging technologies such as artificial intelligence (AI) and machine learning are being used to automate performance management processes, including performance reviews, goal setting, and tracking progress. This approach makes the process more efficient, accurate and eliminates the bias associated with manual processes.

4. **Emphasis on Employee Wellbeing:** Employee well-being has become a top priority for many organizations, and performance management has a role to play in supporting this. Organizations are beginning to use performance management to assess employee engagement, job satisfaction, and stress levels. This approach helps to identify potential sources of stress and burnout and take proactive steps to address them.
5. **Shift from Annual Reviews to Frequent Check-ins:** Many organizations have realized that annual performance reviews are not an effective way to manage employee performance. As such, they are moving away from annual reviews and embracing frequent check-ins as a way of keeping track of employee performance. Frequent check-ins allow for more immediate feedback and course correction, leading to better performance outcomes.

Overall, performance management continues to evolve, and organizations need to keep up with the emerging trends to ensure that they are getting the most out of their employees.

Questions for Discussion

Short Questions

1. What is Performance Management Analytics, and Why is Performance Management Analytics important for organizations?
2. What are some common metrics used in Performance Management Analytics?
3. How can Performance Management Analytics help improve employee engagement?
4. What is the significance of Employee Turnover as a metric in Performance Management Analytics?
5. What are Key Performance Indicators (KPIs) in Performance Management Analytics?
6. What is the role of data-driven decision-making in Performance Management Analytics?
7. What is employee engagement? Name five factors that contribute to employee engagement.
8. How can organizations use employee engagement data to improve their performance management strategies?
9. What are some potential areas for improvement that performance management analytics can identify for high-performing employees?
10. How can performance management analytics help in aligning performance goals with business objectives?
11. What is the significance of using diverse data sources in performance management analytics to prevent bias?
12. What are some technological limitations that organizations may encounter when implementing performance management analytics?

Long Questions

1. Explain the concept of Performance Management Analytics and its role in organizational improvement.
2. How does Performance Management Analytics support decision-making within organizations? Can you provide real-world instances?
3. What are the key steps involved in effectively using Key Performance Indicators (KPIs) in Performance Management Analytics, and why are they important?
4. Discuss the significance of Employee Turnover as a metric in Performance Management Analytics, and provide strategies for reducing turnover.
5. Explain the various metrics related to Employee Turnover and how they can be calculated and utilized for performance improvement.
6. Define employee engagement and explain its significance in performance management analytics. Provide examples of how engaged employees can positively impact an organization.
7. Describe various methods for measuring employee engagement. Discuss the advantages and disadvantages of each method.
8. Outline the steps involved in using employee engagement as a metric in performance management analytics. Provide a detailed explanation of each step.
9. Discuss the importance of continuously monitoring and improving employee engagement. Provide examples of strategies that organizations can implement to enhance employee engagement over time.
10. What are the key challenges and limitations associated with performance management analytics, and how can organizations address them to ensure the success of their analytics programs?
11. How can organizations prevent bias and discrimination in performance management analytics, and what role does data quality and diversity play in this process?
12. What are the best practices for organizations to establish and maintain effective performance management analytics, and how can these practices lead to better decision-making and performance optimization?

CHAPTER

5

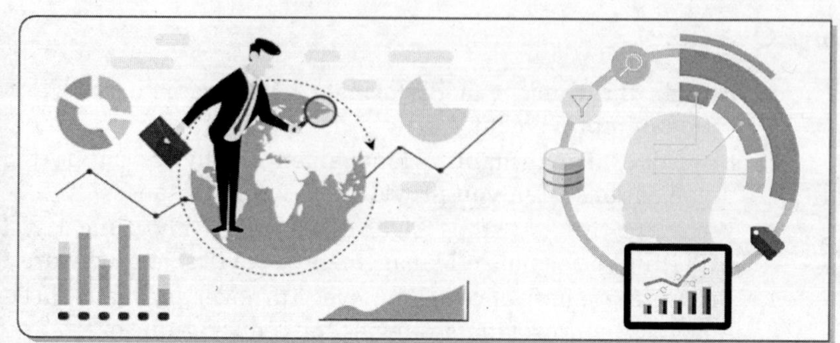

Employee Engagement Analytics

Employee Engagement Analytics refers to the systematic collection, measurement, analysis, and interpretation of data related to employee engagement within an organization. In today's data-driven world, organizations recognize the crucial role that engaged employees play in achieving business success and maintaining a positive work culture. Employee Engagement Analytics leverages various quantitative and qualitative methods to gain insights into the levels of employee engagement, the factors influencing it, and its impact on overall organizational performance.

By using advanced data analytics methods, companies can learn more about the thoughts, feelings, and actions of their employees. In order to do this, data from sources such as employee surveys, job reviews, feedback systems, social media interactions, and more must be examined. The goal is to find patterns, trends, and connections that can help us figure out what motivates employees and what might be getting in the way of their involvement.

The information gathered from Employee Engagement Analytics can help businesses figure out what they need to change, make their HR policies more effective, and carry out focused actions that will make employees more engaged. A few of these strategies can include training and development initiatives, adjustments to management procedures, modifications to work procedures, and efforts to make the workplace more inclusive and friendly.

In the end, employee engagement analytics gives businesses the ability to make decisions based on data-driven insights, which improves employee engagement, productivity, lowers attrition, and creates a happier workplace culture overall.

DEFINITIONS OF EMPLOYEE ENGAGEMENT

Employee engagement refers to the emotional commitment and connection employees have towards their organization. It's characterized by their level of enthusiasm, dedication, and involvement in their work and the overall goals of the company. Engaged employees are motivated to go beyond their basic job responsibilities, they feel a sense of ownership in their roles, and they are more likely to contribute proactively to the organization's success.

Few definitions of employee engagement are:

Gallup: "Employee engagement is the involvement with, commitment to, and enthusiasm for the job."

Aon Hewitt: "Employee engagement is the level of an employee's psychological investment in their organization. In simplest terms, it measures the extent of an employee's commitment, loyalty, and willingness to go above and beyond for their organization."

Harvard Business Review: "Employee engagement is the emotional commitment the employee has to the organization and its goals. This emotional commitment means engaged employees actually care about their work and their company."

Tower Watson: "Employee engagement is the extent to which employees are motivated to contribute to organizational success and are willing to apply discretionary effort to accomplishing tasks important to the achievement of organizational goals."

Alec Levenson: "Employee engagement is a management concept that describes an employee's emotional commitment to an organization's goals. It goes beyond financial compensation and is not just happiness or satisfaction. True engagement results in employees who are willing to make an extra effort to contribute to the organization's success."

These definitions collectively emphasize the emotional and psychological connection employees have with their work and the organization. Employee engagement is not just about job satisfaction or happiness; it's about fostering a deep sense of commitment, dedication, and a willingness to go the extra mile for the betterment of both the employee and the organization.

Employee involvement includes the following essential components:

1. *Emotional Connection:* Engaged employees feel a strong emotional connection to their workplace. They genuinely care about the company's success and are motivated to contribute positively.
2. *Job Satisfaction:* Engaged employees tend to be satisfied with their roles, responsibilities, and the overall work environment. Their satisfaction is driven by factors like job clarity, growth opportunities, and a supportive work culture.
3. *Commitment:* Engaged employees are committed to the organization's long-term success. They are more likely to stay with the company, reducing turnover rates and related costs.
4. *Effort and Initiative:* Engaged employees consistently put in extra effort to achieve their goals. They are proactive, take initiative, and often contribute innovative ideas to improve processes and outcomes.
5. *Alignment with Values:* Engaged employees find alignment between their personal values and the organization's mission and values. This alignment enhances their sense of purpose and motivation.
6. *Communication and Collaboration:* Engaged employees are more likely to engage in open communication and collaborative efforts with colleagues. They foster positive working relationships and contribute to a supportive team environment.

7. *Recognition and Feedback:* Engaged employees value recognition and feedback. Regular acknowledgment of their contributions and opportunities for growth and development are important factors in maintaining their engagement.
8. *Well-Being:* Engaged employees' well-being is considered. Organizations that prioritize employee wellness and work-life balance tend to have more engaged and motivated staff.

In essence, employee engagement represents a mutual relationship between employees and their organizations. It involves creating an environment where employees feel valued, supported, and empowered to contribute their best efforts, resulting in mutual benefits for both the individual and the organization.

HOW TO MEASURE AND IMPROVE EMPLOYEE ENGAGEMENT

Measuring and improving employee engagement involves a systematic approach that combines data collection, analysis, and strategic interventions. Here's a step-by-step guide on how to effectively measure and enhance employee engagement:

Measuring Employee Engagement

- **Select Measurement Tools:** Choose appropriate tools for gathering employee feedback, such as surveys, focus groups, one-on-one interviews, or even analysis of employee feedback on internal communication platforms.
- **Design Surveys:** Create well-structured surveys with a mix of quantitative and qualitative questions. Include questions that assess overall satisfaction, alignment with company values, job satisfaction, work-life balance, communication, and opportunities for growth.
- **Administer Surveys:** Distribute surveys to employees, ensuring anonymity to encourage honest responses. Use a mix of periodic surveys (annual or bi-annual) and pulse surveys for more frequent check-ins.
- **Collect Data from Multiple Sources:** Besides surveys, gather insights from performance reviews, employee feedback platforms, and other communication channels.
- **Quantitative Analysis:** Analyse survey data quantitatively to identify trends, areas of concern, and strengths. Calculate engagement scores and benchmark them against industry standards or past data.
- **Qualitative Analysis:** Review open-ended responses and qualitative feedback to gain deeper insights into the reasons behind engagement levels.

Improving Employee Engagement

- **Identify Key Areas:** Based on the analysis, identify specific areas where engagement is lacking or needs improvement. This could be related to communication, leadership, career development, work-life balance, etc.

TABLE 5.1 Methods for measuring employee engagement

Measurement method	*Description*
1. Conduct employee surveys	• Conducted regularly through various means such as online surveys, paper-based surveys, or interviews. • Questions designed to assess aspects like job satisfaction, leadership, communication, and growth opportunities. • Provides direct feedback from employees regarding their engagement and satisfaction.
2. Analyze employee turnover	• Examining the rate at which employees leave the organization. • Frequent turnover can be indicative of low engagement, dissatisfaction with work, management, or company culture. • A higher turnover rate suggests the need to address underlying issues.
3. Monitor absenteeism & productivity	• Tracking employee absenteeism (unscheduled leaves) and productivity levels. • High absenteeism and reduced productivity may indicate disengaged employees who lack motivation and commitment. • An increase in these metrics can trigger a closer look into employee engagement factors.

- **Set Clear Goals:** Define clear, measurable goals for improving engagement in these identified areas. These goals should be specific, achievable, relevant, and time-bound (SMART).
- **Leadership Involvement:** Engage senior leadership to lead by example and actively communicate the organization's commitment to employee engagement.
- **Effective Communication:** Enhance communication channels between leadership and employees. Regularly share updates on company goals, successes, and challenges.
- **Recognition and Rewards:** Implement recognition programs that celebrate employee accomplishments and contributions. These can include peer recognition, spot awards, or public acknowledgments.
- **Professional Development:** Provide opportunities for learning and growth. This can involve training, mentorship, career advancement pathways, and cross-functional projects.
- **Work-Life Balance:** Encourage a healthy work-life balance by offering flexible work arrangements, remote work options, and initiatives to manage workload.
- **Managerial Support:** Train managers to provide constructive feedback, set clear expectations, and offer support to their teams.
- **Employee Well-being:** Prioritize employee well-being by offering wellness programs, mental health support, and initiatives that foster a positive workplace culture.
- **Feedback Loop:** Continuously collect feedback on the effectiveness of your engagement initiatives. Adjust strategies based on the feedback received and changing organizational dynamics.

- **Celebrate Progress:** Celebrate improvements in engagement levels and communicate them to employees. This demonstrates that their feedback is valued and changes are being implemented.

Increasing employee involvement is a constant process that needs hard work and a real desire to make the workplace a good place to be. It's about creating a place where workers feel appreciated, given the freedom to do their best work, and pushed to do so.

IMPORTANCE OF EMPLOYEE ENGAGEMENT

Employee engagement holds significant importance for both employees and organizations. Following are some key reasons why employee engagement is crucial:

1. **Enhanced Productivity:** Engaged employees are more committed to their work, leading to increased productivity. They are willing to put in extra effort to achieve the organization's goals, leading to improved efficiency and output.
2. **Higher Job Satisfaction:** Engaged employees tend to be more satisfied with their jobs. When employees feel a sense of purpose and connection to their work, they experience higher levels of job satisfaction and contentment.
3. **Reduced Turnover:** Engaged employees are less likely to leave the organization. They have a stronger attachment to their roles and the company, reducing turnover rates and the associated costs of recruitment and training.
4. **Improved Customer Satisfaction:** Engaged employees provide better customer service. Their positive attitude and commitment translate into better interactions with customers, leading to improved customer satisfaction and loyalty.
5. **Innovation and Creativity:** Engaged employees are more likely to contribute innovative ideas. They feel empowered to share their insights and are invested in the organization's success, fostering a culture of innovation.
6. **Better Employee Morale:** Engaged employees have higher morale and a more positive outlook. This positive attitude is contagious and can uplift the overall work environment, contributing to a healthier organizational culture.
7. **Higher Employee Retention:** Engaged employees are loyal to the organization and more likely to stay long-term. This stability contributes to the continuity of institutional knowledge and expertise.
8. **Increased Profitability:** Engaged employees directly impact the bottom line. Studies have shown that companies with engaged workforces tend to be more profitable due to increased productivity, reduced turnover costs, and improved customer satisfaction.
9. **Stronger Teamwork:** Engaged employees collaborate effectively with colleagues. They are more willing to share information, support team members, and contribute to a positive team dynamic.
10. **Positive Employer Branding:** Organizations with high levels of employee engagement have a positive reputation as employers. This can attract top talent, making it easier to recruit skilled individuals.
11. **Adaptability to Change:** Engaged employees are more adaptable to changes within the organization. Their commitment helps in navigating transitions and transformations smoothly.

12. **Health and Well-being:** Employee engagement is linked to better physical and mental well-being. Engaged employees experience lower stress levels and better overall health.
13. **Alignment with Organizational Goals:** Engaged employees understand and align with the organization's goals and values. This alignment ensures that their efforts are contributing to the company's success.
14. **Employee Development:** Engaged employees are more likely to seek opportunities for growth and development. This leads to a skilled and capable workforce.

Basically, employee engagement is a key part of organizational success. It creates a positive feedback loop where engaged employees drive better outcomes, leading to increased job satisfaction, stronger commitment, and ultimately, a healthier and more prosperous organization.

ROLE OF EMPLOYEE ENGAGEMENT ANALYTICS

Employee engagement analytics is the process of collecting and analysing data on employee engagement levels within an organization. It involves using various metrics to assess how committed, motivated, and satisfied employees are with their work, their colleagues, and their workplace.

The role of employee engagement analytics is to provide organizations with insights into how to improve employee engagement levels. By analysing the data, organizations can identify areas of weakness in their employee engagement strategies and develop targeted interventions to address them.

Employee Engagement Analytics plays a crucial role in understanding, measuring, and improving employee engagement within an organization.

1. **Data-driven Insights:** Employee Engagement Analytics allows organizations to gather quantitative and qualitative data on various aspects of employee engagement. This data provides insights into what motivates and demotivates employees, helping organizations make informed decisions.
2. **Identifying Patterns and Trends:** Analytics help identify patterns and trends in employee engagement data over time. This helps in recognizing whether engagement levels are improving, declining, or remaining stable. These insights can guide strategies for improvement.
3. **Pinpointing Engagement Drivers:** By analysing engagement data, organizations can pinpoint the factors that have the most significant impact on engagement. This information enables targeted interventions in areas that matter the most to employees.
4. **Customized Interventions:** Engagement analytics help tailor interventions based on specific insights. For instance, if the data indicates that a particular team lacks communication, efforts can be focused on improving communication channels for that team.
5. **Benchmarking and Comparison:** Analytics allow organizations to benchmark their engagement levels against industry standards or competitors. This provides context for understanding whether engagement efforts are effective and competitive.

6. **Feedback Loop for Improvement:** Analytics create a feedback loop. Organizations can analyse the results of engagement initiatives and adjust their strategies based on the outcomes. Continuous improvement becomes possible.
7. **Predictive Insights:** Advanced analytics can predict future engagement trends based on historical data. This helps organizations anticipate challenges and proactively address potential issues.
8. **Measuring Impact of Initiatives:** Organizations can measure the impact of specific engagement initiatives. For example, if a wellness program is introduced, analytics can help assess whether it positively affects engagement and overall well-being.
9. **Aligning with Business Goals**: Engagement analytics allow organizations to align engagement strategies with broader business goals. For instance, if innovation is a priority, engagement initiatives can be tailored to promote a culture of innovation.
10. **Demonstrating ROI:** Engagement analytics can show the return on investment (ROI) of engagement initiatives. Organizations can quantify the impact of improved engagement on productivity, turnover, and other business metrics.
11. **Personalizing Employee Experience:** Analytics enable a personalized employee experience. By understanding individual preferences and engagement drivers, organizations can cater to employees' needs more effectively.
12. **Transparency and Communication:** Sharing engagement data with employees promotes transparency. It shows that the organization values their input and is committed to improvement.
13. **Long-term Strategy Development:** Engagement analytics aid in developing long-term engagement strategies. Instead of reacting to short-term issues, organizations can focus on sustained engagement improvement.

Employee Engagement Analytics transforms engagement efforts from subjective measures to data-driven strategies. It empowers organizations to take a targeted, evidence-based approach to engagement, leading to a more motivated, committed, and productive workforce.

IDENTIFYING DRIVERS OF ENGAGEMENT

Identifying drivers of engagement involves understanding the key factors that motivate people to engage with a particular activity, brand, or organization. Following are some common drivers of engagement:

1. **Purpose:** People are more likely to engage with a brand or organization when they feel it aligns with their values and beliefs. Communicating a clear purpose can help build trust and loyalty.
2. **Personalization:** Customizing experiences based on individual preferences and needs can increase engagement. Personalization can range from tailored product recommendations to personalized email campaigns.
3. **Convenience:** Making it easy for people to engage can increase participation. This includes things like a user-friendly website or mobile app, easy checkout processes, and convenient customer service options.

4. **Social Proof:** People are often influenced by the opinions and actions of others. Incorporating social proof, such as testimonials or user-generated content, can increase engagement by building trust and credibility.
5. **Gamification:** Adding game-like elements, such as rewards or leader boards, can increase engagement by making the experience more fun and interactive.
6. **Clear Communication:** Providing clear and concise communication about what is expected and how to participate can help increase engagement by reducing confusion and uncertainty.
7. **Feedback and Recognition:** Providing feedback and recognition for participation can increase engagement by making people feel valued and appreciated.

By identifying and understanding these drivers of engagement, businesses and organizations can create strategies that increase engagement and build long-term relationships with customers and stakeholders. Identifying the drivers of engagement involves understanding the specific factors that have the most significant impact on motivating and engaging employees within an organization. Below mentioned are the ways to identifying these drivers:

1. **Employee Surveys:** Conduct comprehensive employee engagement surveys with carefully crafted questions. Analyse the survey data to identify patterns and correlations between different aspects of the work environment and engagement levels.
2. **Focus Groups and Interviews:** Conduct focus groups or one-on-one interviews with employees to gain qualitative insights. This can provide a deeper understanding of their perspectives on what motivates them and what challenges they face.
3. **Analyse Historical Data:** Look at historical engagement data and compare it with different organizational changes, events, or initiatives. This can help you identify any trends or correlations between engagement levels and specific factors.
4. **Exit Interviews:** When employees leave the organization, conduct exit interviews to understand their reasons for leaving and any factors that contributed to their disengagement. This can provide valuable insights into areas needing improvement.
5. **Managerial Feedback:** Engage managers in conversations about their teams' engagement levels. Managers often have direct insights into what drives their team members and what challenges they encounter.
6. **Peer-to-Peer Feedback:** Encourage employees to provide feedback to each other. Peers often have a good understanding of what motivates their colleagues and can offer valuable insights.
7. **Review Best Practices:** Look at industry research and best practices related to employee engagement. While not every practice will directly apply to your organization, they can provide ideas for potential drivers.
8. **Analyse High-Performing Teams:** Examine teams or departments with consistently high engagement levels. What specific practices, leadership styles, or work processes might be contributing to their engagement?
9. **Employee Suggestions:** Encourage employees to provide suggestions for improving engagement. This can give you direct insights into what they believe would make a positive impact.

10. **Analyse Engagement Metrics:** If you're using any engagement measurement tools or platforms, analyse the data they provide. Look for patterns and trends in responses to different questions or sections.
11. **Leadership Engagement:** Assess how engaged the leadership team is. Leaders who demonstrate a commitment to employee well-being and development often positively influence engagement.
12. **Employee Resource Groups:** Engage with employee resource groups or affinity groups to understand the specific needs and motivations of various demographic groups within the organization.
13. **Regular Check-ins:** Foster a culture of open communication where employees feel comfortable discussing their engagement levels and what factors are influencing them during regular check-ins with their managers.

The drivers of engagement can vary from one organization to another. It's important to approach this process with an open mind and a willingness to adapt your strategies based on the insights you gather. Regularly reassessing and refining your understanding of engagement drivers will help to maintain a motivated and committed workforce.

TYPES OF EMPLOYEE ENGAGEMENT ANALYTICS

Employee Engagement Analytics encompasses various types of data analysis methods and approaches to gain insights into employee engagement levels and factors. Following are some key types of employee engagement analytics:

1. **Survey Analysis:** This involves analysing data collected from employee surveys. It includes quantifying responses, identifying trends, and understanding correlations between different survey questions and engagement levels.
2. **Text Analytics:** Text analytics involves analysing open-ended survey responses, comments, and feedback from employees. Natural language processing (NLP) techniques are used to understand sentiment, themes, and topics within the text data.
3. **Predictive Analytics:** Predictive analytics uses historical engagement data to forecast future engagement levels. It can help organizations anticipate potential challenges and proactively address them.
4. **Benchmarking Analysis:** Benchmarking involves comparing your organization's engagement data with industry standards or competitors. This provides context for understanding your performance relative to others.
5. **Heat Map and Visualization Analysis:** Using visual representations like heat maps, graphs, and charts, this analysis helps to present engagement data in an easily understandable format, highlighting trends and patterns.
6. **Segmentation Analysis:** Segmentation involves dividing the employee population into different groups based on characteristics such as department, role, tenure, or demographics. This helps identify specific engagement patterns within different segments.
7. **Driver Analysis:** This analysis identifies which factors have the most impact on employee engagement. It involves using statistical techniques to determine which variables are strongly correlated with engagement levels.

8. **Network Analysis:** Network analysis focuses on understanding the relationships and interactions among employees. It helps identify key influencers, communication patterns, and how these factors affect engagement.
9. **Pulse Surveys and Real-time Analysis:** Pulse surveys provide quick, frequent feedback on engagement levels. Real-time analysis of these data points helps organizations respond swiftly to emerging engagement trends.
10. **Social Media and Collaboration Platform Analysis:** Analysing employee interactions on internal collaboration platforms or social media can provide insights into engagement-related discussions, trends, and sentiments.
11. **Attrition Analysis:** Analysing the engagement levels of employees who leave the organization can provide insights into factors contributing to turnover and disengagement.
12. **Managerial and Leadership Analysis:** Assessing how different managers impact employee engagement can help identify effective leadership practices and areas for improvement.
13. **Longitudinal Analysis:** Longitudinal analysis involves tracking engagement data over an extended period to identify trends and changes in engagement levels and their potential causes.
14. **Gap Analysis:** Gap analysis compares desired engagement levels (as indicated by surveys or benchmarks) with actual engagement levels. This highlights areas where improvements are needed.
15. **Actionable Insights Analysis:** This approach focuses on generating actionable insights from engagement data, providing specific recommendations for interventions and improvements.

Each of these types of analytics can provide unique insights into employee engagement, allowing organizations to tailor their strategies to foster a more engaged workforce and achieve better outcomes.

BENEFITS OF EMPLOYEE ENGAGEMENT ANALYTICS

Employee Engagement Analytics offers several benefits that can contribute to a more informed, effective, and strategic approach to managing and improving employee engagement within an organization. Following are some key advantages:

1. **Data-driven Decision Making:** Engagement analytics provides objective data that guides decision-making. It helps leaders base their actions on concrete insights rather than assumptions or subjective opinions.
2. **Targeted Interventions:** By identifying specific areas that impact engagement, analytics enable organizations to design targeted interventions and initiatives. This ensures resources are directed where they are most needed.
3. **Early Issue Identification:** Analytics can identify early signs of disengagement or negative trends. This allows organizations to address issues before they escalate and negatively impact the work environment.

4. **Continuous Improvement:** Engagement analytics promotes a culture of continuous improvement. Organizations can track the impact of engagement initiatives over time and adjust strategies based on real-time data.
5. **Customization of Strategies:** With insights from engagement analytics, organizations can tailor engagement strategies to different employee segments, teams, or departments, recognizing that different groups may have varying engagement drivers.
6. **Measurable ROI:** Analytics help quantify the return on investment (ROI) of engagement initiatives. Organizations can demonstrate how improved engagement positively affects business metrics such as productivity, retention, and customer satisfaction.
7. **Evidence-Based Communication:** Analytics provide evidence for communication with stakeholders. Leaders can present engagement data to executives, boards, and shareholders, showing the organization's commitment to employee well-being.
8. **Alignment with Business Goals:** Engagement analytics allows organizations to align their engagement strategies with broader business objectives. This integration reinforces the understanding that employee engagement is directly linked to organizational success.
9. **Insights into Leadership Effectiveness:** Analytics can reveal how different leadership styles impact engagement levels. This information helps organizations invest in leadership development that supports engagement.
10. **Employee Involvement and Transparency:** Sharing engagement data with employees promotes transparency and demonstrates that their opinions matter. It encourages a sense of involvement and ownership in improving engagement.
11. **Evaluation of Changes:** When organizational changes occur, engagement analytics can help assess their impact on engagement levels. This guides the refinement of change management strategies.
12. **Proactive Problem Solving:** Predictive analytics can anticipate potential engagement challenges, enabling organizations to proactively address issues before they occur.
13. **Employee-Centric Approach:** Engagement analytics keep the focus on employees' needs and preferences. Organizations can create more tailored experiences that resonate with their workforce.
14. **Competitive Advantage in Talent Acquisition:** Organizations known for using analytics to enhance engagement may have a competitive edge in attracting top talent, as potential employees seek workplaces that prioritize engagement and well-being.
15. **Holistic View of Engagement:** Analytics allow organizations to take a comprehensive look at engagement from multiple angles, considering various factors that contribute to employee satisfaction and motivation.

CHALLENGES IN EMPLOYEE ENGAGEMENT ANALYTICS

Employee engagement analytics is the process of analysing data related to employee engagement to better understand and improve engagement levels in an organization. While it can provide valuable insights, there are several challenges that organizations may face when implementing employee engagement analytics:

1. **Data Collection:** Gathering employee engagement data can be a significant challenge for organizations. Surveys are a common method of collecting data, but it can be difficult to get employees to participate, and the quality of the data collected can be affected by factors such as survey design and the timing of the survey.
2. **Data Quality:** Even when data is collected, it may not be of sufficient quality to provide useful insights. For example, if the survey questions are poorly designed or if employees don't feel comfortable providing honest feedback, the resulting data may be inaccurate or incomplete.
3. **Data Analysis:** Analysing employee engagement data requires expertise in statistical analysis, data visualization, and other analytical techniques. Organizations may lack the necessary resources or expertise to perform this analysis effectively.
4. **Data Interpretation:** Even if data is analysed effectively, it can be difficult to interpret the results and identify actionable insights. There may be a lack of understanding of what the data is telling us or how to use it to improve engagement.
5. **Data Privacy:** Employee engagement data can be sensitive and personal. Organizations need to ensure that they are collecting and handling this data in a way that protects employee privacy.
6. **Actionability:** Finally, even if organizations are able to collect high-quality data and analyse it effectively, they need to be able to take action based on the insights they gain. This may require changes to organizational policies or processes, which can be difficult to implement.

TABLE 5.2 Common challenges in employee engagement analytics

Challenge	*Description*
Defining employee engagement	There is no universally agreed-upon definition of employee engagement, which can make it difficult to measure consistently.
Choosing relevant metrics	There are many possible metrics to measure employee engagement, such as satisfaction, loyalty, and commitment. Organizations must determine which metrics are most relevant for their goals and culture.
Obtaining accurate data	Data collection can be challenging, as employees may be reluctant to provide honest feedback or may not understand the questions being asked. Additionally, organizations may struggle to gather data from remote or distributed teams.
Ensuring data quality	Even when data is collected, it may be incomplete or inaccurate, which can undermine the usefulness of analytics.
Analysing and interpreting data	Organizations must have the expertise and resources to analyse and interpret data effectively. They must be able to identify patterns, trends, and outliers, and make informed decisions based on that analysis.
Taking action on insights	Finally, organizations must be willing and able to take action based on the insights gleaned from employee engagement analytics. This can be challenging if the insights require significant changes to the organization's culture, policies, or processes.

Addressing these challenges requires a multifaceted approach that involves engaging employees in the data collection process, ensuring the quality of the data collected, building the necessary expertise to analyse and interpret the data, protecting employee privacy, and taking concrete action based on the insights gained from the data.

TABLE 5.3 Limitations of employee engagement analytics

Limitations of employee engagement analytics	*Description*
1. Limited contextual understanding	Data may lack context, making it challenging to understand the underlying reasons for certain trends.
2. Incomplete data	Not all aspects of engagement can be quantified, potentially leading to an incomplete picture.
3. Self-reporting Bias	Employees might provide responses they think are expected rather than their genuine feelings.
4. Voluntary participation bias	Survey participation might be higher among employees who are more engaged or discontented, skewing data.
5. Change over time	Employee engagement is dynamic; what's true today might not hold true in the future.
6. Overreliance on technology	Relying solely on technology can depersonalize the process and miss out on nuances.
7. Cultural and language barriers	Different cultural backgrounds and languages can impact the accuracy of survey responses.
8. Lack of actionable insights	Data analysis might not always provide clear action points for improving engagement.
9. Disengaged workforce	A disengaged workforce might not provide accurate or meaningful data on their engagement levels.
10. Fluctuating employee emotions	Employee emotions can change rapidly, impacting survey responses and engagement metrics.
11. Resistance to change	Employees might resist engagement initiatives derived from data, leading to implementation challenges.
12. Lack of data quality	Inaccurate or incomplete data can lead to flawed conclusions and ineffective strategies.
13. Lack of long-term impact assessment	Analytics might not always show the long-term impact of engagement efforts on organizational outcomes.
14. Potential for misinterpretation	Misinterpreting data or drawing incorrect conclusions can lead to ineffective decision-making.
15. Neglect of qualitative factors	Analytics may overlook qualitative aspects like personal growth and intrinsic motivation.

These limitations highlight the need for a balanced approach, combining analytics with qualitative insights, employee feedback, and contextual understanding to make well-informed decisions about employee engagement strategies.

BEST PRACTICES IN EMPLOYEE ENGAGEMENT ANALYTICS

Implementing employee engagement analytics effectively requires following best practices to ensure accurate, insightful, and actionable results. Following are some key best practices:

1. **Clearly Define Objectives:** Clearly outline your goals for using engagement analytics. Define what you want to measure, why you're measuring it, and how the data will be used to improve engagement.
2. **Select Relevant Metrics:** Choose metrics that align with your organization's goals and the drivers of engagement that are most important for your workforce. Avoid measuring for the sake of measurement.
3. **Design Comprehensive Surveys:** Craft surveys with a mix of quantitative and qualitative questions that cover various aspects of engagement. Include questions that assess both satisfaction and the factors driving engagement.
4. **Ensure Data Privacy:** Prioritize data privacy and ensure that all employee data is anonymized and secured. Transparency about data usage builds trust among employees.
5. **Encourage Honest Feedback:** Create a culture where employees feel safe providing honest feedback. Assure them that their input is valued and will be used for positive change.
6. **Regular and Consistent Data Collection:** Collect engagement data regularly and consistently to track trends over time. This enables you to identify shifts and patterns more effectively.
7. **Segment Data for Insights:** Segment data by department, location, tenure, and other relevant factors. This helps you identify specific areas that need attention and design targeted interventions.
8. **Combine Quantitative and Qualitative Insights:** Integrate both quantitative survey results and qualitative feedback to gain a holistic understanding of engagement levels and underlying reasons.
9. **Use Benchmarking Wisely:** Benchmark against industry standards but don't rely solely on them. Your organization's context and culture can significantly impact engagement.
10. **Employ Advanced Analytics:** Leverage advanced techniques like predictive analytics to anticipate engagement trends and proactively address issues.
11. **Regularly Communicate Results:** Share engagement analytics findings with employees, managers, and leadership. Transparency builds a sense of ownership and collective responsibility.
12. **Actionable Insights:** Ensure that the insights derived from analytics are actionable. Identify clear steps that can be taken to improve engagement based on the data.
13. **Involve Employees in Solutions:** Engage employees in creating and implementing solutions based on the analytics. Their input enhances the effectiveness of interventions.

14. **Continuously Review and Refine Strategies:** Review the impact of your engagement strategies and analytics-driven interventions regularly. Adjust your approaches based on results.
15. **Executive Involvement:** Engage leadership in the process. When executives prioritize engagement analytics, it sends a strong message throughout the organization.
16. **Training and Support:** Equip HR teams and managers with the necessary training to interpret analytics correctly and take appropriate actions.
17. **Focus on Long-term Impact:** While short-term changes are important, also consider the long-term impact of engagement initiatives on employee morale and organizational success.
18. **Embrace Flexibility:** Engagement analytics should be adaptable to changes in the organization's goals, structure, and workforce composition.

Remember, the goal of employee engagement analytics is to foster a positive work environment that benefits both employees and the organization. By following these best practices, you can leverage analytics to drive meaningful improvements in engagement and overall workplace culture.

TABLE 5.4 Future trends in employee engagement analytics

Future trends in employee engagement analytics	*Description*
1. AI and machine learning integration	AI and machine learning will be used to predict engagement trends, personalize interventions, and analyse sentiment.
2. Real-time feedback and pulse analytics	Continuous feedback through pulse surveys and real-time analytics will provide instant insights into engagement.
3. Wearable technology integration	Wearable devices may offer physiological data to gauge employee stress levels, mood, and overall well-being.
4. Sentiment analysis and emotion recognition	Advanced sentiment analysis tools will assess employee sentiments from text, tone, and facial expressions.
5. Integration of external data	Employee engagement data may be integrated with external data, such as market trends, for a broader perspective.
6. Predictive modelling for turnover	Analytics will predict potential turnover based on engagement patterns, helping organizations take preventive measures.
7. Real-time dashboards and visualization	Interactive dashboards will provide real-time engagement insights, enabling quick decision-making.
8. Diversity, equity, and inclusion metrics	Analytics will focus on tracking engagement of diverse groups, evaluating the effectiveness of inclusion efforts.
9. Well-being and mental health analytics	Tools will monitor employee well-being, offering insights into stressors and mental health challenges.
10. Employee experience journey mapping	Analysing the entire employee journey will help identify touchpoints where engagement can be enhanced.

(*Contd.*)

Future trends in employee engagement analytics	*Description*
11. Gamification of engagement data	Gamified approaches will make engagement data more engaging, encouraging active participation and feedback.
12. Remote work analytics	Analytics will adapt to remote work, tracking engagement in virtual settings and identifying challenges.
13. Integration of HR tech stack	Employee engagement analytics will be seamlessly integrated with broader HR tech solutions for holistic insights.
14. Continuous learning and development metrics	Tracking engagement related to learning and development initiatives to enhance employee growth.
15. Social impact and sustainability metrics	Organizations will measure engagement in social responsibility efforts, aligning with employee values.

EXAMPLES OF SUCCESSFUL IMPLEMENTATION OF EMPLOYEE ENGAGEMENT ANALYTICS AND LESSONS LEARNED FROM THEM

Employee engagement analytics can help organizations identify areas of strength and areas for improvement in employee engagement, as well as help them develop strategies for improving engagement levels. Following are some examples of successful implementation of employee engagement analytics and the lessons learned from them:

1. **IBM:** IBM uses employee engagement data to keep an eye on how engaged its workers are and find places where engagement is low. The study helped IBM figure out that workers who were close to their bosses were more likely to be interested in their jobs. Because of this, IBM worked on making connections between managers and employees better through coaching and training programmes. This led to a 20% rise in the level of involvement among workers.
   Lesson learned: Organisations should use employee engagement data to figure out what makes employees interested in their jobs and then work on making those things better.
2. **Hilton:** Hilton used employee engagement analytics to identify areas where employees were not engaged and developed programs to address those areas. For example, Hilton found that employees who worked the night shift were less engaged than those who worked during the day. As a result, Hilton developed a program that provided night-shift employees with additional training and opportunities for career advancement. This program resulted in a 22% increase in engagement levels among night-shift employees.
   Lesson learned: Organizations should use employee engagement analytics to identify specific groups of employees that are less engaged and develop programs to address their needs.
3. **Southwest Airlines:** Southwest Airlines uses employee engagement analytics to monitor the engagement levels of its employees and identify areas for improvement.

Through this analysis, Southwest found that employees who were recognized for their work were more engaged. As a result, Southwest developed a program that provided employees with frequent recognition and rewards for their work. This program resulted in a 15% increase in engagement levels among employees.

Lesson learned: Organizations should use employee engagement analytics to identify the specific behaviours that drive engagement and develop programs that promote those behaviours.

Overall, these examples demonstrate the importance of using employee engagement analytics to identify areas for improvement and develop programs that address those areas. By doing so, organizations can improve employee engagement levels and ultimately, their bottom line.

EMPLOYEE ATTITUDE SURVEYS

Employee attitude surveys, also known as employee satisfaction surveys or employee engagement surveys given in the annexure, are valuable tools used by organizations to gauge the overall sentiments, perceptions, and attitudes of their workforce. These surveys play a pivotal role in helping companies understand their employees' experiences, opinions, and concerns, which, in turn, enable them to make informed decisions to enhance workplace satisfaction, productivity, and overall performance.

The employee attitude survey process typically involves the following key steps:

1. **Survey Design:** Incorporating a combination of closed-ended and open-ended inquiries into a meticulously organised questionnaire constitutes the initial phase. Job satisfaction, work-life balance, communication, leadership, and organisational culture are a few of the subject matters addressed in these inquiries regarding the employee experience. With care, the design ought to be devoid of bias and comprise pertinent inquiries.
2. **Data Collection:** Employee attitude surveys can be conducted through various methods, such as paper-based surveys, online surveys, or phone interviews. The anonymity of respondents is often ensured to encourage honest and candid feedback.
3. **Survey Distribution:** Surveys are distributed to all employees, ensuring that it is comprehensive and representative of the entire workforce. It's important to communicate the purpose and significance of the survey to employees to encourage their participation.
4. **Data Analysis:** Once the responses are collected, the data is analysed to identify patterns, trends, and areas of concern. Quantitative data can be used to measure satisfaction levels, while qualitative data from open-ended questions provides context and deeper insights.
5. **Feedback and Reporting:** Survey results are typically shared with employees in a transparent and constructive manner. Organizations may hold feedback sessions to discuss the findings and gather additional input or suggestions.
6. **Action Planning:** Perhaps the most critical step, organizations use survey results to develop action plans aimed at addressing areas of concern and improving overall employee satisfaction. This could involve changes in policies, processes, or communication strategies, as well as specific interventions in areas where improvement is needed.

7. **Follow-up Surveys:** Employee attitude surveys are often conducted periodically to track progress and measure the effectiveness of implemented changes. This ongoing feedback loop helps organizations make necessary adjustments and ensures they stay aligned with their employees' evolving needs.

Following are some benefits of employee attitude surveys:

1. **Improved Employee Engagement:** Understanding employee attitudes helps in designing strategies to increase engagement, leading to a more motivated and productive workforce.
2. **Identifying Problem Areas:** These surveys can pinpoint specific areas of concern, such as poor management, communication issues, or work-related stress, which can then be addressed.
3. **Enhanced Retention:** By addressing employee concerns and improving job satisfaction, organizations can reduce turnover and retain their top talent.
4. **Productivity Gains:** Satisfied and engaged employees are more likely to be productive, which positively impacts the organization's bottom line.
5. **Enhanced Organizational Culture:** These surveys can help organizations in aligning their culture with employee expectations, leading to a healthier workplace environment.
6. **Legal Compliance and Ethical Considerations:** Employee attitude surveys can help organizations comply with labour laws and ethical standards by addressing concerns like discrimination, harassment, or unfair treatment.

It's essential for organizations to approach employee attitude surveys with sensitivity, confidentiality, and a genuine commitment to action. A poorly managed survey can lead to distrust among employees, so transparency in the process and the use of data is crucial. Moreover, organizations should recognize that the work doesn't end with the survey results but with the ongoing effort to foster a positive and productive work environment based on the feedback received from their employees.

WORKFORCE PERCEPTION

Workforce perception, also known as employee perception or workplace perception, is a crucial aspect of organizational dynamics. It refers to how employees view and interpret various elements of their work environment, including their jobs, colleagues, supervisors, company culture, and the organization's overall mission and values. Understanding and managing workforce perception is essential for fostering a positive and productive work environment.

Importance of Workforce Perception

1. **Employee Engagement:** A positive workforce perception is closely linked to high levels of employee engagement. Engaged employees are more committed, productive, and likely to stay with the organization. When employees perceive their work as meaningful and rewarding, they are more likely to be engaged.

2. **Organizational Culture:** Workforce perception plays a significant role in shaping an organization's culture. When employees share a positive perception of the company's values and principles, it helps reinforce and strengthen the desired culture.
3. **Performance and Productivity:** Employees who perceive that their contributions are valued and that they have the necessary tools and support are more likely to perform at their best. This leads to higher productivity and better business outcomes.
4. **Retention:** Employee turnover is costly and disruptive. When employees have a favourable perception of their workplace, they are more likely to stay with the company, reducing recruitment and training expenses.

Factors Influencing Workforce Perception

1. **Leadership:** Employees' perception of their leaders, including their competence, communication skills, and approachability, greatly influences how they feel about their work environment.
2. **Company Culture:** The organizational culture, values, and the extent to which these are practiced influence workforce perception. A disconnect between stated values and actual behaviours can lead to negative perceptions.
3. **Work-Life Balance:** A balance between work and personal life significantly impacts workforce perception. Employers who promote work-life balance are likely to have employees with a positive view of their jobs.
4. **Job Satisfaction:** The extent to which employees find their job meaningful, challenging, and in line with their skills and interests affects their perception of the workplace.
5. **Communication:** Effective and transparent communication from management fosters trust and a sense of belonging, leading to more positive perceptions.
6. **Recognition and Rewards:** Perceptions of fairness in terms of recognition, rewards, and promotions can either boost or diminish morale.

Enhancing Workforce Perception

1. **Leadership Development:** Invest in leadership training to ensure managers are capable of fostering positive perceptions among their teams.
2. **Transparency:** Maintain open and honest communication about the company's goals, challenges, and decisions to build trust and reduce uncertainty.
3. **Employee Feedback:** Actively seek and respond to employee feedback. Understanding their concerns and needs can lead to improvements in the workplace.
4. **Recognition and Rewards:** Implement fair and transparent systems for recognizing and rewarding employees' contributions.
5. **Professional Development:** Offer opportunities for skill development and career advancement, demonstrating a commitment to employee growth.
6. **Wellness Programs:** Support employees' well-being by offering wellness programs and promoting work-life balance.
7. **Diversity and Inclusion:** Create a diverse and inclusive work environment that values differences, and ensure policies and practices promote equality.

Workforce perception is a multifaceted aspect of organizational success. A positive perception among employees can lead to increased engagement, better performance, and lower turnover rates. Therefore, organizations must actively manage and cultivate a favourable workforce perception by addressing key factors and consistently working to improve the overall employee experience. This not only benefits individual employees but also contributes to the long-term success and sustainability of the organization as a whole.

Questions for Discussion

Short Questions

1. What is Employee Engagement Analytics?
2. Why is employee engagement important for organizations?
3. How can organizations measure employee engagement?
4. What are some key drivers of employee engagement?
5. What role does leadership play in employee engagement?
6. How can organizations use employee engagement analytics to improve their workforce?
7. What are the benefits of using employee engagement analytics?
8. How can organizations align their engagement strategies with business goals?

Long Questions

1. Can you explain the concept of Employee Engagement Analytics and its significance in detail?
2. What are the different methods and tools organizations can use to measure employee engagement, and how do they analyse the data collected?
3. Can you provide a comprehensive overview of the key drivers of employee engagement and their impact on the organization?
4. How can organizations implement targeted interventions to improve employee engagement based on insights from analytics?
5. What are the potential challenges and limitations of Employee Engagement Analytics, and how can organizations address them?
6. Can you share some examples of organizations that have successfully leveraged Employee Engagement Analytics to achieve positive outcomes?
7. How can organizations use predictive analytics to anticipate and proactively address employee engagement challenges?
8. What steps can organizations take to ensure the ethical and responsible use of employee data in engagement analytics?

CHAPTER 6

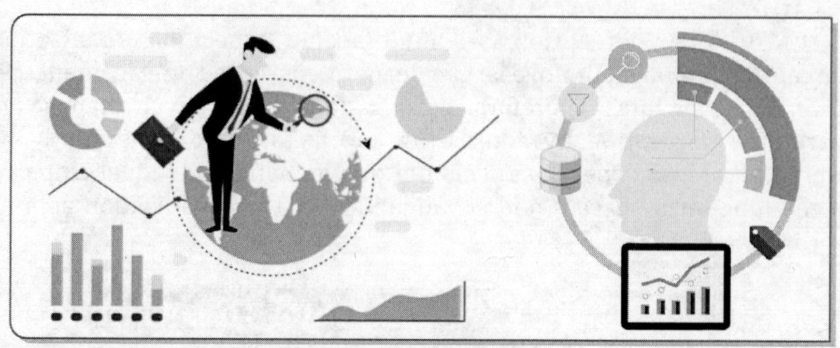

Diversity, Equity and Inclusion (DEI) Analytics

Diversity analysis, often referred to as diversity and inclusion (D&I) analysis, is a process that involves the examination of various aspects of diversity within an organization or a community. It aims to assess, understand, and measure the representation, experiences, and opportunities of individuals from different demographic backgrounds, such as race, gender, age, sexual orientation, and more. The primary objectives of diversity analysis are to promote equality, identify areas of improvement, and create more inclusive and equitable environments.

Diversity, Equity, and Inclusion (DEI) Analytics refers to the systematic collection, analysis, and interpretation of data related to diversity, equity, and inclusion efforts within an organization. In recent years, there has been a growing recognition of the importance of fostering a diverse and inclusive workplace that promotes equal opportunities for all employees, regardless of their background, identity, or characteristics.

DEI analytics aims to provide organizations with actionable insights to measure the effectiveness of their diversity and inclusion initiatives, identify disparities, and create strategies to promote a more equitable workplace. It involves quantifying and assessing various aspects of diversity (such as gender, ethnicity, age, and more), equity (fair treatment and opportunities), and inclusion (sense of belonging and involvement) through data-driven methods.

With this data-driven approach, companies can do more than just surface-level projects. They can make smart choices that will help everyone do their best at work. Not only does DEI analytics help organisations find places to improve, it also lets them track their progress and show internal and external partners that they are committed to building a diverse and welcoming workforce.

Companies can use DEI data to learn more about how their strategies are working, make changes to help fix specific problems, and keep track of how well their efforts are working overtime to make the workplace fairer and welcoming for everyone.

IMPORTANCE OF DEI IN MODERN ORGANIZATIONS

Diversity, Equity, and Inclusion (DEI) have become increasingly important in modern organizations due to their significant impact on business success, employee well-being, innovation, and societal responsibility. Following are some key reasons highlighting the importance of DEI:

1. **Business Performance and Innovation:** Diverse teams bring a range of perspectives, experiences, and skills to the table. This diversity fosters innovative thinking, problem-solving, and creativity, leading to better decision-making and a competitive edge in a rapidly changing business landscape.
2. **Talent Attraction and Retention:** A commitment to DEI is attractive to top talent. Potential employees seek organizations that prioritize inclusion and offer equal opportunities for growth. Retaining a diverse workforce improves overall employee satisfaction and reduces turnover.
3. **Improved Employee Engagement and Productivity:** An inclusive work environment where employees feel valued and respected enhances their engagement and job satisfaction. Engaged employees are more productive, committed, and likely to contribute positively to the organization's goals.
4. **Better Customer Understanding and Relationships:** Diverse teams can better understand and connect with a diverse customer base. This understanding leads to improved products, services, and customer relationships, ultimately driving business growth.
5. **Global Market Relevance:** In a globalized world, diverse organizations can effectively navigate international markets and understand cultural nuances. DEI initiatives position companies to connect with diverse consumers and clients.
6. **Ethical and Social Responsibility:** Promoting equity and inclusion aligns with ethical principles and demonstrates social responsibility. Organizations have a role in addressing systemic inequalities and contributing to positive social change.
7. **Legal and Compliance Requirements:** Many jurisdictions mandate non-discrimination and equal opportunity practices. Organizations that prioritize DEI mitigate legal risks and ensure compliance with anti-discrimination laws.
8. **Creativity and Problem-solving:** Diverse teams bring a range of perspectives that challenge the status quo and encourage innovative problem-solving. This leads to fresh ideas and solutions that might otherwise be overlooked.
9. **Cultural Competence and Sensitivity:** An inclusive workplace fosters cultural competence, where employees understand and respect differences. This skill is crucial in a globalized world, reducing misunderstandings and conflicts.
10. **Reputation and Brand Enhancement:** Organizations that champion DEI build a positive reputation as inclusive and progressive employer. This enhances their brand image and attracts customers who share similar values.
11. **Leadership Development:** Promoting diverse talent in leadership positions fosters different leadership styles and approaches. Diverse leaders can better connect with diverse employees and drive organizational growth.
12. **Innovation and Adaptability:** Inclusive cultures encourage employees to voice their ideas and concerns. This feedback loop drives innovation, and organizations can more effectively adapt to market changes.

13. **Reducing Bias and Discrimination:** DEI efforts challenge biases and discrimination, fostering a more respectful and accepting environment where all employees can thrive without fear of prejudice.

DEI is crucial not only for creating an equitable workplace but also for driving business success, fostering innovation, and contributing to positive societal change. Organizations that prioritize and actively invest in DEI initiatives stand to gain numerous benefits across various aspects of their operations.

ROLE OF ANALYTICS IN DRIVING DEI EFFORTS

Analytics plays a crucial role in driving Diversity, Equity, and Inclusion (DEI) efforts within organizations. It provides the necessary insights, data-driven strategies, and measurement tools to create a more equitable and inclusive workplace. Following points shows how analytics contributes to DEI initiatives:

1. **Data-driven Decision-making:** Analytics provides objective data to guide DEI efforts. It helps organizations move beyond assumptions and gut feelings, making decisions based on concrete information and trends.
2. **Identifying Disparities and Gaps:** Analytics allows organizations to identify disparities in representation, pay, promotions, and other areas. It highlights where inequities exist and where targeted interventions are needed.
3. **Intersectional Analysis:** Analytics enables the exploration of how different aspects of diversity intersect. For instance, it can help understand the unique experiences of employees who belong to multiple marginalized groups.
4. **Monitoring Progress and Impact:** DEI initiatives require ongoing evaluation. Analytics tracks the progress of these initiatives, measuring changes in key metrics over time and assessing their effectiveness.
5. **Tailoring Strategies:** Analytics helps organizations tailor their DEI strategies to address specific gaps and challenges. Insights from data guide the development of interventions that are aligned with actual needs.
6. **Uncovering Unconscious Bias:** Analytics can reveal patterns of unconscious bias in hiring, promotion, and performance evaluation processes. This awareness prompts organizations to take corrective actions.
7. **Performance Evaluation Equity:** Analytics helps ensure that performance evaluations are fair and unbiased, reducing the likelihood of disproportionately negative outcomes for underrepresented groups.
8. **Transparency and Accountability:** Data-driven reporting demonstrates an organization's commitment to DEI. It provides a transparent way to communicate progress and hold the organization accountable.
9. **Customizing Training Programs:** DEI training can be tailored based on data insights. Analytics identifies areas where employees may need more education about biases and inclusion.
10. **Recruitment and Hiring Practices:** Analytics guides inclusive recruitment strategies, ensuring job descriptions are unbiased, recruitment sources are diverse, and interview processes are fair.

11. **Pay Equity Analysis:** Analytics is crucial in identifying pay gaps across demographic groups. It helps ensure that compensation is equitable and aligned with employee contributions.
12. **Employee Engagement and Retention:** Analytics measures the impact of DEI efforts on employee engagement and retention. It helps organizations understand how inclusive environments affect overall job satisfaction.
13. **Monitoring ERG Impact:** Analytics tracks the impact of Employee Resource Groups (ERGs) and affinity groups on employee engagement and inclusivity efforts.
14. **Predictive Analysis:** Advanced analytics can predict potential issues or challenges in DEI efforts, allowing organizations to take proactive measures.
15. **Demonstrating ROI:** Analytics quantifies the return on investment (ROI) of DEI initiatives. It shows how improvements in DEI metrics positively impact business outcomes.

Thus, analytics is a strong tool for checking out, putting into action, and improving DEI projects. It turns vague goals into measured results, which helps companies make their workplaces fairer and open to everyone.

DEFINING DEI ANALYTICS

Diversity, Equity, and Inclusion (DEI) Analytics refers to the systematic and data-driven process of collecting, analysing, and interpreting relevant data to assess, monitor, and improve diversity, equity, and inclusion efforts within an organization. It involves the use of quantitative and qualitative methods to measure various aspects of diversity, such as representation of different demographic groups, pay equity, promotion rates, employee satisfaction, and the overall sense of inclusion within the workplace.

DEI analytics goes beyond simply gathering data; it involves deriving meaningful insights and actionable recommendations from the data collected. It empowers organizations to make informed decisions, develop targeted strategies, and track progress in their pursuit of creating a more diverse, equitable, and inclusive work environment.

Key Components of DEI Analytics Include

1. **Data Collection:** Gathering data from various sources such as HR records, employee surveys, performance evaluations, and other relevant sources. This data may include information about demographics, compensation, employee experiences, and more.
2. **Data Analysis:** Applying analytical techniques to examine the collected data and identify patterns, trends, disparities, and potential areas for improvement. This could involve statistical analysis, data visualization, and qualitative coding.
3. **Metric Definition:** Defining and measuring key DEI metrics, which could include diversity representation percentages, pay ratios, promotion rates, turnover rates by demographic groups, employee engagement scores, and inclusion index scores.
4. **Benchmarking:** Comparing organization-specific DEI metrics against industry benchmarks or best practices to gain insights into how the organization is performing relative to others.

5. **Identifying Disparities:** Using analytics to identify disparities and gaps in representation, compensation, and opportunities among different demographic groups.
6. **Developing Strategies:** Using data insights to develop targeted strategies and interventions aimed at addressing identified disparities and fostering an inclusive environment.
7. **Measuring Impact:** Continuously evaluating the impact of DEI initiatives by monitoring changes in relevant metrics over time and assessing the effectiveness of implemented strategies.
8. **Predictive Analysis:** Utilizing advanced analytics techniques to predict potential future trends related to diversity, equity, and inclusion, enabling proactive interventions.
9. **Communication:** Effectively communicating DEI data and insights to employees, leadership, and stakeholders to foster transparency and accountability.
10. **Continuous Improvement:** Using data-driven feedback loops to refine strategies, adapt to changing circumstances, and ensure that the organization's DEI efforts remain aligned with its goals.

DEI analytics empowers organizations to move beyond anecdotal evidence and make evidence-based decisions to foster a more inclusive workplace that values and respects individuals from all backgrounds.

HOW TO USE ANALYTICS TO ASSESS AND IMPROVE DIVERSITY, EQUITY, AND INCLUSION IN THE WORKPLACE

Using analytics to assess and improve diversity, equity, and inclusion (DEI) in the workplace involves a strategic and data-driven approach. Following are the steps to assess and improve diversity, equity, and inclusion (DEI) in the workplace:

1. **Establish a Data-driven Culture:** Promote the use of data and analytics in decision-making across the organization. Emphasize the importance of DEI data for driving positive changes.
2. **Define Key Metrics and Indicators:** Identify the specific DEI metrics you want to measure, such as representation by demographic groups, pay equity, promotion rates, employee satisfaction, and inclusion index.
3. **Collect and Clean Data:** Gather data from HR records, surveys, performance evaluations, and other relevant sources. Ensure the data is accurate, consistent, and up-to-date.
4. **Identify Baseline Data:** Establish a baseline of your current DEI metrics. This will serve as a point of comparison to measure progress over time.
5. **Analyse Data for Gaps:** Use analytics tools to analyse the collected data. Identify disparities in representation, pay, promotions, and other relevant areas. Look for patterns that suggest systemic issues.
6. **Conduct Intersectional Analysis:** Analyse data across different dimensions of diversity (e.g., gender, ethnicity, age) to understand how various identities intersect and impact experiences.

7. **Benchmark Against Industry Standards:** Compare your DEI metrics against industry benchmarks to gain a broader perspective on your organization's performance.
8. **Track Progress Over Time:** Continuously monitor your DEI metrics to track progress. Use visualizations and dashboards to make trends and changes easily understandable.
9. **Identify Root Causes:** Dig deeper to identify the root causes of gaps and disparities. Use qualitative methods like surveys, focus groups, and interviews to gain insights.
10. **Develop Targeted Strategies:** Based on the insights from your analysis, design strategies to address identified gaps and root causes. Ensure these strategies are specific and actionable.
11. **Set Goals and KPIs:** Define specific goals and key performance indicators (KPIs) for your DEI initiatives. These should be measurable and aligned with your organization's values.
12. **Implement Interventions:** Implement your strategies across the organization. Provide training, resources, and support to ensure successful implementation.
13. **Monitor Interventions:** Continuously assess the impact of your interventions. Use analytics to measure changes in DEI metrics and assess whether your strategies are effective.
14. **Adjust Strategies as Needed:** If your interventions are not producing the desired results, be prepared to adjust your strategies based on ongoing data analysis.
15. **Address Systemic Issues:** Systemic issues require long-term solutions. Engage leadership and create a culture of accountability to address biases and structural barriers.
16. **Promote Transparency:** Share progress and data with employees, stakeholders, and leadership. Transparency builds trust and demonstrates commitment to DEI.
17. **Continuous Learning and Improvement:** DEI is an ongoing process. Encourage learning, adaptability, and a willingness to evolve based on new insights and challenges.
18. **Celebrate Wins and Progress:** Celebrate milestones and improvements in your DEI efforts. Recognize and acknowledge the positive changes that are taking place.

By integrating analytics into your DEI initiatives, you can assess the current state of diversity, equity, and inclusion, track progress, and develop targeted strategies to create a more inclusive and equitable workplace for all employees.

TABLE 6.1 Key DEI (Diversity, Equity, and Inclusion) metrics and indicators

DEI Metric or Indicator	*Description*
Representation metrics	
Workforce composition	Breakdown of employees by demographic categories (e.g., gender, ethnicity, age).
Leadership representation	Representation of diverse groups at different leadership levels.

(Contd.)

DEI Metric or Indicator	*Description*
Pay equity metrics	
Gender pay gap	Difference in average earnings between men and women in similar roles.
Ethnicity pay gap	Similar to gender pay gap, but focusing on earnings differences among different ethnic groups.
Promotion and advancement metrics	
Promotion rates	Comparing promotion rates for diverse groups to identify disparities.
Retention rates	Tracking retention of employees from diverse backgrounds and assessing turnover patterns.
Employee engagement metrics	
Inclusion index	Measurement of employees' sense of belonging and inclusion within the organization.
Engagement scores	Assessment of employee engagement with their work and the organization, broken down by demographic groups.
Diversity in recruitment metrics	
Diversity in applicant pool	Evaluation of the diversity of candidates applying for job positions.
Offer acceptance rates	Tracking whether diverse candidates accept job offers at the same rate as others.
Supplier diversity metrics	
Diverse supplier spend	Monitoring the proportion of procurement spending going to diverse-owned businesses.
ERG engagement metrics	
Participation rates	Measurement of employee engagement in Employee Resource Groups (ERGs) or affinity groups.
Erg impact	Assessment of the impact of ERGs on employee engagement, professional development, and inclusivity efforts.
Accessibility metrics	
Accessibility accommodations	Tracking the provision of accommodations for employees with disabilities to ensure an inclusive work environment.
Training and development metrics	
Diversity training participation	Measurement of employee participation in diversity and inclusion training programs.

(*Contd.*)

DEI Metric or Indicator	*Description*
Leadership development	Evaluation of the inclusion of diverse employees in leadership development programs.
Exit interviews and turnover metrics	
Exit reasons	Analysis of reasons for employee departures and identification of patterns among diverse groups.
Inclusive policies metrics	
Usage of policies	Tracking the utilization of inclusive policies (e.g., flexible work arrangements, parental leave) across different demographic groups.
Employee feedback metrics	
Survey responses	Analysis of survey responses on diversity and inclusion-related questions to understand employee perceptions.
Representation in high-visibility projects	
Project participation	Assessment of the participation of diverse employees in high-profile projects and initiatives.

COLLECTING AND PREPARING DATA

Collecting and preparing data for Diversity, Equity, and Inclusion (DEI) analytics involves several critical steps, including identifying sources of data, addressing data privacy and security considerations, and ensuring data cleaning and validation.

1. *Sources of DEI Data*

Identifying the sources of DEI data is the first step in the data collection process. Below mentioned are the sources that provide the raw information needed for DEI analysis:

- **Human Resources (HR) Records:** HR databases contain valuable demographic data such as gender, ethnicity, age, and job roles.
- **Employee Surveys:** Surveys can gather employee perceptions, experiences, and feedback related to DEI topics.
- **Performance Evaluations:** Data on employee performance, promotions, and compensation can help assess equity in career advancement.
- **Payroll and Compensation Data:** Information about salaries, bonuses, and benefits can be used to analyse pay equity.
- **Recruitment and Hiring Records:** Data on job applicants, hiring decisions, and applicant demographics can inform recruitment strategies.
- **Exit Interviews:** Feedback from departing employees can reveal insights into the reasons for turnover and potential DEI-related issues.

- **Employee Resource Group (ERG) Data:** ERGs may track their membership, activities, and contributions to DEI initiatives.
- **Diversity Reports:** Publicly available reports, such as Equal Employment Opportunity (EEO) reports, may provide industry or regional benchmarks.

2. *Data Privacy and Security Considerations*

Maintaining data privacy and security is paramount when collecting and handling DEI data:

- **Legal Compliance:** Ensure compliance with data protection laws (e.g., GDPR, CCPA) and DEI reporting requirements (e.g., EEO-1 reporting).
- **Anonymization and Aggregation:** Anonymize individual-level data and aggregate data when necessary to prevent the identification of individuals.
- **Access Control:** Restrict access to sensitive DEI data to authorized personnel only, and implement user access controls.
- **Data Encryption:** Encrypt data both in transit and at rest to protect it from unauthorized access.
- **Data Retention Policies:** Establish policies for data retention and secure disposal of data that is no longer needed.
- **Informed Consent:** If collecting employee survey data, ensure that employees provide informed consent and understand how their data will be used.

3. *Data Cleaning and Validation*

Data collected for DEI analytics must be accurate, consistent, and reliable. Data cleaning and validation are essential to ensure the quality of the data:

- **Data Verification:** Verify the accuracy of demographic data through cross-referencing with official records, if available.
- **Addressing Missing Data:** Develop strategies for handling missing data, such as imputation techniques or flagging missing values.
- **Outlier Detection:** Identify and address outliers in the data that may skew analysis results.
- **Standardization:** Standardize data formats and coding schemes to ensure consistency.
- **Data Quality Metrics:** Define and track data quality metrics to assess the overall reliability of DEI data.
- **Validation Checks:** Implement validation checks to verify that data entries fall within acceptable ranges.
- **Regular Auditing:** Conduct regular audits to maintain data quality and identify areas for improvement.

By carefully selecting data sources, addressing privacy and security concerns, and implementing robust data cleaning and validation procedures, organizations can ensure that the data used for DEI analytics is both reliable and ethically handled, laying the foundation for meaningful insights and actionable strategies to promote diversity, equity, and inclusion within the workplace.

ANALYSING DEI DATA

Analysing Diversity, Equity, and Inclusion (DEI) data involves a combination of quantitative and qualitative analysis methods to gain a comprehensive understanding of the organization's DEI landscape. Here's an overview of the analysis methods, including intersectional analysis:

Quantitative Analysis Methods

- **Descriptive Statistics:** Descriptive statistics provide a summary of key DEI metrics, such as mean, median, mode, and standard deviation. They offer an overview of the current state of diversity, equity, and inclusion within the organization.
- **Correlation Analysis:** Correlation analysis examines relationships between variables. For example, it can assess whether there is a correlation between employee engagement scores and diversity representation.
- **Regression Analysis:** Regression analysis explores the impact of one or more independent variables (e.g., demographics) on an outcome variable (e.g., promotion rates or pay). It helps identify factors contributing to disparities.
- **Trend Analysis:** Trend analysis tracks changes in DEI metrics over time. It allows organizations to assess whether DEI efforts are making a positive impact and whether disparities are decreasing.
- **Comparative Analysis:** Comparative analysis involves benchmarking your organization's DEI metrics against industry or peer benchmarks. It provides context for understanding how your organization performs relative to others.
- **Pay Equity Analysis:** Quantitative analysis is crucial for assessing pay equity. It involves statistical methods to identify and rectify gender or ethnicity-based pay gaps.

Qualitative Analysis Methods

- **Content Analysis:** Content analysis involves examining qualitative data, such as open-ended survey responses, to identify recurring themes and patterns related to DEI experiences and perceptions.
- **Thematic Analysis:** Thematic analysis is a qualitative method that involves coding and categorizing qualitative data into themes or patterns, allowing for a deeper understanding of employee experiences and concerns.
- **Interviews and Focus Groups:** Qualitative data can be gathered through interviews and focus groups with employees. These methods provide in-depth insights into individual experiences and allow for the exploration of nuances.
- **Narrative Analysis:** Narrative analysis focuses on stories and narratives shared by employees. It helps uncover the lived experiences of individuals and their interactions with DEI initiatives.

Intersectional Analysis

Intersectional analysis is an approach that considers how multiple dimensions of diversity intersect and interact. It recognizes that individuals hold multiple social identities (e.g., gender, race, age), and the combination of these identities can result in unique experiences and challenges. For example:

- An intersectional analysis might explore how the experiences of women of colour differ from those of white women or men of colour.
- It can identify disparities faced by LGBTQ+ individuals within specific racial or ethnic groups.
- It can reveal how age intersects with gender to impact career progression.

To do intersectional analysis, companies need to gather information on different aspects of diversity and then look at how these aspects interact with each other to give workers different experiences and problems. This way of doing things makes sure that DEI programmes are designed to meet the specific needs of people whose identities overlap.

When you use both quantitative and qualitative analysis tools together with intersectional analysis, you can get a full picture of an organization's DEI environment. These methods help find differences, track progress, and create focused plans to promote variety, fairness, and inclusion at work.

IDENTIFYING GAPS AND DISPARITIES

Identifying gaps and disparities in Diversity, Equity, and Inclusion (DEI) efforts is a crucial step in improving workplace inclusivity. Following are some strategies for identifying patterns and trends, conducting root cause analysis for disparities, and analysing bias in hiring and promotions:

1. *Identifying Patterns and Trends*

- **Data Visualization:** Use data visualization tools to create charts, graphs, and dashboards that illustrate DEI metrics over time. Visual representations make it easier to spot trends and anomalies.
- **Comparative Analysis:** Compare DEI metrics across different departments, teams, or geographic locations within your organization. This can reveal disparities that may be masked in aggregate data.
- **Intersectional Analysis:** Analyse DEI data by considering multiple dimensions of diversity simultaneously (e.g., race, gender, age). This approach helps uncover nuanced disparities experienced by individuals with intersecting identities.
- **Employee Feedback:** Review qualitative data from surveys, interviews, or focus groups to identify recurring themes related to DEI challenges and experiences. Patterns in employee narratives can highlight areas of concern.

2. *Root Cause Analysis for Disparities*

- **Data Segmentation:** Segment your data to understand where disparities exist. For example, break down pay gap data by job level, department, and tenure to pinpoint where the disparities are most significant.

- **Stakeholder Interviews:** Conduct interviews with employees, especially those from underrepresented groups, to gain qualitative insights into the root causes of disparities. Ask about their experiences, challenges, and suggestions for improvement.
- **Process Mapping:** Map out key HR processes, such as hiring, performance evaluations, and promotions, to identify potential points where bias or discrimination may occur. Look for bottlenecks and inconsistencies.
- **Historical Analysis:** Review historical data to understand the evolution of disparities. This can reveal trends and patterns that have persisted over time.
- **Benchmarking:** Compare your organization's DEI metrics to industry benchmarks to understand how you stack up against others. This can help identify areas where improvements are needed.

3. *Analysing Bias in Hiring and Promotions*

- **Resume and Application Analysis:** Examine resumes and job applications for potential bias, such as gendered language or assumptions. Implement blind recruitment practices to reduce bias during the initial screening process.
- **Interview Process Analysis:** Evaluate interview questions and processes for bias. Standardize interview questions and scoring to ensure consistency and fairness.
- **Promotion Criteria Review:** Review the criteria used for promotions to ensure they are objective and equitable. Establish clear guidelines for career advancement that minimize opportunities for bias.
- **Unconscious Bias Training:** Provide training to hiring managers and decision-makers on recognizing and mitigating unconscious bias. Awareness is the first step in addressing bias in decision-making.
- **Promotion Transparency:** Ensure that promotion decisions are transparent and communicated clearly to employees. This helps reduce perceptions of bias and favouritism.
- **Diverse Hiring Panels:** Include diverse members on hiring and promotion panels to provide different perspectives and minimize potential bias.
- **Data-driven Audits:** Regularly audit hiring and promotion data to identify disparities in candidate selection and career progression. Use this data to inform corrective actions.

Identifying gaps, conducting root cause analysis, and addressing bias in hiring and promotions require a combination of quantitative and qualitative methods, as well as a commitment to ongoing monitoring and improvement. By systematically addressing disparities and bias, organizations can create more equitable and inclusive environments for their employees.

INDUSTRY BENCHMARKS FOR DEI METRICS

Benchmarking in the context of Diversity, Equity, and Inclusion (DEI) involves comparing your organization's DEI metrics to industry or sector-wide standards or averages. Following are some common industry benchmarks for DEI metrics:

1. **Gender and Ethnicity Representation:** Compare the gender and ethnicity demographics of your workforce to industry averages or regional demographics. This helps identify underrepresentation or overrepresentation of certain groups.
2. **Gender Pay Gap:** Benchmark your organization's gender pay gap against industry averages. This can highlight areas where gender-based pay disparities may exist.
3. **Promotion Rates:** Compare the promotion rates of underrepresented groups (e.g., women, ethnic minorities) to industry norms. Identify if there are disparities in advancement opportunities.
4. **Employee Engagement Scores:** Measure employee engagement scores and compare them to industry benchmarks. This can help gauge how engaged your workforce is relative to similar organizations.
5. **Diversity in Leadership:** Assess the diversity of your organization's leadership positions (e.g., board of directors, executive leadership) and compare it to industry standards.
6. **Supplier Diversity:** Benchmark your supplier diversity efforts against industry standards to assess your organization's commitment to diverse supplier partnerships.

Benefits of Benchmarking

1. **Performance Assessment:** Benchmarking allows organizations to assess their DEI performance objectively. It provides a clear picture of where the organization stands in comparison to peers.
2. **Identifying Disparities:** Benchmarking helps identify disparities and areas of improvement by highlighting gaps between your organization and industry standards.
3. **Goal Setting:** Benchmarks provide a basis for setting realistic and achievable DEI goals. They help organizations establish targets that align with industry best practices.
4. **Tracking Progress:** Over time, benchmarking enables organizations to track their progress in improving DEI metrics. It provides a basis for measuring the impact of DEI initiatives.
5. **Informed Decision-making:** Benchmarking data informs data-driven decision-making. It helps organizations prioritize DEI efforts and allocate resources effectively.
6. **Competitive Advantage:** Achieving or surpassing industry benchmarks in DEI can be a source of competitive advantage, attracting top talent and demonstrating commitment to diversity and inclusion.

Limitations of Benchmarking

1. **Data Variability:** Industry benchmarks may not account for differences in regional demographics, industry-specific challenges, or organizational culture. Comparing against benchmarks that are not directly relevant can lead to skewed conclusions.
2. **Context Matters:** Benchmarks do not provide context for why disparities exist or how to address them. They offer a snapshot of performance but not necessarily a solution.
3. **Focus on Averages:** Benchmarking often focuses on averages, which can mask disparities within an organization. Averages may not reflect the experiences of specific groups.

4. **Benchmark Data Quality:** The quality of industry benchmark data can vary widely. Inaccurate or outdated benchmark data can lead to misguided conclusions.
5. **Overemphasis on Comparison:** Excessive focus on benchmarking can lead to a "check-the-box" mentality where organizations prioritize meeting industry norms rather than genuinely addressing DEI issues.
6. **Lack of Customization:** Industry benchmarks are general by nature and may not align with an organization's unique DEI goals, culture, or context. Customization is often necessary.

DESIGNING TARGETED DEI STRATEGIES

Designing targeted Diversity, Equity, and Inclusion (DEI) strategies is essential for creating a workplace that is diverse, equitable, and inclusive. These strategies should be tailored to address specific gaps and challenges identified through data analysis. Following are the steps to guide on how to design targeted DEI strategies:

1. **Identify Areas for Improvement:** Review the findings from your DEI data analysis. Identify specific areas where disparities or challenges exist. This could include representation, pay equity, promotion rates, or inclusion metrics.
2. **Set Clear Objectives:** Define clear and measurable objectives for your targeted DEI strategies. Your objectives should align with the areas you identified for improvement. For example, if you found gender disparities in leadership roles, your objective could be to increase the representation of women in leadership positions by a certain percentage within a specified time frame.
3. **Conduct Root Cause Analysis:** Understand the underlying factors contributing to the identified disparities. This might involve qualitative research, surveys, focus groups, or interviews to gain insights from employees and stakeholders. For instance, if pay disparities exist, determine whether it's due to biased hiring practices, unequal promotion opportunities, or other factors.
4. **Engage Stakeholders:** Involve key stakeholders, including employees, managers, and leadership, in the design of your strategies. Seek their input and feedback to ensure a collaborative approach and increase buy-in.
5. **Tailor Interventions:** Develop interventions that directly address the root causes of the disparities. These interventions should be specific and targeted. For example:
   - If biases in hiring are identified, implement blind recruitment practices.
   - If underrepresented groups lack access to mentorship, create mentorship programs.
   - If pay disparities exist, conduct pay equity audits and make necessary adjustments.
6. **Prioritize Inclusion Training:** Implement mandatory diversity and inclusion training programs for all employees and leadership. Ensure that these programs address unconscious bias, macroaggressions, and inclusive communication.
7. **Create Affinity Groups and ERGs:** Establish Employee Resource Groups (ERGs) and affinity groups to provide support and a sense of belonging for underrepresented employees. These groups can also serve as forums for sharing feedback and suggestions.

8. **Monitor Progress and Adjust:** Continuously monitor the impact of your targeted strategies. Use analytics to measure changes in DEI metrics and assess the effectiveness of your interventions. Be prepared to make adjustments based on ongoing data analysis.
9. **Promote Accountability:** Hold leaders and managers accountable for the progress of DEI initiatives in their respective areas. Incorporate DEI goals into performance evaluations and compensation decisions.
10. **Communication and Transparency:** Communicate your DEI strategies, goals, and progress to all employees. Transparency builds trust and encourages employees to engage in the process.
11. **Evaluate and Learn:** Periodically evaluate the outcomes of your targeted DEI strategies. Assess what worked, what didn't, and what can be improved. Use these insights to inform future initiatives.
12. **Sustain the Effort:** DEI efforts are ongoing. Commit to the long-term sustainability of your strategies. DEI should be integrated into the culture and values of the organization.

Remember that targeted DEI strategies should be data-driven, tailored to your organization's unique context, and continuously refined based on the evolving needs of your workforce and the insights gained through analytics.

MEASURING PROGRESS AND IMPACT

Measuring progress and impact in the context of Diversity, Equity, and Inclusion (DEI) initiatives is crucial to assess the effectiveness of your efforts and ensure that they are creating a positive change within your organization. Following are the ways to measure progress and impact:

1. **Define Clear Metrics and Key Performance Indicators (KPIs):**
   - Identify specific DEI metrics and KPIs that align with your organization's goals. These could include metrics related to representation, pay equity, promotion rates, employee satisfaction, diversity in leadership roles, and more.
   - Ensure that your metrics are specific, measurable, achievable, relevant, and time-bound (SMART).
2. **Establish a Baseline:** Before you can measure progress, establish a baseline by collecting data on your chosen DEI metrics at the beginning of your initiative. This will serve as a point of comparison.
3. **Regular Data Collection and Analysis:**
   - Continuously collect and analyse data related to your DEI metrics. This includes data from HR records, employee surveys, performance evaluations, and other relevant sources.
   - Use analytics tools to identify trends, changes, and disparities in your data.
4. **Set Progress Milestones:**
   - Define clear milestones and objectives for your DEI initiatives. These should be tied to your chosen metrics and KPIs.
   - Ensure that these milestones are realistic and attainable within your specified timeframe.

5. **Monitor Changes Over Time:**
    - Track changes in your DEI metrics and KPIs over time. This could involve monthly, quarterly, or annual assessments, depending on the nature of the metrics.
    - Visualize your data through charts and dashboards to make trends and changes easily understandable.
6. **Assess Impact on Organizational Goals:** Evaluate how changes in DEI metrics align with broader organizational goals. For example, assess whether an increase in diversity has led to improvements in innovation, employee satisfaction, or customer relations.
7. **Seek Employee Feedback:**
    - Incorporate employee feedback through surveys, focus groups, and interviews. Employee experiences and perceptions are valuable indicators of progress.
    - Use qualitative data to gain insights into the lived experiences of employees and identify areas for improvement.
8. **Conduct Intersectional Analysis:** Analyse data across different dimensions of diversity, such as gender, ethnicity, age, and more. Understand how various identities intersect and influence experiences within your organization.
9. **Adjust Strategies as Needed:** If your data analysis reveals that progress is not being made or that disparities are persisting, be prepared to adjust your DEI strategies. Tailor interventions to address specific challenges.
10. **Celebrate Wins and Recognize Progress:** Acknowledge and celebrate milestones and positive changes in DEI metrics. Recognize and appreciate the efforts of individuals and teams who have contributed to these improvements.
11. **Promote Transparency:** Share progress and data with employees, leadership, and stakeholders. Transparency builds trust and demonstrates a commitment to DEI initiatives.
12. **Review and Refine Goals:** Regularly review and refine your DEI goals and objectives based on new insights and changing organizational needs.

DATA-DRIVEN INTERVENTIONS

Data-driven interventions in the context of Diversity, Equity, and Inclusion (DEI) refer to strategies and actions that are guided by insights and patterns obtained through data analysis. These interventions aim to address specific DEI challenges, disparities, or opportunities within an organization based on empirical evidence rather than assumptions. Following are the steps to implement data-driven interventions effectively:

1. **Analyse Data Thoroughly:**
    - Begin by conducting a comprehensive analysis of your DEI data. Look for trends, patterns, and disparities in areas like representation, pay equity, promotion rates, and employee satisfaction.
    - Use quantitative and qualitative data to gain a holistic understanding of the issues.

2. **Identify Root Causes:**
   - Once you've identified areas of concern, delve deeper to determine the root causes behind the disparities or challenges. This might involve further data analysis, employee surveys, focus groups, or interviews.
   - Understand whether the issues are related to organizational policies, biases, culture, or other factors.
3. **Set Clear Goals and Objectives:** Based on your data analysis and the identified root causes, set clear and specific goals for your interventions. Define what success looks like and establish key performance indicators (KPIs).
4. **Tailor Interventions to Data:**
   - Develop interventions that directly address the specific issues uncovered by your data analysis. Ensure that your strategies are aligned with your goals and KPIs.
   - For example, if pay equity is a concern, design compensation adjustments or policies to rectify disparities.
5. **Pilot Interventions:** Before implementing interventions organization-wide, consider piloting them in smaller groups or departments. This allows you to test their effectiveness and make necessary adjustments.
6. **Implement and Monitor Progress:**
   - Roll out your data-driven interventions and closely monitor their progress. Continuously track relevant DEI metrics and KPIs to assess whether your strategies are making a difference.
   - Use analytics tools to measure changes over time and identify early signs of success or areas that need improvement.
7. **Employee Training and Awareness:** Implement training programs and awareness campaigns that target specific DEI issues. For instance, if bias in hiring is a concern, provide training on unconscious bias to hiring managers.
8. **Employee Resource Groups (ERGs):** Support and encourage the formation of Employee Resource Groups (ERGs) that focus on DEI. These groups can provide valuable insights and drive positive change.
9. **Accountability and Leadership Involvement:**
   - Ensure that leaders and managers are held accountable for the success of DEI initiatives. Leadership involvement is critical for driving cultural change.
   - Leaders should champion DEI efforts and lead by example.
10. **Adjust and Iterate:** Regularly review the impact of your data-driven interventions. If they are not producing the desired results, be willing to adjust and iterate based on ongoing data analysis. Continuously learn from your interventions and apply lessons to future strategies.
11. **Communicate Progress:** Share the progress and impact of your data-driven interventions with employees, leadership, and stakeholders. Transparent communication builds trust and encourages engagement.

Data-driven interventions empower organizations to address DEI challenges with precision and evidence-based decision-making. By continuously analysing data, tailoring strategies, and monitoring progress, organizations can create a more equitable and inclusive workplace for all employees.

ADDRESSING SYSTEMIC ISSUES

Addressing systemic issues within an organization is a critical aspect of Diversity, Equity, and Inclusion (DEI) efforts. Systemic issues often involve deep-rooted biases, structural barriers, and cultural norms that perpetuate inequalities and hinder progress in DEI. Following are steps and strategies for addressing systemic issues:

1. **Acknowledge the Existence of Systemic Issues:** Begin by acknowledging that systemic issues exist within the organization. Denial or avoidance only perpetuates the problem.
2. **Conduct a Comprehensive DEI Assessment:** Perform a thorough assessment of the organization's policies, practices, and culture to identify systemic issues. This may include analysing hiring practices, promotion processes, compensation structures, and more.
3. **Establish Clear DEI Goals:** Define specific DEI objectives that address systemic issues. Goals should be actionable, measurable, and tied to eliminating systemic disparities.
4. **Engage Leadership Commitment:** Obtain visible commitment from senior leadership to address systemic issues. Leaders should champion DEI initiatives and communicate their importance.
5. **Conduct Training and Education:** Provide training on topics such as unconscious bias, cultural competency, and inclusive leadership. Ensure that employees at all levels understand the impact of systemic issues.
6. **Review and Revise Policies and Practices:** Examine HR policies, recruitment procedures, performance evaluations, and any practices that may perpetuate systemic issues. Make necessary revisions to promote equity.
7. **Implement Inclusive Recruitment and Promotion:** Create diverse candidate pipelines through inclusive recruitment practices. Ensure that promotions are based on merit and not biased criteria.
8. **Establish Fair Compensation Practices:** Analyse compensation data to identify pay disparities. Implement fair compensation practices that eliminate gender, ethnicity, or age-based wage gaps.
9. **Foster a Culture of Inclusion:** Create a culture where every employee feels valued and included. Encourage open dialogue, diverse perspectives, and a sense of belonging.
10. **Support Employee Resource Groups (ERGs):** Empower ERGs to provide insights, support, and advocacy for underrepresented groups within the organization. Recognize their contributions.
11. **Conduct Regular DEI Audits:** Periodically evaluate progress and impact using DEI audits. Monitor changes in key metrics and make adjustments as needed.
12. **Hold Accountable for Results:** Establish accountability mechanisms for leaders and managers to ensure they actively address systemic issues. Include DEI objectives in performance evaluations.
13. **Promote Transparency:** Communicate DEI initiatives and progress transparently with employees, stakeholders, and the public. This builds trust and accountability.

14. **Seek External Guidance:** Consider bringing in external DEI consultants or experts to provide an objective assessment of systemic issues and recommend strategies for improvement.
15. **Commit to Long-term Change:** Understand that addressing systemic issues is a long-term commitment. Sustainable change takes time, persistence, and ongoing effort.
16. **Measure and Share Success Stories:** Continuously measure the impact of your efforts and share success stories. Highlighting positive changes reinforces the importance of addressing systemic issues.
17. **Empower Employees as Change Agents:** Encourage employees at all levels to be advocates for change. Empower them to speak up about systemic issues and contribute to solutions.

Addressing systemic issues is a complex but essential part of creating a more equitable and inclusive workplace. By taking deliberate and sustained actions, organizations can work towards eliminating systemic biases and fostering an environment where everyone has equal opportunities and feels valued.

TABLE 6.2 Strategies for inclusive leadership

Inclusive leadership strategies	*Description*
1. Self-awareness and reflection	Leaders should regularly self-reflect on their biases, beliefs, and behaviours that may impact inclusivity. This awareness forms the foundation of inclusive leadership.
2. Empathy and active listening	Inclusive leaders actively listen to others, seeking to understand their perspectives and emotions. They show empathy and validate others' experiences.
3. Cultivating a growth mind-set	Encourage a culture of learning and continuous improvement. Embrace challenges and view failures as opportunities for growth.
4. Creating psycholo-gical safety	Foster an environment where employees feel safe to voice their opinions, ask questions, and make mistakes without fear of retribution.
5. Diverse talent development	Invest in the development of diverse talent. Provide mentorship, coaching, and opportunities for advancement to underrepresented groups.
6. Inclusive decision-making	Involve a diverse range of voices in decision-making processes. Seek input from various backgrounds and perspectives before finalizing decisions.
7. Inclusive communication	Use inclusive language and communication styles. Ensure that messages are accessible and resonate with a diverse audience.
8. Addressing micro aggressions	Educate employees on macroaggressions and provide tools for addressing and preventing them. Encourage open conversations about their impact.

(*Contd.*)

Inclusive leadership strategies	*Description*
9. Conflict resolution skills	Develop skills for resolving conflicts in an inclusive manner. Encourage constructive dialogues and mediate when necessary to maintain harmony.
10. Employee resource groups (ergs)	Support and actively engage with ERGs representing various demographics. Recognize their value in promoting inclusion.
11. Accountability and measurement	Set clear DEI goals, track progress, and hold leaders accountable for results. Regularly assess the impact of inclusive leadership initiatives.
12. Modelling inclusivity	Lead by example. Demonstrate inclusive behaviours and attitudes in your interactions with others. Showcase the expected standard of behaviour.
13. Cultural competence	Develop cultural competence by learning about different cultures, customs, and traditions. Understand the impact of culture on communication and teamwork.
14. Feedback and adaptability	Be open to feedback regarding your leadership style. Adapt and refine your approach based on feedback to better serve your team's needs.
15. Recognizing and celebrating diversity	Acknowledge and celebrate diversity within your team. Embrace the unique strengths and perspectives that each member brings.

USING TECHNOLOGY AND AI FOR DEI

Leveraging technology and artificial intelligence (AI) can be instrumental in advancing diversity, equity, and inclusion (DEI) efforts within an organization.

1. *Leveraging AI for Unbiased Recruitment*

- **Resume Screening:** Implement AI-driven resume screening tools to anonymize resumes by removing personally identifiable information (PII) like names, gender, and age. This reduces the potential for unconscious bias during the initial screening process.
- **Job Posting Analysis:** Use AI to analyse job postings and identify gendered language or biased terminology that might discourage diverse candidates from applying. This can help in creating more inclusive job descriptions.
- **Predictive Hiring Models:** Develop predictive hiring models using AI algorithms that consider various factors to predict a candidate's likelihood of success in a role. This approach can reduce reliance on traditional proxies and promote equitable hiring.
- **Interview Insights:** Implement AI tools that analyse interview transcripts or videos to identify any bias in interviewer behaviour, such as interrupting candidates or asking biased questions. This feedback can guide interviewers in providing a fairer experience.

2. *AI Tools for Analysing Language and Communication*

- **Sentiment Analysis:** Employ sentiment analysis tools to assess the sentiment of internal and external communications, such as emails, chat messages, and social media posts. Identify potential issues related to discrimination or exclusionary language.
- **Inclusive Language Scanners:** Use AI-driven language scanners that flag biased or non-inclusive language in written materials, including company documents, training materials, and emails.
- **Bias Detection in AI Algorithms:** Ensure that AI algorithms used in decision-making (e.g., promotions, performance evaluations) are regularly audited for bias. Implement mechanisms to correct any detected bias.

3. *Tech Solutions for Tracking and Improving Inclusion*

- **Inclusive Culture Surveys:** Implement tech solutions to conduct surveys that measure the inclusivity of the workplace culture. Analyse survey data to identify areas that need improvement.
- **Collaboration Analytics:** Use collaboration analytics tools to track patterns of interaction and collaboration within teams. Identify whether certain groups are excluded from key projects or decision-making processes.
- **Inclusion Dashboards:** Develop dashboards that provide real-time insights into DEI metrics, such as representation, inclusion scores, and pay equity. Make these dashboards accessible to leadership and employees for transparency.
- **Employee Resource Group (ERG) Platforms:** Leverage technology to support ERGs and affinity groups. Provide them with platforms to organize, share resources, and track their own impact on DEI initiatives.
- **Feedback and Reporting Tools:** Offer anonymous reporting tools for employees to report instances of bias, discrimination, or harassment. Use technology to ensure confidentiality and facilitate prompt resolution.
- **Training and Development Platforms:** Implement e-learning platforms that offer diversity and inclusion training modules. Use analytics to track employee participation, completion rates, and knowledge gain.
- **Remote Work Inclusion Tools:** Adapt tech solutions to ensure inclusion in remote work environments. Provide accessibility features and tools that promote virtual team-building and collaboration.
- **Data-driven Goals:** Set data-driven DEI goals and use technology to monitor progress toward these goals. Regularly update stakeholders on progress and areas that need improvement.

Leveraging technology and AI for DEI initiatives can enhance objectivity, reduce biases, and facilitate a more inclusive workplace. However, it's essential to continuously evaluate and fine-tune these tools and processes to ensure that they align with your organization's DEI objectives and do not inadvertently introduce new biases or challenges.

TABLE 6.3 Communicating DEI (Diversity, Equity, and Inclusion) data and progress effectively

Aspect	*Description*
Transparency	• Be transparent about DEI data collection and analysis methods.
	• Communicate the organization's commitment to openness and accountability.
	• Explain the purpose of sharing DEI data and the benefits it brings.
Audience consideration	• Tailor your communication to various stakeholders (employees, leadership, shareholders, etc.).
	• Highlight the relevance of DEI data to each audience's interests and concerns.
	• Use language and formats that are accessible and understandable to all stakeholders.
Regular reporting	• Establish a regular reporting schedule for DEI updates.
	• Consistency in reporting builds trust and demonstrates long-term commitment.
	• Include both quantitative metrics and qualitative narratives for a comprehensive view.
Visual representation	• Use charts, graphs, and infographics to visualize data trends and progress.
	• Visuals make complex data more digestible and engaging for the audience.
Storytelling	• Share real-life stories and examples that illustrate the impact of DEI initiatives.
	• Personal narratives humanize the data and connect emotionally with the audience.
Highlight achievements	• Celebrate milestones and successes in DEI efforts.
	• Acknowledge individuals and teams that have contributed to progress.
	• Positive reinforcement motivates continued engagement.
Address challenges	• Acknowledge areas where challenges persist and where progress has been slow.
	• Show a commitment to addressing these challenges with concrete plans.
	• Transparency about challenges builds credibility and trust.
Set future goals	• Outline future DEI goals and objectives that the organization aims to achieve.
	• Setting clear goals provides a roadmap for the future and demonstrates a forward-thinking approach.
Engagement	• Encourage employees and stakeholders to provide feedback and ask questions about DEI data.
	• Foster an open dialogue to address concerns and gather input for improvement.

(*Contd.*)

Aspect	*Description*
Accessibility	• Ensure DEI data and progress reports are accessible to all, including those with disabilities.
	• Comply with accessibility standards in document formatting and online presentation.
Interactive platforms	• Use digital platforms for interactive reporting, allowing users to explore data and trends.
	• Interactive tools can enhance engagement and understanding.
Cultural sensitivity	• Be mindful of cultural nuances and sensitivities when discussing DEI data.
	• Respect diverse perspectives and encourage an inclusive dialogue.
Feedback loop	• Establish a feedback mechanism for stakeholders to share their thoughts on DEI reporting.
	• Use feedback to refine future communications and data collection.
Compliance reporting	• If applicable, include information about regulatory compliance with DEI reporting requirements.
	• Demonstrate the organization's commitment to legal obligations.

Effective communication of DEI data and progress is critical for building trust, fostering understanding, and ensuring that all stakeholders are engaged and informed about an organization's efforts in promoting diversity, equity, and inclusion.

TABLE 6.4 Challenges and ethical considerations related to DEI initiatives

Challenge/Ethical consideration	*Description*
Data privacy and security	• Protecting sensitive employee data is paramount.
	• Ethical consideration: Ensure data is used responsibly, and individuals' privacy rights are respected.
Bias in data collection	• Data collected may reflect existing biases in the organization.
	• Ethical consideration: Strive to collect unbiased data and address any systemic bias in the process.
Data accuracy	• Inaccurate data can lead to incorrect conclusions and actions.
	• Ethical consideration: Ensure data accuracy and transparency in reporting.
Resistance and backlash	• Some employees or stakeholders may resist DEI initiatives.
	• Ethical consideration: Respect diverse perspectives, engage in dialogue, and address concerns respectfully.

(*Contd.*)

Challenge/Ethical consideration	*Description*
Overreliance on technology	• Relying solely on technology may depersonalize DEI efforts.
	• Ethical consideration: Balance technology with human interaction and empathy.
Tokenism	• Superficial efforts to demonstrate diversity without substantive change.
	• Ethical consideration: Ensure DEI initiatives are genuine and not mere token gestures.
Cherry-picking data	• Selectively presenting data to create a biased narrative.
	• Ethical consideration: Present data transparently, including both positive and challenging aspects.
Inequitable impact	• DEI initiatives may inadvertently benefit some groups more than others.
	• Ethical consideration: Monitor impacts and adjust strategies to ensure equity for all.
Data invisibility	• Some employees may feel uncomfortable sharing their identity data.
	• Ethical consideration: Respect individual choices while encouraging voluntary disclosure.
Reactive vs. Proactive	• DEI efforts may become reactive, addressing issues only when problems arise.
	• Ethical consideration: Foster a proactive culture of inclusion and continuous improvement.
Measurement challenges	• Difficulty in measuring qualitative aspects of inclusion and equity.
	• Ethical consideration: Combine quantitative data with qualitative insights for a holistic view.
Reporting bias	• Fear of retaliation may lead employees to provide inaccurate feedback.
	• Ethical consideration: Create safe channels for reporting and protecting whistle-blowers.
Accountability	• Lack of accountability can undermine DEI efforts.
	• Ethical consideration: Establish clear lines of responsibility and hold individuals accountable for DEI goals.
Cultural sensitivity	• Different cultures may have unique perspectives on DEI.
	• Ethical consideration: Promote cultural competency and respect diverse viewpoints.

(Contd.)

Challenge/Ethical consideration	*Description*
Data sharing risks	• Sharing DEI data externally may lead to reputation risks or misuse.
	• Ethical consideration: Safeguard data, share responsibly, and communicate intentions clearly.
Balancing short-term and long-term	• Focusing on quick wins at the expense of long-term cultural change.
	• Ethical consideration: Strive for a balanced approach that considers both immediate and enduring impacts.
DEI fatigue	• Employees may become fatigued with DEI initiatives over time.
	• Ethical consideration: Maintain engagement by demonstrating consistent commitment and progress.

TESTING THE IMPACT OF DIVERSITY

Diversity, in the context of organizations and society, has become an increasingly prominent and critical topic. It encompasses various dimensions, including but not limited to race, gender, ethnicity, age, sexual orientation, physical abilities, and socioeconomic backgrounds. The impact of diversity, especially in the workplace, is a subject of significant interest and research. Organizations, governments, and scholars are keen to understand the implications of diverse workforces and communities. Diversity is a multifaceted concept, and its dimensions extend beyond mere demographics. It also includes cognitive diversity, which encompasses different perspectives, problem-solving approaches, and experiences. While visible diversity (e.g., racial and gender diversity) is crucial, cognitive diversity can be equally impactful. Research has shown that a diverse team or workforce can lead to increased creativity, better problem-solving, and improved decision-making.

The Significance of Diversity Testing

Testing the impact of diversity is crucial for several reasons:

1. **Business Benefits:** Diverse teams are believed to be more innovative, creative, and better at problem-solving. Businesses are keen to understand how diversity can enhance productivity, profitability, and competitiveness.
2. **Social Equity:** Evaluating diversity's impact is central to creating fair and equitable workplaces and societies. It can help identify and address disparities in opportunities, wages, and career advancement.
3. **Legal Compliance:** In many countries, anti-discrimination laws necessitate monitoring and assessing diversity to ensure compliance. Understanding the impact of diversity can help organizations avoid legal pitfalls.

4. **Inclusive Environments:** Testing the impact of diversity is crucial for building inclusive environments that promote acceptance, tolerance, and belonging. This, in turn, improves employee satisfaction and engagement.

Methodologies for Testing Diversity Impact

To comprehensively test the impact of diversity, various methodologies can be employed:

1. **Statistical Analysis:** Analysing demographic data within an organization or community can reveal correlations between diversity and various outcomes, such as productivity, retention, or innovation. This can be done through quantitative tools like regression analysis.
2. **Surveys and Interviews:** Gathering qualitative data through surveys and interviews can uncover personal experiences and perspectives related to diversity. This provides valuable insights into the psychological and emotional impact of diversity.
3. **Case Studies:** Examining specific organizations or communities can provide in-depth understanding. It involves investigating how diversity initiatives have affected their culture, performance, and bottom line.
4. **Experimental Studies:** Controlled experiments can be conducted to isolate the impact of diversity on various variables. This may involve creating diverse and non-diverse groups and comparing their performance under similar conditions.
5. **Longitudinal Research:** Monitoring diversity initiatives and their impact over an extended period can reveal trends and evolution in outcomes, offering a more complete picture of diversity's effects.

Outcomes of Diversity Testing

The impact of diversity testing can yield a range of outcomes, depending on the focus and methods used. Some of the key findings include:

1. **Innovation and Creativity:** Many studies have shown that diverse teams are more innovative and creative, bringing different perspectives and ideas to the table.
2. **Problem-solving:** Diverse groups tend to be better at problem-solving and decision-making due to their varied experiences and viewpoints.
3. **Employee Satisfaction:** Inclusive environments tend to boost employee satisfaction and engagement, leading to higher retention rates and improved organizational performance.
4. **Market Reach:** Diverse workforces can help organizations understand and cater to a broader range of customers, expanding their market reach.
5. **Challenges and Conflicts:** Diversity can also lead to challenges and conflicts, especially if not managed well. However, addressing these issues through effective diversity and inclusion strategies can lead to growth and development.
6. **Social Equality:** Testing the impact of diversity can also reveal disparities and discrimination that need to be addressed. It can help policymakers create more equitable societies and workforces.

The Impact of Diversity on Innovation

One of the primary ways to test the impact of diversity is by examining its role in fostering innovation. Diverse teams often bring a broader range of ideas, experiences, and viewpoints to the table. When individuals from various backgrounds collaborate, they can challenge the status quo and generate creative solutions to complex problems.

A study conducted by McKinsey & Company in 2015 found that companies with more diverse executive boards were 35% more likely to outperform their industry peers in terms of profitability. This supports the idea that diversity at the decision-making level can lead to innovative strategies that give organizations a competitive edge.

Additionally, diverse organizations are more likely to hire the best people because they make people from underrepresented groups feel valued and included, which creates a wider range of possible workers. On the other hand, this makes the organisation better at coming up with new ideas.

The Impact of Diversity on Decision-making

Another aspect to consider when testing the impact of diversity is its effect on decision-making. Diverse groups are more likely to engage in thorough and critical discussions when making choices. The presence of individuals with different viewpoints encourages a broader examination of alternatives and can help identify potential biases or blind spots.

Research by the Harvard Business Review indicates that diverse teams tend to make more accurate and effective decisions compared to homogeneous groups. This is because diversity promotes a culture of constructive conflict, where varying perspectives are encouraged and valued, ultimately leading to better-informed choices.

However, it's important to note that the benefits of diversity in decision-making are not automatic. Inclusion and an environment where individuals feel safe to express their opinions are essential to realize these advantages fully.

The Impact of Diversity on Overall Performance

Organizations that embrace diversity often experience improvements in their overall performance. Several key factors contribute to this positive impact:

1. **Enhanced Employee Engagement:** A diverse and inclusive work environment can lead to higher employee engagement. When individuals feel valued and respected for their unique contributions, they tend to be more motivated and committed to their work.
2. **Improved Customer Relations:** Diverse teams can better understand and connect with a wider range of customers, leading to improved customer relations and market reach.
3. **Adaptability and Resilience:** Diverse organizations are often more adaptable and resilient in the face of change. The ability to draw from diverse experiences and perspectives can help navigate turbulent times more effectively.
4. **Global Perspective:** In an increasingly globalized world, organizations with diverse workforces are better positioned to understand and respond to international markets and challenges.

Testing the impact of diversity is a complex and multifaceted endeavour. It requires a combination of quantitative and qualitative methodologies to assess the influence of diversity in organizations and society. While diversity can bring numerous benefits, it also presents challenges that require careful management. In the pursuit of a more inclusive and equitable world, understanding the impact of diversity remains an essential task for businesses, policymakers, and researchers. By comprehensively examining diversity's effects, we can better shape policies, practices, and environments that harness the full potential of diverse perspectives and experiences.

WORKFORCE SEGMENTATION AND SEARCH FOR CRITICAL JOB ROLES

In today's rapidly evolving business landscape, the ability to effectively manage and optimize a workforce is paramount. Organizations must ensure they have the right talent in the right places to remain competitive and agile. One of the key strategies that companies use to achieve this is workforce segmentation, which involves categorizing and prioritizing job roles within the organization. This process allows companies to identify critical job roles and search for individuals who can fill these positions effectively.

Workforce Segmentation

Workforce segmentation is the process of dividing an organization's workforce into distinct categories based on various criteria. These criteria can include job function, skillset, level of responsibility, performance, and potential. The primary purpose of workforce segmentation is to gain a better understanding of the diverse needs and characteristics of different employee groups within an organization.

Importance of Workforce Segmentation

1. **Talent Management:** Workforce segmentation enables organizations to effectively manage their talent pool. By categorizing employees based on their skills and potential, HR and management can make informed decisions about promotions, training, and development opportunities.
2. **Resource Allocation:** It helps in allocating resources strategically. Organizations can identify areas where they need to invest in training, recruitment, or retention efforts, optimizing resource allocation.
3. **Succession Planning:** Workforce segmentation is critical for succession planning. Identifying high-potential employees and grooming them for leadership roles is made more precise through this process.
4. **Diversity and Inclusion:** It plays a role in promoting diversity and inclusion within an organization. Understanding the demographics of different employee groups can inform diversity initiatives.

Search for Critical Job Roles

Once workforce segmentation is complete, the next step is to identify critical job roles within the organization. These roles are essential for the company's success and have a significant impact on its strategic goals and operations.

Significance of Searching for Critical Job Roles

1. **Strategic Alignment:** Identifying critical job roles ensures that the organization's talent aligns with its strategic objectives. This alignment is vital for sustained growth and competitive advantage.
2. **Risk Mitigation:** Recognizing key positions helps in mitigating risks associated with talent shortages. By identifying individuals who can fill these roles or preparing successors, companies can reduce the impact of sudden departures or skill gaps.
3. **Performance Improvement:** Focusing on critical job roles enables organizations to develop and support employees in these positions, ultimately enhancing their performance and productivity.
4. **Employee Engagement:** When employees see their roles as critical and integral to the organization's success, it can boost their engagement and motivation, leading to increased job satisfaction and retention.

Best Practices for Workforce Segmentation and Searching for Critical Job Roles

1. **Data-driven Approach:** Use data and analytics to segment the workforce. This ensures objectivity and minimizes biases in the process.
2. **Regular Review:** Workforce segmentation should be an ongoing process. The business environment evolves, and so do the critical roles within the organization.
3. **Engage Stakeholders:** Involve various stakeholders, including HR, department heads, and senior management, in the segmentation and search processes to gain different perspectives.
4. **Succession Planning:** Combine workforce segmentation with succession planning to ensure a pipeline of talent for critical roles.
5. **Cross-training:** Encourage cross-training and skill development for employees to prepare them for future critical roles.
6. **Communication:** Clearly communicate the criteria for identifying critical roles to all employees to maintain transparency and clarity.

Workforce segmentation and the search for critical job roles are integral components of effective talent management and organizational success. By segmenting the workforce and identifying the roles crucial to the company's objectives, organizations can strategically develop and deploy their talent, ensuring a competitive edge in today's dynamic business environment. These processes demand a data-driven and continuously evolving approach, aligning talent with strategic goals and fostering a culture of employee engagement and development.

FUTURE TRENDS IN DEI ANALYTICS

Some future trends in Diversity, Equity, and Inclusion (DEI) Analytics are:

1. **Predictive Analytics for DEI:** Using machine learning and predictive analytics to forecast future DEI trends, identify potential issues, and proactively design interventions.
2. **AI-Powered Unconscious Bias Detection:** Implementing AI tools that can analyse language, communication patterns, and decision-making processes to detect and address unconscious bias in real-time.
3. **Personalized DEI Interventions:** Tailoring DEI strategies to individual employees based on their specific needs and experiences, creating a more personalized and impactful approach.
4. **Enhanced Intersectional Analysis:** Going beyond single-axis analysis (e.g., gender or ethnicity) to better understand how multiple dimensions of diversity intersect and impact experiences.
5. **Augmented Reality (AR) and Virtual Reality (VR) for Inclusive Training:** Using AR and VR technologies to create immersive, empathy-building experiences that help employees better understand diverse perspectives.
6. **Sentiment Analysis and Emotion Recognition:** Employing advanced sentiment analysis and emotion recognition tools to understand employee sentiments related to DEI issues, both within and outside the workplace.
7. **Integration of External Data Sources:** Combining internal DEI data with external data sources, such as social and economic indicators, to gain a more comprehensive view of DEI challenges and opportunities.
8. **Inclusive Design Thinking:** Applying principles of inclusive design to DEI initiatives, ensuring that products, services, and workplaces are accessible and equitable for all.
9. **DEI in Gig and Remote Workforces:** Developing DEI analytics strategies that cater to the growing gig economy and remote workforce, ensuring equitable opportunities for all workers, regardless of their employment arrangement or location.
10. **Holistic Well-being Metrics:** Expanding DEI analytics to include metrics related to employees' mental, emotional, and physical well-being, recognizing the interconnectedness of DEI and well-being.
11. **Blockchain for Diversity Verification:** Exploring blockchain technology to securely verify and authenticate employees' diverse backgrounds and experiences, reducing the risk of fraud in DEI reporting.
12. **AI-Driven Accessibility Solutions:** Leveraging artificial intelligence to automatically generate accessible content, making digital resources, including job postings and training materials, more inclusive.
13. **Data Storytelling for DEI Impact:** Using data visualization and storytelling techniques to communicate DEI progress and challenges in a compelling and accessible way.
14. **Gamification of DEI Initiatives:** Applying gamification principles to DEI programs to increase engagement and participation, turning DEI initiatives into interactive and enjoyable experiences.

15. **Global DEI Analytics Standards:** Developing and implementing global standards for DEI analytics to enable consistent measurement and benchmarking across industries and regions.

These future trends reflect the evolving nature of DEI analytics, driven by advancements in technology, a growing emphasis on personalization, and a deepening commitment to fostering diverse, equitable, and inclusive workplaces. Organizations that embrace these trends can stay at the forefront of DEI efforts and create more inclusive and equitable environments for their employees.

Questions for Discussion

Short Questions

1. What is DEI Analytics?
2. Why is DEI important in modern organizations?
3. How does DEI analytics contribute to improving workplace diversity and inclusion?
4. What are some key components of DEI Analytics?
5. How can analytics be used to assess pay equity in an organization?
6. What is intersectional analysis in the context of DEI?
7. How does data visualization assist in identifying DEI trends?
8. What strategies can organizations use to mitigate unconscious bias in hiring?
9. What role does transparency play in addressing disparities in the workplace?
10. Why is continuous monitoring important in DEI initiatives?
11. What is benchmarking in the context of Diversity, Equity, and Inclusion (DEI)?
12. How can organizations benefit from benchmarking their DEI metrics?
13. What are some limitations of using industry benchmarks for DEI metrics?
14. What steps are involved in designing targeted DEI strategies?
15. What are some key strategies for inclusive leadership?
16. How can technology and AI be used to improve DEI efforts in recruitment?
17. What are some tools and technologies that can help organizations track and improve inclusion?
18. What should organizations keep in mind when using technology and AI for DEI?

Long Questions

1. Explain the role of analytics in driving Diversity, Equity, and Inclusion (DEI) efforts within organizations. Provide examples of how analytics can be applied in DEI initiatives.
2. Discuss the process of collecting and preparing data for DEI analytics. What are the key considerations for data privacy and security in this context?

3. Analysing DEI data involves quantitative and qualitative methods. Explain how these methods are used to assess and improve diversity, equity, and inclusion in the workplace. Provide examples of each method.
4. How can organizations identify gaps and disparities in their DEI efforts, and what strategies can be employed to conduct root cause analysis for disparities in the workplace?
5. Analysing bias in hiring and promotions is a crucial aspect of DEI analytics. Describe the steps organizations can take to address bias in these processes and ensure fairness in decision-making.
6. Explain the concept of benchmarking in the context of Diversity, Equity, and Inclusion (DEI) metrics. Why is it important for organizations to compare their DEI metrics to industry standards or averages?
7. What are the benefits of benchmarking for DEI metrics, and how can it assist organizations in their DEI efforts? Provide examples.
8. Discuss the limitations of using industry benchmarks for DEI metrics. How can organizations mitigate these limitations to make more informed decisions?
9. Provide a step-by-step guide on how to design targeted DEI strategies, highlighting the importance of data analysis and customization.
10. Explain the concept of data-driven interventions in the context of DEI. How can organizations use data to address specific DEI challenges?
11. Describe the strategies for inclusive leadership and why they are essential for promoting diversity, equity, and inclusion in the workplace.
12. How can technology and AI be leveraged to improve the recruitment process and reduce bias? Provide examples of AI-driven recruitment tools.
13. Discuss the various technology solutions that can be used to track and improve inclusion within an organization. How can these tools enhance the DEI efforts of organizations?
14. What are the potential risks and challenges associated with using technology and AI for DEI? How can organizations ensure that these tools align with their DEI objectives and values?

CHAPTER 7

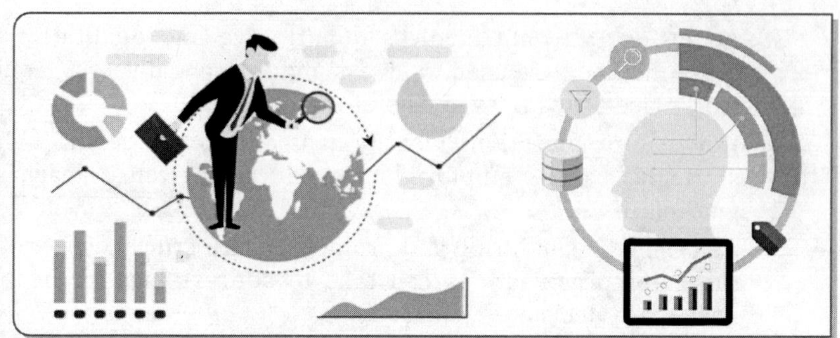

Ethical Considerations in HR Analytics

Using data analytics in human resources management has changed the way companies find, keep, and grow people in the modern era. As technology and data access improve, HR analytics has the potential to give us more information than ever before about the workforce. With these insights, you can make better decisions, improve processes, and get the most out of your human capital, all of which will help your business grow and be more competitive.

HR analytics is changing and becoming more important, but it also brings with it some very important social issues that should not be ignored. Data-driven decision-making is very powerful, but it also comes with a big responsibility: making sure that these insights are learned and used in an honest and responsible way.

This chapter explores deep into the ethical dimensions of HR analytics. It navigates the complex landscape where data-driven insights meet human resources, discussing the key ethical considerations that HR professionals and organizations must grapple with. It examines the delicate balance between reaping the benefits of analytics and safeguarding individual rights, dignity, and fairness in the workplace. Ultimately, the goal is to underscore that while data analytics can undoubtedly drive HR success, the true measure of that success lies in its ethical and responsible application—a commitment to protect and respect the rights and well-being of every employee.

SETTING THE STAGE: THE IMPORTANCE OF ETHICS IN HR ANALYTICS

Using technology and data analytics has greatly changed the field of Human Resources (HR) in today's workplace. HR workers can now access employee data in ways that have never been possible before. This could change how talent is managed, how jobs are filled, how success is evaluated, and how engaged employees are with their work. However, as HR focuses more and more on data-driven insights, it has to deal with a crucial and difficult aspect of this change: the moral issues that HR analytics raise.

Ethics isn't just a theory in HR analytics; it's what makes sure that data is used responsibly to make important HR choices. It's an acknowledgment that the power of data can have big effects on people in the workforce if it's used carelessly. As a result, it is very important to understand and prioritise ethics.

The Significance of HR in Organizations

To understand the importance of ethics in HR analytics, we must first acknowledge the pivotal role that HR plays within any organization. HR is not just a department; it is the custodian of an organization's most invaluable asset—its people. HR is entrusted with the welfare, development, and fair treatment of employees, making it the moral conscience of the workplace.

As HR embraces data-driven practices, it possesses the potential to significantly impact the lives and well-being of employees. These practices can influence hiring decisions, promotions, compensation, and even the overall work environment. With this power comes an ethical imperative: HR must ensure that data-driven decisions are not only accurate but also just and fair.

What HR Analytics can do and What Harm they can do

A lot of good things can come from HR data. It can help businesses find hidden skill gaps, hire the best people more quickly, and make the workplace more diverse and welcoming for everyone. Along with that, it can find trends in how well employees are doing their jobs and how engaged they are with their work, which lets managers take action to boost happiness and productivity.

Such a promise does come with the possibility of danger, though. Personal and sensitive information about workers is often in the data that HR analytics tools gather and look at. Not taking care of this information properly could result in privacy breaches, unfair treatment, and problems at work.

The Need for Ethics

In this age of making decisions based on data, HR workers, data scientists, and business leaders have a moral obligation to do the right thing. They need to understand that behind every piece of data and computer model forecast is a person with rights, worth, and the expectation of being treated fairly.

Ethics in HR Analytics Involves Addressing Critical Questions

- How do we protect employee privacy while extracting valuable insights?
- How can we ensure that algorithms are free from bias and discrimination?
- What measures are in place to maintain transparency and fairness in HR decisions?

Ultimately, ethical HR analytics is about striking a balance between data-driven efficiencies and the ethical responsibilities we owe to our employees. It is about fostering a workplace where every individual is treated with respect, dignity, and equity, regardless of the data that informs HR decisions.

THE RISE OF DATA-DRIVEN HR AND ITS IMPACT ON EMPLOYEE DATA

In recent years, the Human Resources (HR) function has undergone a profound transformation. Traditionally perceived as primarily administrative and people-centric, HR is now increasingly data-driven. This evolution is driven by advancements in technology, the availability of large datasets, and the recognition that data can inform better decision-making. However, the rise of data-driven HR has significant implications for the collection, use, and protection of employee data.

1. *The Evolution of HR into a Data-driven Discipline*

Traditionally, HR decisions were often made based on intuition, experience, and anecdotal evidence. With the advent of technology and the recognition of HR's strategic importance, data analytics has become a cornerstone of HR strategy. This shift is fuelled by several factors:

- **Technological Advancements**: HR now has access to advanced analytics tools, artificial intelligence (AI), and machine learning algorithms that can process vast amounts of data.
- **The Business Case for HR Analytics**: Evidence has shown that data-driven HR practices correlate with improved business outcomes, such as increased productivity, reduced turnover, and better talent acquisition.
- **Increased Data Availability**: HR departments have access to a wealth of data, including employee records, performance metrics, engagement surveys, and external market data.

2. *Employee Data: A Strategic Asset*

As HR becomes more data-driven, employee data is recognized as a strategic asset. It encompasses a wide range of information, from personal details and employment history to performance metrics and sentiment analysis from surveys. This data is used for various purposes such as:

- **Recruitment and Talent Acquisition**: Data helps identify top-performing candidates and optimize recruitment processes.
- **Performance Management**: Metrics enable the assessment of individual and team performance, guiding promotions and development plans.
- **Employee Engagement**: Surveys and sentiment analysis gauge employee satisfaction and engagement levels.
- **Predictive Analytics**: HR leverages data to forecast workforce needs, succession planning, and turnover rates.

3. *Ethical Considerations and Employee Data Privacy*

While the rise of data-driven HR offers numerous benefits, it also raises important ethical considerations, particularly regarding employee data privacy:

- **Informed Consent**: Employees must be informed about the data collected, how it will be used, and provide consent. Transparency is essential to maintain trust.
- **Data Security**: Safeguarding employee data from breaches and unauthorized access is critical. Organizations must implement robust cybersecurity measures.

- **Data Retention**: Ethical data practices include clearly defined data retention policies to protect employees' rights.
- **Bias Mitigation**: Data-driven HR should actively address biases in data collection, algorithms, and decision-making processes.
- **Fairness and Equity**: The use of data for performance evaluation and decision-making must be fair and equitable to avoid discrimination.

The rise of data-driven HR has transformed the function into a strategic partner within organizations. However, this transformation comes with responsibilities. HR professionals must navigate the ethical complexities of data collection, usage, and protection to ensure that the power of employee data is harnessed for the benefit of both the organization and its workforce while respecting privacy and maintaining trust. As data-driven HR continues to evolve, striking this balance will be crucial to its continued success and relevance.

THE NEED FOR ETHICAL FRAMEWORKS IN HR ANALYTICS

The need for ethical frameworks in HR analytics is crucial due to several significant reasons:

1. **Protection of Employee Privacy:** Ethical frameworks establish guidelines for collecting, storing, and handling employee data. This is critical in safeguarding individual privacy rights. Without ethical guidelines, HR analytics could potentially infringe upon personal privacy, leading to mistrust and legal issues.
2. **Bias Mitigation:** Ethical frameworks help identify and mitigate biases in HR analytics. Algorithms and data collection methods can inadvertently perpetuate discrimination. Ethical guidelines promote fairness and non-discrimination, ensuring that HR analytics do not reinforce existing biases.
3. **Transparency and Trust:** Ethical frameworks emphasize transparency in data collection and decision-making processes. When employees understand how their data is used and how decisions are made, they are more likely to trust the organization. Trust is essential for employee engagement and a positive workplace culture.
4. **Legal Compliance:** Adhering to ethical frameworks often aligns with legal requirements. Regulations such as the General Data Protection Regulation (GDPR) and the California Consumer Privacy Act (CCPA) mandate ethical data practices. Failure to comply with these regulations can result in significant fines and legal consequences.
5. **Employee Well-being:** Ethical HR analytics prioritize the well-being of employees. By considering the impact of HR practices on individuals' lives and experiences, organizations can create a more supportive and inclusive work environment.
6. **Equity and Fairness:** Ethical frameworks highlight the importance of equity and fairness in HR decision-making. This is especially critical in areas like recruitment, compensation, and performance evaluations. Ethical guidelines ensure that opportunities are distributed equitably.
7. **Reputation and Brand Image:** Unethical HR analytics practices can damage an organization's reputation and brand image. Negative publicity regarding data breaches, discriminatory practices, or privacy violations can have lasting consequences.

8. **Employee Engagement and Retention:** Ethical HR practices contribute to higher employee engagement and retention. When employees believe they are treated fairly and that their data is handled with care, they are more likely to stay committed to the organization.
9. **Strategic Decision-making:** Ethical HR analytics support strategic decision-making. Ethical frameworks help organizations focus on long-term goals, fostering a workplace culture that is sustainable and aligned with ethical values.
10. **Global Considerations:** In an increasingly globalized world, organizations often operate across borders. Ethical frameworks help navigate the complexities of international data protection laws and cultural differences, ensuring consistency in ethical practices.

Ethical frameworks in HR analytics serve as a guiding light, helping organizations navigate the intricate landscape of data-driven HR practices while prioritizing individual rights, fairness, transparency, and the overall well-being of employees. They not only mitigate risks but also contribute to a positive workplace culture and enhance an organization's reputation.

PRIVACY AND DATA PROTECTION

Privacy and data protection are critical components of ethical considerations in HR analytics. Respecting and safeguarding employee privacy is essential to maintaining trust and compliance with data protection regulations. Following are key aspects of privacy and data protection in HR analytics:

1. **Informed Consent:**
   - Ethical HR analytics begins with obtaining informed consent from employees. Employees should be aware of what data is being collected, why it's being collected, and how it will be used.
   - Consent should be freely given, specific, and revocable without adverse consequences. Employees should have the option to opt in or opt out of data collection and analysis.
2. **Data Minimization:**
   - Collect only the data that is necessary for the stated purpose. Avoid excessive or irrelevant data collection.
   - HR analytics should prioritize collecting data that directly contributes to improving HR practices and employee well-being.
3. **Anonymization and Pseudonymization:**
   - Anonymizing or pseudonymizing data helps protect individual identities while allowing for analysis. Personal identifiers should be removed or replaced with unique identifiers.
   - Ensure that data cannot be re-identified easily, preserving employee anonymity.
4. **Data Security:**
   - Data security is fundamental to data protection. HR analytics data must be stored securely, both physically and electronically, to prevent unauthorized access or breaches.
   - Implement encryption, access controls, and regular security audits to protect employee data.

5. **Transparency:**
   - Transparency is a key ethical principle. Clearly communicate to employees how their data will be used, who will have access to it, and what safeguards are in place.
   - Publish data protection policies and make them easily accessible to employees.
6. **Data Retention and Deletion:**
   - Establish clear data retention policies that specify how long HR data will be retained. Once data is no longer needed for its intended purpose, it should be securely deleted.
   - Respect employees' right to be forgotten, allowing them to request the deletion of their data.
7. **Regular Audits and Compliance:**
   - Conduct regular audits to ensure compliance with data protection regulations and ethical standards. Keep up-to-date with evolving laws, such as GDPR, CCPA, and HIPAA, as they relate to HR data.
   - Appoint a data protection officer or designate someone responsible for data protection.
8. **Third-Party Vendors:**
   - If third-party vendors are involved in HR analytics (e.g., HR software providers, data analytics firms), ensure they also adhere to strict data protection standards.
   - Contracts should include provisions for data security and compliance.
9. **Employee Education:**
   - Educate employees about their rights regarding data protection. Provide training on data security practices and how to report data breaches or concerns.
   - Encourage a culture of data privacy within the organization.
10. **Data Impact Assessments:** Conduct Data Protection Impact Assessments (DPIAs) for HR analytics projects that involve high risks to individuals' privacy. DPIAs help identify and mitigate privacy risks.
11. **Cross-Border Data Transfer:** If HR data is transferred across international borders, ensure compliance with data protection laws in both the originating and receiving countries.

Privacy and data protection in HR analytics are not only ethical imperatives but also legal obligations in many jurisdictions. Organizations that prioritize these principles demonstrate their commitment to protecting employee rights and fostering trust in the workplace.

BIAS AND FAIRNESS IN ETHICAL CONSIDERATIONS IN HR ANALYTICS

Bias and fairness are critical aspects of ethical considerations in HR analytics. Addressing bias and promoting fairness ensures that HR analytics practices are equitable, unbiased, and aligned with ethical principles. Following are the bias and fairness in HR analytics:

1. **Bias in HR Analytics:** Bias in HR analytics refers to the presence of systematic and unfair discrimination in data collection, analysis, or decision-making processes. Bias can manifest in various ways:
   - **Selection Bias:** Occurs when certain groups are overrepresented or under-represented in data, leading to skewed results.

- **Algorithmic Bias:** Arises when machine learning algorithms or predictive models perpetuate existing biases in recruitment, performance evaluations, or promotions.
- **Cultural Bias:** Results from cultural insensitivity in surveys or assessments, making them less accurate or relevant for diverse employee groups.
- **Confirmation Bias:** Occurs when analysts or decision-makers interpret data in a way that confirms their pre-existing beliefs or stereotypes.

TABLE 7.1 Bias in data collection and algorithms

Aspect	*Description*
Definition	Bias refers to systematic and unfair discrimination in data collection, analysis, or decision-making processes.
Types of Bias	• ***Selection Bias:*** Certain groups are overrepresented or under-represented in data.
	• ***Algorithmic Bias:*** Machine learning algorithms perpetuate existing biases.
	• ***Cultural Bias:*** Surveys or assessments may lack cultural sensitivity.
	• ***Confirmation Bias:*** Analysts interpret data to confirm pre-existing beliefs or stereotypes.
Causes	• ***Historical Bias:*** Data reflects historical discrimination.
	• ***Data Collection Methods:*** Biases can be introduced during data collection.
	• ***Sampling Methods:*** Unrepresentative sampling can lead to selection bias.
	• ***Algorithm Training Data:*** Biased training data can lead to algorithmic bias.
Impact	• Reinforces existing inequalities in HR practices.
	• Can lead to discriminatory hiring, promotions, and compensation decisions.
	• Lowers employee morale and engagement, particularly among marginalized groups.
Challenges	• Identifying bias in complex data sets can be challenging.
	• Balancing fairness and accuracy in algorithmic decision-making is complex.
	• Cultural biases are context-dependent and may be challenging to detect.

(*Contd.*)

Aspect	Description
Mitigation	• Regularly review data collection methods and sources for potential bias.
	• Implement debiasing techniques in data pre-processing and model development.
	• Use diverse and representative data to train algorithms.
	• Conduct fairness tests on algorithms to identify and correct bias.
Ethical Considerations	Bias in data collection and algorithms raises ethical concerns about fairness and discrimination.
	Addressing bias aligns with ethical frameworks for responsible HR analytics.

Addressing bias in data collection and algorithms is crucial for ensuring fairness, equity, and ethical HR practices. It requires ongoing monitoring, transparency, and a commitment to promoting diversity and inclusion within organizations.

2. **Fairness in HR Analytics:** Fairness, on the other hand, is the absence of discrimination or bias in HR practices. Fairness involves treating all employees equally and providing equitable opportunities. In HR analytics, fairness can be broken down into several dimensions:
   - **Procedural Fairness:** Ensuring that HR processes, such as hiring and promotions, are transparent, consistent, and free from bias.
   - **Outcome Fairness:** Ensuring that the outcomes of HR decisions are equitable and do not disproportionately benefit or harm any particular group.
   - **Individual Fairness:** Treating each employee as an individual, considering their unique strengths and qualifications, rather than making decisions based on group characteristics.
   - **Opportunity Fairness:** Ensuring that all employees have equal access to opportunities for career advancement, training, and development.

TABLE 7.2 Dimension of fairness

Dimension of fairness	*Description*
Procedural Fairness	Ensures that HR processes, such as hiring, promotion, and performance evaluation, are conducted transparently and consistently.
Outcome Fairness	Ensures that the outcomes of HR decisions, such as compensation, promotions, and termination, are equitable and do not disproportionately benefit or harm any particular group.
Individual Fairness	Focuses on treating each employee as an individual, considering their unique qualifications, skills, and experiences, rather than making decisions based solely on group characteristics.
Opportunity Fairness	Guarantees that all employees have equal access to opportunities for career advancement, training, development, and other benefits, regardless of their background or identity.

3. **The Role of Ethical Frameworks:** Ethical frameworks provide guidance on identifying and mitigating bias while promoting fairness in HR analytics. They help organizations:
   - **Develop Bias Mitigation Strategies:** Ethical frameworks encourage the use of debiasing techniques in data collection and model development to reduce the impact of bias.
   - **Promote Diversity and Inclusion:** Ethical guidelines encourage organizations to actively foster diversity and inclusion, not just in data collection but also in hiring and promotion practices.
   - **Enhance Transparency:** Ethical practices emphasize transparency in explaining how HR decisions are made, ensuring that employees understand the criteria used.
   - **Regular Auditing:** Ethical frameworks may recommend regular audits of HR analytics processes to identify and rectify bias or unfairness.

TABLE 7.3 The role of ethical frameworks in HR analytics

Role of ethical frameworks in HR analytics	*Description*
1. Bias mitigation	• Ethical frameworks guide organizations in identifying and mitigating bias in data collection, analysis, and decision-making.
	• They promote the use of debiasing techniques to reduce the impact of bias in algorithms and data-driven HR practices.
2. Promoting diversity and inclusion	• Ethical guidelines encourage organizations to actively foster diversity and inclusion in all aspects of HR analytics.
	• They emphasize the importance of considering diverse perspectives and experiences in data collection, analysis, and decision-making.
3. Enhancing transparency	• Ethical frameworks stress the need for transparency in explaining how HR decisions are made based on data and analytics.
	• Transparency builds trust among employees by ensuring they understand the criteria and processes used in HR practices.
4. Regular auditing	• Ethical practices may recommend regular audits of HR analytics processes to identify and rectify bias or unfairness.
	• Auditing helps organizations continuously improve their data-driven HR practices and align them with ethical standards.

(*Contd.*)

Role of ethical frameworks in HR analytics	*Description*
5. Ensuring equal opportunities	• Ethical frameworks underscore the importance of ensuring that HR analytics provide equal opportunities and outcomes for all employees.
	• They guide organizations in developing strategies that promote fairness in areas such as recruitment, promotions, and compensation.
6. Training and awareness	• Ethical guidelines encourage organizations to provide training to analysts, decision-makers, and employees on recognizing and addressing bias.
	• They promote awareness of the ethical implications of HR analytics and the role of individuals in upholding ethical standards.
7. Incorporating employee feedback	• Ethical frameworks emphasize the value of soliciting feedback from employees regarding HR practices and analytics.
	• Employee feedback helps identify potential bias or fairness issues and fosters a culture of openness and accountability.

4. **Addressing Bias and Promoting Fairness:** To address bias and promote fairness in HR analytics, organizations should:
   - **Regularly Review Data:** Continuously review data collection methods and data sources to identify and correct bias.
   - **Train Analysts:** Provide training to analysts and decision-makers on recognizing and mitigating bias in data and algorithms.
   - **Use Diverse Data:** Ensure that data used in HR analytics represents diverse employee groups, allowing for more accurate insights.
   - **Test for Fairness:** Implement fairness tests on algorithms to ensure that they provide equal opportunities and outcomes for all groups.
   - **Solicit Employee Feedback:** Encourage employees to provide feedback on HR practices and analytics, enabling the identification of potential bias or fairness issues.
   - **Monitor Outcomes:** Continuously monitor HR outcomes to detect any disparities and take corrective actions promptly.

Addressing bias and promoting fairness in HR analytics is not just an ethical imperative but also a strategic one. Fair and unbiased HR practices contribute to a positive workplace culture, improve employee morale, and support organizational goals related to diversity and inclusion.

TABLE 7.4 De-biasing techniques commonly used in HR analytics, along with their limitations

Debiasing technique	*Description*	*Limitations*
1. Blind recruitment	Removing personally identifiable information (PII) from job applications to reduce bias.	• May not eliminate all biases. • Could lead to other issues such as lack of context.
2. Anonymized resumes	Replacing names with unique identifiers on resumes to hide gender, ethnicity, or other traits.	• Does not address bias in interviews or during actual job performance assessment.
3. Structured interviews	Using a standardized set of questions for all candidates to ensure consistency.	• Interviewer bias can still affect the evaluation process. • Limited flexibility for follow-up questions.
4. Blind auditions	Implementing auditions or trials where candidates are evaluated solely based on performance.	• Feasible in some industries, not all. • May not address biases related to other factors like age or disability.
5. Machine learning fairness tools	Using specialized algorithms to identify and mitigate bias in AI and machine learning models.	• Requires expertise in AI and machine learning. • May not completely eliminate complex biases.
6. Diversity training	Conducting training programs to raise awareness about biases and promote diversity and inclusion.	• Effectiveness varies; some studies suggest limited impact. • Can sometimes reinforce stereotypes.
7. Decision review panels	Involving multiple reviewers to evaluate decisions like promotions to minimize individual bias.	• Can be resource-intensive and time-consuming. • May not fully eliminate collective bias.

If one want to reduce bias in HR data, these debiasing methods are very useful. They do have some problems, though, and it's important to know that a mix of tactics is often needed to fully fix bias in HR practices. These methods also need to be constantly checked and changed so they can adapt to new biases and changing workplace relations.

TRANSPARENCY AND EXPLAIN ABILITY IN ETHICAL CONSIDERATIONS IN HR ANALYTICS

Transparency and explain ability are critical aspects of ethical considerations in HR analytics. They involve making the processes and outcomes of HR analytics clear and understandable to employees, stakeholders, and decision-makers. Following are the points which clarifies why transparency and explain ability are essential:

1. **Building Trust and Confidence:**
   - Transparency in data collection and analysis fosters trust among employees. When they understand how data is used, they are more likely to trust that their information is handled ethically.
   - Explain ability in decision-making processes, especially in recruitment or promotions, helps employees perceive fairness, leading to greater confidence in HR practices.
2. **Accountability and Responsibility:**
   - Transparent HR analytics hold organizations accountable for their data-driven decisions. When employees and stakeholders can trace decisions back to data and analytics, it becomes clear who is responsible for those decisions.
   - Explain ability ensures that organizations can defend their decisions when questioned by employees, regulators, or external parties.
3. **Compliance with Regulations:**
   - Many data privacy regulations, such as GDPR, require transparency in data processing. Organizations must inform individuals about how their data is used and provide mechanisms for opting out or correcting inaccuracies.
   - Explain ability can help organizations comply with regulations that require them to explain automated decisions, especially those with legal or significant consequences.
4. **Avoiding Discrimination and Bias:**
   - Transparency in algorithms and data sources helps identify and mitigate biases. When the inner workings of algorithms are hidden, it's difficult to assess whether they are perpetuating bias.
   - Explain ability allows organizations to identify and rectify biased decision-making processes.
5. **Facilitating Employee Feedback:** When employees understand how HR analytics affect them, they are more likely to provide feedback. This feedback can be invaluable in improving HR practices and refining data collection and analysis methods.
6. **Employee Development and Growth:** Explain ability in performance evaluations and promotions enables employees to see how they can improve and grow within the organization. Clear feedback promotes professional development.
7. **Inclusivity and Diversity:** Transparent hiring and promotion processes that are well-explained can attract a diverse range of candidates. When individuals believe they have an equal opportunity, they are more likely to apply for positions.
8. **Ethical Decision-making:** Transparency and explain ability serve as ethical guardrails. They ensure that HR analytics adhere to ethical principles and do not make opaque or questionable decisions.
9. **Avoiding Legal Consequences:** Lack of transparency and explain ability can result in legal challenges. Organizations that cannot provide a clear rationale for HR decisions may face legal action for discrimination or privacy violations.
10. **Ethical Reputation:** Transparent and explainable HR practices contribute to an ethical reputation. Organizations known for ethical HR analytics are more likely to attract top talent and gain the trust of customers and partners.

Transparency and explain ability are not only ethical imperatives but also practical necessities in HR analytics. They enhance trust, accountability, and fairness while helping organizations navigate legal requirements and attract a diverse and talented workforce.

ETHICAL DECISION-MAKING

Ethical decision-making in HR analytics is essential to ensure that data-driven HR practices align with moral principles, respect employee rights, and promote fairness. Following are steps and considerations for ethical decision-making in HR analytics:

1. **Define Ethical Principles:** Establish clear ethical principles and values that guide HR analytics practices within your organization. These principles should prioritize respect for individuals, fairness, transparency, and the protection of privacy.
2. **Identify Ethical Dilemmas:** Recognize potential ethical dilemmas in HR analytics, such as issues related to data privacy, bias, transparency, and fairness. Be proactive in identifying situations where ethical concerns may arise.
3. **Gather Relevant Information:** Before making any decisions, gather all relevant information about the HR analytics process in question. Understand the data being collected, the algorithms used, and the potential impact on employees.
4. **Assess the Consequences:** Consider the potential consequences of your HR analytics decisions. How might they affect employees' privacy, job opportunities, or well-being? Assess both short-term and long-term impacts.
5. **Consider Legal and Regulatory Requirements:** Ensure that your HR analytics practices comply with applicable laws and regulations, such as data protection laws (e.g., GDPR, CCPA). Legal compliance is a fundamental aspect of ethical HR analytics.
6. **Involve Stakeholders:** Engage with relevant stakeholders, including HR professionals, data scientists, employees, and legal experts, in the decision-making process. Collect diverse perspectives to ensure a well-rounded understanding of the ethical implications.
7. **Evaluate Data Sources and Methods:** Scrutinize the sources of data and the methods used for data collection, analysis, and decision-making. Identify any potential biases or sources of unfairness in the process.
8. **Promote Transparency:** Emphasize transparency throughout the HR analytics process. Communicate openly with employees about the data being collected, how it will be used, and the potential impacts on their employment.
9. **Mitigate Bias and Ensure Fairness:** Implement strategies to minimize biases in data collection and algorithms. Regularly audit and test your analytics models for fairness and equity. Be prepared to make adjustments when biases are detected.
10. **Seek Ethical Guidance:** When faced with complex ethical dilemmas, seek guidance from experts in ethics, legal professionals, or industry organizations that specialize in HR ethics.
11. **Document Ethical Decisions:** Maintain clear records of your ethical decision-making processes. Document the rationale behind your choices and the steps taken to address ethical concerns.

12. **Continuously Monitor and Improve:** Ethical HR analytics is an ongoing process. Continuously monitor the impact of your analytics initiatives and make improvements as needed to align with ethical standards.
13. **Training and Education:** Provide training and education to HR professionals and data analysts on ethical considerations in HR analytics. Raise awareness of the importance of ethical decision-making.
14. **Encourage Whistleblowing:** Establish channels for employees and stakeholders to report ethical concerns witout fear of retaliation. Encourage a culture of ethical accountability.
15. **Review and Revise Ethical Guidelines:** Periodically review and revise your organization's ethical guidelines and principles to adapt to evolving HR analytics practices and emerging ethical challenges.

By following these steps and considerations, HR professionals can make ethical decisions in the realm of HR analytics, ensuring that data-driven HR practices respect individuals' rights and promote a fair and inclusive workplace.

CODES OF CONDUCT AND GUIDELINES

Codes of conduct and guidelines in HR analytics serve as essential frameworks that guide professionals and organizations in the ethical use of data and analytics in human resources. They ensure that HR analytics processes are fair, transparent, and respectful of employee rights and privacy. Following are some prominent codes of conduct and guidelines in HR analytics:

1. **Society for Human Resource Management (SHRM) Code of Ethics**: SHRM provides a comprehensive code of ethics that emphasizes the importance of HR professionals' ethical behaviour in all aspects of HR, including HR analytics. It encourages practitioners to uphold the highest standards of integrity, fairness, and confidentiality when using data for HR decisions.
2. **The European General Data Protection Regulation (GDPR)**: GDPR is a robust framework for data protection and privacy, applicable to HR analytics within the European Union (EU). It outlines strict requirements for handling employee data, including transparency, consent, data minimization, and the right to be forgotten.
3. **The General Data Protection Regulation (GDPR) HR Guidelines**: The EU's GDPR also provides specific guidelines for HR data processing. These guidelines address consent, data protection impact assessments, and data subject rights concerning HR analytics.
4. **The Institute for Operations Research and the Management Sciences (INFORMS) Code of Ethics**: While not specific to HR, INFORMS provides ethical guidelines for analytics professionals. HR analysts can draw upon these principles, which include transparency, accountability, and ensuring that models do not perpetuate discrimination.
5. **The International Association for Privacy Professionals (IAPP) Code of Conduct**: This organization focuses on data privacy and protection. Their code of conduct outlines principles related to privacy and data protection that are highly relevant to HR analytics professionals.

6. **The AI Ethics Guidelines for the European Commission**: These guidelines include principles and requirements for trustworthy AI. While not specific to HR analytics, they address issues such as bias, transparency, and accountability, which are crucial considerations in the use of AI in HR.
7. **The Human Resources Professionals Association (HRPA) Code of Ethics**: HRPA, based in Ontario, Canada, offers a code of ethics for HR professionals, which includes provisions related to respecting confidentiality, maintaining competence, and avoiding conflicts of interest in HR analytics.
8. **The Ethical Guidelines for Statistical Practice by the American Statistical Association**: These guidelines, although not HR-specific, offer ethical principles that statisticians and data analysts, including HR analysts, can apply. They emphasize transparency, honesty, and accountability in data analysis.
9. **The Data and Marketing Association (DMA) Code of Ethics**: While primarily focused on marketing, DMA's code includes principles relevant to HR analytics, such as data privacy, transparency, and consent.

HR professionals and organizations should familiarize themselves with these codes of conduct and guidelines to ensure that their HR analytics practices align with ethical standards and legal requirements. It's essential to stay updated with evolving regulations and best practices to maintain ethical and responsible data usage in HR analytics.

THE IMPORTANCE OF ADHERING TO INDUSTRY STANDARDS

It is very important for HR statistics to follow industry standards for a number of reasons:

1. **Legal Compliance:** Industry standards often align with legal requirements and regulations related to data privacy, security, and employment practices. Compliance with these standards helps organizations avoid legal issues, fines, and penalties.
2. **Data Protection:** Many industry standards provide guidelines for handling and protecting employee data. Adhering to these standards ensures that sensitive personal information is safeguarded, fostering trust among employees.
3. **Risk Mitigation:** Failure to comply with industry standards can lead to data breaches, privacy violations, and reputational damage. Adherence reduces the risk of these negative consequences.
4. **Ethical Considerations:** Industry standards often incorporate ethical principles, emphasizing fairness, non-discrimination, and transparency. Adhering to these standards ensures that HR analytics practices align with ethical norms.
5. **Consistency:** Industry standards promote uniformity and consistency in data collection, analysis, and reporting. This consistency enables meaningful comparisons across organizations and industries.
6. **Benchmarking:** Organizations can use industry standards as benchmarks to evaluate their HR analytics practices. This allows them to assess their performance relative to peers and competitors.
7. **Employee Trust:** When employees know that their data is handled in accordance with industry standards, they are more likely to trust the organization. Trust is essential for open communication and engagement.

8. **Stakeholder Confidence:** Adherence to industry standards enhances the confidence of stakeholders, including investors, customers, and partners, in the organization's commitment to responsible HR analytics.
9. **Quality Assurance:** Standards often include best practices for data quality, analysis, and reporting. Following these practices ensures that HR analytics efforts produce accurate and reliable results.
10. **Continuous Improvement:** Industry standards evolve to reflect emerging trends, technologies, and ethical considerations. Adhering to these standards encourages organizations to stay updated and continuously improve their HR analytics practices.
11. **Global Operations:** For organizations with a global presence, adherence to industry standards helps navigate the complexities of data protection and privacy laws in different countries.
12. **Competitive Advantage:** Demonstrating compliance with industry standards can be a competitive advantage. It signals to potential employees, customers, and partners that the organization takes data privacy and ethical considerations seriously.

ETHICAL DECISION-MAKING TOOLS FOR HR PROFESSIONALS

Ethical decision-making in HR analytics is critical to ensure that data-driven initiatives respect individuals' rights, maintain fairness, and uphold transparency. HR professionals can utilize various tools and approaches to guide ethical decision-making in this context. Following are some ethical decision-making tools and strategies for HR professionals in HR analytics:

1. **Ethical Frameworks:**
   - **Utilitarianism:** Assess the consequences of a decision and choose the one that maximizes overall well-being for employees and the organization.
   - **Deontology:** Apply a set of ethical rules and principles, such as respect for autonomy and fairness, when making HR analytics decisions.
   - **Virtue Ethics:** Focus on developing virtues like honesty, transparency, and empathy in HR analytics practices.
2. **Ethical Decision-making Models:**
   - **The Ethical Decision-making Model by Rest:** This model involves steps such as recognizing the ethical issue, gathering relevant information, considering alternative courses of action, making a decision, and reflecting on the decision's consequences.
   - **The PLUS Ethical Decision-making Model:** PLUS, stands for People, Legal, Unethical, and Societal. It guides professionals to consider the impact on individuals, legal implications, unethical aspects, and broader societal consequences of their decisions.
3. **Codes of Ethics and Guidelines:** Refer to established HR associations' codes of ethics and ethical guidelines, such as those provided by the Society for Human Resource Management (SHRM) or the Chartered Institute of Personnel and Development (CIPD). These codes offer principles and standards for ethical HR analytics practices.

4. **Stakeholder Analysis:** Consider the interests and perspectives of all stakeholders involved in HR analytics, including employees, leadership, customers, and regulatory authorities. Analyse how decisions may affect each group.
5. **Privacy Impact Assessments (PIAs):** Conduct PIAs to evaluate the impact of HR analytics initiatives on individual privacy. Assess the necessity of data collection, the security measures in place, and the potential risks to employees.
6. **Data Ethics Committees:** Establish cross-functional committees within the organization dedicated to reviewing and providing ethical guidance on HR analytics projects. Include experts from HR, legal, IT, and ethics departments.
7. **Ethical Training and Education:** Provide ongoing training to HR professionals on ethical considerations in HR analytics. Include case studies, scenario-based learning, and discussions on real-world ethical dilemmas.
8. **Ethical Auditing and Compliance Checks:** Regularly audit HR analytics practices to ensure compliance with ethical standards and relevant laws. Address any identified ethical issues promptly.
9. **Fairness Impact Assessments:** Evaluate the fairness of HR analytics models and decisions using fairness impact assessments. Check for bias and disparities in outcomes, especially regarding protected characteristics.
10. **Ethical Data Governance:** Establish data governance practices that prioritize ethics, including clear data collection, storage, and usage policies. Ensure that employees understand how their data is used.
11. **Open and Inclusive Decision-making:** Involve a diverse group of stakeholders in the decision-making process related to HR analytics initiatives. Encourage input from employees and seek diverse perspectives.
12. **Continuous Ethical Reflection:** Encourage HR professionals to engage in continuous ethical reflection and discussion. Foster a culture where employees can raise ethical concerns without fear of retaliation.

These tools and strategies can help HR professionals navigate the complex ethical landscape of HR analytics. By integrating ethical considerations into every step of the HR analytics process, organizations can build trust with employees, mitigate risks, and ensure that data-driven decisions align with ethical principles and values.

FUTURE TRENDS AND CHALLENGES

As we look to the future of ethics issues in HR analytics, we can see both positive trends and difficult problems.

Trends

1. **AI Ethics:** With the increasing use of artificial intelligence (AI) in HR analytics, there will be a growing focus on AI ethics. Organizations will need to ensure that AI-driven decisions are transparent, fair, and free from biases. Ethical AI design and responsible AI practices will become essential.

2. **Responsible Data Use:** The responsible use of employee data will be a top priority. This includes not only collecting and storing data ethically but also ensuring that data is used in ways that benefit employees and the organization without compromising privacy.
3. **Global Data Governance:** As data flows across borders, organizations will need to navigate a complex landscape of international data protection laws. Ethical considerations will include complying with diverse regulations and respecting cultural differences in data handling.
4. **Ethical AI Audits:** Ethical audits of AI algorithms and HR analytics processes will become more common. Organizations will need to regularly assess the ethical implications of their data-driven decisions and make necessary adjustments.
5. **Employee Consent and Control:** Giving employees more control over their data and how it's used will be a growing trend. This might include allowing employees to opt in or out of certain data collection practices and providing them with more transparency.
6. **Collaboration with Ethical Experts:** Organizations will collaborate with ethicists, data ethicists, and privacy experts to ensure that HR analytics practices align with ethical principles. Ethical expertise will become a crucial part of HR analytics teams.

Challenges

1. **Algorithmic Bias:** Ensuring that algorithms used in HR analytics are free from bias remains a significant challenge. Bias can lead to discriminatory outcomes in areas like recruitment and performance evaluations.
2. **Data Security:** The more data organizations collect, the greater the risk of data breaches. Ethical challenges will involve maintaining data security to protect employee information.
3. **Informed Consent Complexity:** Obtaining informed consent for data collection can be challenging, especially in cases where employees may not fully understand the implications of data usage. Organizations will need to find ways to obtain meaningful consent.
4. **Transparency in AI:** Achieving transparency in AI and machine learning algorithms can be difficult, especially in complex models. Ethical challenges will revolve around making AI decisions more understandable to employees.
5. **Balancing Automation and Human Oversight:** As HR analytics becomes more automated, finding the right balance between automation and human oversight to ensure ethical practices will be a challenge.
6. **Data Ethics Education:** There is a shortage of professionals with expertise in data ethics. Organizations will face challenges in educating their workforce about ethical considerations in HR analytics.
7. **Continuous Ethical Review:** Keeping pace with evolving ethical standards and regulations in HR analytics will require ongoing attention and resources.

In conclusion, ethical considerations in HR analytics will continue to evolve in response to technological advancements and changing data privacy regulations. To navigate these trends and challenges successfully, organizations must prioritize ethics as an integral part of their HR analytics strategies and seek to strike a balance between data-driven insights and ethical responsibility.

INTERNATIONAL PERSPECTIVES ON HR ANALYTICS ETHICS

International perspectives on HR analytics ethics vary due to differences in cultural norms, legal frameworks, and business practices. Following are some key considerations and perspectives from various regions:

1. **Europe—GDPR Compliance:** European countries, particularly those in the European Union (EU), place a strong emphasis on data privacy and protection. The General Data Protection Regulation (GDPR) has a significant impact on HR analytics. Employers must obtain explicit consent for data collection, ensure data accuracy, and notify individuals about data breaches. There's also a focus on data minimization, meaning that only necessary data should be collected. EU countries stress the importance of employees' right to access and rectify their personal data, making transparency a crucial element of HR analytics.
2. **United States—Equal Employment Opportunity (EEO) Compliance:** In the United States, the Equal Employment Opportunity Commission (EEOC) enforces anti-discrimination laws. HR analytics must comply with these regulations to avoid bias and discrimination in hiring, promotion, and termination decisions. While there's no single data privacy law like the GDPR, employers must be cautious about collecting, storing, and using employee data. Ethical considerations often revolve around ensuring equal opportunities for all, minimizing bias in algorithms, and maintaining employee consent for data usage.
3. **Asia—Data Privacy and Cultural Sensitivity:** Asian countries, including Japan, South Korea, and Singapore, have their data privacy laws and regulations. Ethical concerns often centre around cultural sensitivities and the handling of sensitive personal information. In countries like China, where AI is heavily used in HR analytics, there's a growing concern about transparency and fairness in algorithmic decision-making. Ethical HR analytics in Asia also involves addressing diversity and inclusion, given the diverse workforce in many countries.
4. **Latin America—Data Protection and Consent:** In Latin American countries like Brazil and Mexico, data protection regulations are becoming more stringent. Consent, data security, and transparency are central ethical considerations. HR analytics must respect individuals' rights to privacy and provide clear explanations of data usage. Cultural nuances also play a role, as there's often an emphasis on interpersonal relationships in HR practices.
5. **Africa—Emerging Concerns:** Africa is an emerging market for HR analytics, and ethical considerations are evolving. Data privacy and consent are becoming more critical as analytics practices grow. HR professionals in African countries must navigate the balance between data-driven decision-making and ethical considerations, particularly in addressing diversity and inclusion.

6. **Global Organizations—Standardization:** Multinational companies operating across borders must adhere to various data protection and HR regulations. Many are adopting global HR analytics ethics standards to ensure consistency and fairness. They are increasingly mindful of cultural differences, striving for inclusive practices that respect local values and norms.

International perspectives on HR analytics ethics reflect a balance between data-driven decision-making and the protection of individual rights and values. Adherence to local regulations and global ethical standards is essential for organizations operating in multiple regions. Additionally, HR professionals must remain adaptable and culturally sensitive in their HR analytics practices to navigate diverse global landscapes.

NAVIGATING CROSS-BORDER DATA ISSUES ETHICALLY

Navigating cross-border data issues ethically is a critical consideration, especially in HR analytics, where employee data is often involved. Following are some ethical principles and strategies for handling cross-border data issues:

1. **Compliance with International Data Protection Laws:**
   - Understand and comply with the data protection laws of the countries where your organization operates and where data is processed. This includes GDPR in Europe, CCPA in California, and many others.
   - Appoint a Data Protection Officer (DPO) or equivalent, where required by law.
2. **Data Minimization and Purpose Limitation:**
   - Collect and process only the data that is necessary for the intended purpose.
   - Clearly define the purpose of data processing and ensure it aligns with lawful and ethical standards.
3. **Informed Consent Across Borders:**
   - Ensure that you have obtained informed consent from employees to process their data, especially when data is transferred across borders.
   - Clearly communicate to employees how their data will be used, where it will be stored, and if it will be transferred internationally.
4. **Secure Data Transfer Mechanisms:**
   - Use secure methods for transferring data across borders, such as encryption and secure data transfer protocols.
   - Consider data residency requirements and choose data centres and cloud providers that comply with local regulations.
5. **Cross-Border Data Transfer Agreements:**
   - Implement Standard Contractual Clauses (SCCs) or Binding Corporate Rules (BCRs) when transferring data between regions.
   - Ensure these agreements uphold the rights and privacy of data subjects.
6. **Vendor Selection and Due Diligence:**
   - When working with third-party vendors, conduct due diligence to ensure they comply with data protection regulations and ethical data practices.
   - Include data protection clauses in contracts with vendors to hold them accountable.

7. **Data Impact Assessments (DPIAs):**
    - Conduct Data Protection Impact Assessments to evaluate the potential risks to data subjects when transferring data across borders.
    - Mitigate identified risks to protect the rights and interests of employees.
8. **Data Localization and Storage:**
    - If data localization laws apply, store data within the borders of the respective country.
    - Balance this requirement with the need for efficient data management and security.
9. **Cross-Border Employee Training:**
    - Train employees about the implications of cross-border data transfers and the organization's commitment to data protection.
    - Ensure that employees are aware of their rights regarding their data.
10. **Incident Response Planning:**
    - Develop and communicate an incident response plan in case of data breaches or other cross-border data issues.
    - Promptly report data breaches to authorities and affected individuals as required by law.
11. **Regular Auditing and Monitoring:**
    - Regularly audit data practices and cross-border data transfers to ensure compliance with evolving regulations.
    - Monitor changes in international data protection laws and adjust strategies accordingly.
12. **Transparency and Accountability:**
    - Be transparent with employees about data practices and demonstrate accountability by adhering to ethical standards.
    - Foster a culture of responsibility and data ethics within the organization.
13. **Consult Legal and Compliance Experts:** Consult with legal and compliance experts who specialize in data protection to navigate complex cross-border data issues effectively.

Ethical handling of cross-border data issues is not only a legal requirement but also crucial for maintaining trust with employees and stakeholders. Organizations that prioritize data ethics are better positioned to manage the complexities of global HR analytics while upholding individual rights and privacy.

Questions for Discussion

Short Questions

1. What is the significance of ethics in HR analytics in the modern workplace?
2. How has data-driven HR transformed traditional HR practices?
3. What is the role of ethical frameworks in HR analytics?

4. Why is transparency crucial in HR analytics?
5. How can organizations mitigate bias in HR analytics?
6. What is the importance of explain ability in HR analytics?
7. How does ethical decision-making impact HR analytics practices?
8. Why should organizations seek guidance from experts in HR ethics?
9. How does SHRM's Code of Ethics influence HR analytics practices?
10. What are the key principles of GDPR as it relates to HR analytics?
11. What is the role of the International Association for Privacy Professionals (IAPP) in HR analytics?
12. Why is adherence to industry standards important in HR analytics?
13. How do industry standards promote transparency in data analysis?
14. What ethical decision-making tools can HR professionals use in HR analytics?
15. What is the significance of continuous ethical reflection in HR analytics?

Long Questions

1. In the context of HR analytics, what are the potential ethical dilemmas that organizations might face, and how can they address these challenges while respecting employee rights and ensuring fairness?
2. Explain the evolution of HR from an intuition-based discipline to a data-driven one. What factors have driven this transformation, and what ethical considerations arise from this shift?
3. Discuss the ethical principles and values that organizations should define to guide their HR analytics practices. How do these principles prioritize transparency, fairness, and privacy protection?
4. How can organizations promote transparency throughout the HR analytics process, and why is this important for building trust and confidence among employees and stakeholders?
5. What steps can HR professionals take to ensure that their data-driven HR practices comply with legal and regulatory requirements, particularly in the context of data protection laws like GDPR and CCPA?
6. Explain the role of explain ability in HR analytics and how it relates to employee development, inclusivity, and ethical decision-making.
7. How can organizations create a culture of ethical accountability in HR analytics, and why is it essential to encourage whistleblowing and open reporting channels?
8. Provide examples of strategies and techniques for mitigating bias in HR analytics, and explain why these measures are crucial for ethical data-driven decision-making.
9. Can you explain the specific requirements and principles outlined in the European General Data Protection Regulation (GDPR) that impact HR analytics, and how can organizations ensure compliance with these regulations?

10. What are some common ethical principles found in the codes of conduct and guidelines provided by organizations like INFORMS and the International Association for Privacy Professionals (IAPP), and how can HR professionals apply these principles in their analytics practices?
11. What promising trends and complex challenges can we expect in the future of ethical considerations in HR analytics, especially with the increasing use of AI and the need for responsible data use?
12. What ethical principles and strategies should organizations employ when navigating cross-border data issues in HR analytics, and how can they ensure compliance with international data protection laws while safeguarding employee rights and privacy?

CHAPTER

8

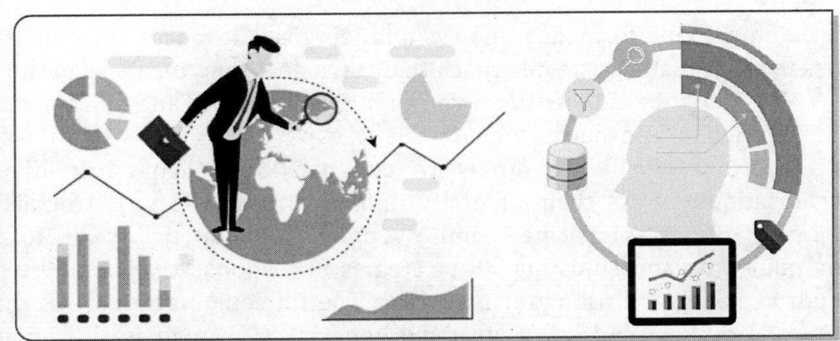

Implementation of HR Analytics

In the last few years, Human Resources (HR) Analytics has become a powerful tool for organisations. It uses insights from data to help HR make better decisions, handle people better, and make sure HR plans are in line with the organization's overall goals. As the world becomes more digital, businesses are realising that HR analytics is a key part of finding, keeping, and growing bright employees. This chapter talks about the most important parts of putting HR Analytics into practice in businesses and the advantages it offers. Getting and combining data is what HR analytics is all about. Human Resource Information Systems (HRIS), recruitment tools, performance management systems, employee polls, and even outside sources like market trends and rival insights must all be used by organisations to collect data. Putting all of this info on one single platform is necessary to get useful insights.

Keeping employee privacy and making sure data is correct are the most important things. The people who work at HR Analytics should follow the rules for protecting data and being responsible. To stop data leaks and keep workers' trust, it's important to clean and verify data and make personal information anonymous. After gathering and organising data, advanced analytics methods like predictive models, machine learning, and data visualisation can be used to find patterns, trends, and connections. These studies can help you figure out how to predict employee loss, measure the diversity of your workforce, and see how HR efforts affect business results.

It is very important to make sure that HR KPIs are in line with the organization's goals. Metrics like success ratings, time-to-hire, and employee engagement numbers can help HR pros keep track of their progress and make smart choices. By improving the hiring process, HR analytics can completely change the way people are hired. Predictive models can find the best places to find new employees, judge how useful job postings are, and even guess how well a candidate will do based on past data.

HR needs to know what motivates and keeps employees working hard. Analytics can find the things that affect job happiness and involvement, which helps companies keep their best employees. Personalised learning and development plans can be made for each employee based on their performance reviews and job goals. It makes sure that money spent on training goes to areas that help people reach their own goals and the goals of the organisation as a whole.

HR Analytics can identify high-potential employees and build succession plans accordingly. This proactive approach reduces talent gaps during leadership transitions and enhances organizational resilience. Analytics can provide insights into diversity metrics, helping organizations assess their diversity and inclusion efforts. It can also identify areas where diversity initiatives may need improvement. HR Analytics is an iterative process. Regularly analysing data and adjusting HR strategies in response to changing trends and organizational needs is essential for long-term success. The implementation of HR Analytics in organizations is not merely a trend but a strategic imperative. It enables HR departments to evolve from traditional administrative roles to strategic partners in achieving organizational goals. By harnessing the power of data and analytics, organizations can create a more agile, data-driven, and employee-centric work environment, ultimately leading to improved performance and sustainable growth.

BENEFITS OF HR ANALYTICS IMPLEMENTATION

1. **Informed Decision-making:** Data-driven insights empower HR professionals to make informed decisions, reducing the guesswork and subjectivity in HR management.
2. **Cost Savings:** By optimizing hiring processes, reducing turnover, and aligning training with employee needs, organizations can save costs associated with recruitment, on boarding, and training.

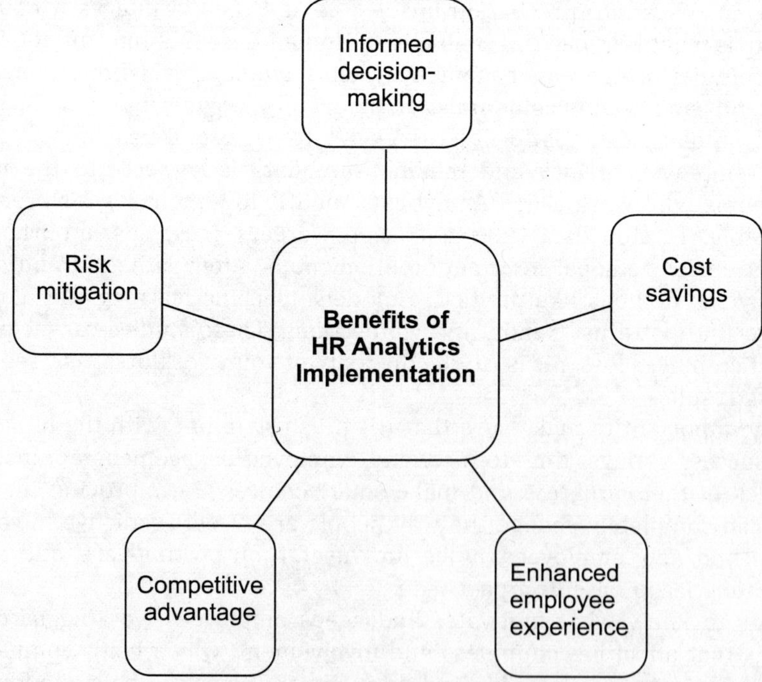

FIGURE 8.1 Benefits of HR analytics implementation.

3. **Enhanced Employee Experience:** Personalized development plans, improved work-life balance, and targeted interventions lead to a better employee experience, which, in turn, boosts retention rates and productivity.
4. **Competitive Advantage:** Organizations that effectively implement HR Analytics gain a competitive edge by attracting and retaining top talent and responding quickly to changing market demands.
5. **Risk Mitigation:** Identifying potential HR issues such as turnover or employee dissatisfaction early on allows organizations to take proactive measures to mitigate risks.

IMPLEMENTING HR ANALYTICS IN ORGANIZATIONS

Implementing HR analytics in organizations involves using data and analytics tools to make data-driven decisions about human resources management. HR analytics can help organizations improve employee performance, recruitment, retention, and overall organizational effectiveness. Following are the steps to implement HR analytics:

1. **Define Objectives and Goals**: Make it clear what its goals are for using HR data. There could be any HR-related goal, like keeping employees longer, making them more productive, optimizing workforce planning, or any other specific HR-related goal.
2. **Data Collection and Integration**:
   - Identify the relevant data sources within your organization. This may include HR systems, employee surveys, performance reviews, time and attendance records, and more.
   - Ensure data quality and accuracy. Data cleansing and integration may be necessary to combine data from different sources.
3. **Select Key Metrics**: Choose the key performance indicators (KPIs) that align with your objectives. These could include turnover rate, employee engagement, time-to-fill vacancies, absenteeism rate, or any other metrics relevant to your goals.
4. **Analytics Tools and Technology**: Invest in the right analytics tools and technology. This may involve purchasing specialized HR analytics software or developing custom solutions, depending on your budget and requirements.
5. **Build an Analytics Team**: Assemble a team of data analysts, data scientists, and HR professionals who understand the data and the HR domain. Cross-functional collaboration is crucial.
6. **Data Analysis and Modelling**:
   - Analyse the data to identify trends, patterns, and correlations. Use statistical and machine learning techniques to gain insights from the data.
   - Develop predictive models if needed, such as attrition prediction models or workforce forecasting models.
7. **Data Visualization**: Create visually appealing and easy-to-understand dashboards and reports to present your findings. Tools like Tableau, Power BI, or custom-built dashboards can be useful for this.

8. **Data Governance and Privacy**: Implement data governance policies to ensure data security, compliance with privacy regulations (e.g., GDPR, CCPA), and ethical data handling practices.
9. **Continuous Monitoring and Feedback**:
   - Continuously monitor the HR analytics program's effectiveness and seek feedback from HR practitioners and business leaders.
   - Make adjustments and improvements based on feedback and evolving business needs.
10. **Communication and Change Management**:
    - Communicate the insights and recommendations effectively to HR professionals and business leaders.
    - Implement changes and initiatives based on the insights gained through HR analytics, and monitor their impact.
11. **Training and Development**: Provide training to HR staff to enhance their data literacy and analytical skills, enabling them to use HR analytics effectively.
12. **Evaluation and ROI Measurement**: Evaluate the impact of HR analytics on your organization's HR-related goals and overall business performance. Calculate the return on investment (ROI) to justify the resources invested in HR analytics.
13. **Iterate and Improve**: Continuously iterate on your HR analytics processes, expanding the scope and improving the accuracy and relevance of your analyses.

HR analytics is an ongoing process, and it's essential to align it with the organization's strategic goals. By leveraging data and analytics, organizations can make more informed decisions regarding their human resources, ultimately leading to better workforce management and business outcomes.

BUILDING A STRONG DATA CULTURE

In today's data-driven world, organizations that thrive are those that embrace data as a strategic asset. A strong data culture is not just a buzzword but a fundamental shift in the way an organization thinks and operates. It represents an environment where data is not just collected, but it's harnessed, respected, and central to decision-making at all levels. Building a strong data culture is essential, not only for effective data management but for staying competitive and agile in a rapidly changing business landscape.

Building a strong data culture is not something that happens overnight; it's a journey that requires commitment from leadership, education for employees, and a willingness to embrace change. However, the rewards in terms of improved decision-making, efficiency, and competitiveness are well worth the effort. In today's data-driven world, a strong data culture is not a luxury but a necessity for organizations that want to thrive and grow.

Understanding the Importance of Data Culture

In the age of information, data is often hailed as the new currency. Organizations that understand and embrace the concept of a data culture have a distinct advantage in today's competitive landscape. But what exactly is a data culture, and why is it so crucial? Let's explore the importance of fostering a data culture within organizations.

Defining Data Culture

A data culture refers to the collective mind-set, values, practices, and behaviours within an organization regarding the collection, analysis, and utilization of data. It's an environment where data is not just seen as a by-product of operations but as a strategic asset that drives decision-making, innovation, and continuous improvement.

The Importance of a Data Culture

1. **Informed Decision-making:** A data-driven culture places data at the heart of decision-making processes. This ensures that decisions are based on evidence rather than intuition or personal biases. Informed decisions lead to better outcomes.
2. **Competitive Advantage:** Organizations that leverage data effectively gain a competitive edge. They can spot trends, identify opportunities, and adapt to changes in the market faster than their competitors. This agility can be a game-changer.
3. **Efficiency and Productivity:** Data helps organizations identify inefficiencies and areas for improvement. By optimizing processes based on data insights, companies can enhance productivity and reduce operational costs.
4. **Customer-Centricity:** Data provides insights into customer behaviour and preferences. Organizations with a data culture can better understand their customers, tailor their offerings, and provide superior customer experiences.
5. **Innovation:** Data often reveals unexpected patterns, opportunities, or problems. In a data culture, employees are encouraged to explore data creatively, leading to innovations in products, services, and processes.
6. **Risk Mitigation:** Data can help organizations identify and mitigate risks proactively. Whether it's financial risks, compliance risks, or cybersecurity risks, data can be a powerful tool for risk management.
7. **Continuous Improvement:** Data fosters a culture of continuous improvement. When employees have access to data that shows how they're performing, they are more likely to seek ways to improve their work.

Key Elements of a Strong Data Culture

1. **Data Transparency:** In a strong data culture, data is not hidden away in silos. It's accessible to those who need it, when they need it. Transparency ensures that data isn't seen as a weapon but as a tool for improvement.
2. **Data Literacy:** Everyone in the organization, from top executives to front-line employees, should have a basic understanding of data. This doesn't mean everyone needs to be a data scientist, but they should know how to interpret and use data in their roles.
3. **Data-driven Decision-making:** In a data culture, decisions are based on evidence, not gut feelings. Leaders encourage and require data to support proposals, strategies, and actions.

4. **Continuous Learning:** Data technologies and methodologies evolve rapidly. A strong data culture encourages continuous learning and adaptation to new tools and techniques.
5. **Accountability:** Individuals and teams are responsible for the data they generate and the insights they derive from it. This fosters a sense of ownership and a commitment to data accuracy.
6. **Innovation:** Data can be a catalyst for innovation. In a data culture, employees are encouraged to explore data to find new opportunities, whether it's in product development, customer service, or process improvement.
7. **Data Security and Ethics:** Strong data cultures also prioritize data security and ethical data practices. This ensures that data is used responsibly and that privacy and compliance are maintained.

Why Building a Strong Data Culture Matters?

1. **Informed Decision-making:** Organizations with a strong data culture can make more informed decisions. They have a clear view of what's happening, why it's happening, and what might happen in the future.
2. **Competitive Advantage:** A data-driven organization can spot trends and opportunities faster than competitors. This agility can be a significant competitive advantage.
3. **Efficiency and Productivity:** Data can reveal inefficiencies and bottlenecks. By addressing these issues, organizations can improve productivity and reduce costs.
4. **Customer Insights:** Data can provide deep insights into customer behaviour and preferences. This can lead to more personalized and effective marketing and customer service.
5. **Risk Management:** Data can help identify and mitigate risks before they become major issues. Whether it's financial risks, operational risks, or compliance risks, data can be a valuable tool.
6. **Innovation:** Data can spark innovation by revealing new product ideas, process improvements, or market opportunities that might otherwise go unnoticed.

LEADERSHIP AND ADVOCACY

As an organisation works to create a data culture, leadership and support play the most important roles. Leadership support and advocacy are key drivers that can make or break the successful adoption of a data-centric mind-set and practices across all levels of an organization. How important leadership and advocacy are for creating a data culture is explained below:

1. **Setting the Example:** Leadership sets the tone for the entire organization. When leaders demonstrate a commitment to data-driven decision-making and actively use data in their own roles, it sends a powerful message. Employees are more likely to embrace data when they see their leaders doing the same.
2. **Gaining Executive Support:** To implement data initiatives effectively, leaders need to secure buy-in and support from top executives. This support includes financial

backing, resources, and time allocated for data-related projects. When leadership recognizes the strategic value of data, it becomes easier to drive data culture initiatives forward.

3. **Communicating the Vision:** Leaders should articulate a clear vision of what a data culture means for the organization. This vision should outline the benefits of data-driven decision-making, such as improved performance, innovation, and better customer experiences. Communicating this vision helps employees understand why a data culture is essential.
4. **Removing Barriers:** Leaders should actively identify and remove barriers that hinder the adoption of a data culture. This includes addressing resistance to change, ensuring data accessibility, and investing in training and resources for employees to develop data-related skills.
5. **Fostering Collaboration:** Leadership can promote collaboration between different departments and teams. Data is often generated and used across various functions, and a collaborative approach ensures that data is leveraged optimally for organizational benefit.
6. **Recognizing Data Champions:** Leaders can identify and celebrate individuals or teams who champion data initiatives. Recognizing and rewarding those who actively contribute to building a data culture can motivate others to follow suit.
7. **Data-driven Strategy:** Leadership should incorporate data-driven strategies into the organization's overall business plans. This includes setting key performance indicators (KPIs) that are measurable, attainable, and relevant, and regularly reviewing progress based on data.
8. **Providing Resources:** Leaders need to allocate resources for data infrastructure, analytics tools, and training programs. Adequate resources ensure that employees have the tools and knowledge necessary to work with data effectively.
9. **Encouraging Learning and Development:** Leaders can encourage continuous learning and development related to data. This includes supporting employees in attending data-related courses, workshops, and conferences to stay updated on best practices and emerging trends.
10. **Sustained Commitment:** Building a data culture is not a one-time effort but an ongoing commitment. Leaders must ensure that the data culture remains a priority over time and continue to advocate for its importance.

Leadership and advocacy play a pivotal role in nurturing a data culture within an organization. When leaders champion data-driven decision-making, secure executive support, and create an environment that encourages data use, they pave the way for the successful adoption of a data culture. This culture, in turn, enhances an organization's ability to make informed decisions, adapt to changing circumstances, and drive innovation and growth.

EMPLOYEE TRAINING AND DEVELOPMENT IN BUILDING A DATA CULTURE

Employee training and development are essential components of building a data culture within an organization. In a world where data plays an increasingly vital role in decision-making and performance improvement, ensuring that employees have the necessary skills and knowledge to work effectively with data is crucial. Below mentioned points illustrates why employee training and development are essential in the context of building a data culture:

1. **Enhancing Data Literacy:** Data Literacy is the ability to read, understand, and communicate data effectively. Many employees may not be familiar with data concepts, terminology, or analysis techniques. Training programs can bridge this knowledge gap, enabling employees to interpret data, draw meaningful insights, and make informed decisions.
2. **Promoting Confidence and Competence:** Effective training boosts employees' confidence in handling data. When employees feel competent in working with data, they are more likely to embrace data-driven decision-making and proactively seek out data for problem-solving.
3. **Demystifying Data Tools:** Data tools and software can be intimidating for those unfamiliar with them. Training programs can introduce employees to data analytics tools, making them comfortable with data manipulation, visualization, and analysis.
4. **Cultivating Analytical Thinking:** Data analysis is not just about numbers; it's about critical thinking and problem-solving. Training programs can teach employees how to approach data analytically, ask the right questions, and derive meaningful insights from data.
5. **Ensuring Data Quality and Integrity:** Employees need to understand the importance of data quality and integrity. Training can emphasize data governance practices, ensuring that employees contribute to maintaining data accuracy and consistency.
6. **Fostering a Data-driven Mind-set:** Training programs can instil a data-driven mind-set in employees. This means encouraging them to seek data to support their arguments, rather than relying solely on intuition or past experiences.
7. **Staying Current with Technology:** Data-related technologies and tools are continually evolving. Training and development initiatives ensure that employees are up to date with the latest advancements, allowing them to leverage new tools and techniques effectively.
8. **Customization to Roles:** Different roles within an organization may require different levels of data expertise. Tailored training programs can address the specific needs of various departments, ensuring that employees gain skills relevant to their job functions.
9. **Creating a Learning Culture:** Investing in employee training and development sends a clear message that the organization values learning and growth. This can help create a broader culture of continuous learning, where employees are encouraged to seek out new knowledge and skills.
10. **Increasing Data-driven Contributions:** Trained employees are more likely to contribute valuable insights and ideas based on data analysis. This can lead to more effective problem-solving, improved processes, and innovation within the organization.
11. **Measuring and Assessing Progress:** Training programs should include mechanisms to measure the impact of training on employees' data skills and its effects on the organization's data culture. Regular assessments can help identify areas for improvement.

Employee training and development are pivotal in establishing and sustaining a data culture within an organization. By investing in training initiatives that enhance data literacy, promote analytical thinking, and ensure data quality, organizations can empower their employees to harness the power of data effectively. This, in turn, leads to more informed decision-making, improved performance, and a competitive edge in today's data-driven business environment.

SELECTING THE RIGHT TECHNOLOGY FOR HR ANALYTICS IMPLEMENTATION

Selecting the right technology is a critical step in successfully implementing HR analytics within an organization. The technology you choose should align with your specific needs, support efficient data processing, and ensure data security and compliance. Following are the steps to guide you to make the right technology choices:

Assessing Technological Needs

Before diving into the selection of HR analytics technology, it's essential to thoroughly assess your organization's technological requirements. This involves:

- **Defining Objectives:** Clearly outline your HR analytics goals and objectives. What do you intend to achieve with HR analytics, and what specific challenges are you trying to address?
- **Identifying Data Sources:** Determine the sources of HR data within your organization. This might include HRIS (Human Resources Information System), payroll systems, performance management tools, and more.
- **Scalability:** Consider whether the technology can scale to accommodate the increasing volume of HR data as your organization grows.
- **Integration Capability:** Assess how well the technology can integrate with existing HR systems and data sources. Seamless integration is crucial for efficient data flow.
- **User Requirements:** Understand the needs of HR professionals and other stakeholders who will be using HR analytics technology. Identify essential features and functionalities.
- **Budget:** Determine the budget available for technology investments. Balance your requirements with available resources.

Choosing HR Analytics Tools

Selecting the appropriate HR analytics tools is a pivotal step. The way to go about this is as follows:

- **Needs Assessment:** Match your organization's needs and objectives with the features offered by HR analytics tools. Consider factors such as reporting capabilities, data visualization, predictive analytics, and user-friendliness.
- **Vendor Evaluation:** Research and evaluate different HR analytics tool vendors. Seek user reviews, case studies, and industry reports to assess reputation and reliability.

- **Data Integration:** Ensure that the chosen tools can seamlessly integrate with your existing HR systems and data sources. Compatibility is essential for efficient data flow.
- **Scalability:** Opt for tools that can grow alongside your organization. Scalable solutions can accommodate increased data volumes and evolving analytical needs.
- **User Training:** Consider the ease of training HR professionals and other users to utilize the selected tools effectively. User-friendly interfaces and available training resources are crucial.
- **Security:** Assess the security features of the tools, including data encryption, user access controls, and compliance with data protection regulations.
- **Cost-Benefit Analysis:** Evaluate the total cost of ownership, encompassing licensing, support, and maintenance costs, against the expected benefits of the tools.
- **Pilot Testing:** If feasible, conduct pilot tests or trials of shortlisted HR analytics tools to assess their performance in a real organizational context.

DATA SECURITY AND COMPLIANCE

Ensuring data security and compliance with relevant regulations is paramount in HR analytics. One can deal with this issue in the following ways:

- **Data Governance:** Establish robust data governance policies and procedures to ensure data quality, integrity, and security. Define roles and responsibilities for data management.
- **Data Privacy:** Adhere to data privacy regulations, such as GDPR or HIPAA, depending on your location and the nature of HR data you handle. Implement consent mechanisms and data anonymization practices.
- **Data Encryption:** Ensure that sensitive HR data is encrypted both in transit and at rest to protect it from unauthorized access.
- **Access Controls:** Implement user access controls to restrict data access based on roles and responsibilities. Only authorized personnel should have access to sensitive HR information.
- **Regular Audits:** Conduct periodic data security audits and assessments to identify vulnerabilities and ensure compliance with data protection regulations.
- **Data Retention:** Define data retention policies and practices to manage HR data throughout its lifecycle, including secure disposal when data is no longer needed.

By following these steps and considering your organization's specific requirements, you can select the right technology for HR analytics implementation that aligns with your objectives while safeguarding data security and compliance.

PARTNERING WITH KEY STAKEHOLDERS IN HR ANALYTICS IMPLEMENTATION

Effective collaboration with key stakeholders is crucial for the successful implementation of HR analytics within an organization. HR professionals can achieve more significant results when they work closely with other departments and teams. Following are the steps to guide on how to partner with key stakeholders effectively:

Collaboration with IT Department

The IT department is a critical partner in HR analytics implementation. Following are the ways to foster a productive collaboration:

- **Align Objectives:** Ensure that HR analytics goals align with the overall IT strategy and objectives of the organization.
- **Data Integration:** Collaborate with IT to integrate HR systems with other organizational databases and applications seamlessly.
- **Technical Support:** Leverage IT's expertise in managing data, security, and infrastructure to ensure the smooth functioning of HR analytics tools and systems.
- **Communication:** Maintain open communication channels with the IT team to address technical issues and resolve them promptly.

Working with Finance and Operations

Finance and operations departments play a vital role in HR analytics implementation. Collaborate effectively by:

- **ROI Demonstration:** Explain how HR analytics initiatives can lead to cost savings or revenue generation, aligning with financial objectives.
- **Budget Allocation:** Work with the finance department to secure the necessary funding for HR analytics projects.
- **Operational Efficiency:** Collaborate with operations to identify opportunities for process improvement through data-driven insights.
- **Reporting Metrics:** Define and track key performance indicators (KPIs) that are relevant to both HR and finance/operations.

Engaging HR Business Partners

HR business partners work closely with different business units. Collaboration with them can help tailor HR analytics initiatives to specific departmental needs:

- **Needs Assessment:** Consult HR business partners to understand the unique data requirements and challenges of various business units.
- **Customized Solutions:** Develop customized analytics solutions that address the specific needs of different departments or teams.
- **Feedback Loop:** Establish a feedback loop with HR business partners to continuously refine HR analytics strategies based on their input.
- **Education:** Provide training and support to HR business partners so they can effectively utilize HR analytics insights in their decision-making.

Effective Communication

Effective communication is a cornerstone of successful collaboration with key stakeholders:

- **Clear Objectives:** Clearly communicate the objectives and benefits of HR analytics initiatives to all stakeholders, emphasizing how it aligns with the organization's overall goals.
- **Regular Updates:** Provide regular updates on the progress of HR analytics projects and share success stories to maintain engagement and interest.
- **Feedback Mechanisms:** Create mechanisms for stakeholders to provide feedback and suggestions, fostering a sense of ownership and involvement.
- **Customized Reporting:** Tailor HR analytics reports and insights to the specific needs and preferences of different stakeholder groups.

Change Management

HR analytics initiatives often bring about organizational change. Manage this change effectively:

- **Change Champions:** Identify and empower change champions within each stakeholder group to drive adoption and acceptance.
- **Training and Support:** Offer training and ongoing support to help stakeholders adapt to new data-driven processes and tools.
- **Addressing Concerns:** Address concerns and resistance to change proactively, highlighting the benefits and addressing misconceptions.

Cross-Functional Teams

Consider forming cross-functional teams that include representatives from HR, IT, finance, operations, and other relevant departments. These teams can collaborate closely on HR analytics projects, ensuring a holistic approach and shared ownership of outcomes.

By collaborating effectively with key stakeholders and fostering a culture of cooperation, HR professionals can maximize the impact of HR analytics and drive positive organizational change.

IMPLEMENTATION OF BEST PRACTICES FOR HR ANALYTICS

Implementing HR analytics effectively is crucial for leveraging data-driven insights to improve HR processes and make informed workforce decisions. Following are some best practices to ensure a successful HR analytics implementation:

Creating a Roadmap

- **Define Clear Objectives:** Clearly outline your HR analytics goals and objectives. What specific outcomes are you aiming to achieve, such as improved talent acquisition, employee retention, or workforce planning?

- **Set Achievable Milestones:** Break down your HR analytics implementation into manageable phases and set achievable milestones. This helps track progress and ensures that each step is completed successfully.
- **Establish Timelines:** Develop a timeline for each phase of the implementation. Timelines provide a sense of urgency and help manage expectations regarding when results can be expected.

Data Collection and Quality Assurance

- **Identify Relevant Data Sources:** Determine the data sources required for your HR analytics initiatives. These may include HRIS, performance data, employee surveys, and external data sources.
- **Data Cleaning and Validation:** Implement robust data cleaning and validation processes to ensure data accuracy and reliability. Inaccurate or incomplete data can lead to misleading insights.
- **Data Governance:** Establish data governance policies and practices to maintain data quality and integrity over time. Define roles and responsibilities for data management.

Data Analysis and Reporting

- **Advanced Analytics:** Utilize advanced analytics techniques such as predictive modelling and machine learning to derive valuable insights from HR data. These techniques can uncover trends and patterns that may not be apparent through traditional analysis.
- **Visualization:** Use data visualization tools to present HR analytics findings in a visually compelling and understandable manner. Visualizations make complex data more accessible to a broader audience.
- **Actionable Insights:** Ensure that HR analytics reports and insights are actionable. Recommendations should be based on data-driven evidence and provide clear steps for improvement.
- **Regular Reporting:** Establish a regular reporting schedule to keep stakeholders informed about HR analytics progress and outcomes. Consistency in reporting builds trust and engagement.

Change Management

- **Change Champions:** Identify and empower change champions within the organization. These individuals can help drive adoption and acceptance of HR analytics initiatives among employees and stakeholders.
- **Training and Education:** Provide training and educational resources to HR professionals and other users to enhance their data literacy and analytical skills. This empowers them to make data-driven decisions effectively.
- **Addressing Resistance:** Anticipate and address resistance to change. Communicate the benefits of HR analytics, address concerns, and involve employees in the implementation process.

Continuous Improvement

- **Feedback Loop:** Create mechanisms for gathering feedback from users and stakeholders. Use this feedback to make continuous improvements to HR analytics processes and tools.
- **Adapt to Changing Needs:** HR analytics is an evolving field. Be prepared to adapt to changing organizational needs, technological advancements, and emerging best practices.
- **Benchmarking:** Compare your HR analytics outcomes with industry benchmarks and best-in-class practices. Benchmarking helps identify areas for improvement and sets performance standards.

Executive Support

- **Engage Executives:** Maintain ongoing engagement with executive leadership. Regularly update them on the impact of HR analytics on organizational performance and align HR initiatives with broader strategic goals.
- **Demonstrate ROI:** Clearly demonstrate the return on investment (ROI) of HR analytics initiatives. Show how data-driven decisions have led to cost savings, improved employee engagement, or enhanced talent acquisition.

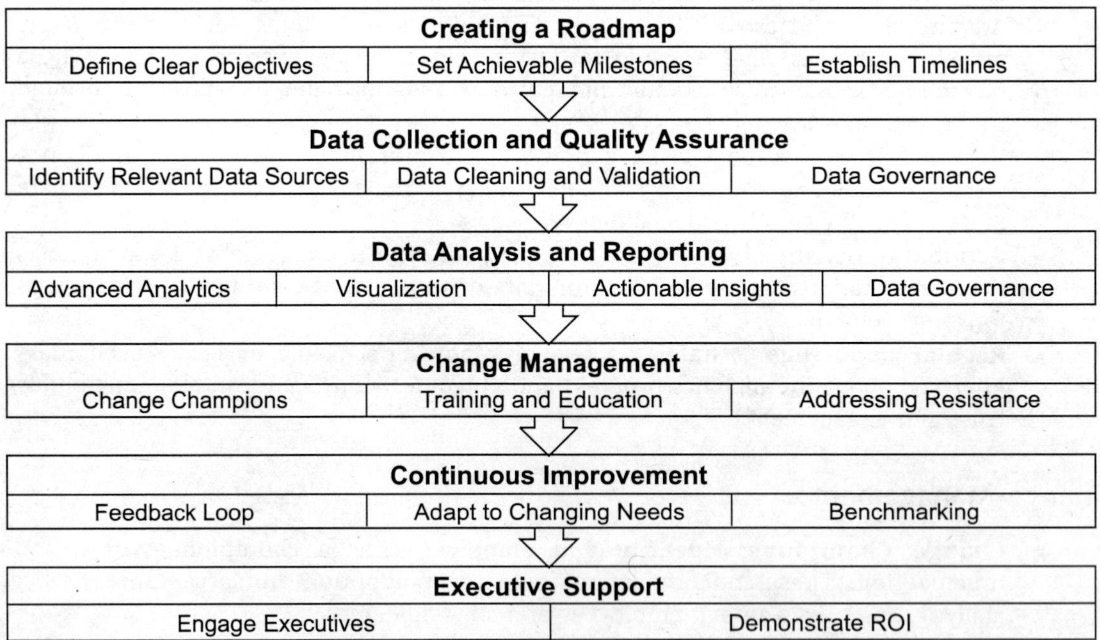

FIGURE 8.2 Implementation of best practices for HR analytics.

By following these implementation of best practices, organizations can unlock the full potential of HR analytics, improving HR processes, optimizing workforce management, and ultimately driving business success.

OVERCOMING CHALLENGES AND PITFALLS IN HR ANALYTICS IMPLEMENTATION

Implementing HR analytics can be a transformative process, but it's not without its challenges and potential pitfalls. Identifying and addressing these challenges is essential for a successful HR analytics implementation. Following are some common challenges and strategies to overcome them:

Data Quality and Integration Challenges

Challenge: Poor data quality, inconsistent data sources, and difficulties in data integration can hinder accurate analysis.

Solution:

- **Data Governance:** Establish robust data governance practices to ensure data accuracy, consistency, and reliability.
- **Data Cleaning:** Implement data cleaning processes to identify and rectify data errors, inconsistencies, and duplicates.
- **Data Integration:** Invest in integration tools and techniques to connect disparate HR systems and data sources seamlessly.

Lack of Data Skills

Challenge: Many HR professionals may not have the necessary data skills to work effectively with analytics tools.

Solution:

- **Training and Development:** Provide training and development opportunities to enhance the data literacy and analytical skills of HR staff.
- **Cross-Functional Teams:** Encourage collaboration between HR and IT or data science teams to leverage their expertise.
- **User-Friendly Tools:** Select HR analytics tools that are user-friendly and require minimal technical expertise.

Resistance to Change

Challenge: Employees may resist the adoption of HR analytics, fearing that it could impact job security or privacy.

Solution:

- **Change Management:** Implement a robust change management strategy that includes communication, education, and addressing concerns proactively.
- **Transparency:** Be transparent about the purpose and benefits of HR analytics, emphasizing its role in improving decision-making and not as a tool for punitive action.
- **Engagement:** Involve employees and stakeholders in the process, seek their input, and emphasize the value they can gain from data-driven insights.

Privacy and Compliance Concerns

Challenge: Collecting and analysing HR data may raise privacy and compliance issues, especially with regulations like GDPR and CCPA.

Solution:

- **Data Privacy Policies:** Develop and enforce clear data privacy policies and practices, ensuring that HR data is handled in compliance with relevant regulations.
- **Data Anonymization:** Anonymize sensitive HR data to protect individual privacy while still allowing for analysis.
- **Legal Consultation:** Seek legal counsel to ensure that your HR analytics practices are in compliance with all applicable laws.

Overcoming Silos

Challenge: Data and insights can become siloed within departments or teams, limiting their impact.

Solution:

- **Cross-Functional Collaboration:** Foster collaboration between HR, IT, finance, operations, and other relevant departments to break down data silos.
- **Centralized Reporting:** Develop a centralized reporting structure that allows for the sharing of insights across the organization.
- **Communication:** Promote a culture of open communication to encourage the sharing of insights and best practices.

Measuring Impact

Challenge: Demonstrating the ROI of HR analytics initiatives can be challenging.

Solution:

- **Define Metrics:** Establish clear key performance indicators (KPIs) to measure the impact of HR analytics on organizational objectives.
- **Benchmarking:** Compare your HR analytics outcomes with industry benchmarks to provide context for your results.
- **Continuous Evaluation:** Continuously assess the effectiveness of HR analytics initiatives and make adjustments as needed.

Technology Selection

Challenge: Selecting the right HR analytics technology can be daunting with many options available.

Solution:

- **Needs Assessment:** Thoroughly assess your organization's requirements and objectives before choosing technology.
- **Vendor Evaluation:** Research and compare different vendors to find a solution that aligns with your needs and budget.

- **Pilot Testing:** If possible, conduct pilot tests to evaluate the performance of shortlisted HR analytics tools.

By addressing these challenges with well-thought-out solutions and strategies, organizations can navigate the complexities of HR analytics implementation and realize the full potential of data-driven HR decision-making.

TABLE 8.1 Common challenges and pitfalls in HR analytics implementation

Challenges and Pitfalls	*Strategies for overcoming them*
Lack of data quality.	1. Establish data quality assurance processes. 2. Regularly audit and clean data.
Data privacy and compliance	1. Adhere to relevant data privacy regulations. 2. Implement data anonymization and encryption.
Insufficient data integration	1. Collaborate with IT to ensure seamless integration. 2. Invest in data integration tools.
Lack of data governance	1. Develop data governance policies and procedures. 2. Define roles and responsibilities for data management.
Resistance to change	1. Identify and empower change champions. 2. Provide training and support for employees adapting to new processes.
Data silos and fragmentation	1. Create cross-functional teams to break down silos. 2. Implement centralized data repositories.
Inadequate data literacy	1. Offer data literacy training programs. 2. Foster a culture of continuous learning.
Tool selection challenges	1. Assess organizational needs before selecting tools. 2. Pilot test shortlisted tools. 3. Involve IT in tool evaluation.
Lack of executive support	1. Regularly engage with executive leadership. 2. Demonstrate the ROI of HR analytics initiatives.
Overemphasis on technology	1. Prioritize people and processes alongside technology. 2. Focus on the strategic use of data rather than just tool adoption.
Inadequate communication	1. Clearly communicate HR analytics objectives and benefits. 2. Maintain regular reporting and feedback mechanisms.
Lack of scalability	1. Choose scalable technology solutions. 2. Plan for future growth in data volume and analytical needs.

THE IMPORTANCE OF ONGOING EVALUATION AND REFINEMENT OF HR ANALYTICS INITIATIVES

Implementing HR analytics initiatives is not a one-time effort; it's an ongoing process that requires continuous evaluation and refinement. This ongoing commitment is crucial for several reasons:

1. **Ensuring Alignment with Organizational Goals:** Organizational goals and priorities can change over time. Regular evaluation ensures that HR analytics initiatives remain aligned with the evolving strategic objectives of the organization. It helps verify that the insights and actions derived from HR data continue to contribute to the overall success of the company.
2. **Maximizing ROI and Impact:** HR analytics represents an investment of resources, including time, technology, and personnel. Regular evaluation allows organizations to assess the return on this investment (ROI). By identifying which analytics initiatives deliver the most significant impact, organizations can optimize resource allocation for maximum efficiency.
3. **Adapting to Changing Workforce Dynamics:** The workforce is dynamic, with employees entering and exiting the organization, changing roles, and evolving skillsets. Ongoing evaluation of HR analytics initiatives enables organizations to adapt to these changes effectively. This includes adjusting talent acquisition strategies, optimizing training and development programs, and addressing turnover issues as they arise.
4. **Improving Data Quality and Governance:** Data quality and governance are ongoing concerns in HR analytics. Continuous evaluation helps identify data quality issues and areas where data governance processes may need improvement. Regular data audits and assessments can lead to more accurate and reliable HR data, which is the foundation of effective analytics.
5. **Enhancing Predictive Capabilities:** Predictive analytics is a powerful aspect of HR analytics, but it becomes more accurate with time and additional data. Continuous evaluation allows organizations to refine predictive models, making them more precise and actionable. As more data is collected, predictive capabilities can improve, leading to better workforce planning and decision-making.
6. **Addressing Feedback and Concerns:** Employees and stakeholders may provide valuable feedback and express concerns regarding HR analytics initiatives. Ongoing evaluation provides a mechanism to address these issues promptly. Addressing feedback not only improves the perception of HR analytics within the organization but also enhances the quality of the initiatives themselves.
7. **Staying Competitive:** The business landscape is continually evolving, and organizations must adapt to stay competitive. Ongoing evaluation ensures that HR analytics initiatives remain current and responsive to industry trends, technological advancements, and changes in the competitive landscape.
8. **Promoting a Culture of Continuous Improvement:** Ongoing evaluation and refinement of HR analytics initiatives foster a culture of continuous improvement. When employees see that their feedback leads to positive changes and that data-driven insights drive progress, they are more likely to embrace data-driven decision-making and actively participate in HR analytics initiatives.

In conclusion, the importance of ongoing evaluation and refinement of HR analytics initiatives cannot be overstated. It ensures that HR analytics remains relevant, aligned with organizational goals, and capable of delivering actionable insights that drive business success. By committing to continuous improvement, organizations can harness the full potential of HR analytics in optimizing their workforce and achieving strategic objectives.

Questions for Discussion

Short Questions

1. What is the significance of building a strong data culture in HR analytics implementation?
2. How can leadership play a pivotal role in promoting a data-driven culture?
3. Why is employee training and development crucial in HR analytics adoption?
4. What are the key considerations when assessing technological needs for HR analytics?
5. How can organizations choose the right HR analytics tools that align with their objectives?
6. What steps should be taken to ensure data security and compliance in HR analytics?
7. Why is collaboration with the IT department essential for successful HR analytics implementation?
8. What are the benefits of engaging HR business partners in data-driven decision-making?

Long Questions

1. Explain the concept of a data culture and its importance in HR analytics implementation. How can organizations foster a data-driven culture?
2. Discuss the role of leadership in advocating for HR analytics and promoting data-driven decision-making. What strategies can be employed to gain executive support for HR analytics initiatives?
3. Describe the significance of employee training and development in building a data culture. How can organizations educate HR teams and employees about the benefits and best practices of data utilization?
4. What steps should organizations take when assessing their technological needs for HR analytics implementation? How can they ensure that their chosen technology aligns with their organizational goals?
5. Discuss the importance of data security and compliance in HR analytics. How can organizations ensure the privacy and security of HR data while complying with relevant data protection regulations?
6. How can HR analytics demonstrate its ROI to finance and operations teams? What strategies can be employed to align HR initiatives with operational efficiency objectives?
7. Describe the role of HR business partners in data-driven decision-making. How can organizations effectively engage HR business partners in HR analytics initiatives?
8. Discuss the challenges and pitfalls commonly encountered in HR analytics implementation. Provide examples of organizations that have successfully overcome these challenges.

CHAPTER

9

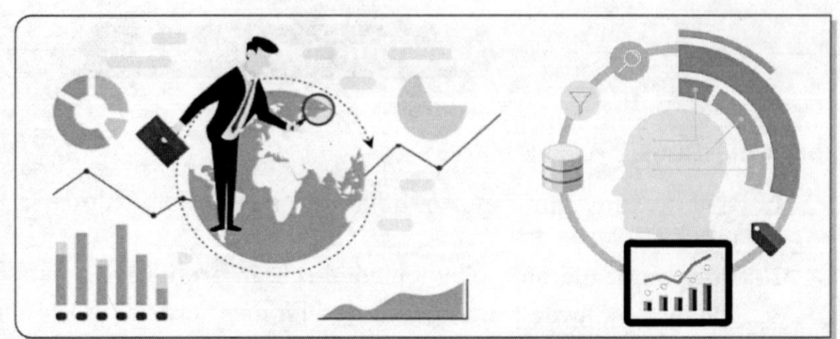

Workforce Planning and Succession Planning

In today's dynamic and rapidly changing business landscape, workforce planning and succession planning have emerged as pivotal components of human resource management. These strategic practices are essential for organizations seeking to thrive, adapt, and remain resilient in the face of uncertainties, retirements, and talent shortages. Workforce planning and succession planning are critical components of strategic human resource management. They involve ensuring that an organization has the right talent in place today and for the future to meet its business goals. Workforce planning and succession planning have evolved over time in response to changing organizational needs, labour markets, and business environments.

Workforce planning, in some form, has likely existed as long as organizations themselves. However, formalized workforce planning as we know it today was not a widespread practice in the pre-industrial era. The Industrial Revolution marked a significant shift in the nature of work and labour. As factories and large-scale manufacturing became prevalent, organizations began to consider labour needs more systematically. The mid-20th century saw the rise of modern personnel departments within organizations. These departments were responsible for various HR functions, including basic workforce planning, to ensure that organizations had the right number of employees with the right skills. During this period, workforce planning became more sophisticated. It involved analysing labour supply and demand, considering factors like turnover, retirement, and skills gaps. Technology played a role in making data analysis more accessible. From Late 20th Century to Present, Workforce planning has continued to evolve, incorporating more advanced data analytics, predictive modelling, and the use of technology platforms. It has become a strategic HR function closely tied to organizational goals and objectives.

In earlier times, succession planning often cantered around dynasties, royal families, and aristocracies, where leadership roles were passed down through bloodlines. The concept of succession planning started to emerge in the context of businesses during the industrial era. Family-owned companies often had succession plans in place to transition leadership within the family. Succession planning began to gain importance in larger corporations as they recognized the need to identify and develop talent for key leadership positions. It was often a manual and informal process within organizations. In recent decades, succession planning has become a more formalized and strategic process. Organizations realized the critical role of leadership continuity in their long-term success. Succession planning now involves identifying high-potential employees, providing them with development opportunities, and ensuring a seamless transition for key roles. In the 21st century, organizations have faced challenges related to demographic shifts (e.g., the aging workforce), changing skill requirements, and increased competition for top talent. Succession planning has become even more crucial as a means to address these challenges.

Today, both workforce planning and succession planning are integral parts of strategic human resource management. They help organizations align their talent needs with their business objectives, ensuring they have the right people in the right positions to achieve long-term success. Advanced data analytics and technology continue to play a significant role in enhancing the effectiveness of these practices.

WORKFORCE PLANNING

Workforce planning is the process of aligning an organization's current and future workforce needs with its strategic objectives. It involves analysing the current workforce, identifying gaps in skills and capabilities, and planning for the recruitment, development, and retention of employees to bridge those gaps. Key elements of workforce planning include:

- **Analysis of Current Workforce:** This involves assessing the skills, experience, and performance of current employees. It may also include demographic data like age, tenure, and diversity.
- **Identifying Future Needs:** Workforce planners look at the organization's strategic goals and forecast the skills and talent required to achieve those goals. This may involve considering factors like expansion, technological changes, or shifts in market demand.
- **Gap Analysis:** Comparing the current workforce to future needs helps identify gaps in skills, knowledge, and numbers. This gap analysis informs recruitment, training, and development strategies.
- **Recruitment and Development:** Based on the analysis, organizations can plan recruitment efforts and training programs to address skill gaps and ensure a future-ready workforce.
- **Succession Planning Integration:** Workforce planning often integrates with succession planning, as both involve preparing for future talent needs.

SUCCESSION PLANNING

Succession planning is a subset of workforce planning that focuses on identifying and developing internal talent to fill key leadership and critical roles within an organization. The goal is to ensure a smooth transition when current leaders or key employees retire, resign, or are promoted. Key elements of succession planning include:

- **Identification of Critical Roles:** Organizations identify roles that are critical to their success, including executive positions, technical experts, and specialized roles.

- **Talent Assessment:** Identifying high-potential employees who have the potential to fill these roles in the future. This assessment includes evaluating their skills, performance, and leadership potential.
- **Development Plans:** Once high-potential employees are identified; organizations create individual development plans to prepare them for future leadership roles. This may involve training, mentoring, job rotations, and stretch assignments.
- **Monitoring and Evaluation:** Succession plans are dynamic and require ongoing monitoring and evaluation. As employees progress in their development, adjustments may be made to the plan.
- **Emergency Succession Planning:** Preparing for unexpected departures of key personnel, such as due to illness or sudden resignation.
- **Communication:** Clear communication with employees about succession plans, career paths, and development opportunities is essential to maintain morale and motivation.

Both workforce planning and succession planning are crucial for ensuring organizational stability and continuity. They help organizations adapt to changing business environments and ensure they have the right talent in place to achieve their strategic goals.

TABLE 9.1 Overview of the significance of workforce planning and succession planning in modern HR management

Aspect	*Workforce Planning*	*Succession Planning*
Definition and purpose	A strategic process to ensure the right people with the right skills are available when needed.	Focused on developing a pipeline of talent to fill key leadership positions in the future.
Business continuity	Ensures business continuity by addressing talent gaps and reducing the impact of workforce disruptions.	Mitigates risks associated with leadership gaps by having prepared successors ready for critical roles.
Strategic alignment	Aligns the workforce with the organization's strategic goals and objectives.	Develops leaders who can execute the organization's strategy effectively.
Talent optimization	Optimizes the allocation of human resources to maximize productivity and efficiency.	Grooms high-potential employees to assume leadership roles, contributing to long-term success.
Adaptation to change	Helps organizations adapt to changing market conditions, industry trends, and technological advancements.	Ensures a steady supply of leaders capable of steering the organization through evolving challenges.
Risk reduction	Minimizes risks associated with talent shortages, skill gaps, and workforce imbalances.	Reduces the risk of leadership vacuums during unexpected departures or retirements.

(*Contd.*)

Aspect	*Workforce Planning*	*Succession Planning*
Talent development and engagement	Identifies opportunities for employee development and engagement.	Fosters employee engagement through clear career paths and development opportunities.
Cost efficiency	Reduces recruitment and training costs by proactively managing workforce needs.	Minimizes the need for costly external hires for leadership positions.
Organizational resilience	Enhances organizational resilience by preparing for future talent challenges.	Increases the organization's ability to weather leadership transitions and crises effectively.
Competitive advantage	Provides a competitive advantage by ensuring access to the right talent at the right time.	Positions the organization for a competitive edge through a pool of skilled leaders.

THE INTERRELATIONSHIP BETWEEN WORKFORCE PLANNING AND SUCCESSION PLANNING

The interrelationship between workforce planning and succession planning is essential for effective talent management and organizational success. These two practices are closely interconnected and complement each other in various ways:

- **Data Sharing:** Workforce planning and succession planning rely on data analysis. Workforce planning uses data to predict future talent needs and assess current workforce capabilities. Succession planning utilizes data to identify high-potential employees and assess their readiness for leadership roles. The data used in workforce planning can inform the identification of high-potential employees in succession planning.
- **Alignment with Organizational Goals:** Both practices need to align with the organization's strategic objectives. Workforce planning ensures that the workforce composition supports the organization's strategic goals, while succession planning grooms' leaders who can effectively execute those strategies.
- **Skill Development:** Workforce planning identifies skill gaps and development needs across the organization, which can inform the focus of leadership development efforts in succession planning. High-potential employees identified in succession planning may also be targeted for specific skill development in workforce planning.
- **Retention and Engagement:** Effective workforce planning includes strategies to retain critical talent. In succession planning, retaining high-potential employees is crucial for ensuring a steady pipeline of potential leaders. Both practices aim to retain and engage top talent, and they can collaborate to develop strategies for talent retention.

- **Risk Mitigation:** Both workforce and succession planning are risk mitigation strategies. Workforce planning reduces risks associated with talent shortages and skills gaps. Succession planning mitigates the risks of leadership vacuums during unexpected departures or retirements. Together, they ensure the organization is prepared for both workforce and leadership-related risks.
- **Leadership Transition:** Succession planning is a subset of workforce planning that specifically focuses on leadership transition. It ensures a smooth transfer of leadership by preparing successors in advance. Workforce planning, in a broader sense, encompasses all levels of employees and their transitions.
- **Communication and Transparency:** Both practices require clear communication and transparency with employees. Employees should be aware of their development opportunities, whether in terms of skill development (workforce planning) or leadership progression (succession planning). Clear communication is vital in building trust and engagement.
- **Long-term Organizational Resilience:** Both workforce planning and succession planning contribute to long-term organizational resilience. Workforce planning ensures that the organization has the right talent mix to adapt to changing circumstances. Succession planning ensures that leadership positions are continuously filled with capable individuals who can guide the organization through challenges.
- **Feedback Loop:** The interrelationship includes a feedback loop between the two practices. Insights from succession planning can inform workforce planning, ensuring that the development of high-potential employees aligns with future talent needs. For example, if succession planning identifies a need for specific leadership skills in the future, workforce planning can tailor training programs accordingly.

To sum up, succession planning and workforce planning are connected tasks that, when combined and matched effectively, make up a full talent management plan. They make sure that an organisation not only has the right people with the right skills at all levels but also a leadership pool that can handle the difficulties of the future.

PREDICTING FUTURE TALENT NEEDS

Predicting future talent needs is a critical aspect of workforce planning and talent management. It involves using data, analysis, and strategic thinking to anticipate the skills and workforce requirements an organization will need to achieve its goals and objectives in the future. Following are the key steps and considerations involved in predicting future talent needs:

- **Alignment with Organizational Strategy:** Begin by aligning talent planning with the organization's strategic objectives. Understanding the company's mission, vision, and long-term goals is crucial.
- **Environmental Scanning:** Conduct an environmental scan of the internal and external factors that could impact the organization's workforce needs. Consider market trends, technological advancements, economic conditions, and industry-specific factors.

- **Data Analysis:** Utilize historical and current workforce data to identify trends and patterns. Analyse workforce demographics, turnover rates, and skills gaps. Quantitative data is essential for making informed predictions.
- **Qualitative Assessment:** Combine quantitative data with qualitative assessments. Engage with department heads, subject matter experts, and other stakeholders to gain insights into the skills and competencies that will be required in the future.
- **Scenario Planning:** Develop different scenarios for the future, considering various possibilities such as rapid growth, economic downturns, technological disruptions, and changes in industry regulations. Each scenario should outline the corresponding talent needs.
- **Skills and Competencies Identification:** Based on the data and assessments, identify the specific skills, competencies, and qualifications that will be in demand in the future. This includes both technical and soft skills.
- **Talent Gap Analysis:** Compare the future skills and competencies required with the current workforce's capabilities. Identify gaps between the current state and the future needs.
- **Workforce Planning Models:** Use workforce planning models and tools, such as workforce analytics software, to visualize the data and make predictions. These tools can help quantify the talent gap and assist in decision-making.
- **Flexibility and Adaptability:** Plan for flexibility in your talent strategy. Recognize that the future is uncertain, and your predictions may need adjustment. Ensure that your workforce planning strategies are adaptable to changing circumstances.
- **Implementation Planning:** Develop strategies for addressing talent gaps and acquiring the needed skills. This may involve recruitment, training and development, promotions, and external partnerships.
- **Communication and Collaboration:** Share the findings and predictions with relevant stakeholders within the organization. Collaboration between HR, department heads, and senior leadership is vital to ensure buy-in and alignment with the talent strategy.
- **Monitoring and Review:** Continuously monitor the progress of talent planning and make adjustments as needed. Regularly review the predictions and adapt to changing conditions.

Predicting future talent needs is an ongoing process that requires a blend of data-driven analysis and strategic vision. By anticipating and addressing talent gaps and staying aligned with the organization's strategic goals, organizations can better position themselves to meet future workforce requirements and succeed in a dynamic business environment.

Table 9.2 provides a structured overview of the key components of predicting future talent needs and the respective subcomponents associated with each aspect. It illustrates how workforce planning involves aligning with organizational goals, scanning the external environment, conducting data-driven analysis, and preparing for multiple future scenarios. These steps collectively form a strategic approach to workforce planning, helping organizations anticipate and meet their talent requirements in an ever-changing and dynamic business landscape.

TABLE 9.2 Key components of predicting future talent need, including their subcomponents

Aspect	*Subcomponent*
1.1. Anticipating organizational goals	• Aligning workforce planning with organizational objectives. • Defining short-term and long-term talent needs.
1.2. Environmental scanning	• Analysing industry trends, economic factors, and technological advancements. • Identifying external factors influencing talent requirements.
1.3. Data-driven analysis	• Leveraging historical data and predictive analytics to forecast staffing needs. • Utilizing quantitative and qualitative data to make informed predictions.
1.4. Scenario planning	• Preparing for various future scenarios and their talent implications. • Creating flexible workforce strategies to adapt to changing circumstances.

Identifying High-Potential Employees

Identifying high-potential employees is a critical component of succession planning and talent development within an organization. High-potential employees are individuals who demonstrate the ability and willingness to grow, take on leadership roles, and make a significant impact on the organization's future. Following are the key steps and considerations involved in identifying high-potential employees:

1. **Defining High-Potential Talent:** Begin by establishing clear and well-defined criteria for what constitutes a high-potential employee in your organization. This might include attributes like leadership potential, adaptability, and a commitment to organizational values.
2. **Assessment and Evaluation:** Use various assessment methods to evaluate employees' potential. This can include performance evaluations, competency assessments, personality assessments, and feedback from managers and peers.
3. **Talent Review and Calibration:** Conduct talent review meetings where HR, senior leadership, and department heads come together to review and discuss employees' potential. Calibrate assessments to ensure consistency in identifying high-potential employees.
4. **Development and Engagement:** Once high-potential employees are identified, design tailored development plans for them. These plans may include special projects, leadership training, mentorship programs, and opportunities for growth and exposure to different parts of the organization.
5. **Performance and Behaviour Observation:** Observe not only what employees achieve but also how they achieve it. High-potential employees often exhibit positive behaviours such as problem-solving, teamwork, and a willingness to take on challenges.

6. **Career Ambition and Commitment:** Consider an employee's career aspirations and commitment to the organization. High-potential employees are typically driven to advance their careers and are committed to the long-term success of the organization.
7. **Feedback and Regular Review:** Provide constructive feedback to high-potential employees, helping them understand their strengths and areas for improvement. Regularly review their progress and adjust development plans as needed.
8. **Inclusivity and Diversity:** Ensure that the identification of high-potential employees is based on objective and fair criteria. Avoid biases and promote diversity and inclusion in the process.
9. **Leadership Potential:** Assess employees' readiness and potential for leadership roles. High-potential employees should not only excel in their current roles but also exhibit the potential to assume greater responsibilities in the future.
10. **Communication and Transparency:** Communicate with high-potential employees about their status and development plans. Be transparent about the organization's commitment to their growth.
11. **Ongoing Monitoring:** Identifying high-potential employees is not a one-time activity. Continuously monitor and reassess their progress and potential as they develop in their roles.

Identifying high-potential employees is essential for building a leadership pipeline and ensuring the organization's long-term success. It requires a combination of objective assessments, feedback, tailored development, and a commitment to fostering a culture that recognizes and supports talent with the potential to lead and make a significant impact.

Developing Succession Plans Based on Data

Developing succession plans based on data is a critical aspect of talent management and organizational continuity. Succession planning involves identifying and developing individuals within the organization who have the potential to fill key leadership roles in the future. Data-driven succession planning takes this process a step further by using quantitative and qualitative data to make informed decisions about leadership development and transitions.

Data as the Foundation

Data is at the core of effective succession planning. It serves as the foundation for identifying and preparing future leaders. This data can include a range of information, from performance reviews and skills assessments to feedback from managers, co-workers, and even potential successors themselves.

Establishing a Succession Planning Framework

Before data can be effectively used, organizations must establish a structured framework for succession planning. This framework outlines the process, roles and responsibilities, and the objectives of the succession plan. Data plays a critical role in every step of this framework.

Data-driven Succession Decisions

1. **Identifying Potential Successors:** The first step is to identify individuals within the organization who have the potential to step into key leadership roles. Data-driven assessments, including performance data, potential assessments, and skills matrices, provide valuable insights into an individual's readiness and suitability for leadership positions.
2. **Leadership Development Initiatives:** Once high-potential employees are identified; data helps in crafting tailored development plans. These plans are based on the skills and competencies identified as essential for future leadership roles. This can include leadership training, coaching, mentoring, and other developmental opportunities.
3. **Creating a Talent Pool:** A data-driven approach helps organizations build a talent pool of potential successors for various roles. This talent pool is dynamic and can be updated based on ongoing assessments and changes in organizational needs.

Communication and Transparency

Data-driven succession planning is effective when there is clear communication with employees about the succession process. Employees who are part of the talent pool should be aware of their inclusion and the organization's commitment to their growth and development.

Addressing Development Gaps

One of the key advantages of data-driven succession planning is that it helps in pinpointing specific development gaps in potential successors. When employees understand where they need improvement, they can work on these areas to become better-prepared leaders.

Risk Mitigation

Data-driven succession planning is also a risk mitigation strategy. It reduces the risk of leadership vacuums when key leaders depart or retire unexpectedly. By having a talent pool ready, organizations are better prepared for unforeseen circumstances.

Regular Review and Adjustment

The data used in succession planning isn't static. It's dynamic and should be reviewed and adjusted regularly. Changes in an employee's performance, the evolving needs of the organization, and shifts in industry dynamics all necessitate updates to the succession plan.

On the whole, using data to make succession plans is a smart way to make sure that an organisation has long-term success and leadership stability. To find, train, and keep the next crop of leaders, there is a clear, standardised, and flexible method that uses objective interviews and performance data. Because it is based on data, this method makes it easier for an organisation to handle changes in leadership and deal with the complicated nature of the constantly evolving business world.

The Table 9.3 outlines the key elements and considerations involved in developing succession plans based on data, with a focus on using data-driven assessments, leadership development, and transparent communication to groom potential successors for key organizational roles.

TABLE 9.3 Developing succession plans based on data

Aspect	*Succession Plans Based on Data*
Definition and purpose	A structured process to identify and groom potential successors for key leadership positions based on data-driven assessments and insights.
Data collection and analysis	Gathering data related to employee performance, potential, and skills. Analysing this data to identify high-potential individuals.
Skill and competency assessment	Assessing employees' skills, competencies, and leadership potential using both quantitative and qualitative methods.
Leadership development programs	Designing programs to develop the skills and knowledge needed for potential successors to excel in leadership roles.
Succession pool identification	Creating a pool of individuals identified as potential successors, based on data-driven assessments.
Mentoring and coaching	Providing one-on-one support and guidance for high-potential employees to accelerate their leadership development.
Communication and transparency	Transparently communicating the organization's succession planning process to potential successors and other stakeholders.
Flexibility and adaptation	Creating flexible succession plans that can adapt to changing circumstances and emerging leadership needs.
Continuous monitoring and evaluation	Regularly reviewing and adjusting succession plans based on the progress and development of potential successors.
Diversity and inclusion considerations	Ensuring diversity and inclusion are considered when identifying potential successors and developing leadership programs.
Integration with workforce planning	Aligning succession planning with the organization's workforce planning to ensure a cohesive talent management strategy.
Leadership transition strategies	Preparing for leadership transitions by ensuring potential successors are ready to assume key roles when needed.
Performance metrics and KPIs	Defining and tracking key performance indicators related to succession planning and leadership development programs.
Case studies and best practices	Learning from real-world examples and best practices in developing succession plans based on data.
References and resources	Citing relevant sources, research, and tools that support the data-driven approach to succession planning.

REINFORCING THE ROLE OF WORKFORCE AND SUCCESSION PLANNING IN ENSURING ORGANIZATIONAL RESILIENCE

Organisational resilience is a key factor in determining success in today's constantly changing business world, which is marked by technological changes, economic uncertainty, and fast-moving market dynamics. In order to deal with these problems well, businesses need to handle their most important asset: their people. Succession planning and workforce planning are very important for making sure that an organisation is resilient because they give people the tools and methods they need to change, grow, and do well in uncertain times.

Workforce Planning: The Foundation of Resilience

Workforce planning is the process of assessing an organization's current workforce, predicting its future talent needs, and developing strategies to meet those needs. It is the cornerstone of organizational resilience for several reasons:

- **Anticipating Change:** Workforce planning allows organizations to anticipate changes in the business environment. By analysing industry trends, economic factors, and technological advancements, organizations can prepare for shifts in talent demand and adapt proactively.
- **Skill Alignment:** It aligns workforce skills with organizational goals. Resilient organizations ensure their workforce possesses the right skills and competencies to adapt to evolving requirements, be it in adopting new technologies or responding to shifting customer expectations.
- **Contingency Planning:** Workforce planning is about preparing for contingencies. By scenario planning and creating flexible workforce strategies, organizations can withstand unforeseen events and respond swiftly to changing circumstances.
- **Cost Management:** Resilience is often tied to financial stability. Workforce planning minimizes costs by efficiently allocating human resources, reducing the risk of overstaffing or understaffing, and avoiding costly external hires.

Succession Planning: Fostering Leadership Resilience

Succession planning, a subset of workforce planning, focuses on developing a pipeline of talent to fill critical leadership positions. It is a cornerstone of leadership resilience for several reasons:

- **Mitigating Leadership Gaps:** Succession planning ensures that leadership positions are continuously filled with capable individuals who can steer the organization through challenges. It reduces the risk of leadership vacuums during unexpected departures or retirements.
- **Leadership Development:** By investing in the development of high-potential employees, succession planning fosters a culture of adaptability and innovation. These future leaders are equipped to guide the organization through crises and drive it toward long-term success.
- **Organizational Memory:** It allows organizations to capture institutional knowledge. Succession planning involves knowledge transfer from experienced leaders to successors, ensuring the preservation of critical insights and expertise.
- **Resilience through Diversity:** A diverse and inclusive succession planning process promotes diversity in leadership roles, leading to a broader range of perspectives and ideas that enhance organizational resilience.

The Resilient Organization

In an era where change is the only constant, organizational resilience is the key to survival and success. Workforce planning and succession planning, when intertwined seamlessly, serve as the pillars of this resilience. They provide organizations with the capability to anticipate and adapt to change, effectively allocate human capital, and ensure that the right leaders are ready to steer the ship through turbulent waters. These practices are not mere HR functions; they are strategic instruments that can transform an organization's ability to thrive in the face of adversity and uncertainty. In today's unpredictable business environment, the organizations that embrace workforce and succession planning as the linchpins of their resilience will undoubtedly emerge as the leaders of tomorrow.

EMPHASIZING THE CONTINUOUS NATURE OF WORKFORCE AND SUCCESSION PLANNING IN ADAPTING TO A CHANGING BUSINESS LANDSCAPE

Workforce planning and succession planning are not one-time events or isolated processes. Instead, they are ongoing, dynamic practices that adapt and evolve in lockstep with the changing business landscape. The continuous nature of these practices is paramount in ensuring an organization's ability to thrive, adapt, and succeed in an environment marked by uncertainty, innovation, and constant transformation. This adaptability is crucial for long-term sustainability and resilience. This is why the continuity of workforce and succession planning is so important:

Evolving Business Needs

The business landscape is in a perpetual state of flux. New technologies emerge, markets shift, and customer preferences change. Workforce planning must continuously assess how these factors impact talent requirements. Roles that were essential yesterday might become obsolete, and new positions may emerge. Continual assessment ensures that the workforce remains aligned with the organization's strategic goals.

Talent Development

Succession planning is a process of identifying and grooming future leaders. Leadership requirements change as the organization evolves. Continual development and refinement of leadership pipelines are essential to keep up with changing leadership skill sets and capabilities. As leaders progress in their careers, they need new skills and experiences. Succession planning must adapt to these shifting needs.

Emerging Skills and Competencies

In a rapidly changing world, new skills and competencies become essential. Organizations need to identify these skills early and develop strategies for acquiring or developing them within the workforce. Continuous assessment ensures that the organization remains at the forefront of industry trends and technological advancements.

Crisis Preparedness

Unexpected events can disrupt business operations and leadership continuity. The continuous aspect of succession planning means that organizations are always prepared for leadership transitions, whether planned or sudden. This proactive approach is crucial for maintaining stability in times of crisis.

Incorporating Feedback

Feedback is a valuable source of information for improvement. By continually gathering feedback from employees, leaders, and stakeholders, organizations can refine their workforce and succession planning processes. This feedback loop ensures that strategies remain relevant and effective.

Adaptive Decision-making

Continuous workforce and succession planning enable organizations to make adaptive decisions based on real-time data and circumstances. It allows them to pivot quickly in response to new challenges or opportunities, rather than relying on rigid, outdated strategies.

Cultivating a Talent-centric Culture

Organizations that embrace continuous talent management practices create a culture of adaptability and resilience. It sends a clear message to employees that the organization values talent development, agility, and long-term success.

Competitive Advantage

In a competitive business landscape, organizations that continuously invest in their people and leadership development have an edge. They are better prepared to seize opportunities and respond to threats, giving them a competitive advantage.

In summary, workforce and succession planning are not static activities but rather dynamic, ongoing processes that align an organization's talent with its strategic goals and prepare for leadership continuity. In a world where change is constant, the adaptability and continuity of these practices are key drivers of long-term success, resilience, and competitive advantage. By emphasizing their continuous nature, organizations can stay ahead of the curve and thrive in the ever-evolving business landscape.

Questions for Discussion

Short Questions

1. What is workforce planning, and why is it important in today's business landscape?
2. How has workforce planning evolved over time in response to changing organizational needs and technology?
3. What is succession planning, and when did it become a more formalized and strategic process?

4. How do workforce planning and succession planning work together to benefit organizations?
5. What role does data play in both workforce planning and succession planning?
6. How do workforce planning and succession planning help organizations mitigate risks?
7. What is the significance of aligning talent planning with an organization's strategic objectives?
8. How can organizations prepare for unforeseen leadership departures through succession planning?
9. What are some key considerations in identifying high-potential employees?
10. How does data-driven succession planning contribute to organizational resilience?

Long Questions

1. Explain the evolution of workforce planning from pre-industrial times to the present, and highlight the factors that drove this evolution.
2. Discuss the interrelationship between workforce planning and succession planning, and how they collaborate to ensure organizational stability and continuity.
3. Describe the process of predicting future talent needs and the key steps involved in this critical aspect of workforce planning.
4. Explain the steps and considerations involved in identifying high-potential employees and why this is essential for talent development.
5. Provide a detailed overview of developing succession plans based on data, highlighting the role of data in effective succession planning.
6. Explain the importance of workforce planning and succession planning in reinforcing organizational resilience and how they contribute to adaptability and growth.
7. Highlight the continuous nature of workforce and succession planning, and discuss why adaptability and ongoing assessment are crucial in a rapidly changing business landscape.

CHAPTER

10

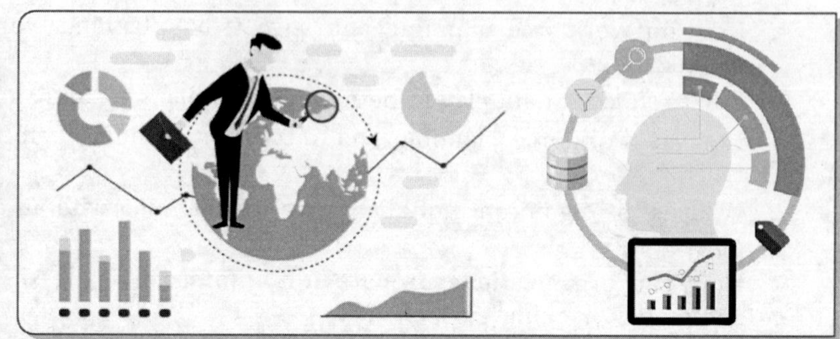

Employee Wellness and Well-being

In an era defined by rapid technological advancements and the ever-increasing demands of the modern workplace, the well-being of employees has become a paramount concern for organizations and companies have started caring a lot about their workers' health and happiness these days. An engaged and healthy staff is not only an advantage but also a key factor in the success of a business. This introduction goes over the main ideas of employee health and well-being, focusing on how important they are and how they affect people and the companies they work for.

Today's workplaces are very different from those of the past. These differences are caused by globalisation, digital development, and changing employee standards. A strict nine-to-five routine is no longer the only way to work. These days, people can be more flexible and adapt to their surroundings. Workers today want more than just a pay check; they want to be happy at work, have a good mix between work and life, and be surrounded by people who care about them. As a result, businesses are focused more and more on tactics that improve the health and happiness of their employees.

DEFINING EMPLOYEE WELLNESS AND WELL-BEING

Employee Wellness

At its core, employee wellness refers to the state of being in good physical health. It encompasses elements such as regular exercise, proper nutrition, and overall physical health. Wellness programs often include initiatives like fitness challenges, health screenings, and access to gym facilities. These programs aim to reduce health risks and improve the overall health of employees.

Employee Well-being

Well-being takes a broader perspective, encompassing not only physical health but also emotional, mental, and social well-being. It addresses factors like job satisfaction, stress management, work-life balance, and mental health. Well-being initiatives extend beyond traditional wellness programs to create a supportive work culture that acknowledges the holistic needs of employees.

The Business Case for Employee Well-being

The link between employee well-being and organizational performance is well-established. When employees are healthy, engaged, and have a sense of well-being, organizations benefit in several ways:

- *Increased Productivity:* Healthy and happy employees are more productive and tend to be more engaged in their work.
- *Reduced Absenteeism:* Well-being programs can help reduce the number of sick days and absenteeism due to health issues.
- *Enhanced Employee Engagement:* Well-being initiatives contribute to higher employee morale and commitment to the organization.
- *Talent Attraction and Retention:* Organizations that prioritize well-being are more likely to attract and retain top talent.
- *Cost Savings:* Healthy employees incur lower healthcare costs for organizations.

THE ROLE OF HR IN PROMOTING EMPLOYEE WELL-BEING

Employee well-being is a critical component of a healthy and productive workforce. It encompasses physical, mental, and emotional health, as well as overall job satisfaction. Human Resources (HR) departments play a pivotal role in championing employee well-being. HR professionals are responsible for designing, implementing, and overseeing wellness and well-being programs. They also foster a culture that values well-being and mental health, promotes work-life balance, and addresses issues that can negatively affect employees' overall quality of life. In recent years, organizations have come to recognize that promoting employee well-being is not just a matter of goodwill; it's a strategic imperative. This is where the Human Resources (HR) department plays a pivotal role. HR professionals are uniquely positioned to champion and facilitate the promotion of employee well-being in the workplace.

Designing and Implementing Well-being Programs

HR is responsible for conceptualizing, developing, and implementing well-being programs that cater to the diverse needs of employees. This includes crafting initiatives related to physical fitness, mental health, stress management, nutrition, and work-life balance. HR professionals collaborate with wellness experts, insurance providers, and external consultants to create comprehensive programs that can positively impact employee health and happiness.

Culture and Policy Development

HR is instrumental in shaping the organizational culture. They design policies and practices that foster an environment where employee well-being is valued. This may involve flexible work arrangements, paid time off, family-friendly policies, and stress reduction strategies. By creating a supportive culture, HR helps in reducing workplace stress and burnout.

Communication and Education

HR acts as a conduit for disseminating information about well-being programs and resources. They engage in effective internal communication to ensure that employees are aware of the available wellness initiatives. HR professionals also organize workshops, seminars, and training sessions on topics like mental health, nutrition, and stress management. This education empowers employees to take control of their well-being.

Mental Health Support

Mental health issues are prevalent in the workplace, and HR plays a crucial role in addressing them. HR professionals are trained to recognize signs of distress and can guide employees toward appropriate resources. They establish confidential channels for employees to seek help, connecting them with counsellors or mental health professionals when needed. By promoting mental health awareness, HR contributes to a more inclusive and compassionate workplace.

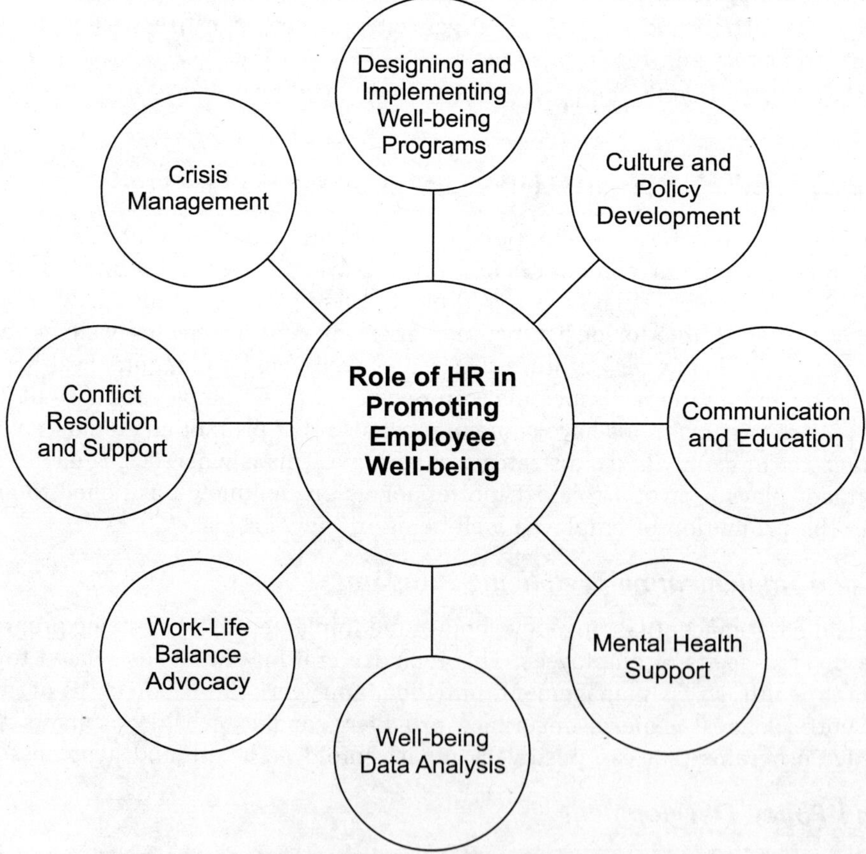

FIGURE 10.1 Role of HR in promoting employee well-being.

Well-being Data Analysis

HR collects and analyses data related to employee well-being. This data informs decision-making and helps in assessing the effectiveness of well-being programs. For instance, they can evaluate the impact of wellness initiatives on absenteeism, productivity, and job satisfaction. This data-driven approach allows HR to make continuous improvements in well-being strategies.

Work-Life Balance Advocacy

HR is an advocate for work-life balance. They encourage and support initiatives such as flexible work arrangements, telecommuting, and family support programs. These efforts enable employees to better manage their personal and professional lives, reducing stress and improving overall well-being.

Conflict Resolution and Support

HR is often the first point of contact for employees facing work-related conflicts or stressors. HR professionals are trained in conflict resolution and can help mediate disputes, provide support, and offer guidance on problem-solving. By addressing these issues, HR contributes to a healthier workplace environment.

Crisis Management

During crises such as the COVID-19 pandemic, HR is at the forefront of managing the impact on employee well-being. They play a key role in establishing remote work policies, mental health support systems, and communication strategies to keep employees informed and connected during challenging times.

The role of HR in promoting employee well-being is multifaceted and essential for maintaining a thriving and resilient workforce. HR professionals serve as advocates, educators, facilitators, and data-driven decision-makers, working in tandem with employees to create an environment where well-being is prioritized. By investing in employee well-being, organizations not only enhance their employees' quality of life but also boost productivity, engagement, and overall business success.

THE SIGNIFICANCE OF EMPLOYEE WELL-BEING

The significance of employee well-being cannot be overstated in the modern workplace. Employee well-being encompasses physical, mental, and emotional health, and it goes beyond merely avoiding illness or burnout. It is about creating a work environment that fosters a sense of purpose, engagement, and balance. Following are some of the key reasons why employee well-being is of utmost importance for both individuals and organizations:

Enhanced Productivity and Performance

- Healthy and well-balanced employees are more likely to be productive and perform at their best.
- Reduced stress and burnout lead to higher concentration, creativity, and problem-solving abilities.

Employee Engagement

- Well-being initiatives contribute to higher levels of employee engagement.
- Engaged employees are more committed to their work and the organization's goals.

Talent Attraction and Retention

- Organizations that prioritize employee well-being are more attractive to top talent.
- Well-being programs are a competitive advantage in recruiting and retaining skilled employees.

Healthcare Cost Reduction

- A focus on wellness can lead to lower healthcare costs for both employees and the organization.
- Prevention and early intervention can mitigate the need for costly medical treatments.

Reduced Absenteeism and Presenteeism

- Well-being initiatives reduce the number of sick days taken by employees.
- Improved well-being also diminishes presenteeism, where employees are present at work but not fully productive due to health issues.

Improved Organizational Culture

- An organization that cares about well-being fosters a positive culture.
- Employees feel valued, supported, and part of a community, leading to higher job satisfaction.

Mental Health and Emotional Well-being

- Promoting mental health and emotional well-being reduces the stigma surrounding these issues.
- It helps employees seek help and support when needed, leading to healthier minds and lives.

Work-Life Balance

- A healthy work-life balance is crucial for overall well-being.
- It allows employees to devote time to family, hobbies, and personal growth, reducing stress and enhancing satisfaction.

Organizational Resilience

- Well-being initiatives create a more resilient workforce that can adapt to change and handle stress more effectively.
- In times of crisis, employees with strong well-being are better equipped to navigate challenges.

Legal and Ethical Considerations

- In many regions, there are legal and ethical obligations for employers to provide a safe and healthy work environment.
- Neglecting employee well-being can lead to legal issues and damage an organization's reputation.

Social Responsibility

- Organizations are increasingly expected to demonstrate social responsibility.
- Promoting employee well-being is seen as a responsible and ethical practice.

Long-term Sustainability

- Prioritizing well-being ensures the long-term sustainability of an organization.
- Healthy, satisfied employees are more likely to stay with the organization and contribute to its long-term success.

In short, employee well-being is not just a feel-good concept but a critical driver of organizational success. It is the foundation upon which a productive, engaged, and resilient workforce is built. When organizations invest in their employees' well-being, they reap the rewards of a healthier, happier, and more productive workforce, contributing to their own success and the well-being of their employees.

TABLE 10.1 The link between employee well-being and organizational performance

Aspect	*Employee Well-being*	*Organizational Performance*
Definition	Employee well-being refers to the physical, mental, and emotional health and contentment of employees within the workplace.	Organizational performance refers to the ability of an organization to achieve its strategic goals and objectives, which may include financial success, productivity, innovation, and customer satisfaction.
Key indicators	• Physical health • Mental health • Work-life balance • Job satisfaction • Stress levels • Engagement • Job security.	• Productivity • Employee retention • Innovation and creativity • Customer satisfaction • Profitability • Market competitiveness.
Causal relationship	Positive employee well-being positively affects organizational performance. When employees are healthy, satisfied, and engaged, they are more likely to contribute to the organization's success.	Strong organizational performance can also have a positive impact on employee well-being. A thriving company can provide job security, competitive compensation, and opportunities for professional growth, enhancing employee well-being.
Impact on productivity	• Employees with good well-being are more focused and less likely to be absent due to illness. • Reduced stress and anxiety lead to improved concentration and task completion.	• High-performing organizations can afford to invest in employee development, training, and wellness programs, which can enhance productivity. • A culture of excellence and success often motivates employees to perform at their best.

(*Contd.*)

Aspect	*Employee Well-being*	*Organizational Performance*
Employee engagement	• Satisfied and healthy employees are more likely to be engaged and committed to their work. • They tend to be more proactive and dedicated to organizational goals.	• Organizations with strong performance often have a compelling mission and a track record of success, which can increase employee pride and commitment. • High-performance cultures typically emphasize engagement and continuous improvement.
Employee retention	• Employees with good well-being are less likely to seek opportunities elsewhere. • Job satisfaction and work-life balance contribute to higher retention rates.	• Successful organizations often provide competitive compensation, benefits, and advancement opportunities, which reduce employee turnover. • A reputation for excellence can make the organization an attractive place to work.
Innovation and creativity	• Employees with better well-being are more likely to be creative and innovative, contributing fresh ideas and solutions.	• High-performing organizations typically foster a culture of innovation and reward creative thinking, encouraging employees to contribute to the organization's success.
Customer satisfaction	• Satisfied, engaged employees are more likely to provide excellent customer service. • Low employee stress levels can lead to more positive interactions with customers.	• High-performing organizations often deliver quality products and services that meet or exceed customer expectations, resulting in higher customer satisfaction and loyalty.
Profitability	• Healthy, satisfied employees are typically more productive and contribute to cost savings through reduced absenteeism and turnover.	• Organizational performance, when characterized by efficiency, effectiveness, and competitiveness, tends to lead to higher profitability.
Key initiatives	• Wellness programs • Employee assistance programs • Work-life balance policies • Mental health support • Employee engagement initiatives.	• Performance measurement and management systems • Competitive compensation and benefits • Employee development programs • Leadership and culture that promotes excellence and innovation.
Case studies	• Google offers a range of wellness programs and employee benefits that contribute to employee well-being, resulting in a creative and innovative work environment.	• Apple Inc. is known for its strong organizational performance, driven by product innovation, customer loyalty, and competitive profitability.

This table highlights the interconnectedness between employee well-being and organizational performance, illustrating how positive well-being influences performance and how strong performance can enhance employee well-being. Employers who understand and leverage this relationship can create a more successful and fulfilling work environment.

ANALYSING EMPLOYEE WELL-BEING PROGRAMS

Employee well-being programs have become a cornerstone of modern organizations' efforts to support their workforce, enhance engagement, and improve productivity.

Understanding Well-being Programs

Definition and Objectives: Employee well-being programs, often referred to as workplace wellness programs, are structured initiatives designed to improve and maintain the health and overall well-being of an organization's employees. The primary objectives of these programs include:

- Promoting physical health by encouraging regular exercise, proper nutrition, and health screenings.
- Enhancing mental health and emotional well-being by providing resources for stress management and work-life balance.
- Fostering a culture of well-being that supports employee happiness and engagement.
- Reducing health-related absenteeism and healthcare costs for both employees and the organization.

Common Elements of Well-being Programs: Well-being programs encompass a variety of elements aimed at addressing different facets of employee health and happiness. Common elements include:

- **Health Assessments:** Employees are often encouraged to participate in health assessments to identify potential health risks and areas for improvement.
- **Fitness Initiatives:** These may include gym access, fitness challenges, or onsite exercise classes to promote physical health.
- **Mental Health Resources:** Providing access to counselling, stress management programs, and support for emotional well-being.
- **Nutrition Programs:** Offering guidance on healthy eating habits and sometimes providing healthy snacks or meals.
- **Work-Life Balance Initiatives:** Encouraging employees to balance their work commitments with personal and family life.
- **Preventive Health Measures:** Promoting vaccinations, regular check-ups, and screenings for early detection of health issues.

Designing Effective Well-being Programs

Tailoring Programs to Employee Needs: Effective well-being programs recognize that a one-size-fits-all approach may not work for all employees. Organizations should:

- Conduct surveys and assessments to understand the specific needs and preferences of their workforce.
- Customize programs to address the most pressing concerns, whether they be physical, mental, or emotional health.
- Provide options and flexibility within the program to accommodate diverse needs and lifestyles.

Assessing Program Goals and Metrics: Before implementing a well-being program, organizations should define clear goals and metrics to measure the program's success:

- Identify the key performance indicators (KPIs) that align with program objectives, such as reduced absenteeism or increased employee engagement.
- Regularly assess and adjust the program's goals and metrics to ensure that it remains effective and relevant.
- Benchmark the program against industry standards to gauge its success relative to similar organizations.

Well-being Program Implementation

Communicating the Program to Employees: Successful implementation starts with effective communication:

- Clearly and transparently communicate the program's objectives, benefits, and how employees can participate.
- Use a variety of communication channels, such as emails, intranet, posters, and in-person meetings, to reach all employees.
- Encourage leaders and managers to lead by example and actively promote the program.

Integrating Well-being into Organizational Culture: The most effective well-being programs are those that are woven into the fabric of an organization's culture:

- Leadership should champion well-being and encourage employees to prioritize their health and happiness.
- Create a supportive work environment that includes flexibility, stress reduction, and a positive work-life balance.
- Ensure that well-being is reflected in organizational policies, practices, and decision-making.

MEASURING THE IMPACT OF WELLNESS INITIATIVES

In order to create a company that cares about its employees' well-being, it is important to not only start wellness programmes but also evaluate how well they work. Organisations need to measure the results of health programmes to see how they help their workers and the business as a whole.

Key Metrics for Measuring Employee Well-being

Employee Engagement Surveys

Employee engagement is a cornerstone of well-being. Employee engagement surveys gauge employees' emotional commitment to their work, the organization, and their overall job satisfaction. By regularly conducting these surveys, organizations can track changes in engagement levels and identify areas that require improvement.

Health and Lifestyle Assessments

Assessing the health and lifestyle choices of employees provides valuable data on their physical well-being. These assessments typically include factors like diet, exercise, stress levels, and smoking habits. The results help in identifying potential health risks and allow organizations to tailor wellness programs to address specific needs.

Absenteeism and Presenteeism

The rates of absenteeism (employees being absent from work) and presenteeism (employees working while unwell or not at their best) are critical indicators of well-being. High absenteeism and presenteeism can be signs of underlying health or work-related issues. Tracking these metrics helps in identifying patterns and potential causes that need addressing.

Data Collection and Analysis

The Role of Data in Assessing Well-being

Data plays a central role in assessing the effectiveness of wellness initiatives. It provides quantitative and qualitative insights into employee well-being. Data allows organizations to monitor changes over time, compare results across different initiatives, and make informed decisions.

Tools and Methods for Data Collection

There are various tools and methods for collecting well-being data. These include surveys, questionnaires, interviews, wearable devices, and HR software that can track employee health and engagement. Organizations should choose methods that best align with their goals and employee preferences.

Interpreting Data and Identifying Trends

Identifying Successes and Areas for Improvement

Data alone is not sufficient; it must be interpreted to extract meaningful insights. Successes and areas for improvement become apparent when trends are identified. For example, a consistent improvement in employee engagement scores can indicate the success of wellness programs, while a sudden increase in absenteeism may signal emerging issues.

Using Data for Informed Decision-making

Data-driven decision-making is at the heart of effective wellness program management. When organizations interpret data and identify trends, they can make informed decisions about program adjustments, reallocation of resources, and the introduction of new initiatives to better support employee well-being.

Continuous Improvement of Wellness Initiatives

Iterative Approach to Wellness Programs

Measuring the impact of wellness initiatives should not be a one-time effort but an ongoing process. Organizations should adopt an iterative approach, continually reassessing and adapting programs based on the data and feedback received. This approach ensures that wellness initiatives remain relevant and effective.

Feedback and Employee Involvement

Employees are valuable sources of feedback about wellness programs. Organizations should actively seek input from employees to understand their needs, preferences, and concerns. Involving employees in program design and improvement fosters a sense of ownership and ensures that programs align with their well-being aspirations.

In short, measuring the impact of wellness initiatives is a multifaceted process that combines the collection and analysis of well-being data with the interpretation of results and a commitment to continuous improvement. By adopting a data-driven, employee-centric approach, organizations can not only gauge the effectiveness of their wellness programs but also make informed decisions that lead to improved employee well-being and overall organizational success.

PROMOTING WORK-LIFE BALANCE AND MENTAL HEALTH

Work-Life Balance

Work-life balance is a concept that refers to the equilibrium an individual seeks to strike between their professional and personal life. It is the ability to manage the demands of work alongside personal and family life, without one infringing on the other. The significance of work-life balance cannot be overstated, as it affects the physical, mental, and emotional well-being of employees and has broader implications for organizational success.

Importance of Work-Life Balance

1. **Enhanced Well-being:** Maintaining work-life balance is fundamental to the overall well-being of employees. It reduces stress, anxiety, and burnout, promoting better mental and physical health.
2. **Increased Productivity:** A balanced life allows employees to recharge and recuperate, leading to higher job performance and productivity. Rested and motivated individuals tend to work more efficiently.
3. **Improved Job Satisfaction:** Employees with work-life balance are generally more satisfied with their jobs and are more likely to stay with the organization.
4. **Talent Attraction and Retention:** Organizations that support work-life balance are more appealing to potential hires. It's a key factor for attracting and retaining top talent.

5. **Reduced Absenteeism and Presenteeism:** A balanced life results in fewer sick days and reduced instances of presenteeism, where employees are physically present but not fully engaged due to exhaustion or stress.
6. **Healthier Relationships:** Maintaining work-life balance is essential for maintaining healthy relationships with family and friends. It helps individuals nurture personal connections and find emotional support.
7. **Long-term Sustainability:** Organizations benefit from employees who maintain work-life balance. Such employees are less likely to burn out, more likely to stay with the company, and contribute to the organization's long-term success.

Strategies for Promoting Work-life Balance

Promoting work-life balance is not just a benefit for employees; it's a strategic imperative for organizations. Following are some strategies for creating an environment that fosters work-life balance:

1. **Flexible Work Arrangements**:
   - Allow employees to have flexible work hours or remote work options.
   - Encourage job-sharing or part-time work for those who seek it.
2. **Clear Communication**:
   - Establish open and transparent communication channels.
   - Encourage employees to express their needs and boundaries regarding work.
3. **Set Realistic Expectations**:
   - Encourage reasonable workloads and deadlines.
   - Ensure employees are not consistently overburdened.
4. **Encourage Time Management**:
   - Train employees in time management skills.
   - Promote setting priorities and boundaries.
5. **Promote Unplugging**:
   - Encourage employees to disconnect from work when not on the clock.
   - Discourage sending work-related emails during non-working hours.
6. **Support for Caregivers**:
   - Provide support and resources for employees who are caregivers.
   - Offer family-friendly policies, such as parental leave and childcare assistance.
7. **Wellness Programs**:
   - Implement wellness programs that focus on stress management, mindfulness, and overall health.
   - Encourage physical fitness and healthy eating.
8. **Leadership Role Modelling**:
   - Leaders should set the example by prioritizing their own work-life balance.
   - Recognize and reward employees who maintain balance effectively.
9. **Mental Health Support**:
   - Address mental health issues proactively by providing access to counselling services and resources.
   - Promote a stigma-free environment where employees feel comfortable seeking help.

In summary, work-life balance is an essential component of a happy, engaged, and productive workforce—it is not just a trendy word. Prioritising work-life balance allows organisations to profit from their employees' well-being as well as develop a successful and resilient workforce that can survive in a cutthroat and dynamic business climate.

Mental Health Support: Recognizing and Addressing Mental Health Issues

In today's fast-paced and high-pressure work environments, the importance of addressing mental health issues cannot be overstated. Mental health support in the workplace is a crucial aspect of employee well-being.

Recognizing and Addressing Mental Health Issues

Mental health issues can affect anyone, regardless of their position or seniority within an organization. It's essential for both employees and employers to recognize the signs of mental health issues. These signs may include increased absenteeism, reduced productivity, changes in behaviour, mood swings, and withdrawal from social interactions. Creating an environment where employees feel comfortable discussing their mental health concerns is the first step in addressing these issues.

- **Open Dialogue:** Encouraging open and non-judgmental conversations about mental health is crucial. Employees should feel safe discussing their concerns with their managers or HR without fear of reprisal.
- **Mental Health Training:** Providing training to both employees and management on recognizing mental health issues is essential. It equips individuals with the knowledge and skills to support their colleagues and seek help when needed.
- **Access to Resources:** Organizations should offer resources such as Employee Assistance Programs (EAPs), counselling services, or access to mental health professionals. This demonstrates a commitment to addressing mental health issues and provides concrete support.
- **Reasonable Accommodations:** Offering accommodations, such as flexible work arrangements or reduced workloads, can help employees manage their mental health while remaining productive.

Destigmatizing Mental Health in the Workplace

The stigma associated with mental health problems continues to be a major obstacle to getting treatment and assistance. Organisations need to take proactive steps to lessen this stigma if they want to foster a psychologically healthy work environment.

- **Leadership Role:** Company leadership should set an example by discussing their own mental health challenges. This not only destigmatizes the issue but also encourages employees to be open about their struggles.
- **Education and Awareness:** Regularly providing educational programs and awareness campaigns can help employees understand mental health better. By addressing common misconceptions and promoting empathy, organizations can create a more supportive environment.

- **Inclusive Policies:** Organizations should implement policies that explicitly support mental health, including reasonable accommodations, job protection during treatment, and leave policies.
- **Mental Health Days:** Offering mental health days as part of leave policies acknowledges that mental health is just as important as physical health. This small gesture can make a big difference.

FLEXIBLE WORK ARRANGEMENTS: TELECOMMUTING AND FLEXIBLE HOURS

The concept of a traditional nine-to-five, in-office workday is evolving. Flexible work arrangements, such as telecommuting and flexible hours, have gained prominence. The benefits and challenges of these arrangements and their impact on employee well-being are discussed below:

Telecommuting and Flexible Hours

- **Telecommuting:** This arrangement allows employees to work from remote locations, such as home or co-working spaces. It provides greater flexibility and reduces the need for daily commutes.
- **Flexible Hours:** Flexible hours permit employees to set their own work schedules, within certain constraints. This flexibility accommodates diverse personal needs and preferences.

Benefits of Flexible Work Arrangements

- **Improved Work-Life Balance:** Flexible work arrangements empower employees to better balance work and personal life, reducing stress and improving overall well-being.
- **Increased Job Satisfaction:** Employees value the autonomy and trust associated with flexible work arrangements, leading to higher job satisfaction.
- **Talent Attraction and Retention:** Organizations offering such flexibility are more appealing to a diverse talent pool. They also retain experienced employees who might otherwise leave due to rigid work schedules.
- **Productivity and Efficiency:** Many employees find they are more productive in a comfortable, self-chosen environment, resulting in increased efficiency.
- **Cost Savings:** Reduced commuting expenses and office space requirements can lead to cost savings for both employees and employers.

Challenges of Flexible Work Arrangements

- **Communication Challenges:** Remote work can sometimes lead to communication issues, especially in collaborative roles that require constant interaction.
- **Work-Life Boundaries:** Without clear boundaries, employees may struggle to disconnect from work, leading to burnout.

- **Security and Privacy Concerns:** Organizations need to address data security and privacy concerns when employees work outside traditional office settings.
- **Team Building and Company Culture:** Building a cohesive team and maintaining a company culture can be more challenging with remote or dispersed employees.

Thus, recognizing and addressing mental health issues and embracing flexible work arrangements are essential components of a holistic approach to employee well-being. By creating an environment that supports mental health and offers flexibility in work arrangements, organizations not only improve the overall well-being of their employees but also enhance productivity, engagement, and their ability to attract and retain top talent.

SUPPORTING EMPLOYEE WELL-BEING DURING AND AFTER CRISIS

Organisations need to be ready to react to crises quickly and efficiently in the turbulent and unpredictable world of today. A crisis can take many different forms, such as a natural disaster, an economic slump, or, more recently, a worldwide epidemic. Employee welfare becomes a top priority during these difficult times. The strategies and resources that organizations can employ to support employee well-being during and after crises are discussed below:

Coping with Pandemics and Other Crises

Crises, whether they are pandemics, natural disasters, economic recessions, or other emergencies, can exact a heavy toll on employees' physical and mental health. The impact of crises can be profound, affecting both personal and professional lives. Organizations play a crucial role in helping employees navigate these turbulent waters.

1. **Transparent Communication:** Open and transparent communication is key during a crisis. Employees need to know that the organization is aware of the situation, taking steps to address it, and prioritizing their safety and well-being.
2. **Flexible Work Arrangements:** During crises, employees may face challenges such as school closures or health concerns. Offering flexible work arrangements, such as remote work or adjusted hours, can ease the burden and reduce stress.
3. **Access to Healthcare and Mental Health Support:** Providing access to healthcare resources, including COVID-19 testing and treatment, is essential. Mental health support is equally crucial, as crises can trigger anxiety, depression, and stress. Employee assistance programs (EAPs) and virtual counselling services can be invaluable.
4. **Support for Caregivers:** Many employees are also caregivers for children, elderly family members, or individuals with special needs. Offering support, including guidance on balancing work and caregiving responsibilities, can ease the strain.
5. **Financial Support and Counselling:** Economic crises can lead to financial stress. Organizations can offer financial counselling and resources to help employees manage their finances during challenging times.
6. **Remote Work Resources:** For organizations shifting to remote work, ensuring that employees have the necessary technology, ergonomics, and support for remote collaboration is essential.

Crisis Management and Mental Health Resources

Crisis management is an essential aspect of maintaining employee well-being during and after crises. Following are some strategies to consider:

1. **Wellness Check-ins:** Regular check-ins with employees can help organizations gauge their well-being. These check-ins can be both formal (surveys or interviews) and informal (team meetings). The data collected can inform well-being support initiatives.
2. **Mental Health Training:** Training managers and HR personnel to recognize signs of mental health struggles and respond appropriately is crucial. Mental health first aid courses can provide valuable knowledge and skills.
3. **Clear Mental Health Policies:** Organizations should have clear policies on mental health support. These policies should detail available resources, confidentiality, and anti-discrimination measures.
4. **Peer Support Programs:** Peer support programs, where employees are trained to provide support to their colleagues, can be effective in normalizing conversations about mental health.
5. **Resilience Training:** Resilience training equips employees with tools to cope with stress and adversity. These programs can enhance employees' ability to navigate crises.
6. **Post-Crisis Debriefing:** After a crisis has passed, it's important to conduct debriefing sessions to learn from the experience and identify areas for improvement in crisis management and support initiatives.
7. **Creating a Culture of Support:** Building a culture that values well-being and encourages employees to seek help when needed is an ongoing effort. It starts with leadership setting an example and fostering an environment of trust.

Hence supporting employee well-being during and after crises is a critical aspect of organizational resilience and responsible management. Crises can be disruptive, but they also provide opportunities for organizations to demonstrate their commitment to their employees' health and well-being. By implementing comprehensive crisis management strategies and mental health resources, organizations can help employees navigate adversity, ultimately emerging stronger and more resilient on the other side.

THE ONGOING EVOLUTION OF EMPLOYEE WELL-BEING PROGRAMS

Employee well-being programs have come a long way from traditional workplace wellness initiatives, which often focused solely on physical health. Today, these programs have evolved to encompass a holistic approach that considers the physical, mental, and emotional well-being of employees. The ongoing evolution of employee well-being programs is driven by several factors:

1. **Holistic Approach:** Earlier programs predominantly concentrated on physical health, like exercise and nutrition. Modern programs recognize the interconnectedness of physical, mental, and emotional well-being and aim to address all these facets.

2. **Customization:** Organizations now recognize that one-size-fits-all well-being programs may not be effective. Customization and personalization are key trends, allowing employees to choose the initiatives that resonate with their unique needs.
3. **Technological Advancements:** Technology plays a crucial role in the evolution of well-being programs. Mobile apps, wearable devices, and online platforms facilitate easy access to well-being resources, tracking progress, and providing interactive experiences.
4. **Data-driven Insights:** Well-being programs are increasingly data-driven. By collecting and analysing data, organizations can tailor programs to specific employee needs and measure the impact of these initiatives more accurately.
5. **Mental Health Focus:** With a growing awareness of mental health issues, well-being programs now include resources and support for managing stress, anxiety, and depression. Providing access to mental health professionals and services has become a norm.
6. **Work-life Integration:** The lines between work and personal life are blurring. Well-being programs recognize the importance of promoting work-life integration and offer resources for maintaining balance.
7. **Cultural Inclusivity:** Well-being programs are evolving to be more inclusive, respecting diverse cultures and backgrounds. This means recognizing different perspectives on well-being and accommodating various preferences.

TABLE 10.2 The ongoing evolution of employee well-being programs

The Ongoing Evolution of Employee Well-being Programs	*Key Points*
1. Historical perspective	• Early well-being programs focused on physical health.
	• Today's programs encompass mental, emotional, and social aspects.
2. Holistic approach	• Well-being programs now address the whole person.
	• Promote emotional well-being, stress management, and work-life balance.
3. Technology and data	• Technology-driven platforms enable personalized programs.
	• Data analytics help tailor initiatives for maximum impact.
4. Remote work and flexibility	• Well-being programs adapt to the changing work landscape.
	• Promote well-being in remote and hybrid work environments.
5. Inclusivity and diversity	• Inclusivity is a cornerstone; programs cater to diverse needs.
	• Recognize the importance of cultural and identity well-being.

(*Contd.*)

The Ongoing Evolution of Employee Well-being Programs	*Key Points*
6. Employee-centric culture	• Well-being is integrated into an organization's culture.
	• Employees are actively involved in shaping well-being initiatives.
7. Sustainability	• Well-being programs focus on long-term employee health.
	• Ensure well-being sustainability for a resilient workforce.

The Business Case for Prioritizing Employee Well-being

Prioritizing employee well-being is not just a compassionate endeavour; it's a sound business strategy. The business case for investing in employee well-being is supported by a wealth of research and practical evidence:

1. **Enhanced Productivity:** Healthy, well-balanced employees are more productive, resulting in increased output and higher quality work.
2. **Talent Attraction and Retention:** Organizations that prioritize well-being are more appealing to top talent, reducing recruitment costs and improving employee retention rates.
3. **Reduced Healthcare Costs:** Employee wellness programs can lead to lower healthcare costs for both employees and employers by encouraging preventive care and healthy lifestyles.

TABLE 10.3 The business case for prioritizing employee well-being

The Business Case for Prioritizing Employee Well-being	*Key Points*
1. Increased productivity	• Healthy, engaged employees are more productive.
	• Employee well-being positively impacts an organization's bottom line.
2. Talent attraction and retention	• Well-being programs attract and retain top talent.
	• Reduced turnover and recruitment costs.
3. Health care cost reduction	• Promoting well-being leads to lower healthcare expenses.
	• Preventing illnesses reduces medical costs.
4. Reduced absenteeism and presenteeism	• Fewer sick days and increased on-the-job productivity.
	• Improves overall workforce availability.
5. Organizational culture	• A culture of well-being fosters positive workplace morale.
	• Increases job satisfaction and employee engagement.
6. Mental health and emotional well-being	• Prioritizing mental health reduces stigma and enhances support.
	• Employees are more likely to seek help when needed.

4. **Lower Absenteeism and Presenteeism:** Well-being initiatives reduce sick days and the phenomenon of presenteeism, where employees are at work but not fully productive.
5. **Improved Employee Engagement:** Engaged employees are more likely to contribute their best to the organization. Well-being initiatives foster a sense of commitment and engagement.
6. **Positive Organizational Culture:** A culture that values well-being is more attractive to employees and contributes to job satisfaction, reducing turnover.
7. **Enhanced Reputation:** Organizations known for prioritizing employee well-being enjoy a positive reputation, which can attract customers and partners.
8. **Legal and Ethical Compliance:** Meeting legal obligations and ethical responsibilities regarding employee well-being helps avoid legal troubles and ethical breaches.

The Future of Employee Well-being in the Workplace

The future of employee well-being holds exciting possibilities and challenges:

1. **AI and Data Analytics:** Artificial intelligence and data analytics will play a crucial role in personalizing well-being programs and predicting employee needs.
2. **Remote and Flexible Work:** The rise of remote and flexible work arrangements will necessitate new strategies for promoting well-being among virtual teams.
3. **Mental Health Emphasis:** Mental health will continue to be a primary focus, with more proactive measures to support employees' emotional well-being.
4. **Well-being Technology:** Technology will enable more accessible and interactive well-being programs, with wearable devices and mobile apps becoming integral.
5. **Cultural Inclusivity:** Organizations will increasingly focus on accommodating diverse cultural perspectives on well-being and fostering inclusivity.
6. **Community and Social Well-being:** Well-being programs will extend beyond the workplace to promote community and social well-being through corporate social responsibility initiatives.
7. **Flexible Benefits:** Employee benefits packages will become more flexible, allowing employees to customize their well-being benefits.

The ongoing evolution of employee well-being programs is reshaping the workplace to prioritize the comprehensive well-being of employees. The business case for this prioritization is clear, as it enhances performance, engagement, and overall organizational success. Looking to the future, employee well-being will continue to adapt to the changing needs of the workforce and the broader societal context, embracing technology and inclusivity while emphasizing holistic well-being.

TABLE 10.4 The future of employee well-being in the workplace

Future of Employee Well-being	*Key Points*
1. Technological advancements	• Continued integration of technology and data analytics.
	• Personalized well-being programs through AI and wearables.
2. Hybrid work models	• Adaptation to evolving work arrangements (remote, hybrid).
	• Remote well-being programs and flexible support.
3. Greater emphasis on mental health	• Heightened focus on mental health awareness and support.
	• Mental health parity and reducing stigma.
4. Inclusivity and diversity	• Customized well-being programs to cater to diverse needs.
	• Acknowledging cultural and identity well-being.
5. Employee well-being as a core business strategy	• Integrated well-being into business strategy and decision-making.
	• Recognizing well-being as a driver of long-term success.
6. Adaptation to changing workforces	• Well-being programs that cater to multi-generational workforces.
	• Accommodating evolving expectations and needs.

Questions for Discussion

Short Questions

1. What are the core elements of employee wellness programs?
2. How does employee well-being differ from employee wellness?
3. What is the role of Human Resources (HR) in promoting employee well-being?
4. How does HR contribute to work-life balance in organizations?
5. What are the key benefits of promoting mental health in the workplace?
6. How do organizations collect and analyse data related to employee well-being?
7. What is the role of HR in crisis management for employee well-being?
8. How can employee well-being programs help reduce healthcare costs?
9. Why is work-life balance essential for employee well-being?
10. What are some key metrics for measuring employee well-being?
11. How can absenteeism and presenteeism be indicators of employee well-being?

12. What role does data play in assessing the effectiveness of wellness initiatives?
13. What are some tools and methods for collecting well-being data?
14. What is work-life balance, and why is it important for employee well-being?
15. What are some strategies for promoting work-life balance in the workplace?

Long Questions

1. Explain the difference between employee wellness and employee well-being. How can organizations effectively address both aspects?
2. Describe the multifaceted role of Human Resources (HR) in promoting employee well-being, and provide examples of HR initiatives in this regard.
3. What are the primary objectives and common elements of employee well-being programs? How do these programs contribute to a healthier workforce?
4. How can organizations tailor well-being programs to the diverse needs of their employees? What steps should they take to ensure program effectiveness?
5. What are the key considerations for effectively implementing well-being programs in organizations? How can communication and culture integration play a vital role?
6. In what ways can a focus on employee well-being benefit organizations, their employees, and society as a whole? Provide examples and real-world cases to support your explanation.
7. How can organizations measure the success of their well-being programs? What key performance indicators (KPIs) are commonly used in this context?
8. Discuss the legal and ethical considerations associated with neglecting employee well-being in the workplace. How can organizations ensure they meet their obligations in this regard?
9. Explain the concept of work-life balance and its importance for employee well-being. How can organizations support work-life balance effectively?
10. In times of crisis, such as the COVID-19 pandemic, what specific actions can HR take to manage the impact on employee well-being and maintain organizational resilience?
11. Can you explain the importance of measuring the impact of wellness initiatives in detail and how it contributes to both employee well-being and organizational success?
12. How does data collection and analysis play a central role in assessing the effectiveness of wellness initiatives, and what are some best practices for organizations in this regard?
13. What are the challenges and benefits of flexible work arrangements, and how do they contribute to employee well-being?
14. How do crises impact employee well-being, and what strategies and resources can organizations employ to support employees during and after crises effectively?
15. What are the key trends in the ongoing evolution of employee well-being programs, and how are they reshaping the workplace?

CHAPTER

11

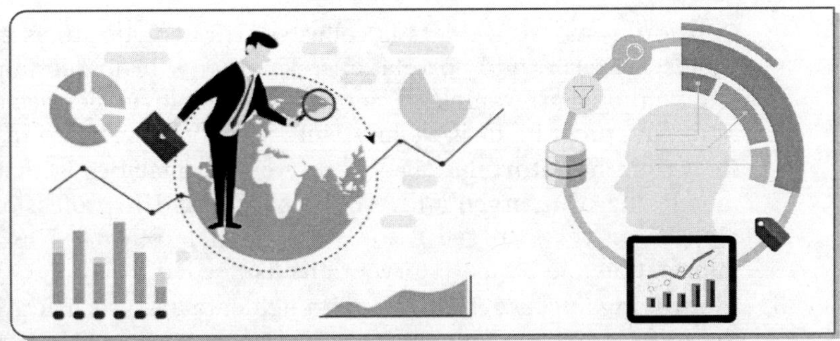

Monitoring the Impact of Interventions

Human Resources (HR) divisions/departments are of utmost importance in the contemporary and highly competitive business environment. They are tasked with the critical responsibility of not only attracting and retaining exceptional personnel but also diligently supporting the overarching goals of the organisation. Implementing a variety of interventions designed to enhance employee engagement, well-being, and performance is one method by which HR accomplishes this. The scope of these interventions is extensive, including initiatives for wellness, diversity and inclusion, and training and development programmes, among others. How can human resources professionals, however, quantify the efficacy and ramifications of these interventions on the organisation? This is a frequently asked and crucial inquiry.

HR analytics is relevant in this context. The systematic gathering, evaluation, and interpretation of human resources data in order to inform decisions based on that data constitutes HR analytics. HR analytics enables organisations to refine interventions in real-time, on the basis of data and insights obtained in the process, in addition to evaluating their efficacy. Monitoring the effectiveness of interventions is illustrated in the following section using HR analytics:

1. **Setting Clear Objectives:** The first step in monitoring the impact of interventions is to set clear objectives. What is the desired outcome of the intervention? These objectives need to be specific, measurable, attainable, relevant, and time-bound (SMART). HR analytics assists in defining these objectives and ensuring that they align with the organization's strategic goals.
2. **Data Collection:** HR professionals need to collect relevant data before, during, and after the intervention. This data can encompass a variety of metrics, such as employee performance, engagement levels, turnover rates, and more. Automated HR systems and software can simplify the data collection process, making it easier to track key performance indicators.

3. **Data Analysis**: Once data is collected, HR analytics tools can analyse it to identify trends, patterns, and correlations. This helps in understanding the impact of the intervention. For example, it can reveal if employee performance has improved after a training program or if wellness initiatives have resulted in decreased absenteeism.
4. **Real-time Monitoring**: The beauty of HR analytics is that it allows for real-time monitoring of interventions. This means that HR professionals don't have to wait months or years to see the results of their efforts. They can access up-to-date information and adjust interventions as needed.
5. **Identifying Success Factors:** Through data analysis, HR professionals can pinpoint the success factors of an intervention. What aspects of the program are working well, and which ones need improvement? This information is invaluable for refining and optimizing interventions.
6. **Return on Investment (ROI):** HR analytics enables organizations to calculate the ROI of their interventions. They can determine whether the resources invested in an intervention are providing a substantial return, both in terms of employee well-being and the organization's bottom line.
7. **Continuous Improvement:** Armed with data-driven insights, HR professionals can make informed decisions on whether to continue, modify, or discontinue interventions. Continuous improvement is a fundamental aspect of HR analytics, and it ensures that interventions remain effective and aligned with the organization's evolving needs.
8. **Evidence-based Decision-making:** By relying on data and evidence, HR professionals can justify the value of their interventions to stakeholders within the organization. Data-driven insights help in decision-making and garnering support for HR initiatives.
9. **Predictive Analytics**: HR analytics doesn't just look at the past and present; it can also provide insights into the future. Predictive analytics can help HR professionals anticipate potential challenges and tailor interventions accordingly.

HR analytics is an indispensable tool for monitoring the impact of interventions in the HR domain. It empowers HR professionals to set clear objectives, collect and analyse data, make real-time adjustments, and continuously improve their initiatives. Through HR analytics, HR departments become agile and responsive, ensuring that their interventions contribute to organizational success and employee well-being. This data-driven approach is not just a trend but a fundamental shift in how HR professionals strategize and deliver value to their organizations.

TRACKING IMPACT INTERVENTIONS

The implementation of HR analytics has resulted in a substantial paradigm shift in the way organisations handle talent acquisition, employee involvement, and overarching workforce strategies within the dynamic domain of Human Resources (HR). The monitoring of the effects of interventions has emerged as a critical component of HR analytics. HR professionals have implemented these targeted initiatives and strategies as interventions to enhance organisational performance and employee satisfaction across multiple dimensions. Monitoring and assessing the effects of these interventions is critical for both determining their efficacy and informing data-driven planning for subsequent endeavours.

Defining Impact Interventions

Impact interventions encompass a wide array of HR initiatives, from onboarding and training programs to diversity and inclusion efforts, employee wellness initiatives, performance management enhancements, and everything in between. These interventions are designed to address specific challenges or capitalize on opportunities within the organization, ultimately aiming to enhance employee well-being, productivity, and overall business outcomes.

The Role of HR Analytics in Tracking Impact Interventions

Tracking the impact of these interventions is where HR analytics plays a vital role. By leveraging data and analytics, organizations can evaluate the effectiveness of these HR strategies and initiatives in a systematic and objective manner. Key HR analytics components that facilitate the monitoring of impact interventions are as follows:

1. **Data Collection:** The first step is to gather relevant data, which may include employee feedback, performance metrics, engagement surveys, and more. The data collected should align with the specific goals and KPIs of the intervention.
2. **Analysis:** Once the data is collected, HR professionals and data analysts can use a variety of analytical techniques to assess the impact of the intervention. Descriptive analytics can provide an overview of what has happened, while predictive analytics can help forecast future outcomes.
3. **KPIs and Metrics:** Key Performance Indicators (KPIs) and metrics are established to measure the intervention's success. These metrics could be related to employee turnover, engagement levels, productivity, or other relevant factors.
4. **Comparative Analysis:** By comparing the data before and after the intervention, organizations can gain valuable insights into the impact of the intervention. This might involve analysing trends, identifying correlations, or conducting more sophisticated statistical analyses.
5. **Feedback and Adjustments:** Tracking impact interventions also allows for continuous improvement. If the intervention is not producing the desired results, HR professionals can make data-informed adjustments to their strategies.

Benefits of Tracking Impact Interventions

There are numerous benefits to monitoring the effectiveness of interventions using HR analytics:

1. **Evidence-based Decision-making:** HR analytics provides concrete evidence of whether an intervention is working or not. This enables HR professionals to make informed decisions based on data rather than gut feeling.
2. **Optimized Resource Allocation:** By understanding which interventions are most effective, organizations can allocate resources more efficiently, focusing on what truly drives improvement.
3. **Employee Engagement:** Effective interventions positively impact employee engagement and satisfaction, contributing to a more motivated and productive workforce.

4. **Cost Savings:** By identifying and addressing issues through impactful interventions, organizations can reduce costs associated with turnover, absenteeism, and underperformance.
5. **Sustainability:** Successful impact interventions can be integrated into the company culture and practices, creating lasting improvements.

Challenges in Tracking Impact Interventions

While the benefits are clear, tracking impact interventions also comes with its share of challenges:

1. **Data Quality:** Accurate and reliable data is essential for meaningful analysis. Inaccurate or incomplete data can lead to incorrect conclusions.
2. **Time and Resources:** Implementing HR analytics to track interventions can be time-consuming and may require additional resources, such as data analysts and specialized software.
3. **Privacy and Ethics:** Handling employee data must be done with the utmost respect for privacy and in compliance with data protection regulations.
4. **Complexity:** Analysing the impact of some interventions can be complex, especially when multiple variables are involved.

Tracking impact interventions through HR analytics is a dynamic and evolving process. As organizations increasingly rely on data-driven decision-making, understanding the effects of HR initiatives becomes essential. By leveraging HR analytics to monitor and evaluate the impact of interventions, organizations can optimize their workforce strategies, improve employee experiences, and ultimately drive better business outcomes. It's a journey that involves challenges but promises a brighter, data-informed future for HR professionals and the organizations they serve.

TABLE 11.1 How to track the impact of interventions, including the key steps and considerations

Step	*Description*
1. Set Clear Objectives and Goals	Define specific, measurable objectives for the intervention.
2. Data Collection	Gather relevant data before, during, and after the intervention.
3. Key Performance Indicators (KPIs)	Identify and establish KPIs that align with the objectives.
4. Data Analysis	Analyse collected data to assess the impact of the intervention.
5. Comparison Groups	Use control or comparison groups to distinguish intervention effects.
6. Feedback and Stakeholder Input	Collect input from participants and stakeholders.

(*Contd.*)

Step	*Description*
7. Documentation	Maintain detailed records of the intervention process.
8. Regular Reporting	Provide regular updates and reports to stakeholders.
9. Adjustment and Learning	Make necessary adjustments based on monitoring results.
10. Long-term Monitoring	Consider the long-term impact of the intervention.
11. Scale or Pivot	Decide to scale up, replicate, or pivot based on results.
12. Communication and Reporting	Share findings with stakeholders and the community.
13. Continuous Improvement	Use insights for improving future interventions.
14. Ethical Considerations	Ensure ethical practices throughout the process.
15. Resource Allocation	Allocate resources based on impact assessment results.

The Table 11.1 provides a concise overview of the steps involved in tracking the impact of interventions, helping organizations and initiatives ensure that their efforts are effective and align with their goals.

STRESS AND ITS TYPES

Stress is a natural physiological and psychological response to challenging or threatening situations. It is a part of the body's "fight or flight" mechanism, which prepares us to react to stressors. While some level of stress can be beneficial and motivating, chronic or excessive stress can have negative effects on physical and mental health.

Key aspects of stress are as follows:

1. **Types of Stress:** There are two main types of stress:
   - **Acute Stress:** Short-term stress that arises from specific situations or events. It can be motivating and is usually manageable.
   - **Chronic Stress:** Ongoing, long-term stress that can result from continuous life challenges, such as work pressure, financial issues, or relationship problems. Chronic stress can have detrimental effects.
2. **Common Stressors:** Stressors, or the events or circumstances that cause stress, can vary widely from person to person but often include work-related pressures, family issues, financial concerns, major life changes, and health problems.
3. **Physical Symptoms of Stress:** Stress can manifest physically, leading to symptoms like headaches, muscle tension, increased heart rate, stomach issues, and fatigue.
4. **Mental and Emotional Symptoms:** Stress can also impact mental and emotional well-being, leading to symptoms like anxiety, irritability, mood swings, and difficulty concentrating.
5. **Coping Strategies:** Effective stress management strategies include regular exercise, relaxation techniques (e.g., deep breathing or meditation), a balanced diet, maintaining a support network, and time management.

6. **Long-term Effects of Chronic Stress:** Prolonged exposure to chronic stress can contribute to health issues like heart disease, high blood pressure, depression, and anxiety disorders. It can weaken the immune system and affect overall well-being.
7. **Mindfulness and Stress Reduction:** Practicing mindfulness, which involves being fully present in the moment and managing thoughts and emotions without judgment, can be an effective way to reduce stress.
8. **Seeking Professional Help:** In cases where stress becomes overwhelming or is accompanied by severe symptoms like panic attacks or clinical depression, it's important to seek help from a healthcare professional or mental health specialist.
9. **Balancing Work and Life:** Achieving a healthy work-life balance is essential for reducing work-related stress and preventing burnout.
10. **Self-care:** Engaging in self-care activities, such as hobbies, spending time with loved ones, and getting enough sleep, can help manage stress and improve overall well-being.

It's important to recognize that some level of stress is a normal part of life, but it's crucial to develop healthy coping mechanisms and seek help when needed to prevent the negative impact of chronic stress on physical and mental health.

STRESS AND ITS IMPACT ON EMPLOYEE PERFORMANCE

Stress is a prevalent aspect of the modern workplace, affecting employees across various industries and job roles. It can be triggered by a multitude of factors, such as high workloads, tight deadlines, interpersonal conflicts, and the constant pressure to meet expectations. While some level of stress can be motivating and drive performance, chronic or excessive stress can have a significant negative impact on employee performance and overall well-being.

Understanding the relationship between stress and employee performance is crucial for both employers and employees. Listed below are some ways in which stress impacts productivity on the job:

1. **Cognitive Impairment:** Chronic stress can impair cognitive functions such as memory, attention, and decision-making. Employees under stress may find it challenging to focus, remember critical details, and make rational decisions, leading to a decline in productivity and job performance.
2. **Reduced Creativity and Problem-solving:** Stress can stifle creativity and hinder problem-solving abilities. In high-stress environments, employees may struggle to think outside the box, which can be detrimental in roles that require innovation and adaptability.
3. **Decreased Motivation and Engagement:** Prolonged stress can erode an employee's motivation and enthusiasm for their work. A lack of motivation can result in reduced effort, leading to lower quality work and decreased productivity.
4. **Physical Health Issues:** Stress has a direct impact on physical health. It can lead to various health problems, including sleep disturbances, headaches, and even chronic conditions like heart disease and obesity. When employees are not in good health, their ability to perform optimally is compromised.

5. **Absenteeism and Presenteeism:** High levels of stress can cause employees to miss work due to illness or burnout, leading to absenteeism. On the other hand, those who continue to work while stressed may experience "presenteeism," where they are physically present but not fully engaged or productive.
6. **Interpersonal Conflicts:** Stress often spills over into workplace relationships. Employees under stress may become irritable, impatient, or prone to conflicts with colleagues, affecting teamwork and collaboration, which are essential for many job roles.
7. **High Turnover Rates:** Organizations with stressful work environments may experience higher turnover rates as employees seek less stressful opportunities. Constantly replacing staff can be expensive and disruptive to business operations.
8. **Burnout and Mental Health Issues:** Prolonged exposure to stress can lead to burnout, a state of emotional, mental, and physical exhaustion. Employees experiencing burnout are more likely to suffer from mental health issues like anxiety and depression, further impacting their performance.
9. **Quality of Work:** Stress can result in a decrease in the quality of work produced. Employees may rush through tasks, make more errors, and deliver subpar results due to the pressure they're under.
10. **Productivity Loss:** Ultimately, the cumulative effect of stress on employee performance can lead to a significant loss in productivity, which impacts an organization's bottom line.

Employers have a vested interest in addressing stress in the workplace to ensure their employees are performing at their best. This can be achieved through the implementation of stress management programs, creating a supportive work environment, offering work-life balance initiatives, and fostering open communication.

Finally, there is a strong correlation between stress and poor performance in the workplace, with long-term or extreme stress negatively impacting an individual's capacity to work efficiently and consistently. Stress reduction and employee mental and emotional health should be top priorities for businesses since these factors have a multiplicative effect on a company's bottom line.

EVALUATING STRESS LEVELS AND VALUE CHANGE

Stress is a ubiquitous aspect of human life, and it often plays a significant role in our decision-making processes. From daily life choices to major life transitions, stress can impact our values and priorities. The evaluation of stress levels and the subsequent changes in values is a complex and fascinating area of study that touches on psychology, sociology, and even economics. Check out how stress influences our values:

Understanding Stress Levels

Stress can be defined as the body's natural response to a perceived threat or challenge. It triggers a physiological and psychological reaction that readies us to confront or escape from a situation. While stress can be beneficial in certain situations, chronic or excessive stress can have detrimental effects on both physical and mental health.

The Impact of Stress on Values

When we experience stress, our values and priorities may shift. Here's how this process unfolds:

1. **Re-evaluation of Priorities:** Stress often prompts individuals to re-evaluate their life priorities. In times of stress, people may place greater importance on immediate needs and security, sometimes at the expense of longer-term goals.
2. **Change in Perspective:** Stress can lead to a change in one's perspective on life. This shift may involve placing more value on personal well-being, relationships, and stress reduction as opposed to career or material pursuits.
3. **Reassessment of Values:** Individuals may reconsider what truly matters to them. Stress can lead to the realization that certain values and ambitions are less significant than previously thought.
4. **Altered Decision-making:** The stress-induced change in values can affect decision-making processes. Choices made under high-stress conditions may prioritize immediate relief or solutions.
5. **Shifts in Lifestyle and Behaviour:** In response to heightened stress, individuals may adopt different lifestyles and behaviours. For example, they might pursue relaxation techniques, change careers, or engage in more pro-social activities.

Factors Influencing Value Change

Several factors contribute to how stress influences our values:

1. **Individual Differences:** Not everyone responds to stress in the same way. Personality traits, coping strategies, and resilience levels play a significant role in how individuals adapt to and experience stress.
2. **Magnitude of Stress:** The intensity and duration of stressors impact the extent of value change. Severe, long-lasting stressors are more likely to cause substantial shifts in values.
3. **Social Support:** The presence of a supportive social network can mitigate the impact of stress on values. A strong support system can help individuals maintain their core values during challenging times.
4. **Crisis Moments:** Major life events, such as illness, loss, or financial hardship, can serve as catalysts for profound value changes.

Evaluating Stress Levels and Value Change

The evaluation of stress levels and the associated value changes can be conducted through various methods:

1. **Psychological Assessments:** Self-report questionnaires and interviews can help individuals reflect on their stress levels and any corresponding shifts in values.
2. **Behavioural Observation:** Monitoring changes in behaviour, such as spending habits, social interactions, and lifestyle choices, can provide insights into value change.
3. **Longitudinal Studies:** Researchers can conduct long-term studies to track the relationship between chronic stress and evolving values.

4. **Comparative Analysis:** Comparative studies between individuals experiencing high and low stress levels can shed light on the impact of stress on values.

Applications and Implications

Understanding the relationship between stress levels and value change has several practical applications:

1. **Counselling and Therapy:** Therapists can help clients navigate value changes in response to stress, providing guidance and support during challenging times.
2. **Career Transitions:** The assessment of stress-related value changes can assist individuals in making informed career decisions or transitions.
3. **Economic Behaviour:** Economists study how stress influences consumer behaviour, saving habits, and investment decisions.
4. **Societal Implications:** At the societal level, understanding stress-induced value changes can inform public policy, social services, and community support programs.

In short, the relationship between stress levels and value change is a multifaceted and evolving area of study. It underscores the dynamic nature of human behaviour and the need to consider psychological and social factors when evaluating the impact of stress on our lives. Recognizing the potential for value changes during stressful periods is an essential step in promoting well-being and resilience in individuals and communities.

FORMULATING EVIDENCE-BASED PRACTICES AND RESPONSIBLE INVESTMENT IN HR ANALYTICS

In the realm of Human Resources (HR) Analytics, evidence-based practices are crucial for informed decision-making and responsible investment. To optimize HR processes and enhance organizational performance, it is essential to rely on data-driven insights and ethical considerations. How to formulate evidence-based practices and responsible investment in the context of HR Analytics is discussed below:

Evidence-based Practices in HR Analytics

1. **Define Clear Objectives:** Start by defining clear and specific objectives for your HR analytics initiatives. Understand what you want to achieve, such as improving employee retention, enhancing recruitment processes, or fostering diversity and inclusion.
2. **Data Collection and Quality Assurance:** Gather relevant HR data from various sources, ensuring data accuracy, completeness, and reliability. Quality data is the foundation of evidence-based practices.
3. **Data Analysis:** Employ statistical and analytical techniques to uncover meaningful patterns and trends in HR data. This analysis will provide insights into your organization's human capital.

4. **Hypothesis Testing:** Formulate hypotheses based on your data analysis and test them rigorously. For example, you might test if a particular training program improves employee performance.
5. **Experimentation:** Implement controlled experiments to assess the impact of HR interventions. For instance, you could conduct A/B tests to evaluate the effectiveness of different recruitment strategies.
6. **Benchmarking:** Compare your HR data and performance metrics to industry benchmarks and best practices to identify areas for improvement.
7. **Feedback Loops:** Establish feedback loops that continuously monitor the impact of HR initiatives. Regularly review and adjust strategies based on ongoing data analysis.
8. **Employee Surveys and Feedback:** Gather employee feedback through surveys and interviews to understand their experiences and needs. Employee input is valuable evidence.
9. **Ethical Considerations:** Ensure that HR data collection and analysis adhere to ethical standards, respecting employee privacy and data protection regulations.

Responsible Investment in HR Analytics

1. **Ethical Data Handling:** Invest in data handling practices that prioritize data privacy, security, and transparency. Ensure that employee data is protected and used responsibly.
2. **Training and Development:** Invest in the training and development of HR professionals and data analysts to enhance their skills in data collection, analysis, and interpretation.
3. **Technology and Tools:** Invest in advanced HR analytics tools and technologies that allow for more comprehensive data collection and in-depth analysis.
4. **Diversity and Inclusion:** Allocate resources to diversity and inclusion initiatives, including those that promote equal opportunities in hiring, development, and advancement.
5. **Talent Acquisition:** Invest in modern recruitment technologies that support fair and unbiased hiring decisions and minimize discrimination.
6. **Employee Well-being:** Allocate resources to programs and initiatives that promote employee well-being, mental health, and work-life balance.
7. **Regular Audits:** Conduct regular audits and reviews of HR analytics practices to ensure that data is being used ethically and responsibly.
8. **Transparency:** Maintain transparent communication with employees about the purpose and methods of HR analytics, addressing any concerns they may have.
9. **Continuous Improvement:** Invest in a culture of continuous improvement, where HR practices are regularly assessed and refined based on evidence and feedback.

Benefits of Evidence-based Practices and Responsible Investment

1. **Improved Decision-making:** Evidence-based practices lead to more informed and effective HR decisions, resulting in improved organizational performance.

2. **Ethical and Inclusive Work Environment:** Responsible investment in HR analytics fosters an ethical and inclusive workplace, promoting diversity and respecting employee rights.
3. **Competitive Advantage:** Organizations that invest in HR analytics and ethical practices gain a competitive edge in attracting and retaining top talent.
4. **Sustainable Growth:** Responsible investment contributes to the long-term sustainability and success of an organization, as it aligns with societal and ethical expectations.
5. **Employee Satisfaction:** Evidence-based practices that prioritize employee well-being and development contribute to higher employee satisfaction and engagement.

Thus, evidence-based practices and responsible investment in HR analytics are integral to achieving organizational goals while maintaining ethical standards and fostering a thriving and inclusive work environment. By making data-driven decisions and ensuring ethical data handling, organizations can optimize their human capital and drive sustainable growth.

EVALUATING THE MEDIATION PROCESS: NAVIGATING CONFLICTS TOWARD RESOLUTION

Mediation is a structured process for resolving disputes or conflicts by involving a neutral third party—the mediator—who facilitates communication and negotiation between the parties involved. The aim is to reach a mutually agreeable solution without the need for costly, time-consuming, and adversarial litigation. Evaluating the mediation process is essential to ensure its effectiveness and to make improvements as needed.

Understanding the Mediation Process

It's crucial to comprehend & understand the mediation process:

1. **Opening Statements:** The mediation typically begins with an opening statement from the mediator, setting the tone, outlining the process, and establishing ground rules.
2. **Communication and Information Sharing:** Each party is given the opportunity to express their perspectives and concerns without interruption. This phase encourages active listening and open dialogue.
3. **Issue Identification:** The mediator assists the parties in identifying the key issues at the heart of the dispute. Clarifying these issues is essential for constructive problem-solving.
4. **Negotiation:** With the mediator's guidance, the parties engage in negotiation to explore potential solutions, compromises, or trade-offs.
5. **Agreement:** If common ground is reached, the mediator helps formalize the agreement, which is typically a written document outlining the terms and conditions.
6. **Closure:** The mediation concludes with a closing statement, summarizing the agreement and encouraging the parties to adhere to their commitments.

Significance of Evaluating the Mediation Process

Evaluating the mediation process serves multiple important purposes:

1. **Assessing Effectiveness:** Evaluation helps determine whether mediation is an effective method for resolving the specific dispute. It gauges whether parties are satisfied with the process and its outcomes.
2. **Improvement and Learning:** Through evaluation, mediators can identify areas for improvement in their approach, techniques, or communication. It contributes to professional development.
3. **Resource Allocation:** Organizations and institutions can evaluate the efficiency of mediation in handling conflicts, helping them allocate resources wisely.
4. **Client Satisfaction:** Understanding client satisfaction is crucial, as it ensures that mediation services meet the needs and expectations of those involved.

Key Considerations in Evaluating the Mediation Process

When evaluating the mediation process, several considerations should be taken into account:

1. **Participant Feedback:** Feedback from the parties involved is invaluable. It can shed light on their perceptions of fairness, the mediator's effectiveness, and the overall experience.
2. **Agreement Rate:** Measuring the rate at which mediated cases result in agreements is a fundamental evaluation metric.
3. **Duration of the Process:** Assess the time taken for mediation, as prolonged processes may be less desirable for participants.
4. **Cost Savings:** Evaluate the cost-effectiveness of mediation compared to traditional litigation.
5. **Follow-up:** It's important to follow up on agreements reached in mediation to ensure compliance and satisfaction.
6. **Confidentiality:** Evaluate whether confidentiality, a core principle of mediation, is maintained and respected.
7. **Mediator's Neutrality:** Assess the mediator's ability to maintain neutrality and foster a safe environment for open communication.
8. **Organizational or Institutional Goals:** Consider whether mediation aligns with the goals and mission of the organization or institution offering these services.

Methods of Evaluation

Various methods can be employed to evaluate the mediation process, including surveys, interviews, case file reviews, and statistical analysis of outcome data. Both qualitative and quantitative data should be considered to gain a comprehensive understanding.

Continuous Improvement

Evaluating the mediation process should be an ongoing endeavour. Continuous improvement based on feedback and data analysis enhances the quality of services offered and fosters trust in the mediation process.

Thus, evaluating the mediation process is a critical aspect of ensuring that this alternative dispute resolution method is effective, efficient, and meets the needs of the parties involved. By gathering feedback, assessing key metrics, and maintaining a commitment to improvement, mediation can continue to be a valuable tool in resolving conflicts and promoting cooperation and understanding.

MODERATION AND INTERACTION ANALYSIS

Moderation and interaction analysis are essential techniques in the field of statistics and research, particularly in understanding the nuances of relationships between variables. They play a crucial role in uncovering when and for whom certain relationships are more or less pronounced.

Moderation Analysis

Moderation is the process of exploring the conditions under which one variable influences the relationship between two other variables. In simpler terms, it helps us understand when the strength or direction of a relationship changes based on a third, moderating variable. This analysis is crucial for identifying the boundary conditions of an existing relationship and discovering who or under what circumstances a particular effect occurs.

A more comprehensive explanation is as follows:

1. **The Moderated Relationship:** At its core, moderation analysis examines the interaction between the predictor variable (independent variable) and a moderating variable to understand how it impacts the outcome variable (dependent variable).
2. **Significance Testing:** Researchers often use statistical tests to determine whether the moderating variable significantly affects the relationship. This helps answer questions like, "Does gender moderate the relationship between education and income?"
3. **Graphical Representation:** Visualization through interaction plots helps in comprehending how the moderating variable influences the relationship.
4. **Practical Significance:** Beyond statistical significance, researchers need to assess the practical significance of moderation, i.e., does it have real-world implications?
5. **Real-life Examples:** An example could be exploring whether the impact of employee training on performance is moderated by the level of prior experience. In this case, experience is the moderating variable, and it affects the training-performance relationship.

Interaction Analysis

Interaction analysis focuses on understanding how the effect of one variable on the outcome depends on the level or values of another variable. It's about investigating whether the relationship between two variables changes when you consider a third variable. This is especially important in situations where the impact of one variable is not uniform across different levels of another variable.

Key elements of interaction analysis:

1. **Identifying Interactions:** Researchers need to pinpoint which variables interact. This means understanding the conditions under which the effect of one variable varies concerning another variable.
2. **Statistical Assessment:** Various statistical methods, such as ANOVA or regression analysis, can be employed to determine whether an interaction is statistically significant.
3. **Visualization:** Interaction plots and graphs are valuable for illustrating how the relationship between two variables changes based on different levels of a third variable.
4. **Significance Interpretation:** Researchers need to interpret the practical significance of the interaction. Is it a meaningful effect in real-life contexts?
5. **Application:** An example could be examining how the impact of the size of an advertising campaign (small or large) on product sales varies depending on the geographic region. Here, region is the interacting variable that influences the advertising-sales relationship.

Significance and Applications

Both moderation and interaction analyses play a critical role in empirical research across various disciplines, including psychology, economics, sociology, and more. These techniques help us understand the complexities of relationships between variables, enabling us to make informed decisions and draw meaningful conclusions from data.

In short, moderation and interaction analyses are powerful tools for exploring how and when the impact of one variable on another is affected by additional factors. They provide a nuanced understanding of the dynamics at play in complex relationships, contributing to more accurate and context-aware research and decision-making.

SKILLS FOR HR ANALYTICS

In the era of data-driven decision-making, Human Resources (HR) is no exception. The advent of HR analytics has transformed the field, emphasizing the need for professionals with a unique skill set. To effectively harness the power of data in HR, individuals must possess a combination of technical, analytical, and communication skills.

1. *Statistics: Unlocking Data Insights*

Statistics is the cornerstone of HR analytics. It involves the collection, analysis, interpretation, and presentation of data. In the HR context, this skill is indispensable for various reasons:

- **Descriptive Statistics:** HR analysts use descriptive statistics to summarize and make sense of large datasets, providing insights into employee demographics, performance, and other HR-related metrics.
- **Inferential Statistics:** Inferential statistics help HR professionals draw conclusions about the entire workforce based on a sample, allowing for predictions and hypothesis testing.

- **Predictive Analytics:** Statistical models enable HR teams to predict outcomes like employee turnover, performance, or recruitment success, helping organizations proactively address issues.
- **Advanced Techniques:** Proficiency in advanced statistical techniques such as regression analysis, hypothesis testing, and survival analysis is invaluable in uncovering hidden patterns and relationships within HR data.

2. *Programming: Turning Data into Action*

Programming skills are essential for HR analysts who work with large datasets, automate repetitive tasks, and develop customized analytics solutions. Following are the points why programming is crucial:

- **Data Handling:** HR analysts often deal with big data. Programming languages like Python and R enable efficient data manipulation and transformation.
- **Model Building:** Scripting and coding are necessary for building predictive models, which are critical for talent management, recruitment, and employee performance analysis.
- **Data Visualization:** Programming skills are used to create interactive data visualizations that make complex HR analytics results accessible to a non-technical audience.
- **Automation:** Automation of data collection, cleaning, and reporting processes can save significant time and resources, increasing HR efficiency.

3. *Optimization: Maximizing HR Impact*

Optimization skills involve finding the best solution to a problem by considering various constraints and objectives. In HR analytics, optimization is used for:

- **Recruitment:** Optimization models can help HR teams find the best candidates while considering factors like qualifications, location, and salary constraints.
- **Employee Scheduling:** Optimizing work schedules to maximize productivity and employee satisfaction is crucial for shift-based industries.
- **Compensation and Benefits:** HR analysts can use optimization techniques to design compensation packages that align with organizational objectives and employee needs.
- **Resource Allocation:** Optimization aids in allocating resources efficiently, such as training budgets or workforce planning, to meet HR goals effectively.

4. *Communication Skills: Bridging the Gap*

While technical skills are vital, effective communication skills are equally critical in HR analytics. The ability to translate data insights into actionable recommendations and convey their significance is essential for the following reasons:

- **Stakeholder Engagement:** HR analysts must effectively communicate with HR professionals, managers, and executives to make data-driven recommendations that align with the organization's strategic goals.
- **Data Storytelling:** Presenting data in a compelling and understandable manner, often through data visualization and storytelling, helps stakeholders grasp the insights and act on them.

- **Change Management:** Communication skills play a pivotal role in managing change, especially when HR analytics leads to organizational adjustments or policy changes.
- **Ethical Considerations:** Clear and transparent communication is essential when addressing ethical concerns related to employee data privacy and security.

Thus, the skills required for HR analytics are multi-faceted, combining statistical expertise, programming proficiency, optimization techniques, and effective communication. As the role of HR continues to evolve in the age of data, professionals who possess these skills are better equipped to unlock the full potential of HR analytics, driving more informed and strategic workforce decisions.

FOSTERING TRUST WITH EMPLOYEE DATA

In the modern workplace, data-driven decision-making has become increasingly integral to human resources management, giving rise to the field of HR analytics. While this data-driven approach offers numerous benefits, it also raises important ethical considerations, particularly regarding the collection and use of employee data. Building and maintaining trust with employees is paramount. One key element of this trust is obtaining the informed consent of employees when it comes to HR analytics.

The Significance of Trust in HR Analytics

Trust is the cornerstone of effective HR analytics. Employees need to believe that their data will be handled responsibly and ethically. Trust is not only about compliance with data protection laws but also about fostering a culture of transparency and respect for individual privacy.

Obtaining Consent in HR Analytics

Obtaining consent for the collection and use of employee data is a fundamental aspect of building trust. Consent is the explicit permission provided by employees to allow their data to be collected and used for specific purposes. When it comes to HR analytics, this consent can take various forms:

1. **Informed Consent:** Employees are provided with clear and detailed information about what data will be collected, how it will be used, and for what purposes. They must explicitly agree to this data collection.
2. **Opt-in Consent:** Employees actively choose to participate in data collection and analysis. They have the option to opt in or out of certain data collection activities.
3. **Revocable Consent:** Employees have the right to revoke their consent at any time. This means they can withdraw permission for further data collection and processing.

Benefits of Consent in HR Analytics

1. **Respect for Privacy:** Consent respects the privacy and autonomy of employees, ensuring they have control over their data.

2. **Ethical Practices:** It aligns with ethical data handling practices, demonstrating that the organization values individual rights and privacy.
3. **Compliance:** Obtaining consent helps the organization comply with data protection regulations, which vary by region.
4. **Enhanced Trust:** When employees know their data is collected with their informed consent, it enhances their trust in the organization and its HR analytics practices.
5. Improved Data Quality: Employees who are willing participants in data collection may provide more accurate and complete information.

Challenges and Considerations

Consent is obviously important, but there are a lot of considerations to think about and challenges to overcome:

1. **Informed Consent:** Ensuring that employees truly understand the implications of providing consent can be complex. Organizations should provide clear, plain-language explanations.
2. **Transparency:** Organizations must be transparent about the purposes for which the data will be used. This involves clear communication and ongoing updates.
3. **Data Security:** Consent comes with the responsibility to safeguard the data collected. Data breaches can have serious consequences for employee trust.
4. **Revocable Consent:** Organizations must be prepared to honour employees' right to revoke their consent. This requires robust data management and deletion processes.

In HR analytics, trust with employee data is a non-negotiable element. It begins with the respectful and ethical collection of data with informed consent. As organizations navigate the evolving landscape of HR analytics, they should prioritize trust, privacy, and responsible data handling to foster a positive and collaborative relationship with their workforce. This not only ensures compliance with data protection laws but also builds a culture of transparency and respect for individual privacy rights, ultimately contributing to a more engaged and motivated workforce.

CIPD, UK, 2012 STANDARDS AND ANALYST ETHICAL STANDARDS BASED ON SCHWARTZ (2011)

The Chartered Institute of Personnel and Development (CIPD) in the United Kingdom is a prestigious professional body that sets standards for HR and people development practices. Their 2012 standards for the HR profession are comprehensive guidelines that cover a wide range of areas, from professional competence to ethical behaviour. When considering analyst ethical standards based on Schwartz (2011), it's essential to align these with the CIPD's framework, as ethics are at the core of any HR and people development role.

CIPD, UK, 2012 Standards

The CIPD's 2012 standards are a set of principles and guidelines that provide a framework for HR professionals to operate effectively and ethically. These standards emphasize the importance of professionalism, integrity, and ethical conduct within the HR field. Some key components of the CIPD standards are:

1. **Professional Competence:** HR professionals are expected to maintain a high level of competence through ongoing learning and development. They should stay updated with the latest HR practices and trends.
2. **Ethical Behaviour:** HR professionals are expected to act with honesty, integrity, and fairness. They must respect the rights and dignity of individuals and avoid discrimination and bias.
3. **Professional Impact:** HR professionals should make a positive impact on their organizations and society as a whole. They should work to create inclusive, diverse, and sustainable workplaces.
4. **Employment Relationship:** HR professionals must maintain professional and constructive relationships with employees, promoting well-being and work-life balance.
5. **Ethical Leadership:** HR leaders are encouraged to promote ethical leadership throughout their organizations, fostering a culture of fairness, accountability, and transparency.

Analyst Ethical Standards Based on Schwartz (2011)

Schwartz (2011) presents a model of ten universal values that underlie human behaviour and ethics. These values encompass a wide range of ethical considerations, including benevolence, universalism, self-direction, power, and more. Analysts in HR and people development can apply Schwartz's ethical standards to their work in various ways:

1. **Benevolence:** HR analysts can demonstrate benevolence by prioritizing the well-being of employees and helping create a work environment that supports their physical and psychological health.
2. **Universalism:** Universalist values encourage fairness, social justice, and respect for all individuals. HR analysts should apply universalism by promoting diversity and inclusion and opposing discrimination in all its forms.
3. **Self-Direction:** HR analysts can embrace self-direction by seeking innovative and ethically sound solutions to HR challenges, continuously improving their analytical methods.
4. **Power:** Ethical HR analysts should exercise their influence responsibly and avoid exploiting their position for personal gain. They should use their power to advocate for fair practices and ethical conduct.
5. **Security:** Security values involve ensuring the safety and well-being of employees. HR analysts should prioritize employee security by conducting thorough risk assessments and promoting health and safety measures.
6. **Stimulation:** Stimulation values encourage creativity, curiosity, and a thirst for knowledge. HR analysts can apply these values by exploring innovative approaches to data analysis and HR problem-solving.
7. **Achievement:** Achievement values emphasize striving for excellence and setting high standards. HR analysts should aim for the highest level of accuracy and ethical conduct in their work.

Integration of CIPD Standards and Schwartz's Ethical Values

The CIPD's 2012 standards and Schwartz's ethical values can be effectively integrated into HR analytics practices. HR analysts must align their work with the CIPD's principles, emphasizing professional competence, ethical behaviour, and a positive professional impact. At the same time, they should embrace Schwartz's universal values, incorporating benevolence, universalism, and self-direction into their analytical processes. By doing so, HR analysts can drive ethical and responsible HR and people development practices that benefit both organizations and employees, fostering a culture of integrity and respect.

Questions for Discussion

Short Questions

1. What role do Human Resources (HR) interventions play in today's competitive business landscape?
2. Why is it essential for HR professionals to measure the effectiveness of interventions?
3. What is HR analytics, and how does it contribute to monitoring the impact of interventions?
4. How does HR analytics assist in setting clear objectives for interventions?
5. What types of data do HR professionals need to collect before, during, and after interventions?
6. How can HR analytics help in identifying success factors of interventions?
7. Why is real-time monitoring crucial in assessing the impact of HR interventions?
8. What is the significance of calculating the Return on Investment (ROI) for HR interventions?
9. How does HR analytics support evidence-based decision-making in the HR domain?
10. What is predictive analytics, and how does it benefit HR professionals in interventions?
11. What steps are involved in formulating evidence-based practices in HR Analytics?
12. What are the key stages involved in the mediation process?
13. Why is evaluating the mediation process important?
14. What skills are essential for effective HR Analytics?
15. What are the benefits of obtaining consent in HR Analytics?
16. What are the key components of the CIPD's 2012 standards?
17. How can Schwartz's ethical values be integrated into HR analytics practices?

Long Questions

1. Discuss the key steps involved in monitoring the impact of HR interventions using HR analytics.
2. How does HR analytics contribute to continuous improvement in HR interventions, and why is it essential?

3. Explain the role of comparative analysis in tracking the impact of interventions through HR analytics.
4. What are the benefits and challenges associated with tracking impact interventions using HR analytics?
5. How does stress impact employee performance, and what are the various ways it manifests in the workplace?
6. What strategies can employers adopt to address and manage stress in the workplace effectively?
7. Discuss the long-term effects of chronic stress on physical and mental health.
8. How does stress influence decision-making processes and priorities?
9. What are the practical applications and implications of understanding the relationship between stress levels and value change?
10. Discuss the significance of responsible investment in HR Analytics, outlining the methods and strategies that contribute to ethical and effective HR practices.
11. Explain the stages of the mediation process and why evaluating this process is crucial for its effectiveness.
12. How do moderation and interaction analyses enhance our understanding of complex relationships between variables, and what methods are commonly used to conduct these analyses?
13. Describe the essential skills required for effective HR Analytics, emphasizing their individual importance and collective impact on organizational decision-making.
14. How does obtaining consent contribute to ethical data handling in HR Analytics, and what considerations should organizations keep in mind when implementing this practice?
15. Compare and contrast the key components of the CIPD's 2012 standards and Schwartz's ethical values, emphasizing their relevance and application in HR Analytics.
16. How can HR analysts effectively integrate both the CIPD's standards and Schwartz's ethical values into their practices to ensure ethical conduct and professional impact?

CHAPTER

12

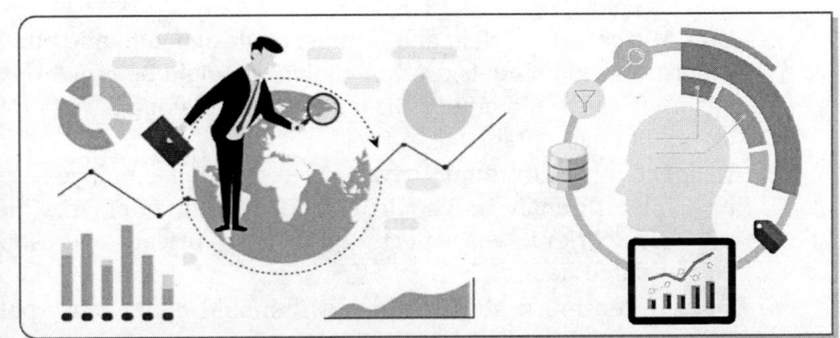

Ethical and Legal Considerations in HR Analytics

Human Resources (HR) analytics has revolutionized the field of HR management by leveraging data and technology to make informed decisions about employees. However, this power also comes with a responsibility to handle employee data ethically and in compliance with legal regulations. Ethical and legal considerations in HR analytics are crucial aspects that organizations must navigate to protect employee rights, ensure data privacy, and maintain trust within the workforce.

ETHICAL CONSIDERATIONS IN HR ANALYTICS

Ethical considerations in HR analytics refer to the principles, standards, and guidelines that govern the responsible and ethical use of data and analytics in the field of human resources. HR analytics involves the collection, analysis, and utilization of vast amounts of data related to employees and candidates, and ethical considerations are crucial to ensure that this process respects the rights and privacy of individuals, avoids discrimination, and upholds principles of fairness and transparency. Here are some key aspects of ethical considerations in HR analytics:

1. **Transparency and Informed Consent**: Employers should be transparent about data collection and analysis practices. Employees should be informed about what data is being collected and how it will be used. Informed consent ensures employees are aware of the implications and can make informed decisions regarding their participation.
2. **Data Minimization**: HR should only collect and retain data that is necessary for the intended purpose. Collecting excessive or irrelevant data can breach privacy and may not be ethically justifiable.
3. **Data Security**: Safeguarding employee data is a fundamental ethical obligation. HR must implement robust security measures to protect data from breaches, unauthorized access, and misuse. This includes encryption, access controls, and secure storage.

4. **Bias Mitigation**: HR analytics must be designed to mitigate bias and discrimination. Algorithms and models used in analytics should be regularly audited and adjusted to ensure fairness and equity. Biased decision-making based on factors like race, gender, or age is unacceptable.
5. **Respect for Individual Privacy**: Respecting employees' privacy is a key ethical principle. HR analytics should not infringe on employees' personal lives or intrude into non-work-related aspects. Employees' private lives should be separated from work-related data.
6. **Data Retention and Deletion**: HR should define clear policies on data retention and deletion. Keeping data for longer than necessary may breach ethical guidelines. Data should be deleted when it is no longer needed for the purpose for which it was collected.
7. **Accountability and Responsibility**: HR professionals and organizations are accountable for the ethical use of HR analytics. They must take responsibility for any harm caused by data misuse and actively work to prevent unethical practices.

Ethical considerations in HR analytics are essential for building trust with employees and candidates, maintaining legal compliance, and upholding principles of fairness and equity. By adhering to ethical guidelines, organizations can harness the power of HR analytics to make informed, responsible, and just decisions related to human resources management.

LEGAL CONSIDERATIONS IN HR ANALYTICS

Legal considerations in HR analytics refer to the complex web of laws, regulations, and compliance requirements that govern the collection, storage, analysis, and use of employee data in the field of Human Resources. HR professionals and organizations need to be acutely aware of these legal considerations to ensure that their HR analytics practices are in full compliance with applicable laws and regulations. Failing to do so can result in legal consequences, including fines, litigation, and damage to an organization's reputation. Some of the key legal considerations in HR analytics are:

1. **Data Protection Laws**: Various countries have data protection laws that regulate the collection, processing, and storage of personal data, including employee data. Laws such as the General Data Protection Regulation (GDPR) in the European Union and the California Consumer Privacy Act (CCPA) impose strict requirements on data handling.
2. **Non-Discrimination Laws**: Discrimination on the basis of race, gender, age, or other protected characteristics is prohibited by law. HR analytics should not perpetuate discrimination, and organizations can be held legally accountable for discriminatory practices.
3. **Labour Laws**: HR analytics must adhere to labour laws and regulations, including those related to working hours, overtime, wages, and employee rights. Violations can lead to legal consequences.
4. **Legal Obligations in Hiring and Promotion**: Laws govern hiring, promotion, and termination processes, requiring fairness, equal opportunity, and non-discrimination in these areas. HR analytics should align with these legal requirements.

5. **Record Keeping**: Legal requirements often dictate the retention of certain employee records. Failure to maintain these records as mandated by law can result in penalties.
6. **Whistle-blower Protection**: Legal protection should be in place for employees who report unethical or illegal practices within the organization. Retaliatory actions against whistle-blowers are prohibited by law in many jurisdictions.
7. **Third-Party Data Sharing**: HR analytics may involve sharing employee data with third-party service providers. Legal agreements and data protection clauses must be in place to ensure data security and compliance.

Not following these legal concerns can lead to serious financial and legal issues, as well as harm to your reputation. Data privacy and regulatory compliance should be prioritised during the development and maintenance of HR analytics processes in order to reduce the impact of these concerns. Human resource analytics present a challenging and essential challenge for organisations seeking to balance ethical and regulatory issues. Loss of confidence from staff, legal trouble, and a tarnished brand are all possible outcomes of neglecting this responsibility. Human resources professionals and organisations must keep up with evolving ethical standards and legislation and have strong policies and procedures in place to guarantee the responsible, transparent, and lawful use of HR analytics.

ENSURING COMPLIANCE WITH DATA PRIVACY REGULATIONS (e.g., GDPR, CCPA): A COMPREHENSIVE GUIDE

In today's digital age, data has become a valuable commodity, driving business decisions, and powering innovative technologies. However, the collection, use, and protection of personal data have raised concerns about privacy and security. To address these concerns, various data privacy regulations have been enacted worldwide, with two prominent examples being the General Data Protection Regulation (GDPR) in the European Union and the California Consumer Privacy Act (CCPA) in the United States. Ensuring compliance with these regulations is not only a legal obligation but also a fundamental aspect of responsible data management and building trust with customers and users.

Understanding General Data Protection Regulation (GDPR)

The General Data Protection Regulation (GDPR) is a comprehensive data protection and privacy regulation that was enacted by the European Union (EU) and came into effect on May 25, 2018. It is considered one of the most significant and influential pieces of data protection legislation globally, and it applies to all EU member states. GDPR introduces a unified framework for data protection within the EU and grants new rights and protections to individuals regarding the processing of their personal data.

Key Features and Principles of GDPR Include

1. **Territorial Scope:** GDPR applies to organizations located within the EU, as well as those outside the EU that process the personal data of EU residents. This extraterritorial reach means that many businesses worldwide must comply with its provisions.

2. **Consent:** GDPR emphasizes the importance of obtaining clear and unambiguous consent from individuals for the processing of their personal data. Consent must be freely given, specific, and informed.
3. **Data Subject Rights:** GDPR enhances the rights of data subjects (individuals whose data is processed), including the right to access, rectify, and erase their data. It also grants the right to data portability and the right to object to data processing.
4. **Data Protection Officers (DPOs):** Certain organizations, particularly those processing large amounts of personal data, are required to appoint a Data Protection Officer responsible for ensuring GDPR compliance.
5. **Data Breach Notification:** GDPR mandates the reporting of data breaches to the appropriate supervisory authority within 72 hours of discovery. In cases where the breach poses a high risk to individuals, affected data subjects must also be informed without undue delay.
6. **Privacy by Design and by Default:** GDPR encourages organizations to implement data protection measures from the outset when designing systems, products, or services. It also advocates for data protection as the default setting.
7. **Data Impact Assessments (DPIAs):** Organizations are required to conduct Data Protection Impact Assessments when processing operations are likely to result in a high risk to individuals' data rights and freedoms.
8. **Accountability and Governance:** GDPR places a significant emphasis on accountability. Organizations must demonstrate their compliance through documentation, records, and effective data protection policies and practices.
9. **International Data Transfers:** GDPR includes provisions for the transfer of personal data outside the EU, including the use of Standard Contractual Clauses (SCCs) and the establishment of binding corporate rules.
10. **Substantial Penalties:** Non-compliance with GDPR can lead to substantial fines. Depending on the nature and severity of the breach, fines can be as high as €20 million or 4% of the global annual turnover, whichever is higher.

GDPR was designed to provide individuals with greater control over their personal data and to harmonize data protection regulations across the EU. It has had a profound impact on the way organizations collect, store, and process personal data, leading to increased transparency, improved data security measures, and a heightened awareness of data protection rights. GDPR's principles have also influenced data protection regulations and discussions around the world, making it a pivotal piece of legislation in the realm of privacy and data protection.

Key Points

- Enacted in 2018, the GDPR is a comprehensive data privacy regulation that applies to all EU member states.
- It extends protection to the personal data of EU residents, regardless of where the data is processed.
- GDPR focuses on principles such as consent, data subject rights, data minimization, and accountability.
- Organizations can face significant fines for non-compliance, making it essential to understand and adhere to its requirements.

California Consumer Privacy Act (CCPA)

The California Consumer Privacy Act (CCPA) is a data privacy regulation that came into effect on January 1, 2020, in the state of California, United States. CCPA is a significant piece of legislation aimed at safeguarding the privacy rights of California residents and gives them more control over their personal data. It places obligations on businesses that collect, process, or share personal information of California consumers, making it one of the most comprehensive privacy laws in the United States.

Key Features and Principles of CCPA Include

1. **Scope:** CCPA applies to businesses that meet specific criteria. This includes businesses that have annual gross revenues exceeding $25 million, collect personal information on 50,000 or more California consumers, households, or devices, or derive 50% or more of their annual revenues from selling consumers' personal information.
2. **Consumer Rights:** CCPA grants California residents several rights regarding their personal data. These rights include the right to know what personal information is collected, the right to request the deletion of their data, and the right to opt-out of the sale of their data.
3. **Data Transparency:** Covered businesses are required to inform consumers about the categories of personal information collected, the purposes for which it is used, and the categories of third parties with whom the information is shared.
4. **Opt-Out of Data Sales:** CCPA introduces the right for consumers to opt-out of the sale of their personal information. Businesses must provide a "Do Not Sell My Personal Information" link on their websites.
5. **Non-Discrimination:** Businesses cannot discriminate against consumers who exercise their CCPA rights. This means they cannot charge different prices or provide different levels of service based on a consumer's decision to exercise their privacy rights.
6. **Data Security:** Businesses must implement reasonable security practices to protect the personal information they collect and maintain. This includes safeguards against data breaches.
7. **Data Breach Notification:** Businesses are required to notify affected consumers and the California Attorney General in the event of a data breach where consumers' personal information may have been exposed.
8. **Data Minimization:** CCPA encourages businesses to limit the collection of personal information to what is necessary for the purposes for which it is being used.
9. **Third-Party Contracts:** If a business shares personal information with third parties, they must have contractual agreements in place ensuring that those third parties comply with CCPA.
10. **Data Protection Impact Assessments:** For certain types of data processing, businesses may be required to conduct Data Protection Impact Assessments (DPIAs) to assess the potential risks to consumers' privacy.
11. **Penalties:** CCPA includes civil penalties for violations, which can be as high as $7,500 per intentional violation and $2,500 per non-intentional violation.

CCPA was enacted to address growing concerns over the privacy and security of personal data in the digital age. It provides California consumers with greater control over their personal information, forcing businesses to be more transparent about their data collection and sharing practices. CCPA has had a significant impact on data privacy regulations in the United States, inspiring similar laws in other states and pushing data privacy discussions to the forefront of the national agenda. It underscores the importance of data protection and the rights of individuals in an era of rapid technological advancement and digital commerce.

Key Points

- Effective from 2020, the CCPA is a state-level data privacy law in California, applicable to businesses that handle the data of California residents.
- CCPA grants consumers rights regarding their data, including the right to know, delete, and opt-out.
- It requires businesses to disclose their data practices and comply with specific regulations for handling personal information.
- CCPA enforcement can lead to financial penalties and legal actions against non-compliant organizations.

KEY ELEMENTS OF COMPLIANCE WITH DATA PRIVACY REGULATIONS

1. **Data Mapping and Inventory**
    - To comply with GDPR and CCPA, organizations must identify all the personal data they collect and process.
    - Documenting data flows and creating data inventories are crucial steps to understanding data handling practices.
2. **Consent and Data Subject Rights**
    - Obtaining explicit and informed consent is a core requirement under GDPR.
    - Organizations should provide data subjects (individuals) with the ability to access, correct, and delete their data as per their rights.
3. **Data Minimization and Purpose Limitation**
    - Collect only the data that is necessary for a specific, legitimate purpose.
    - Data should not be used for purposes beyond what was initially consented to without informing data subjects.
4. **Data Security and Encryption**
    - Implement robust security measures to protect personal data from breaches.
    - Encryption, access controls, and regular security assessments are essential.
5. **Data Protection Impact Assessments (DPIAs)**
    - Conduct DPIAs to assess and mitigate data privacy risks for high-risk processing activities.
    - Document and address potential risks and safeguards.
6. **Data Transfer Mechanisms**
    - If personal data is transferred internationally, ensure compliance with GDPR's cross-border data transfer requirements, such as Standard Contractual Clauses (SCCs).

7. **Data Protection Officers (DPOs)**
    - Appoint a Data Protection Officer if required by GDPR.
    - DPOs are responsible for monitoring compliance, providing guidance, and acting as a point of contact for data subjects and authorities.
8. **Incident Response and Notification**
    - Establish an incident response plan to report data breaches within the stipulated timeframes to regulatory authorities and affected individuals.

Ensuring Compliance in Practice

1. **Education and Training**
    - Ensure that employees are trained in data protection principles and understand their role in compliance.
2. **Policy and Procedure Development**
    - Develop and maintain data protection policies and procedures aligned with GDPR, CCPA, and other relevant regulations.
3. **Regular Auditing and Assessment**
    - Conduct regular internal audits to evaluate compliance and identify areas for improvement.
4. **Vendor Management**
    - Ensure that third-party vendors also comply with data protection regulations when handling personal data on your behalf.
5. **Documentation and Records**
    - Maintain comprehensive records of data processing activities, consents, and data protection measures.
6. **Regular Updates**
    - Stay informed about changes in data privacy regulations and adjust policies and procedures accordingly.

Benefits of Compliance with Data Privacy Regulations

1. **Enhanced Trust**: Compliance fosters trust with customers and users, who are more likely to engage with organizations they trust to protect their data.
2. **Mitigation of Legal Risks**: Avoiding hefty fines and legal actions is a significant incentive for compliance.
3. **Competitive Advantage**: Organizations that prioritize data privacy can use it as a selling point, attracting customers who value their privacy.
4. **Improved Data Management**: Compliance often necessitates better data management practices, which can lead to improved data accuracy and efficiency.
5. **Global Market Access**: Compliance with GDPR can facilitate access to the vast European market, while adhering to CCPA standards can cater to U.S. customers.

Ensuring compliance with data privacy regulations like GDPR and CCPA is not just a legal requirement but a responsible and ethical approach to data management. By understanding these regulations, implementing the necessary measures, and staying vigilant for changes and updates, organizations can protect the personal data of their customers and users, build trust, and safeguard their reputation in an increasingly data-centric world. Moreover, compliance can be a strategic advantage that positions organizations as responsible stewards of sensitive information.

ETHICAL USE OF HR DATA: FOSTERING TRUST AND RESPONSIBILITY IN HUMAN RESOURCES

Human Resources (HR) departments are increasingly relying on data and analytics to make informed decisions, improve processes, and enhance the overall employee experience. This digital transformation, driven by the proliferation of HRIS (Human Resource Information Systems), data analytics tools, and artificial intelligence (AI), has ushered in a new era of HR management. However, this transformation also comes with the responsibility of ensuring the ethical use of HR data.

Using human resources (HR) data ethically has become crucial in this data-driven age when businesses amass enormous volumes of information on their workforce. A careful balance must be struck when handling HR data in order to protect employee rights and privacy while also using the data to inform strategic HR decisions. Due to the potential for severe legal and cultural repercussions, ethical concerns are of the utmost importance in this situation.

Respect for Privacy and Informed Consent

One of the foundational principles of ethical HR data use is the respect for individuals' privacy. Employees have a reasonable expectation that their personal information will be handled with care and confidentiality. Organizations should obtain informed consent from employees before collecting, processing, or sharing their data. This includes ensuring that employees understand the purpose of data collection, how their data will be used, and the extent to which it will be shared within or outside the organization.

Transparency and Communication

Open and transparent communication is a cornerstone of ethical HR data practices. Organizations should be forthcoming about the data they collect, why they collect it, and how it will be used. This includes being clear about data retention policies and who has access to the data. When employees understand these aspects, it fosters a sense of trust and accountability.

Data Security and Protection

Securing HR data is not only a legal requirement but also a moral imperative. Organizations have a duty to protect sensitive employee information from breaches, theft, or unauthorized access. Proper encryption, access controls, and cybersecurity measures are essential to safeguard the privacy and security of HR data. This extends to the physical security of data as well.

Data Minimization

Ethical data practices also encompass the principle of data minimization. This means collecting only the data that is necessary for a specific, legitimate purpose. Unnecessary data collection is not only invasive but also increases the risk of misuse. Organizations should regularly review the data they collect and purge information that is no longer needed.

Fair and Equitable Use

HR data should be used for fair and equitable purposes, such as making employment decisions, assessing performance, or providing relevant training and development opportunities. Discriminatory practices, such as using data to discriminate based on race, gender, age, or other protected characteristics, are unethical and illegal.

Data Accuracy and Corrective Action

Maintaining accurate HR data is crucial for ethical HR practices. Inaccurate data can lead to misinformed decisions and can harm employees. When inaccuracies are identified, organizations have an ethical obligation to correct them promptly. This includes a transparent process for employees to update their personal information.

Accountability and Oversight

Ethical HR data practices require clear accountability and oversight. This may involve the establishment of data governance policies, assigning responsibility for data management, and regular audits to ensure compliance with ethical guidelines and legal regulations.

Training and Awareness

Educating HR professionals and employees about ethical data use is vital. HR teams should be aware of the ethical implications of data collection and handling. Employees, too, should understand their rights and how their data is being used, empowering them to make informed decisions.

Legal and Ethical Compliance

Finally, ethical HR data practices must align with local and international laws and regulations. Compliance with data protection and privacy laws, such as GDPR (General Data Protection Regulation) in Europe or CCPA (California Consumer Privacy Act) in the United States, is essential. Ignoring legal requirements not only poses legal risks but also ethical ones.

The Significance of Ethical HR Data Use

Ethical use of HR data is of great importance for several reasons:

1. **Employee Trust**: Employees entrust HR departments with sensitive and personal information. Violating this trust by misusing or mishandling their data can lead to a loss of trust and negatively impact the employer-employee relationship.
2. **Legal Compliance**: Laws and regulations, such as GDPR (General Data Protection Regulation) and CCPA (California Consumer Privacy Act), require organizations to handle employee data in a lawful and ethical manner. Non-compliance can result in substantial fines and legal consequences.

3. **Reputation and Brand**: Ethical lapses in HR data management can damage an organization's reputation and brand. News of data breaches or unethical data use can lead to public backlash and loss of business.
4. **Employee Well-being**: Ethical data use ensures that employee well-being is prioritized. Data can be used to identify and address workplace issues, support employee growth, and create a healthier work environment.

Key Principles of Ethical HR Data Use

1. **Transparency**: Organizations should be transparent about how they collect, store, and use HR data. Employees should be informed about data collection practices, the purpose of data usage, and their rights.
2. **Data Minimization**: Collect only the data that is necessary for legitimate HR purposes. Avoid collecting excessive or irrelevant data, which can lead to privacy concerns.
3. **Consent**: Obtain informed consent from employees before collecting and using their data. Consent should be freely given, specific, and revocable.
4. **Data Security**: Implement robust security measures to protect HR data from unauthorized access, breaches, or misuse. This includes encryption, access controls, and regular security audits.
5. **Data Accuracy**: Ensure that HR data is accurate, up-to-date, and reliable. Inaccurate data can lead to incorrect HR decisions and negatively impact employees.
6. **Data Ownership**: Clarify data ownership and control. Employees should have some control over their own data, including the right to access and rectify it.
7. **Purpose Limitation**: Limit data use to the purposes for which it was collected. Using HR data for unrelated or undisclosed purposes can be ethically problematic.
8. **Data Retention**: Define clear data retention policies and delete data when it is no longer needed for its intended purpose.

Examples of Ethical HR Data Use

1. **Diversity and Inclusion**: Ethical data use in HR can help identify disparities and biases in hiring, promotions, and compensation. Organizations can then take steps to promote diversity and inclusion.
2. **Performance Evaluation**: Ethical data use ensures that performance evaluations are based on relevant and accurate data rather than biased or discriminatory factors.
3. **Wellness Programs**: Ethical wellness programs use data to support employees' health and well-being, rather than intrusively monitoring their personal lives.
4. **Learning and Development**: Ethical use of HR data helps tailor training and development programs to individual needs and career goals.
5. **Talent Management**: Ethical talent management uses data to identify high-potential employees and provide them with growth opportunities.

Challenges and Future Considerations

As technology continues to advance, HR data ethics remains an evolving field. Challenges include the ethical use of AI in HR decision-making, protecting employee privacy in the age of remote work, and the potential misuse of employee monitoring tools.

In the future, organizations must continue to prioritize ethical HR data use, invest in data protection measures, and ensure that employees are well-informed about data practices. Ethical HR data use is not just a legal obligation but a moral imperative to foster trust, well-being, and fairness in the workplace. It represents a fundamental commitment to respecting the dignity and rights of employees in an increasingly data-driven world.

DATA SECURITY AND CONFIDENTIALITY

In today's interconnected world, data security and confidentiality have become paramount concerns for individuals, organizations, and governments. The rapid proliferation of digital technology has facilitated the easy sharing and access to information, but it has also exposed sensitive data to a multitude of risks. Protecting data from unauthorized access, breaches, and misuse is not only an ethical obligation but also a legal requirement in many jurisdictions. This essay explores the significance of data security and confidentiality and discusses the measures and best practices that individuals and organizations can implement to safeguard their valuable information.

The Significance of Data Security and Confidentiality

1. **Protection of Privacy**: Data security and confidentiality are fundamental to safeguarding the privacy of individuals. Personal information, including financial records, medical history, and communication data, is vulnerable to unauthorized access, identity theft, and misuse. Protecting this data is essential for maintaining trust and ensuring individuals' rights to privacy.
2. **Business Continuity**: For organizations, data is often their most valuable asset. Loss, theft, or corruption of data can lead to business disruption, financial losses, and damage to reputation. Confidential business information, trade secrets, and intellectual property must be protected to maintain a competitive edge.
3. **Legal and Regulatory Compliance**: Many countries have enacted data protection laws and regulations to govern the handling of sensitive data. Non-compliance can result in severe legal consequences, including fines and litigation. Ensuring data security and confidentiality is crucial for adhering to these laws.
4. **National Security**: Government agencies are responsible for protecting national security and classified information. Leaks of sensitive government data can have far-reaching consequences, including endangering lives and compromising national security.

Measures and Best Practices for Data Security and Confidentiality

1. **Access Control:** Implement strict access controls to ensure that only authorized individuals can access sensitive data. This includes user authentication methods like strong passwords, biometrics, and multi-factor authentication.

2. **Encryption:** Encrypt data both in transit and at rest. Encryption transforms data into a format that is unreadable without the proper decryption key. This technology is essential for securing data during transmission over networks and when stored on devices or servers.
3. **Regular Updates and Patch Management**: Keep software, operating systems, and security tools up to date. Vulnerabilities are often exploited by cybercriminals, and regular updates can help patch these vulnerabilities.
4. **Data Backups**: Regularly back up data to ensure its availability in case of data loss or corruption. Backups should be stored securely and tested periodically to ensure they can be restored when needed.
5. **Employee Training**: Employees play a crucial role in data security. Training programs can educate them about the risks, best practices, and their responsibilities in safeguarding data.
6. **Firewalls and Intrusion Detection Systems**: Implement firewalls and intrusion detection systems to monitor and filter network traffic. These tools can help identify and block suspicious or malicious activities.
7. **Data Classification**: Classify data based on its sensitivity. Not all data requires the same level of protection. Assign access controls and security measures accordingly.
8. **Incident Response Plan**: Develop a comprehensive incident response plan to address data breaches and security incidents promptly. This plan should include reporting, investigation, containment, recovery, and communication procedures.
9. **Vendor and Third-Party Risk Assessment**: Evaluate the security practices of third-party vendors and service providers that handle your data. Ensure they adhere to similar security standards and practices.
10. **Regular Audits and Security Assessments**: Conduct regular security audits and assessments to identify vulnerabilities and weaknesses in your data security practices.

Data security and confidentiality are non-negotiable in the digital age. As data breaches continue to make headlines, it is imperative for individuals, organizations, and governments to take proactive steps to protect sensitive information. Implementing a comprehensive data security strategy, which includes encryption, access controls, employee training, and incident response planning, is essential in safeguarding data from unauthorized access, breaches, and misuse. By prioritizing data security, we can preserve privacy, maintain business continuity, comply with legal requirements, and safeguard national security in an increasingly data-driven world.

Questions for Discussion

Short Questions

1. What are the key aspects of ethical considerations in HR analytics?
2. How does transparency and informed consent play a role in ethical HR analytics?
3. Why is data minimization important in HR analytics from an ethical standpoint?

4. What ethical obligations are associated with data security in HR analytics?
5. What is the importance of respecting individual privacy in HR analytics?
6. Why is accountability and responsibility crucial in ethical HR analytics?
7. How can organizations obtain informed consent for HR data collection?
8. What are the key principles of ethical HR data use?
9. Why is data minimization important in HR data practices?
10. How can organizations maintain accountability in HR data practices?
11. What challenges does the future hold for ethical HR data use?

Long Questions

1. How do ethical considerations in HR analytics impact the relationship between organizations and their employees and candidates?
2. Can you explain the ethical principles related to data retention and deletion in HR analytics and their significance?
3. What are the potential consequences for organizations that neglect ethical considerations in HR analytics?
4. How has the General Data Protection Regulation (GDPR) influenced the global landscape of data protection regulations, and what are its key features and principles?
5. What distinguishes the California Consumer Privacy Act (CCPA) from other data privacy regulations, and what rights does it grant to California residents?
6. What are the essential elements of compliance with data privacy regulations like GDPR and CCPA, and how can organizations put them into practice?
7. Discuss the significance of ethical HR data use, including its impact on employee trust, legal compliance, reputation, and employee well-being.
8. Explain the key principles of ethical HR data use, such as transparency, data minimization, and consent, and how they contribute to responsible HR data management.
9. Discuss the significance of data security and confidentiality, highlighting their role in protecting privacy, business continuity, legal compliance, and national security.
10. Explain the measures and best practices for data security and confidentiality, including access control, encryption, employee training, and incident response planning, and their importance in safeguarding sensitive information in the digital age.

CHAPTER

13

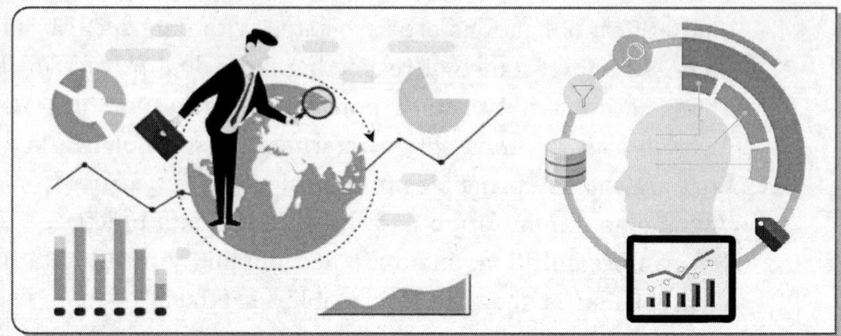

Future of HR Analytics

THE EVOLVING LANDSCAPE OF HR ANALYTICS

In the digital age, the Human Resources (HR) function has undergone a profound transformation. No longer confined to administrative tasks and paperwork, HR has emerged as a strategic partner in driving organizational success. Central to this transformation is the evolution of HR analytics—a field that has transitioned from basic data reporting to predictive and prescriptive analytics.

Today, HR analytics is at the forefront of reshaping the workforce landscape, influencing decision-making, and enhancing the employee experience. It's not just about understanding what happened or why it happened; it's about predicting what will happen and prescribing actions to drive desired outcomes.

As organizations strive to attract, retain, and develop top talent, the need for data-driven decision-making has never been greater. HR analytics is no longer a luxury but a necessity, and its potential is boundless.

THE EVOLUTION OF HR ANALYTICS FROM BASIC REPORTING TO PREDICTIVE AND PRESCRIPTIVE ANALYTICS

The journey of HR analytics has been nothing short of remarkable. It began with basic reporting, where HR professionals primarily collected and summarized data related to employee demographics, attendance, and turnover. These reports were retrospective in nature, offering a historical view of what had already occurred. While they provided some insights, they lacked the depth and foresight needed for strategic decision-making.

The next phase of evolution brought about descriptive analytics. HR teams started to analyse historical data more comprehensively. They could identify trends, patterns, and correlations within their workforce, enabling them to answer questions about the past and present. For example, they could determine which departments had the highest turnover rates or which job roles were the hardest to fill.

However, the real transformation occurred with the advent of predictive analytics. HR professionals began leveraging statistical models and algorithms to forecast future workforce trends and behaviours. Predictive analytics allowed HR to answer questions like, "What factors contribute to employee turnover, and who is at risk of leaving?" By identifying potential issues before they became crises, organizations could proactively take steps to retain talent and improve overall workforce planning.

The latest frontier in HR analytics is prescriptive analytics. This stage goes beyond predicting outcomes; it prescribes actions to optimize HR processes and outcomes. HR teams can now answer questions like, "What specific interventions should we implement to improve employee engagement and productivity?" Prescriptive analytics leverages AI and machine learning to provide evidence-based recommendations, allowing HR to make informed decisions that drive desired results.

THE GROWING IMPORTANCE OF DATA-DRIVEN DECISION-MAKING IN HR

The growing importance of data-driven decision-making in HR cannot be overstated. In an era where information is abundant, organizations that harness the power of data gain a competitive advantage. HR analytics empowers HR professionals and leaders to make strategic, evidence-based decisions that impact the entire employee lifecycle.

Data-driven decision-making in HR offers several benefits:

1. **Improved Talent Acquisition:** HR analytics helps identify the most effective sources for recruiting top talent, reducing time-to-fill, and improving candidate quality.
2. **Enhanced Employee Engagement:** Data enables organizations to pinpoint drivers of engagement, helping them create targeted interventions to boost employee satisfaction and productivity.
3. **Retention and Succession Planning:** Predictive analytics helps identify employees at risk of leaving and high-potential individuals for succession planning.
4. **Pay Equity:** Analytics can identify and rectify gender and ethnic pay gaps, ensuring fairness and compliance.
5. **Learning and Development:** HR can use data to personalize training and development programs, aligning them with individual career goals.
6. **Workforce Planning:** Data-driven insights inform workforce planning strategies, ensuring organizations have the right talent in the right roles.

THE NEED FOR HR TO ADAPT TO EMERGING TRENDS AND TECHNOLOGIES

As HR analytics continues to evolve, HR professionals must adapt to emerging trends and technologies to remain competitive and effective. The following trends and technologies are shaping the future of HR analytics:

1. **Artificial Intelligence (AI):** AI-powered analytics can automate repetitive tasks, analyse unstructured data (like text and voice), and provide insights that enhance decision-making.

2. **Blockchain:** Blockchain technology is revolutionizing HR data management by ensuring the security and integrity of sensitive information like candidate credentials and payroll records.
3. **Augmented Reality (AR) and Virtual Reality (VR):** These technologies are being used in HR for immersive on boarding, training, and development experiences.
4. **Ethical Considerations:** As analytics becomes more pervasive, HR must address ethical concerns related to data privacy, bias, and fairness.

HR analytics has come a long way, transitioning from basic reporting to predictive and prescriptive analytics. Data-driven decision-making is now a cornerstone of effective HR management, and HR must continuously adapt to emerging trends and technologies to remain at the forefront of this transformative field.

AI-POWERED HR ANALYTICS

Artificial Intelligence (AI) and its Impact on HR Analytics

Artificial Intelligence (AI) has emerged as a transformative force in HR analytics, reshaping the way organizations manage their workforce and make HR-related decisions. In this section, we delve into the profound impact of AI on HR analytics, exploring its applications, benefits, and implications.

Understanding AI in HR Analytics

AI refers to the simulation of human intelligence in machines, allowing them to perform tasks that typically require human intelligence, such as learning, reasoning, problem-solving, and decision-making. In the context of HR analytics, AI is revolutionizing the way HR professionals collect, process, and leverage data to make informed decisions.

AI Applications in HR Analytics

AI has found its way into various HR functions, each with its unique set of applications:

1. **Talent Acquisition**: AI-powered Chabot's and virtual assistants streamline candidate interactions, answering inquiries, scheduling interviews, and providing feedback. Machine learning algorithms analyse resumes to identify top candidates quickly.
2. **Employee On-boarding**: Chabot's and AI-driven systems guide new hires through the on-boarding process, offering a personalized experience and answering common questions.
3. **Predictive Analytics**: AI models predict workforce trends and identify potential talent gaps, helping HR teams proactively address recruitment needs.
4. **Performance Management**: AI-driven tools provide continuous feedback, track performance metrics, and suggest personalized development plans for employees.
5. **Employee Engagement**: Sentiment analysis and natural language processing (NLP) tools analyse employee feedback, enabling organizations to gauge engagement levels and identify areas of concern.

6. **Learning and Development**: AI recommends tailored learning paths for employees based on their roles, skill gaps, and career aspirations.
7. **Succession Planning**: AI assesses the skills and potential of employees, aiding in succession planning by identifying high-potential talent.

Benefits of AI in HR Analytics

The incorporation of AI into HR analytics offers several advantages:

1. **Efficiency:** AI automates repetitive tasks, freeing HR professionals to focus on strategic initiatives.
2. **Personalization:** AI tailors HR experiences for individuals, whether in recruitment, on boarding, or learning and development.
3. **Data-driven Decision-making:** AI mines vast datasets to provide actionable insights, supporting evidence-based HR decisions.
4. **Scalability:** AI can handle large volumes of data, making it ideal for organizations with diverse and extensive workforces.
5. **Improved Candidate Experience:** AI-powered Chabot's provide real-time responses, enhancing the candidate experience and speeding up the recruitment process.
6. **Enhanced Predictive Capabilities:** AI's ability to predict trends allows organizations to anticipate HR needs and challenges.

Challenges and Considerations

While the benefits of AI in HR analytics are substantial, there are challenges and considerations to address:

1. **Data Privacy and Ethics:** Protecting employee data and ensuring AI algorithms are free from bias are paramount concerns.
2. **Integration:** Integrating AI tools into existing HR systems can be complex and requires thoughtful planning.
3. **Skill Development:** HR professionals need training to effectively leverage AI tools and interpret their insights.
4. **Change Management:** Employees may resist AI-driven changes if they perceive them as a threat to their roles or privacy.

AI is a game-changer in HR analytics, offering the potential to transform HR processes, enhance decision-making, and create a more personalized and efficient workforce experience. However, organizations must approach AI implementation thoughtfully, addressing privacy, ethics, and skill development to realize its full potential in HR analytics.

AI-DRIVEN TALENT ACQUISITION: TRANSFORMING RECRUITMENT IN THE DIGITAL AGE

In the dynamic landscape of talent acquisition, where the quest for top talent is relentless and the expectations of candidates are ever-evolving, artificial intelligence (AI) has emerged as a game-changer. AI-driven talent acquisition leverages cutting-edge technologies to streamline and enhance every aspect of the recruitment process, from sourcing and screening to the overall candidate experience.

1. **Automating Candidate Sourcing and Screening:** In the traditional recruitment process, identifying and screening potential candidates is often a labour-intensive and time-consuming task. Enter AI, which revolutionizes candidate sourcing and screening:
   (a) **Intelligent Candidate Sourcing:** AI algorithms can comb through vast talent pools, both internally and externally, to identify candidates whose profiles closely match job requirements. By analysing resumes, professional profiles, and even social media data, AI-driven tools can deliver a shortlist of potential candidates within seconds. This not only saves time but also ensures a broader and more diverse talent pool is considered.
   (b) **Predictive Candidate Screening:** AI's machine learning capabilities enable predictive candidate screening. By analysing historical hiring data, AI can identify patterns and characteristics that are indicative of successful hires. This predictive analysis helps in ranking and prioritizing candidates based on their likelihood of success in the role, enhancing the quality of the talent pipeline.
2. **Enhancing Candidate Experience through AI Chabot's:** Candidate experience is a critical aspect of recruitment. AI Chabot's have revolutionized the way candidates interact with employers during the application and interview process:
   (a) **24/7 Support:** AI Chabot's provide round-the-clock support, allowing candidates to ask questions, schedule interviews, and receive instant feedback at their convenience. This ensures a seamless and responsive experience, even outside of traditional working hours.
   (b) **Personalization:** AI-driven Chabot's can personalize interactions with candidates. By analysing candidate data and preferences, Chabot's can tailor messages and responses, creating a more engaging and meaningful experience.
   (c) **Efficient Screening Interviews:** Some AI Chabot's are equipped to conduct preliminary screening interviews. They can ask standardized questions, assess responses, and evaluate a candidate's fit for the role, all while maintaining a consistent and bias-free approach.
3. **Predictive Analytics for Identifying Top Talent:** Predictive analytics has a profound impact on the identification of top talent. By harnessing AI and data analytics, organizations can make more informed decisions about potential hires:
   (a) **Talent Scoring:** AI-powered talent scoring assigns numerical values to candidates based on various factors, including their skills, experience, cultural fit, and performance in assessments. These scores help in objectively evaluating candidates and identifying the most promising ones.
   (b) **Reducing Bias:** Predictive analytics can reduce unconscious bias in the hiring process by focusing on objective criteria. This results in fairer and more equitable hiring decisions, promoting diversity and inclusion.
   (c) **Retention Predictions:** AI can also predict which candidates are likely to stay with the company long-term. This is valuable in identifying individuals who align with the organization's values and are more likely to contribute to its success over time.

In the age of AI-driven talent acquisition, the recruitment process has become more efficient, data-informed, and candidate-centric. As organizations embrace these technologies, they are not only attracting top talent but also fostering a more inclusive and equitable workforce. AI is undoubtedly shaping the future of talent acquisition, and its potential is boundless.

AI IN EMPLOYEE ENGAGEMENT AND RETENTION

In the field of human resources, maintaining high employee engagement levels and holding onto top talent are critical to the success of an organisation. In this sense, artificial intelligence (AI) is turning out to be a game-changer, allowing HR managers to use cutting-edge methods for gauging employee attitude, forecasting flight threats, and formulating individual career development plans. The following explains how artificial intelligence is changing employee engagement and retention methods:

1. **Sentiment Analysis and Natural Language Processing (NLP):**
   (a) **Understanding Employee Sentiment:** In the age of digital communication, employees express their thoughts and feelings through various channels like emails, chats, and feedback forms. AI-powered sentiment analysis and NLP tools can sift through this unstructured textual data to decipher the sentiment behind employee messages.
   (b) **Real-time Feedback Analysis:** With the ability to process vast amounts of text data, AI can provide real-time insights into how employees feel about their work, colleagues, and the organization. Positive sentiments might indicate contentment and engagement, while negative sentiments could signal dissatisfaction or disengagement.
   (c) **Proactive Issue Resolution:** Sentiment analysis enables HR to proactively identify and address issues that affect employee engagement. For example, if a particular department consistently expresses negative sentiment, HR can investigate and implement improvements.
2. **Predictive Analytics for Identifying Flight Risks:**
   (a) **Early Warning System:** AI-driven predictive analytics can help identify employees who are at risk of leaving the organization, often referred to as "flight risks." By analysing historical data and various factors like job satisfaction, performance, and career progression, AI can generate predictive models.
   (b) **Identifying Engagement Red Flags:** Predictive analytics can spot early signs of disengagement, such as a drop in performance, increased absenteeism, or reduced participation in company activities. By identifying these red flags, HR can take proactive measures to re-engage employees.
   (c) **Tailored Retention Strategies:** AI can recommend personalized retention strategies for at-risk employees based on their unique circumstances. For example, it might suggest offering additional training, mentorship, or a change in responsibilities to rekindle their engagement.
3. **AI-Powered Personalized Career Development Plans:**
   (a) **Individualized Skill Assessment:** AI can assess employees' skills, competencies, and career goals. It can analyse their past performance, training history, and current job roles to understand their strengths and areas for improvement.

(b) **Tailored Learning Paths:** With this information, AI can create personalized career development plans for each employee. These plans might include targeted training programs, stretch assignments, or mentoring opportunities.

(c) **Continuous Monitoring and Adaptation:** AI can continually monitor an employee's progress and adapt their career development plan as they acquire new skills or express changing career aspirations.

BLOCKCHAIN IN HR ANALYTICS

Blockchain Technology and its Potential in HR

Blockchain technology, originally designed as the foundation for cryptocurrencies like Bitcoin, has transcended its initial purpose. It has evolved into a versatile and secure method for recording and verifying transactions across a distributed network of computers. Blockchain's inherent characteristics, such as transparency, immutability, and decentralized control, have opened doors to various applications beyond finance, including human resources (HR).

What is Blockchain, and How does it Work?

At its core, a blockchain is a decentralized digital ledger that records transactions across a network of computers. A simple explanation of the process is this:

1. **Decentralization:** Unlike traditional centralized databases, blockchain operates on a decentralized network of computers (nodes). Each node maintains a copy of the entire blockchain.
2. **Blocks:** Transactions are grouped into blocks, and each block contains a list of these transactions.
3. **Cryptography:** Each block is linked to the previous one through a cryptographic hash, creating a chain of blocks, hence the name "blockchain."
4. **Consensus Mechanism:** New transactions must be verified and agreed upon by network participants through a consensus mechanism (e.g., proof of work or proof of stake) before they are added to the blockchain.
5. **Immutability:** Once a block is added to the chain, it is extremely difficult to alter. This immutability ensures the integrity of the data.
6. **Transparency:** The blockchain ledger is transparent and accessible to all network participants. Anyone can view the entire transaction history.

The Security and Transparency Advantages of Blockchain

Blockchain offers several advantages that are particularly relevant to HR data management:

1. **Data Security:** Blockchain uses advanced cryptographic techniques to secure data. Once a record is added to the blockchain, it becomes extremely challenging for malicious actors to alter or delete it. This enhances the security of sensitive HR data.

2. **Data Integrity:** The immutability of blockchain ensures the integrity of HR records. This means that once data is recorded, it cannot be tampered with, ensuring that HR data remains accurate and trustworthy.
3. **Transparency:** Blockchain's transparent nature allows all stakeholders, including employees, to access and verify HR data. This transparency can promote trust and accountability in HR processes.
4. **Reduced Fraud:** HR processes such as background checks and credential verification can benefit from blockchain's ability to securely and efficiently verify information, reducing the risk of fraudulent claims.

Relevance of Blockchain in HR Data Management

The application of blockchain technology in HR data management holds immense promise. It can address various HR challenges and enhance processes in the following ways:

1. **Background Verification:** Blockchain can be used to securely and efficiently verify employee credentials, education, and work history, reducing the risk of resume fraud.
2. **Payroll and Compensation:** Blockchain can facilitate secure and transparent payroll processing, ensuring that compensation is accurate and distributed efficiently.
3. **Digital Identity:** Blockchain can serve as a secure platform for managing employee digital identities, safeguarding sensitive personal information.
4. **Smart Contracts:** These self-executing contracts can automate HR processes such as on boarding, performance evaluations, and benefits administration, reducing administrative burdens and the risk of errors.

As organizations increasingly recognize the importance of data security, integrity, and transparency in HR operations, blockchain technology is poised to play a pivotal role in shaping the future of HR analytics and data management. In the following sections, we will delve deeper into specific applications of blockchain in HR and explore real-world use cases that highlight its transformative potential.

Blockchain in Recruitment and Background Verification

The recruitment and background verification processes are integral parts of human resources management. They involve verifying the qualifications, credentials, and backgrounds of potential candidates to ensure that they meet the requirements for a particular role. Blockchain technology is proving to be a game-changer in these areas due to its ability to enhance transparency, security, and efficiency. Here's how blockchain is transforming recruitment and background verification:

1. **Immutable Records:**
    - Blockchain creates immutable records of an individual's qualifications, work history, and other relevant information. Once verified and added to the blockchain, this data cannot be altered or falsified.
    - This feature is particularly valuable in verifying the accuracy of resumes and preventing resume fraud, which is a common challenge in recruitment.

2. **Credential Verification:**
    - Blockchain can be used to securely verify educational qualifications and certifications. Educational institutions and certifying bodies can issue digital credentials on the blockchain.
    - Candidates can provide access to their blockchain-based credentials, allowing potential employers to instantly verify their authenticity.
3. **Background Checks:**
    - Background checks, including criminal records and employment history, can be conducted more efficiently and securely using blockchain.
    - With the candidate's consent, relevant authorities and organizations can provide access to their data on the blockchain, streamlining the verification process while maintaining data privacy.
4. **Privacy and Consent:**
    - Blockchain-based systems can give individuals control over their data by allowing them to grant or revoke access to their records. This aligns with data privacy regulations such as GDPR.
    - Candidates can choose what information they want to share and with whom, enhancing their privacy and control over their personal data.
5. **Reduced Verification Costs:**
    - Blockchain reduces the administrative costs associated with background checks and verification. There's no need for intermediaries, such as verification agencies, as the data is securely and independently verified on the blockchain.
    - This cost reduction benefits both candidates and employers.
6. **Faster Hiring Processes:**
    - Blockchain's real-time verification capabilities can significantly speed up the hiring process. Employers can quickly confirm a candidate's qualifications and suitability for a role.
    - This speed is especially important in competitive job markets where attracting top talent quickly can make a difference.
7. **Enhanced Trust:** The transparency and security of blockchain instil trust in the hiring process. Employers can have confidence in the accuracy of a candidate's qualifications, reducing the risk of hiring someone who misrepresents their background.
8. **Global Talent Pool:** Blockchain's borderless nature allows organizations to tap into a global talent pool more easily. Verified credentials from one country can be readily accepted by employers in another.
9. **Fraud Prevention:** Blockchain minimizes the risk of identity theft and credential fraud in the hiring process. Candidates are less likely to exaggerate qualifications or provide false information when they know it will be easily verifiable.
10. **Enhanced Candidate Experience:** Candidates benefit from a smoother, more transparent hiring process. They can apply for positions with confidence, knowing their qualifications will be accurately assessed.

Blockchain technology is revolutionizing recruitment and background verification by enhancing data security, reducing fraud, and streamlining processes. As organizations increasingly recognize the value of blockchain in these areas, it's likely to become a standard tool in HR operations, benefiting both employers and candidates.

Blockchain for Payroll and Compensation

Blockchain technology offers numerous advantages when it comes to payroll and compensation management within an organization. It can significantly improve the accuracy, transparency, and security of these critical HR processes. Following are the ways how blockchain can be applied in the realm of payroll and compensation:

1. **Transparent Payroll Processing:**
    - **Smart Contracts:** Blockchain allows the creation of smart contracts, which are self-executing agreements with predefined rules. In the context of payroll, smart contracts can automate the entire payment process. For example, when the payroll period ends, the contract automatically calculates each employee's salary based on their employment agreement and other relevant factors.
    - **Automated Verification:** Smart contracts can also automatically verify various aspects of payroll, such as working hours, overtime, bonuses, and tax withholdings, ensuring that each employee is paid accurately.
2. **Enhanced Security:**
    - **Immutable Records:** Once payroll data is recorded on the blockchain, it becomes immutable. This means that once a transaction is added, it cannot be altered or deleted without consensus from the network. This immutability ensures that payroll data remains tamper-proof and secure.
    - **Cryptographic Security:** Blockchain employs advanced cryptographic techniques to secure data. Employee payment information is encrypted and protected, reducing the risk of data breaches.
3. **Reduced Fraud and Errors:**
    - **Credential Verification:** Blockchain can be used to verify the authenticity of employee credentials, such as degrees, certifications, and work experience. This reduces the risk of hiring individuals with false qualifications.
    - **Elimination of Duplicate Payments:** Blockchain's transparency prevents duplicate payments or errors in compensation, reducing financial losses due to overpayments.
4. **Efficient Cross-Border Payments:**
    - **Global Workforce:** In organizations with employees working in different countries, blockchain can facilitate cross-border payments. Traditional banking systems often incur high fees and lengthy processing times for international transactions. Blockchain can streamline this process, ensuring that employees receive their compensation promptly and with minimal fees.
5. **Compliance and Auditing:**
    - **Real-time Auditing:** Blockchain's transparent and immutable ledger allows for real-time auditing of payroll transactions. Auditors can access and verify payroll records without the need for extensive manual checks.
    - **Tax Compliance:** Blockchain can automate tax calculations and withholdings based on employee profiles and local tax regulations, reducing the risk of non-compliance.

6. **Employee Empowerment:**
    - **Access to Payroll Records:** Blockchain enables employees to access and verify their own payroll records securely. This level of transparency can build trust and confidence among employees regarding their compensation.
7. **Decentralized Control:**
    - **Reduced Dependence on Intermediaries:** Organizations can reduce their reliance on traditional financial intermediaries like banks and payment processors, potentially lowering transaction costs and increasing control over payroll processes.

Real-world Example

Bitwage is a company that uses blockchain technology to streamline international payroll processing. It allows employees and freelancers around the world to receive their salaries in Bitcoin or other cryptocurrencies. By leveraging blockchain, Bitwage ensures faster and more cost-effective cross-border payments while providing users with transparency and control over their compensation.

Blockchain technology has the potential to revolutionize payroll and compensation management by automating processes, increasing security, reducing errors and fraud, and enhancing transparency. As organizations continue to seek efficient and secure methods for managing payroll, blockchain solutions are likely to play an increasingly important role in the HR landscape.

THE FUTURE OF HR ANALYTICS ECOSYSTEM: EMERGING TECHNOLOGIES IN HR ANALYTICS

The landscape of HR analytics is continuously evolving, driven by technological advancements and the ever-increasing importance of data-driven decision-making in the HR field. As organizations strive to attract, retain, and develop top talent, they are looking to emerging technologies to gain deeper insights into their workforce and enhance HR processes.

1. *Artificial Intelligence (AI) and Machine Learning:*

- **Predictive Analytics:** AI and machine learning algorithms are transforming HR analytics by enabling predictive modelling. These technologies can forecast employee turnover, identify high-potential candidates, and predict future workforce needs.
- **Employee Experience Enhancement:** AI-driven Chabot's and virtual assistants enhance the employee experience by providing instant support for HR-related queries, from benefits inquiries to on boarding guidance.
- **Natural Language Processing (NLP):** NLP algorithms analyse employee feedback and sentiment, providing HR professionals with insights into employee satisfaction and areas that need improvement.
- **Resume Screening:** AI-powered resume screening tools help HR teams quickly identify top candidates by analysing resumes and matching qualifications to job requirements.

2. *Data Visualization and Business Intelligence Tools:*

- **Interactive Dashboards:** Advanced data visualization tools create interactive dashboards that allow HR professionals to explore and understand data more easily. These tools provide real-time insights into workforce metrics.
- **Self-Service Analytics:** Business intelligence tools empower HR teams to generate their own reports and analyse data without relying on IT support, enabling faster decision-making.

3. *Augmented Reality (AR) and Virtual Reality (VR):*

- **Training and Development:** R and VR are being used for immersive training experiences, allowing employees to learn and practice new skills in a virtual environment. These technologies can enhance on boarding and development programs.

4. *Internet of Things (IoT):*

- **Employee Well-being:** IoT devices, such as wearables, can track employee well-being metrics like physical activity, stress levels, and sleep patterns. This data can be used to create wellness programs and interventions.

5. *Robotic Process Automation (RPA):*

- **Streamlined HR Processes:** RPA bots can automate repetitive HR tasks, such as data entry, payroll processing, and benefits administration, freeing HR professionals to focus on more strategic initiatives.

6. *Blockchain in HR Data Management:*

- **Security and Transparency:** Blockchain ensures the security and transparency of HR records, making it a valuable tool for verifying credentials, managing digital identities, and securing sensitive employee data.

7. *Ethics and Bias Mitigation:*

- **Ethical AI:** HR analytics is increasingly focused on ensuring fairness and reducing bias in decision-making. Ethical AI frameworks and tools help identify and mitigate bias in algorithms and processes.

8. *Quantum Computing:*

- **Complex Data Analysis:** As quantum computing matures, it holds the potential to revolutionize HR analytics by processing vast amounts of data at unprecedented speeds, enabling complex simulations and analysis.

9. *Continuous Learning and Adaptive Analytics:*

- **Adaptive Algorithms:** HR analytics is moving towards adaptive algorithms that can learn and evolve based on new data, ensuring that insights remain relevant and accurate over time.

10. ***Augmented Analytics:***

- **Automated Insights:** Augmented analytics platforms use AI to automatically generate insights from data, simplifying the process of uncovering actionable information in HR datasets.

As organizations embrace these emerging technologies, the HR analytics ecosystem is becoming more robust and sophisticated. These technologies are not only enhancing traditional HR processes but also driving HR's transformation into a strategic partner within organizations, equipped to make data-driven decisions that optimize the workforce and contribute to overall business success. In the following sections, we will explore practical applications of these technologies in HR analytics and how they are reshaping the HR landscape.

PREPARING FOR THE FUTURE: DEVELOPING HR ANALYTICS CAPABILITIES

Building Data-driven HR Teams

As organizations recognize the critical role of HR analytics in shaping workforce strategies and driving business outcomes, the need to build data-driven HR teams has become paramount. Developing a team with the skills and mind-set to harness the power of data and analytics is essential for success in the evolving HR landscape. The strategies for building data-driven HR teams are explored below:

1. ***Data Literacy and Skill Development:***

- **Assessment:** Begin by assessing the current data literacy and analytical skills of your HR team members. Identify knowledge gaps and areas that require improvement.
- **Training Programs:** Invest in training programs and workshops focused on data analytics, statistics, and data visualization. These programs can be tailored to the specific needs of HR professionals.
- **Continuous Learning:** Encourage continuous learning and provide access to online courses, webinars, and resources to keep HR team members updated on the latest trends and tools in HR analytics.

2. ***Data Integration and Collaboration:***

- **Cross-functional Collaboration:** Foster collaboration between HR and other departments, such as IT and finance, to ensure seamless data integration and access to relevant data sources.
- **Data Governance:** Implement data governance practices to maintain data quality, consistency, and security. Clearly define data ownership and responsibilities within the HR team.

3. ***Analytical Tools and Technology:***

- **Investment in HR Technology:** Provide HR teams with access to advanced HR analytics tools and technologies. These tools should be user-friendly and capable of generating actionable insights.

- **Data Visualization Tools:** Equip HR professionals with data visualization tools that enable them to create interactive dashboards and reports for better data interpretation.

4. ***Business Acumen:***

- **Understanding Organizational Goals:** HR professionals must understand the broader organizational goals and how HR analytics aligns with them. This knowledge helps in framing HR initiatives in a business context.
- **Return on Investment (ROI):** HR teams should be able to demonstrate the ROI of HR analytics initiatives by linking them to improvements in workforce performance, employee engagement, and organizational success.

5. ***Change Management Skills:***

- **Effective Communication:** HR analytics often leads to changes in HR practices. HR professionals need strong communication skills to convey the rationale for these changes and gain buy-in from stakeholders.
- **Change Leadership:** Develop change leadership skills within the HR team to successfully drive and manage the implementation of data-driven initiatives.

6. ***Data-driven Mind-set:***

- **Cultivate Curiosity:** Encourage HR professionals to ask questions and explore data to uncover insights. Cultivate a culture of curiosity within the team.
- **Experimentation:** Promote a culture of experimentation, where HR professionals are open to testing new ideas and analysing the results to inform decisions.

7. ***HR Business Partners as Data Champions:***

- **HR Business Partner Role:** HR business partners are ideally positioned to champion data-driven HR initiatives within their respective business units. Provide them with the necessary training and support.

8. ***Diversity and Inclusion:***

- **Diverse Teams:** Build diverse HR analytics teams to bring varied perspectives and insights. Diverse teams are more likely to identify and address bias in HR analytics.

9. ***Leadership Support:***

- **Executive Buy-In:** Secure support and commitment from HR leadership and top executives. Leadership endorsement is crucial for prioritizing HR analytics initiatives and allocating resources.

10. ***Metrics and KPIs:***

- **Establish Clear Metrics:** Define key performance indicators (KPIs) for HR analytics capabilities. Regularly assess progress and adjust strategies as needed.

By focusing on these strategies, organizations can cultivate HR teams that are proficient in leveraging data and analytics to make informed decisions, drive HR initiatives, and ultimately contribute to achieving organizational objectives. Building data-driven HR teams is not just a matter of technical skills but also a cultural shift toward data-driven thinking and decision-making within the HR function.

INVESTING IN HR TECHNOLOGY

Investing in HR technology is a crucial aspect of developing future-ready HR analytics capabilities. HR technology not only streamlines HR processes but also serves as the foundation for robust data collection and analysis. Following are key considerations when investing in HR technology:

1. **Needs Assessment:**
    - **Identify Pain Points:** Conduct a thorough assessment of HR processes to identify pain points, inefficiencies, and areas where technology can make a significant impact.
    - **Alignment with Strategy:** Ensure that HR technology investments align with your organization's overall HR and business strategies.
2. **Core HR System:**
    - **HRIS (Human Resources Information System):** Invest in a comprehensive HRIS that serves as the central repository for all employee data. Ensure that it is capable of integration with other HR analytics tools.
3. **Analytics Tools:**
    - **Choose the Right Tools:** Select analytics tools that meet your specific HR analytics needs. Consider tools for data visualization, predictive analytics, and reporting.
    - **User-Friendly Interface:** Prioritize tools with user-friendly interfaces to enable HR professionals to easily access and analyse data.
4. **Data Integration:**
    - **Seamless Integration:** Ensure that HR technology systems seamlessly integrate with each other and with other critical systems such as finance and operations.
    - **Data Standardization:** Implement data standardization practices to maintain data consistency across systems.
5. **Cloud-Based Solutions:**
    - **Scalability:** Cloud-based HR technology solutions offer scalability and flexibility to adapt to changing HR needs and accommodate organizational growth.
    - **Security:** Ensure that cloud solutions meet stringent security standards to protect sensitive HR data.
6. **Mobile Accessibility:**
    - **Mobile Apps:** Provide HR professionals and employees with mobile access to HR technology, enabling remote work and on-the-go access to HR data.

7. **Employee Self-service:**
   - **Self-Service Portals:** Invest in employee self-service portals that allow employees to access their HR information, submit requests, and update personal details.
8. **AI and Automation:**
   - **AI-Powered Features:** Explore AI-driven HR technology features like Chabot's for employee inquiries and automation of routine HR tasks.
9. **Vendor Selection:**
   - **Vendor Evaluation:** Conduct thorough vendor evaluations, considering factors such as reputation, customer support, scalability, and long-term viability.
   - **User Feedback:** Seek input from HR professionals who will be using the technology to understand their preferences and needs.
10. **Data Security and Compliance:**
    - **Compliance:** Ensure that the HR technology aligns with data privacy regulations (e.g., GDPR, CCPA) and industry-specific compliance standards.
    - **Data Encryption:** Implement robust data encryption and security measures to protect sensitive HR data.
11. **Training and Support:**
    - **Training Programs:** Provide comprehensive training programs to ensure that HR professionals can effectively use the technology. - **Ongoing Support:** Offer ongoing support and resources to address any issues or questions that may arise.
12. **ROI Assessment:**
    - **Measure ROI:** Continuously assess the return on investment (ROI) of HR technology by tracking improvements in HR processes, data accuracy, and analytics-driven insights.

DEVELOPING A FUTURE–READY HR ANALYTICS STRATEGY

Building a future-ready HR analytics strategy involves aligning HR initiatives with organizational goals and leveraging analytics to drive meaningful change. Following are key steps in developing such a strategy:

1. **Define Clear Objectives:**
   - **Alignment:** Ensure that HR analytics objectives align with overall organizational goals and strategies.
   - **Specificity:** Define specific, measurable, achievable, relevant, and time-bound (SMART) objectives for HR analytics initiatives.
2. **Data Governance:**
   - **Data Quality:** Establish data governance practices to maintain data accuracy, consistency, and security.
   - **Data Ownership:** Clearly define data ownership and accountability within the HR function.

3. **Data Collection and Integration:**
   - **Comprehensive Data Sources:** Identify and integrate data sources from across the organization, including HRIS, performance management, recruitment, and employee surveys.
   - **Data Accessibility:** Ensure that data is easily accessible to HR professionals and analysts for analysis.
4. **Analytics Tools and Techniques:**
   - **Select Tools:** Choose the appropriate analytics tools and techniques for your specific HR analytics goals. Consider predictive analytics, data visualization, and machine learning.
   - **Training:** Provide training to HR professionals on how to effectively use analytics tools and interpret data.
5. **Metrics and KPIs:**
   - **Identify Key Metrics:** Define key performance indicators (KPIs) that align with HR analytics objectives. These may include turnover rates, diversity metrics, and employee engagement scores.
   - **Benchmarking:** Consider benchmarking HR metrics against industry standards for context.
6. **Predictive and Prescriptive Analytics:**
   - **Use Predictive Models:** Leverage predictive analytics to forecast HR trends such as turnover, recruitment needs, and skills gaps.
   - **Prescriptive Insights:** Move beyond predictive to prescriptive analytics, which not only predict outcomes but also recommend actions to achieve desired results.
7. **Ethical Considerations:**
   - **Bias Mitigation:** Implement strategies and tools to identify and mitigate bias in HR analytics, ensuring fairness and equity.
   - **Data Privacy:** Prioritize data privacy and compliance with relevant regulations.
8. **Employee Engagement:**
   - **Employee Feedback:** Use HR analytics to gather and analyse employee feedback, enabling a deeper understanding of employee sentiment and needs.
   - **Action Plans:** Develop action plans based on analytics insights to improve employee engagement and satisfaction.
9. **Change Management:**
   - **Change Communication:** Communicate HR analytics initiatives and findings effectively to HR teams and other stakeholders.
   - **Change Adoption:** Implement change management strategies to ensure that HR professionals and leadership embrace data-driven decision-making.
10. **Continuous Improvement:**
    - **Feedback Loop:** Establish a feedback loop for HR analytics initiatives to continuously improve data quality, analytics processes, and outcomes.
    - **Adaptability:** Be prepared to adapt the HR analytics strategy as the organization's needs and priorities evolve.

A future-ready HR analytics strategy is not a one-time effort but a dynamic process that evolves in tandem with the organization. It empowers HR professionals to harness the power of data to inform decisions, drive workforce strategies, and contribute to the overall success of the organization.

ENCOURAGING HR PROFESSIONALS TO EMBRACE EMERGING TECHNOLOGIES FOR A MORE DATA-DRIVEN AND EFFECTIVE HR FUNCTION

In a time characterised by swift technological progress, the field of human resources is poised to undergo a profound and far-reaching transformation. A new era of human resources practices has begun with the advent of cutting-edge technologies—one that is more agile, data-driven, and efficient than ever before. The message for human resources professionals is unequivocal: adopt these technologies in order to transform your HR function and enhance your standing within the organisation.

The Power of Data-driven HR

Data has become the cornerstone of effective human resource management. It allows HR professionals to make informed decisions, predict trends, and drive organizational success. Following are some compelling reasons why HR professionals should wholeheartedly embrace emerging technologies for a more data-driven HR function:

1. **Enhanced Decision-making:** With the right tools, HR can tap into a wealth of data, providing actionable insights for decision-making. Whether it's predicting turnover, optimizing recruitment strategies, or identifying skills gaps, data-driven HR enables precision and accuracy.
2. **Talent Acquisition and Retention:** Today's technology-driven world has changed the way we attract and retain talent. From AI-powered resume screening to predictive analytics for identifying flight risks, emerging technologies provide the tools to attract and retain top talent.
3. **Employee Engagement and Well-being:** Technology can measure employee engagement in real-time, offering insights into factors affecting morale and productivity. Moreover, it can assist in implementing well-being programs tailored to employee needs, improving overall satisfaction.
4. **Diversity and Inclusion:** Data analytics can uncover bias and disparities within the organization, helping HR professionals design more inclusive recruitment processes and address disparities in pay, promotions, or representation.
5. **Learning and Development:** Personalized learning experiences are possible with technology. AI-driven platforms can recommend training programs tailored to individual needs and career goals, boosting employee development.
6. **Compliance and Risk Management:** HR often deals with sensitive employee data and complex labour laws. Technology can automate compliance checks, mitigating risks and ensuring adherence to legal regulations.

7. **Cost Efficiency:** Streamlining HR processes through automation and data analytics reduces administrative overhead, allowing HR professionals to focus on strategic initiatives.
8. **Agility and Adaptability:** In a rapidly changing business landscape, HR needs to adapt quickly. Data-driven insights provide the agility required to respond to emerging trends and challenges effectively.
9. **Demonstrating Value:** By embracing technology, HR professionals can demonstrate their value within the organization as strategic partners who drive growth, productivity, and innovation.
10. **Future-Proofing the HR Role:** The HR profession is evolving. Embracing technology is not just about enhancing your current role; it's about future-proofing your career by staying relevant in a digital world.

OVERCOMING RESISTANCE TO CHANGE

Embracing emerging technologies in HR may encounter resistance due to concerns about privacy, job security, or unfamiliarity with new tools. However, successful adoption begins with leadership commitment, employee training, and clear communication. HR professionals must champion the cause, emphasizing how technology enhances rather than replaces their roles.

In conclusion, the digital transformation of HR is not a question of 'if' but 'when.' Those who embrace emerging technologies now will be better positioned to harness the advantages they offer in terms of efficiency, effectiveness, and strategic impact. It's time for HR professionals to seize the opportunity to become architects of a data-driven, innovative, and people-centric future. Embrace technology, and watch your HR function flourish like never before.

Questions for Discussion

Short Questions

1. What is HR analytics, and how has it evolved in the digital age?
2. What are the key stages of evolution in HR analytics, from basic reporting to prescriptive analytics?
3. How does predictive analytics benefit HR in workforce planning and talent retention?
4. What are the benefits of data-driven decision-making in HR?
5. How do AI Chabot's enhance the candidate experience in talent acquisition?
6. What ethical considerations should HR address when implementing AI in analytics?
7. How does AI personalize career development plans for employees?
8. What is blockchain, and how does it work?
9. What advantages does blockchain offer for HR data management?
10. How does blockchain improve data security in payroll and compensation management?
11. What role can AI play in HR analytics?

12. Why is data governance important for HR analytics?
13. What challenges might HR professionals face when adopting emerging technologies?
14. What are some key steps in developing a future-ready HR analytics strategy?

Long Questions

1. Can you explain the evolution of HR analytics from basic reporting to prescriptive analytics and the impact of each stage on HR decision-making?
2. How has the growing importance of data-driven decision-making transformed HR practices and improved various aspects of HR management?
3. What are the emerging trends and technologies in HR analytics, and how do they shape the future of HR operations?
4. In what ways does artificial intelligence (AI) impact HR analytics, and how is it transforming various HR functions, including talent acquisition and employee engagement?
5. What are the benefits of AI in HR analytics, and how does it improve efficiency, personalization, and data-driven decision-making in HR?
6. What challenges and considerations should organizations be aware of when implementing AI in HR analytics?
7. How has AI-driven talent acquisition changed the recruitment process, and what are the implications for diversity and efficiency?
8. How does AI contribute to employee engagement and retention through sentiment analysis, predictive analytics, and personalized career development plans?
9. Can you provide examples of AI applications in HR analytics and how they have improved decision-making and the overall employee experience?
10. What do you think the future holds for AI in HR analytics, and how can organizations maximize its potential while addressing ethical concerns and ensuring employee acceptance?
11. What are the security and transparency advantages of blockchain for HR data management, and how do they impact HR processes?
12. How is blockchain technology transforming recruitment and background verification processes in HR, and what benefits does it offer in terms of security and efficiency?
13. In the context of HR analytics, can you elaborate on the role of AI and machine learning, and how they impact predictive modelling and employee experience enhancement?
14. What steps should organizations take to build data-driven HR teams, and why is it essential for HR professionals to possess data literacy and analytical skills?
15. How can HR professionals develop a future-ready HR analytics strategy, and why is it crucial for HR initiatives to align with organizational goals?
16. What are the ethical considerations and strategies for mitigating bias in HR analytics, and how can HR professionals ensure data privacy and compliance with regulations?
17. How can organizations overcome resistance to change when adopting emerging technologies in HR, and what role does leadership commitment and clear communication play in successful adoption?

CHAPTER

14

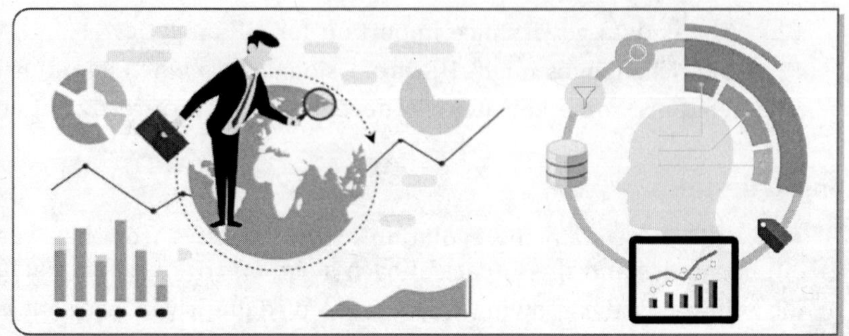

Emerging Trends in HR Analytics

Human Resources (HR) analytics has evolved significantly over the years, and it continues to be at the forefront of transforming the way organizations manage their workforce. In today's data-driven world, emerging trends in HR analytics are shaping the future of HR management, providing valuable insights, enhancing decision-making, and improving employee experiences. Emerging trends in HR analytics reflect the evolving landscape of workforce management, technology, and data-driven decision-making. As organizations recognize the importance of leveraging data to optimize their HR practices, several trends are gaining prominence:

1. **AI and Machine Learning Adoption:** AI and machine learning are playing an increasingly significant role in HR analytics. These technologies are used to predict employee turnover, identify high-potential candidates, personalize learning and development, and enhance the recruitment process through resume parsing and candidate matching.
2. **Predictive Analytics for Employee Retention:** Predictive analytics models are becoming more refined, enabling HR teams to identify early warning signs of employee disengagement and turnover. By analysing a range of data, from performance reviews to sentiment analysis, organizations can proactively address retention issues.
3. **Real-time Analytics:** Real-time data analysis allows HR professionals to respond swiftly to workforce challenges. This is particularly relevant for managing remote or distributed teams and addressing issues like burnout, workload imbalances, and employee well-being.
4. **Employee Experience (EX) Analytics:** Organizations are placing greater emphasis on measuring and enhancing the overall employee experience. This includes tracking employee satisfaction, engagement, well-being, and feedback to create a more positive and productive work environment.

5. **Skills Mapping and Development Analytics:** As the importance of upskilling and reskilling grows, organizations are using HR analytics to map employees' skills, identify skill gaps, and provide targeted learning and development opportunities.
6. **Diversity, Equity, and Inclusion (DEI) Analytics:** DEI analytics is on the rise, enabling organizations to assess and improve diversity and inclusion efforts. HR teams use data to track representation, pay equity, promotion rates, and employee experiences to identify areas for improvement.
7. **Adaptive Workforce Planning:** Traditional workforce planning is evolving into a more adaptive and agile process. HR analytics helps organizations better respond to changes in the business environment by identifying critical talent needs and optimizing resource allocation.
8. **Talent Marketplace Platforms:** Talent marketplace platforms, which facilitate internal mobility and skill-based project assignments, are increasingly powered by HR analytics. These platforms help organizations make the best use of their existing talent.
9. **Employee Sentiment Analysis:** Natural language processing (NLP) and sentiment analysis tools are used to assess employee feedback, sentiment, and social media activity. These insights help HR teams gauge employee morale, identify concerns, and respond proactively.
10. **Blockchain for Verification and Authentication:** Blockchain technology is being explored for background checks, credential verification, and employee on boarding. It offers a secure and immutable way to verify qualifications and employment history.
11. **Workforce Productivity Analytics:** As remote and hybrid work arrangements become more common, organizations are using analytics to assess workforce productivity, collaboration, and engagement in different work settings.
12. **Sustainability and Social Responsibility Metrics:** HR analytics is expanding to include metrics related to sustainability, social responsibility, and ethical practices. Companies are tracking data on environmental impact, diversity initiatives, and corporate social responsibility efforts.
13. **Compliance and Ethics Monitoring:** HR analytics can be used to monitor and enforce compliance with ethics and code of conduct policies, detecting irregular behaviour and promoting a culture of transparency and ethics.
14. **Data Storytelling:** Data storytelling skills are becoming essential in HR analytics. HR professionals are learning to convey data-driven insights in a way that is easily understandable and compelling for decision-makers.

These emerging trends in HR analytics are driven by a growing recognition of the value of data-driven HR practices and the evolving needs of the modern workforce. Organizations that embrace these trends can gain a competitive advantage by making more informed and strategic HR decisions.

CHALLENGES IN THE FIELD OF HR ANALYTICS

The field of HR analytics faces several challenges, ranging from technical and data-related issues to cultural and ethical considerations. Here are some of the key challenges in HR analytics:

1. **Data Quality and Integration**: HR data often comes from various sources and systems, leading to challenges in data integration and consistency. Inaccurate or incomplete data can result in unreliable analysis and decision-making.
2. **Privacy and Compliance:** Data privacy laws, such as GDPR and CCPA, pose challenges for HR analytics. Ensuring compliance with these regulations, especially when handling sensitive employee data, can be complex and demanding.
3. **Data Security:** Protecting HR data from unauthorized access and breaches is a critical challenge. As HR analytics tools and systems become more interconnected, they are exposed to a wider range of potential vulnerabilities.
4. **Bias and Fairness:** Ensuring that HR analytics models are free from bias and discrimination is an ongoing challenge. Biased data or algorithms can lead to unfair treatment of employees, especially in hiring and promotion decisions.
5. **Talent Shortage:** There is a shortage of skilled HR analysts who can extract meaningful insights from data. Organizations often struggle to find and retain professionals with the necessary analytical and data science skills.
6. **Change Management:** Implementing HR analytics requires a cultural shift within an organization. Resistance to data-driven decision-making can be a significant challenge, as employees and leadership may need to adapt to a new way of operating.
7. **Cost and ROI:** HR analytics can be resource-intensive, and organizations may face challenges in demonstrating a clear return on investment (ROI) for their analytics initiatives.
8. **Interpreting Complex Data:** HR professionals must develop the skills to interpret complex data and transform it into actionable insights. This challenge requires ongoing training and education.
9. **Technology Integration:** Integrating HR analytics tools with existing HR systems, such as HRIS (Human Resource Information System), can be challenging. Data silos and compatibility issues may arise.
10. **Global Workforce Challenges:** Managing a global workforce with different legal and cultural considerations adds complexity to HR analytics efforts, especially when dealing with cross-border data transfers and compliance issues.
11. **Ethical Considerations:** Balancing the ethical use of HR analytics with the drive for efficiency and productivity remains an ongoing challenge. Organizations must consider the ethical implications of data collection and usage.
12. **Employee Trust:** Employees may have concerns about data privacy and how HR analytics will impact their careers. Building and maintaining trust is a challenge, as transparency and communication are crucial.
13. **Overcoming Resistance:** HR professionals may encounter resistance from managers and decision-makers who are not accustomed to data-driven HR practices. Convincing stakeholders of the value of analytics can be challenging.
14. **Alignment with Business Objectives:** Ensuring that HR analytics initiatives align with overall business goals and objectives can be a challenge. HR teams need to define key performance indicators (KPIs) that are meaningful to the organization.

Addressing these challenges requires a strategic and holistic approach to HR analytics. Organizations should prioritize data quality, invest in employee training and development, establish strong data security measures, and maintain compliance with relevant regulations. Furthermore, fostering a data-driven culture and promoting ethical practices are essential to overcome many of these challenges and reap the benefits of HR analytics.

These future trends and challenges presented in the Table 14.1 provide insight into the evolving landscape of HR analytics, emphasizing the need to balance technological advancements with legal compliance, data quality, ethical considerations, and workforce readiness.

TABLE 14.1 Future trends and challenges in the field of HR analytics

Future Trends	*Challenges*
1. Predictive Analytics	**1. Data Privacy and Compliance**
Using AI and machine learning to predict employee behaviours and outcomes for better decision-making.	Adhering to increasingly stringent data privacy regulations like GDPR and CCPA.
2. AI-Driven Recruitment	**2. Data Quality and Integrity**
Employing AI to automate and streamline the hiring process, improving efficiency and accuracy.	Ensuring the accuracy and reliability of HR data for meaningful analytics.
3. Diversity and Inclusion	**3. Skills Gap**
Using analytics to measure and improve diversity and inclusion, reducing bias in HR decisions.	Ensuring HR professionals have the necessary skills to harness advanced analytics tools and methods.
4. Employee Well-being	**4. Ethical Dilemmas**
Analysing data to improve employee well-being programs and mental health support.	Balancing the use of data for HR decisions with ethical concerns.
5. Remote Work Analytics	**5. Data Security**
Using data to assess remote work performance, productivity, and engagement.	Protecting employee data from breaches and maintaining data security.
	6. Workforce Resistance
	Overcoming resistance from employees who may be skeptical of HR analytics.
	7. Data Integration
	Integrating data from various HR and organizational sources for a holistic view of HR analytics.

EMERGING TRENDS IN HR ANALYTICS: REVOLUTIONIZING HR MANAGEMENT

Human Resource (HR) analytics is undergoing a profound transformation, driven by advancements in technology, changing workforce dynamics, and the growing recognition of data-driven decision-making in HR practices. These emerging trends in HR analytics are reshaping the way organizations manage their workforce and optimize HR processes. Some of the most significant trends are explained below:

1. **AI and Machine Learning Integration**:
   - AI and machine learning have found a significant role in HR analytics. These technologies enable HR professionals to predict employee turnover, identify high-potential candidates, and enhance the recruitment process.
   - Predictive analytics models powered by AI and machine learning can analyse historical workforce data to identify patterns and forecast future trends. This facilitates proactive decision-making, such as predicting attrition and formulating retention strategies.
2. **Predictive Analytics for Employee Retention**:
   - Predictive analytics in HR is becoming increasingly sophisticated. HR teams can use data to identify early warning signs of employee disengagement or potential turnover.
   - By analysing a wide range of data, including performance metrics, employee feedback, and sentiment analysis, organizations can intervene in real-time to retain their top talent.
3. **Real-time Analytics**:
   - Real-time data analysis is essential for HR teams to address workforce challenges promptly, especially in the context of remote and distributed teams.
   - This capability allows organizations to respond swiftly to issues like burnout, workload imbalances, and employee well-being, thereby enhancing overall productivity.
4. **Employee Experience (EX) Analytics**:
   - The focus on employee experience is growing, with EX metrics becoming central to HR analytics.
   - Metrics like employee satisfaction, well-being, and engagement are being actively tracked and analysed. Organizations are utilizing these insights to create a more positive and productive work environment.
5. **Skills Mapping and Development Analytics**:
   - HR analytics is increasingly being used to map employees' skills and identify skill gaps.
   - With this data, organizations can provide targeted learning and development opportunities, aligning their workforce with the skills required for future success.
6. **Diversity, Equity, and Inclusion (DEI) Analytics**:
   - Organizations are recognizing the importance of diversity and inclusion and are leveraging analytics to assess and improve their DEI efforts.

- HR teams use data to track representation, pay equity, promotion rates, and employee experiences to identify areas for improvement and ensure fair and equitable treatment of all employees.

7. **Adaptive Workforce Planning**: Traditional workforce planning is evolving into a more adaptive and agile process. HR analytics helps organizations respond to changes in the business environment, such as identifying critical talent needs and optimizing resource allocation in real-time.
8. **Talent Marketplace Platforms**:
   - Talent marketplace platforms are gaining traction, allowing organizations to facilitate internal mobility and skill-based project assignments.
   - Powered by HR analytics, these platforms help companies make the best use of their existing talent by matching employees with opportunities that align with their skills and interests.
9. **Employee Sentiment Analysis:** Natural language processing (NLP) and sentiment analysis tools are used to assess employee feedback, sentiment, and social media activity. These insights help HR teams gauge employee morale, identify concerns, and respond proactively.
10. **Blockchain for Verification and Authentication:** Blockchain technology is being explored for background checks, credential verification, and employee on boarding. It offers a secure and immutable way to verify qualifications and employment history.
11. **Workforce Productivity Analytics:** With the growth of remote and hybrid work arrangements, organizations are using analytics to assess workforce productivity, collaboration, and engagement in different work settings.
12. **Sustainability and Social Responsibility Metrics:** HR analytics is expanding to include metrics related to sustainability, social responsibility, and ethical practices. Companies are tracking data on environmental impact, diversity initiatives, and corporate social responsibility efforts.
13. **Compliance and Ethics Monitoring:** HR analytics can be used to monitor and enforce compliance with ethics and code of conduct policies, detecting irregular behaviour and promoting a culture of transparency and ethics.
14. **Data Storytelling:** Data storytelling skills are becoming essential in HR analytics. HR professionals are learning to convey data-driven insights in a way that is easily understandable and compelling for decision-makers.

These trends reflect the ongoing evolution of HR analytics into a vital strategic tool for organizations. By leveraging data, analytics, and technology, HR professionals can gain deeper insights into their workforce, create more inclusive and productive workplaces, and make informed decisions that drive business success. Embracing these trends and the data-driven culture they represent is becoming imperative for HR departments looking to stay competitive and responsive to the evolving demands of the modern workforce.

THE IMPORTANCE OF STAYING UPDATED ON HR ANALYTICS TRENDS

In today's fast-paced and ever-evolving business environment, staying updated on HR analytics trends is not merely a choice but a strategic imperative for organizations. HR analytics, often referred to as people analytics, has rapidly become a cornerstone of modern human resources management. It is the practice of using data, statistical analysis, and technology to make informed decisions about an organization's workforce. The ability to harness HR data effectively and adapt to emerging trends can profoundly impact an organization's ability to attract, retain, and develop talent while maintaining a competitive edge. The significance of staying current with HR analytics trends is discussed below:

1. **Enhanced Decision-making**: HR analytics provides the tools and methodologies to convert data into actionable insights. By staying updated on trends, HR professionals can make informed decisions related to recruitment, talent management, and employee engagement. Access to the latest trends allows HR leaders to take a more strategic and data-driven approach to human resource management, aligning their decisions with organizational goals and objectives.
2. **Talent Attraction and Retention**: Attracting and retaining top talent is a key challenge for organizations. HR analytics trends often revolve around innovative ways to address this challenge. The latest trends can offer insights into how to create more appealing employee value propositions, develop targeted recruitment strategies, and improve employee experiences. By staying informed, organizations can better position themselves in the talent market.
3. **Adaptation to Evolving Work Environments**: The nature of work is changing rapidly, with trends like remote work, gig economy, and hybrid work environments becoming more prevalent. Staying updated on HR analytics trends is essential for adapting to these shifts effectively. New analytics methods and tools can help organizations manage a remote or hybrid workforce, measure productivity, and maintain employee engagement in a virtual setting.
4. **Innovation and Technological Advancements**: HR analytics is closely tied to technological advancements. With the rise of artificial intelligence, machine learning, and advanced data analytics tools, HR professionals have new means to gain deeper insights into employee behaviours and trends. Staying current ensures that HR departments can leverage the latest technology to improve their processes, automate routine tasks, and enhance decision-making.
5. **Compliance and Ethical Considerations**: HR analytics often involves the collection and analysis of sensitive employee data. Staying updated on trends in this field is critical to ensure that organizations remain compliant with evolving data protection regulations, such as GDPR or CCPA. Understanding ethical considerations in data usage is also crucial to maintaining trust and transparency within the organization.
6. **Competitive Advantage**: In a fiercely competitive business landscape, the ability to outperform rivals in attracting, developing, and retaining talent is a source of competitive advantage. Keeping pace with HR analytics trends can provide organizations with that edge. It allows HR professionals to identify and implement best practices and innovative approaches that can set them apart from competitors.
7. **Cost Efficiency**: HR analytics can also help organizations streamline their HR operations and reduce costs. Staying updated on the latest trends enables organizations to identify cost-effective solutions, optimize HR processes, and allocate resources more efficiently.

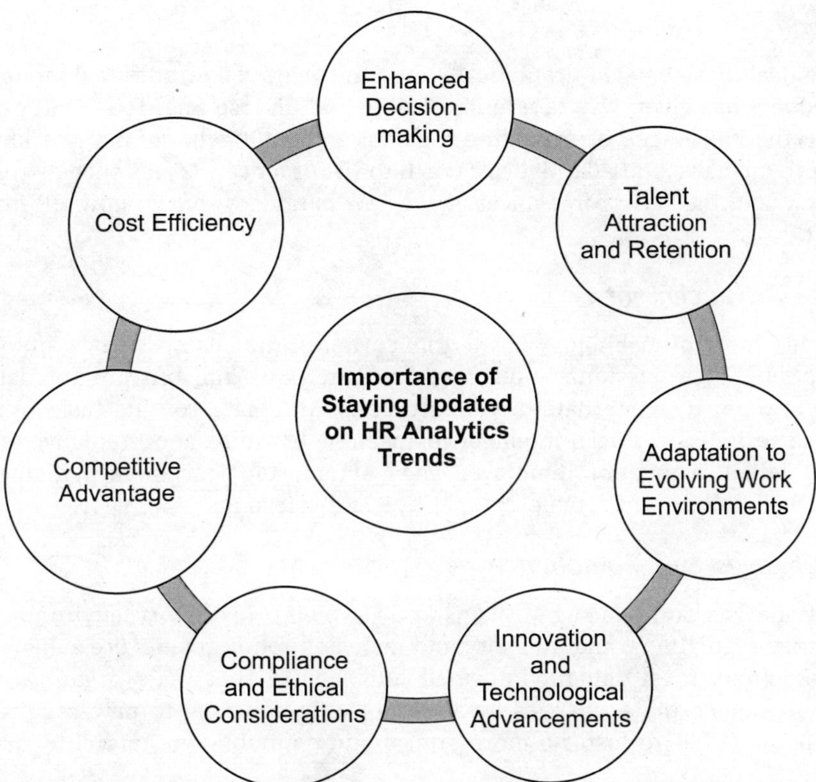

FIGURE 14.1 Importance of staying updated on HR analytics trends.

Thus, HR analytics is not a static field. It is constantly evolving, driven by technological advancements, shifts in the workforce, and changing business dynamics. Staying updated on HR analytics trends is essential for organizations that want to remain agile, competitive, and efficient in their talent management strategies. Those who neglect to adapt and innovate risk falling behind in the increasingly data-centric world of human resources management. Therefore, investing in continuous learning and monitoring of HR analytics trends is not just a choice but a necessity for organizations that aim to thrive in the modern workplace.

THE DYNAMIC NATURE OF THE HR LANDSCAPE: NAVIGATING CHANGE AND ADAPTATION

The human resources (HR) landscape is undergoing a profound transformation, and the only constant within it seems to be change itself. Traditionally viewed as the administrative backbone of organizations, HR has evolved into a strategic partner that plays a critical role in shaping an organization's success. This evolution is driven by a multitude of factors, and it underscores the dynamic nature of the HR landscape.

Evolving Workforce Dynamics

The workforce itself has changed dramatically over the years. The traditional model of a fixed, in-house workforce has given way to a more flexible and diverse one. Today, HR professionals are faced with the challenges of managing a global and multigenerational workforce, which demands a more inclusive and adaptive approach to HR practices. Issues such as remote work, the gig economy, and the rise of freelancers have necessitated a shift in how HR manages and engages talent.

Technological Advancements

The rapid advancement of technology has left no corner of the business world untouched, and HR is no exception. HR professionals now have access to powerful software and data analytics tools that allow them to make data-driven decisions, automate routine tasks, and enhance the employee experience. Artificial intelligence, machine learning, and predictive analytics are revolutionizing talent acquisition, employee engagement, and workforce planning. HR must adapt to these technologies to remain competitive and relevant.

Regulatory Changes and Compliance

The HR landscape is also shaped by a constantly evolving regulatory environment. Labour laws, data privacy regulations, and diversity and inclusion requirements are subject to change, and HR professionals must remain informed and ensure that their organizations are in compliance. Adapting to these changes involves not only adhering to new requirements but also finding opportunities to foster a more ethical and equitable workplace.

Shifting Employee Expectations

Today's employees have different expectations of their employers compared to previous generations. Work-life balance, flexible work arrangements, and a strong commitment to diversity, equity, and inclusion are becoming more critical for attracting and retaining talent. HR must be agile and responsive in addressing these expectations to create a positive employee experience.

Strategic HR

The HR landscape has shifted from a predominantly administrative role to one of strategic significance. HR is increasingly seen as a partner in achieving business goals, and it contributes to organizational success through workforce planning, talent management, and fostering a positive workplace culture. HR professionals are expected to align HR practices with the organization's strategic objectives.

Data-driven Decision-making

Data and analytics have become central to HR's decision-making processes. HR analytics and metrics enable professionals to assess the effectiveness of their programs and initiatives, identify trends, and make informed decisions. This shift towards data-driven HR not only improves efficiency but also enhances HR's impact on the organization.

The dynamic nature of the HR landscape is a testament to the ever-changing nature of business and society. HR professionals must not only adapt to these changes but also actively anticipate and lead them. Success in the HR field now requires continuous learning, a willingness to embrace new technologies, and an agile mind-set that can navigate through the challenges and opportunities presented by the evolving landscape. Ultimately, HR's ability to stay ahead of the curve is crucial to the success of both the HR function and the organizations it serves.

AGILE HR ANALYTICS

Within the dynamic field of Human Resources (HR), conventional methods of data analysis and decision-making are progressively giving way to Agile HR Analytics, a more adaptable and responsive approach. This novel methodology is revolutionising the manner in which human resources practitioners utilise data and analytics to oversee and assist the staff, synchronise HR endeavours with the objectives of the organisation, and generate improved business results.

Understanding Agile HR Analytics

Agile HR Analytics draws inspiration from Agile project management principles commonly used in software development and product management. Its fundamental goal is to enable HR professionals to be more adaptable and responsive to the changing needs of the organization and its employees. Instead of rigid annual HR plans and lengthy data analysis cycles, Agile HR Analytics emphasizes short, iterative cycles of data collection, analysis, and action, all in alignment with the organization's strategic goals.

Key Principles of Agile HR Analytics

1. **Iterative Approach:** Agile HR Analytics breaks down the traditional annual HR planning cycle into shorter, recurring cycles. This iterative approach allows HR teams to gather data, analyse it, make decisions, and implement changes more frequently, often in two-to-four-week sprints.
2. **Cross-functional Teams:** Agile promotes the collaboration of cross-functional teams. In Agile HR Analytics, this means that HR, IT, and business leaders work closely together to define objectives, gather and analyse data, and develop actionable insights.
3. **Customer-centric Focus:** Agile HR places employees and their needs at the centre. The process begins with understanding employee needs, preferences, and pain points, which then guides HR analytics efforts.
4. **Data-driven Decision-making:** Data is the backbone of Agile HR Analytics. HR professionals collect and analyse data regularly, using metrics and key performance indicators (KPIs) to make informed decisions.
5. **Adaptability and Continuous Improvement:** Agile HR is built on the principle of embracing change. HR teams continuously adapt strategies based on data and feedback. Regular retrospectives are held to assess what worked, what didn't, and how to improve.

Benefits of Agile HR Analytics

Agile HR Analytics offers several significant benefits such as:

1. **Faster Response to Change:** The iterative approach allows HR to respond more quickly to changes in the workplace, whether they're driven by industry trends, market conditions, or internal shifts.
2. **Improved Employee Experience:** By focusing on employee needs and using data-driven insights, HR can enhance the employee experience, leading to higher engagement and retention rates.
3. **Better Alignment with Business Goals:** Agile HR Analytics ensures that HR initiatives are closely aligned with the broader organizational goals, promoting synergy between HR and other departments.
4. **Enhanced Data Quality:** Regular data collection and analysis help maintain the accuracy and relevance of HR data, ensuring it remains up-to-date and actionable.
5. **Cost Savings:** By focusing resources on initiatives with the greatest impact, Agile HR Analytics can lead to cost savings through more efficient and effective HR practices.

Challenges and Considerations

Implementing Agile HR Analytics is not without its challenges. It requires a cultural shift within the HR department, support from leadership, and investment in the right technology and data analytics capabilities. Moreover, the process of change itself can be disruptive and may necessitate a learning curve for HR professionals. Agile HR Analytics is a progressive approach to HR management that aligns the HR function with the fast-paced, dynamic nature of the modern workplace. By embracing agility, HR professionals can become more responsive to change, more employee-centric, and better aligned with their organization's strategic objectives. While the transition to Agile HR Analytics may be a journey, the results in terms of improved HR performance and business impact are well worth the effort.

The Agile Approach to HR Analytics

Agile HR Analytics is an approach that borrows its core principles from Agile project management methodologies. It emphasizes adaptability, collaboration, and customer-centricity, enabling HR teams to address evolving organizational needs effectively. Unlike traditional, lengthy data analysis processes, Agile HR Analytics breaks down data into smaller, more manageable pieces, allowing HR professionals to respond to HR challenges promptly.

Iterative Analysis and Adaptation

At the heart of Agile HR Analytics is the concept of iterative analysis and adaptation. Instead of conducting in-depth, lengthy analyses that may be outdated by the time they are completed, HR teams work in short cycles, known as sprints. These sprints allow for the rapid analysis of HR data and the adjustment of strategies based on real-time findings. By breaking down the analysis into smaller, manageable components, teams can identify trends, issues, and opportunities more swiftly and accurately.

The iterative nature of Agile HR Analytics also ensures that HR professionals stay aligned with organizational goals. As priorities shift, HR teams can pivot their efforts, modifying their analytical approach and focus in response to emerging challenges and opportunities. This adaptability enables HR to address workforce issues as they arise, making data-driven decision-making more effective.

Rapid Response to Changing HR Needs

In today's dynamic business environment, HR needs can change rapidly. Whether it's the sudden need for remote work support, adapting to a changing labour market, or addressing employee concerns, HR teams must be agile to keep up. Agile HR Analytics equips HR professionals with the ability to respond rapidly to these changing needs.

Rather than adhering to rigid, pre-defined HR plans, Agile HR Analytics embraces the idea that change is constant. When a new HR challenge arises, Agile HR teams can quickly analyse relevant data, identify potential solutions, and implement changes. This not only enhances HR's agility but also contributes to the organization's overall resilience.

Collaborative Cross-Functional Analytics Teams

In the Agile HR Analytics approach, collaboration is key. HR teams collaborate not only among themselves but also with cross-functional teams within the organization. This collaborative approach encourages diverse perspectives and expertise, leading to more holistic solutions to HR challenges.

Cross-functional teams often include HR professionals, data analysts, IT specialists, and other relevant stakeholders. They work together to identify HR analytics needs, define data collection methods, and analyse results. This collective effort ensures that HR strategies are rooted in data, align with broader organizational goals, and take into account the various perspectives necessary for informed decision-making.

In conclusion, Agile HR Analytics represents a significant shift in the way HR professionals approach data analysis and decision-making. By embracing an agile approach, HR teams can adapt swiftly to changing needs, foster collaboration, and make data-driven decisions that have a more immediate and lasting impact on the organization. This approach ensures that HR remains a dynamic and responsive function, well-prepared to meet the evolving challenges of the modern workplace. As organizations increasingly recognize the value of this approach, Agile HR Analytics is poised to become a cornerstone of effective HR practices.

THE NEED FOR CONTINUOUS LEARNING AND ADAPTATION IN HR ANALYTICS

In today's rapidly evolving business landscape, the role of Human Resources (HR) has transformed dramatically. HR is no longer just about recruitment, payroll, and compliance. It has emerged as a strategic partner in organizations, and one of the key drivers of this transformation is HR analytics. The integration of data-driven decision-making into HR practices has fundamentally changed the way organizations manage their workforce. Unfortunately, HR analytics can only be effective if HR professionals are willing to constantly learn and adapt.

1. *The Dynamic Nature of HR and Business*

The business world is dynamic and constantly changing. Factors such as economic shifts, technological advancements, and societal changes affect the way organizations operate. HR, as a vital component of every business, must adapt to these changes. HR analytics plays a pivotal role in helping organizations respond to these shifts, but to do so effectively, HR professionals must be on a perpetual learning curve.

2. *Rapid Technological Advancements*

Technology is a driving force in HR analytics. From data collection tools to predictive modelling and artificial intelligence, the technology landscape is continually evolving. Staying updated on these advancements is essential for HR professionals to harness the full potential of analytics. Understanding and implementing new technologies can help HR departments automate routine tasks, enhance decision-making, and gain a competitive edge.

3. *Expanding Data Sources*

The volume and sources of data available to HR professionals have grown exponentially. Traditional HR data, such as personnel records and time logs, have been complemented by data from social media, wearables, and even sentiment analysis. The ability to adapt to these new data sources and incorporate them into analytics strategies is crucial. Continuous learning allows HR professionals to effectively manage, analyse, and derive insights from this wealth of information.

4. *Changing Workforce Dynamics*

Workforce dynamics have evolved significantly. Remote work, gig economy jobs, and a multi-generational workforce have become the norm. HR analytics must adapt to account for these changes. Continuous learning in HR analytics enables professionals to understand the unique needs and preferences of a diverse workforce and develop strategies that cater to these dynamics.

5. *Ethical Considerations and Compliance*

With the increasing use of analytics, ethical concerns and compliance requirements are growing. HR professionals need to be well-versed in data privacy regulations, antidiscrimination laws, and best practices in data handling. Continuous learning is essential to ensure that HR analytics initiatives remain ethical and compliant while still delivering value.

6. *Competitive Advantage*

HR analytics provides organizations with a competitive advantage by helping them make data-driven decisions that optimize workforce productivity, reduce turnover, and enhance employee engagement. To maintain this advantage, HR professionals must continually expand their knowledge and skills in analytics. Stagnation in HR analytics practices can lead to a loss of competitive edge.

7. *Adaptation to Organizational Goals*

The goals and strategies of organizations change over time. HR analytics must align with these shifting objectives. Continuous learning ensures that HR professionals can adapt their analytics initiatives to support the evolving goals of the business.

The need for continuous learning and adaptation in HR analytics is not a choice but a necessity. As HR transforms into a strategic partner, the ability to harness the power of data and analytics is paramount. HR professionals who engage in ongoing learning and adaptation are better equipped to navigate the complex and ever-changing landscape of HR analytics, delivering insights that drive business success and ensuring that the HR function remains agile, innovative, and aligned with the goals of the organization.

THE IMPLICATIONS OF EMERGING TRENDS ON HR PROFESSIONALS

The field of Human Resources (HR) has undergone a significant transformation in recent years, driven by emerging trends in HR analytics and technology. These trends have far-reaching implications for HR professionals, reshaping their roles and responsibilities and challenging them to adapt to a rapidly evolving landscape.

TABLE 14.2 The implications of emerging trends on HR professionals

Emerging HR Analytics Trend	*Implications on HR Professionals*
Artificial Intelligence (AI) and Machine Learning	HR professionals need to acquire AI and ML skills or collaborate with data scientists to harness AI's potential.
Predictive Analytics for Employee Well-being	HR professionals must become adept at using predictive analytics to proactively address employee well-being.
Employee Experience (EX) Analytics	HR professionals should invest in EX analytics tools and expertise to improve the employee experience.
Diversity, Equity, and Inclusion (DEI) Analytics	HR professionals must use data to promote diversity, equity, and inclusion and track progress.
HR Analytics in Remote and Hybrid Work Environments	HR professionals need to adapt HR processes for remote and hybrid work and leverage technology for analytics.
Skills and Competency Analytics	HR professionals should invest in tools to identify skill gaps and predict future skill requirements.
Blockchain and HR Data Security	HR professionals must prioritize data security and privacy, exploring blockchain for secure data management.
Agile HR Analytics	HR professionals need to adopt agile approaches, fostering collaboration among cross-functional teams.
Ethical and Responsible HR Analytics	HR professionals should uphold ethical standards, eliminate bias, and ensure legal compliance in data usage.

1. **Evolving Skill Sets:**
   - **Emerging Trend:** With the rise of HR analytics, HR professionals must acquire new skills related to data analysis, statistics, and data visualization. They need to become proficient in using HR technology and data-driven decision-making tools.
   - **Implication:** HR professionals are required to undergo continuous learning and upskilling to remain relevant in their roles. The ability to interpret and leverage data becomes a critical competency.
2. **Strategic Decision-making:**
   - **Emerging Trend:** HR analytics empowers professionals to make data-driven decisions. They can use data to align HR strategies with organizational goals, optimize workforce planning, and enhance employee experience.
   - **Implication:** HR professionals are no longer just administrative gatekeepers but strategic partners within their organizations. They are expected to contribute to the bottom line and participate in high-level business discussions.
3. **Employee Experience Enhancement:**
   - **Emerging Trend:** Employee experience (EX) analytics allows HR professionals to measure, improve, and personalize the employee journey. They can proactively address issues and create a more engaging workplace.
   - **Implication:** HR professionals need to become champions of employee well-being and satisfaction. They are responsible for fostering a positive workplace culture, which can directly impact recruitment, retention, and productivity.
4. **Diversity and Inclusion Advocates:**
   - **Emerging Trend:** HR analytics helps organizations track and improve diversity, equity, and inclusion efforts. HR professionals are expected to take the lead in creating more inclusive workplaces.
   - **Implication:** HR professionals must actively drive DEI initiatives and work to eliminate biases within hiring and talent management processes. They play a critical role in ensuring equal opportunities for all employees.
5. **Remote and Hybrid Work Adaptation:**
   - **Emerging Trend:** Remote and hybrid work arrangements have become more prevalent. HR professionals need to manage and optimize a distributed workforce, utilizing technology to maintain employee engagement and productivity.
   - **Implication:** HR professionals are tasked with developing new policies, processes, and communication strategies to support remote and hybrid workforces. They need to ensure that employees remain connected and aligned with the company's culture and objectives.
6. **Ethical and Legal Considerations:**
   - **Emerging Trend:** As HR professionals harness data and technology, ethical and legal concerns come to the forefront. Data privacy, transparency, and compliance are paramount.
   - **Implication:** HR professionals must navigate complex regulatory landscapes and uphold ethical standards in data management. They are accountable for safeguarding employee data and ensuring that analytics and AI tools are used responsibly.

7. **Agile and Adaptive Approaches:**
   - **Emerging Trend:** Agile methodologies are becoming more popular in HR to address dynamic business needs. HR professionals are embracing iterative, responsive approaches to talent management and development.
   - **Implication:** HR professionals must be adaptable and open to change. They work collaboratively with cross-functional teams and regularly reassess strategies and tactics to respond to evolving organizational requirements.

These implications illustrated in the Table 14.2 highlight the evolving role of HR professionals in the face of emerging trends in HR analytics, emphasizing the need for new skills, adaptability, and a proactive approach to address the changing demands of the field.

TABLE 14.3 How to encourage a forward-looking, innovative HR analytics mind-set

Aspect	*Description*
1. Leadership Support	Gain the endorsement of top leadership for analytics.
	Emphasize the strategic value of HR analytics.
	Encourage leaders to lead by example in data-driven decisions.
2. Continuous Learning	Provide ongoing training in analytics tools and techniques.
	Support HR professionals in gaining data-related certifications.
	Encourage the pursuit of advanced degrees in data analytics.
3. Experimentation	Promote a culture of experimentation and risk-taking.
	Allow HR teams to test innovative analytics approaches.
	Recognize and learn from both successes and failures.
4. Data-driven Decision-making	Make data the foundation of HR decision-making.
	Encourage HR teams to seek data-driven solutions.
	Establish metrics for evaluating HR's impact on the organization
5. Collaboration	Foster collaboration between HR and other departments.
	Create cross-functional analytics teams for holistic insights.
	Share data and insights across the organization.
6. Technology Adoption	Stay current with the latest HR analytics tools and software.
	Invest in technology that facilitates data analysis and visualization.
	Leverage emerging technologies such as AI and machine learning.
7. Ethical Considerations	Prioritize ethical data usage and transparency.
	Implement data privacy and compliance measures.
	Establish guidelines for ethical HR data practices.

(Contd.)

Aspect	*Description*
8. Feedback and Recognition	Provide regular feedback and recognition for innovative ideas.
	Celebrate HR analytics successes within the organization.
	Use positive reinforcement to motivate a forward-thinking mind-set.
9. Incentives and Rewards	Create incentives for HR professionals to innovate with data.
	Reward teams for implementing data-driven improvements.
	Tie innovation to performance evaluations and promotions.
10. Thought Leadership	Encourage HR professionals to participate in industry forums.
	Share thought leadership and best practices in HR analytics.
	Inspire HR to lead in shaping the future of analytics in the field.

Encouraging a forward-looking, innovative HR analytics mind-set involves a combination of leadership support, continuous learning, a culture of experimentation, data-driven decision-making, collaboration, technology adoption, ethical considerations, feedback and recognition, incentives, and thought leadership. These aspects illustrated in the table 14.3 collectively promote a mind-set that embraces innovation and analytics in HR practices.

In conclusion, emerging trends in HR analytics and technology have transformed the role of HR professionals. They are no longer confined to traditional administrative tasks but are expected to be data-savvy, strategic leaders who drive organizational success. The implications of these trends include a shift in skill requirements, a more strategic role within the organization, and a greater responsibility for employee well-being, diversity, ethics, and adaptability. HR professionals who embrace these changes and invest in continuous learning will thrive in the evolving HR landscape.

Questions for Discussion

Short Questions

1. What are some emerging trends in HR analytics?
2. How is AI and machine learning being used in HR analytics?
3. Why is predictive analytics for employee retention important in HR?
4. What is the significance of real-time analytics in HR?
5. How does HR use employee experience (EX) analytics to improve the workplace?
6. What is the purpose of skills mapping and development analytics in HR?
7. How can HR leverage diversity, equity, and inclusion (DEI) analytics?
8. How does HR measure workforce productivity through analytics?
9. Why is data storytelling important in HR analytics?

10. Why is continuous learning and adaptation essential in HR analytics?
11. What role does technology play in HR analytics, and why is staying updated important for HR professionals?
12. What are the implications of expanding data sources on HR analytics, and how can continuous learning help?
13. What ethical and compliance considerations arise in HR analytics, and why is continuous learning crucial in this regard?
14. In what ways should HR analytics adapt to organizational goals, and why is continuous learning relevant?

Long Questions

1. Can you explain the challenges faced in the field of HR analytics and how organizations can address them?
2. How are the emerging trends in HR analytics revolutionizing HR management, and what benefits do they offer to organizations?
3. Why is it important for HR professionals and organizations to stay updated on HR analytics trends, and how can this knowledge be leveraged for competitive advantage?
4. In the context of the dynamic HR landscape, how is HR evolving to navigate change and adaptation, and what are the key factors driving this transformation?
5. What is Agile HR Analytics, and how does it differ from traditional HR analytics? What are the key principles and benefits of this approach?
6. How does Agile HR Analytics enable HR professionals to respond rapidly to changing HR needs, and what role does collaboration play in this approach?
7. How do emerging trends in HR analytics impact the skill sets required by HR professionals, and why is continuous learning and upskilling necessary for them?
8. What role do HR professionals play in enhancing employee experience through analytics, and why is this significant for organizations?
9. What ethical and legal considerations do HR professionals need to address in the age of data and technology, and how can continuous learning help them navigate these challenges?
10. How are HR professionals embracing agile and adaptive approaches to talent management and development, and what are the benefits of such approaches in a dynamic business environment?

CHAPTER

15

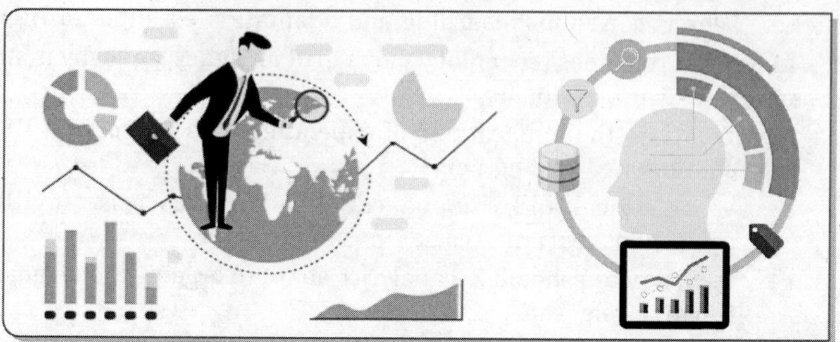

Data Visualization and Reporting in HR Analytics

In today's data-driven world, information is abundant, but its value lies in our ability to extract meaningful insights from it. This is where data visualization and reporting play a pivotal role. Data visualization and reporting are powerful techniques for transforming raw data into accessible and comprehensible formats. They serve as bridges between the data and the human mind, allowing individuals and organizations to make informed decisions. Following are some key reasons why data visualization and reporting are essential:

1. **Enhanced Understanding:** Visual representations of data, such as charts, graphs, and maps, make complex information easier to grasp. Patterns, trends, and outliers become more apparent, enabling better comprehension of data.
2. **Effective Communication:** Visualizations and reports facilitate effective communication of insights to stakeholders. Technical as well as non-technical audiences may easily understand the information they communicate because of their clear and concise style.
3. **Data-driven Decisions:** Informed decision-making relies on accurate and timely data. Data visualization and reporting provide decision-makers with the tools to analyze data, identify opportunities, and address challenges proactively.
4. **Identifying Insights:** Visualizing data often reveals hidden insights that may not be evident in raw data. This can lead to innovative solutions, improved strategies, and a competitive edge.
5. **Error Detection:** Visualizations can help identify data errors or anomalies, allowing organizations to maintain data quality and integrity.

THE ROLE OF DATA IN DECISION-MAKING

Data serves as the foundation for decision-making across various domains, from business and healthcare to government and academia. Informed decisions are based on evidence, and data provides that evidence. Following are the reasons why data plays a central role in decision-making:

1. **Objective Information:** Data is objective and free from biases or opinions. It provides an impartial basis for evaluating situations and options.
2. **Measuring Performance:** Data allows organizations to measure the performance of processes, products, or services, enabling continuous improvement.
3. **Risk Assessment:** Data helps assess risks and uncertainties, enabling organizations to mitigate potential pitfalls.
4. **Resource Allocation:** Effective resource allocation relies on data-driven insights to ensure that resources are used efficiently and effectively.
5. **Competitive Advantage:** Organizations that leverage data for decision-making gain a competitive advantage by being more agile, responsive, and adaptive.

BENEFITS OF USING SPECIALIZED TOOLS FOR DATA VISUALIZATION AND REPORTING

While data is valuable, the process of transforming it into actionable insights can be challenging without the right tools. Specialized data visualization and reporting tools offer several advantages such as:

1. **Efficiency:** These tools streamline the process of creating visualizations and reports, saving time and effort.
2. **Interactivity:** Many tools enable users to interact with data visualizations, drilling down into details or customizing views to answer specific questions.
3. **Scalability:** Specialized tools can handle large and complex datasets, ensuring that insights are not limited by data volume.
4. **Consistency:** Templates and standard formatting in reporting tools help maintain a consistent and professional look in reports and dashboards.
5. **Integration:** Many tools can integrate with data sources, databases, and other software, allowing for real-time or automated reporting.

TYPES OF DATA VISUALIZATION

Data visualization encompasses a wide range of techniques and methods to represent data visually.

1. **Bar Charts:**
   - **When to Use:** Bar charts are suitable for comparing categorical data or showing the distribution of data across categories. They are particularly effective when dealing with discrete categories or nominal data.

   Examples:
   - A bar chart showing the sales performance of different products in a store.
   - Comparing the number of votes for each candidate in an election.

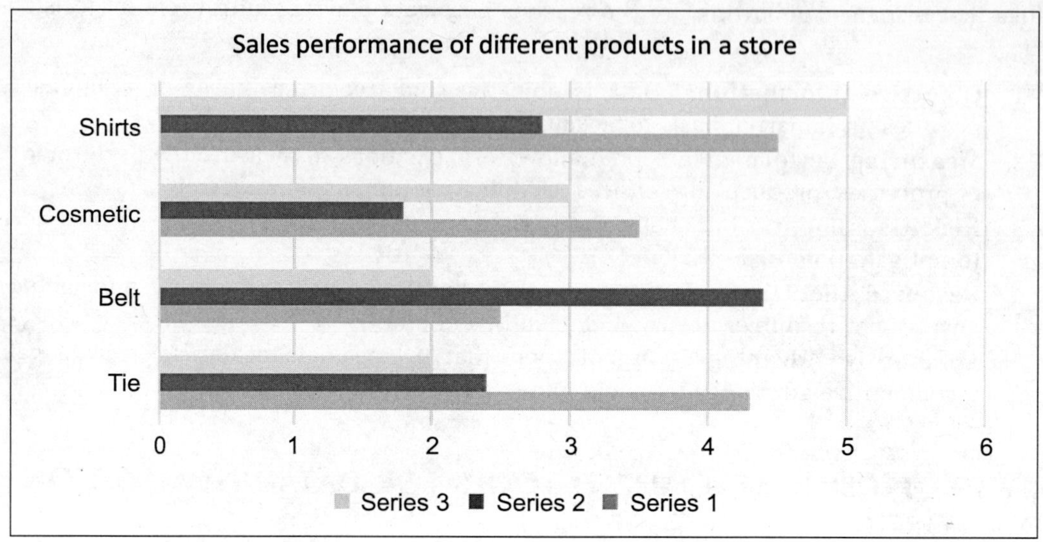

FIGURE 15.1 Bar charts.

2. **Line Charts:**
   - **When to Use:** Line charts show changes and trends over time very well. They are useful for showing data with continuous variables or chronological sequences.

   Examples:
   - A line chart illustrating stock price fluctuations over a year.
   - Tracking temperature variations throughout the day.

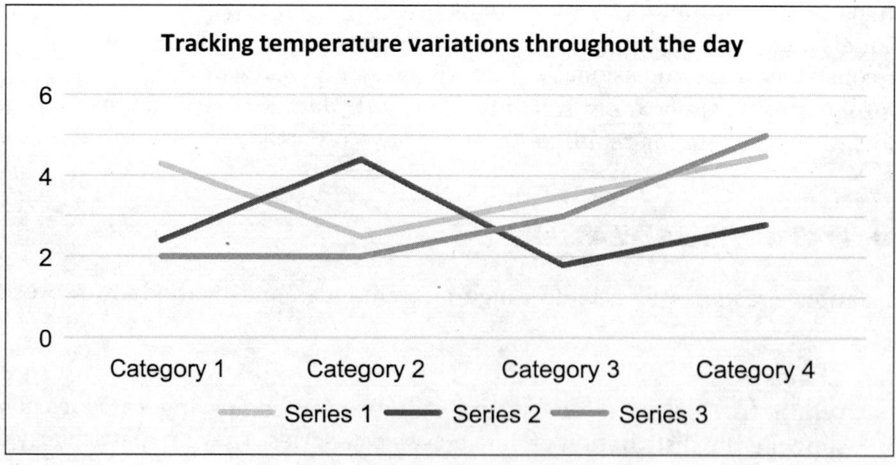

FIGURE 15.2 Line charts.

3. **Scatter Plots:**
   - **When to Use:** To see how two continuous variables are related, one can use a scatter plot. You may use them to find outliers and correlations.

   Examples:
   - Making a graph showing how a person's salary changes as they become older.
   - Looking at how advertising budgets relate to sales figures.

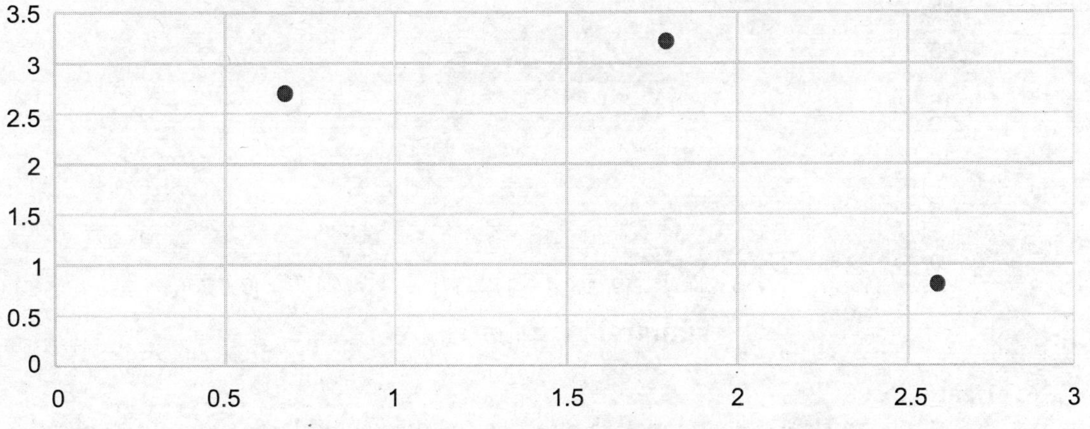

FIGURE 15.3 Scatter plots.

4. **Pie Charts:**
   - **When to Use:** Pie charts are suitable for displaying the parts of a whole. They work best when you want to show the composition of a data set.

   Examples:
   - Visualizing the distribution of expenses in a budget.
   - Displaying the market share of different smartphone brands.

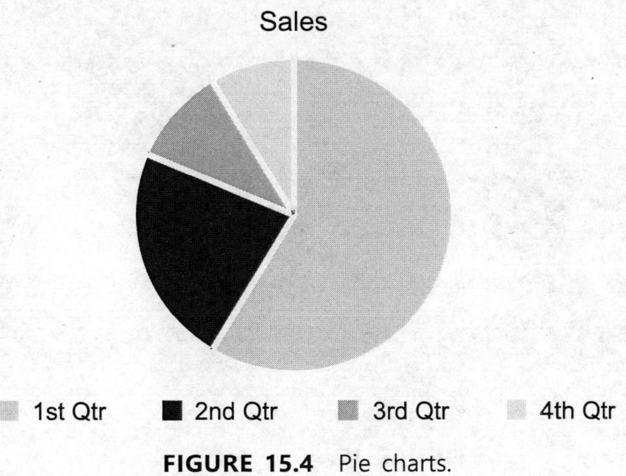

FIGURE 15.4 Pie charts.

5. **Histograms:**
   - **When to Use:** Histograms are used to represent the distribution of continuous data. They help visualize the frequency and spread of values within a dataset.

Examples:

- Showing the distribution of ages in a population.
- Representing the distribution of test scores in a classroom.

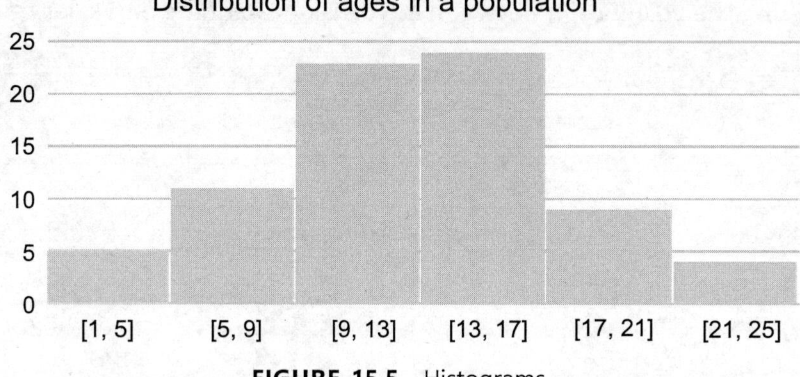

FIGURE 15.5 Histograms.

6. **Heatmaps:**
   - **When to Use:** Heatmaps are effective for displaying large datasets, especially for identifying patterns and trends in multidimensional data.

Average Monthly Temperature (°F) at Central Park, New York

	Jan	Feb	Mar	Apr	May	Jun	Jul	Aug	Sep	Oct	Nov	Dec
2009	27.9	36.7	42.4	54.5	62.5	67.5	72.7	75.7	66.3	55.0	51.2	35.9
2010	32.5	33.1	48.2	57.9	65.3	74.7	81.3	77.4	71.1	58.1	47.9	32.8
2011	29.7	36.0	42.3	54.3	64.5	72.3	80.2	75.3	70.0	57.1	51.9	43.3
2012	37.3	40.9	50.9	54.8	65.1	71.0	78.8	76.7	68.8	58.0	43.9	41.5
2013	35.1	33.9	40.1	53.0	62.8	72.7	79.8	74.6	67.9	60.2	45.3	38.5
2014	28.6	31.6	37.7	52.3	64.0	72.5	76.1	74.5	69.7	59.6	45.3	40.5
2015	29.9	23.9	38.1	54.3	68.5	71.2	78.8	79.0	74.5	58.0	52.8	50.8
2016	34.5	37.7	48.9	53.3	62.8	72.3	78.7	79.2	71.8	58.8	49.8	38.3
2017	38.0	41.6	39.2	57.2	61.1	72.0	76.8	74.0	70.5	64.1	46.6	33.4

FIGURE 15.6 Heatmaps.

Examples:

- Analyzing website traffic by visualizing page views over different times of the day and days of the week.
- Visualizing correlations in a dataset with many variables.

7. **Bubble Charts:**
   - **When to Use:** Bubble charts are an extension of scatter plots. They are used to display three dimensions of data, where the size of the bubble represents the third variable.

Examples:

- Visualizing the relationship between population, GDP, and area for different countries.
- Analyzing data on the number of employees, revenue, and profit for various companies.

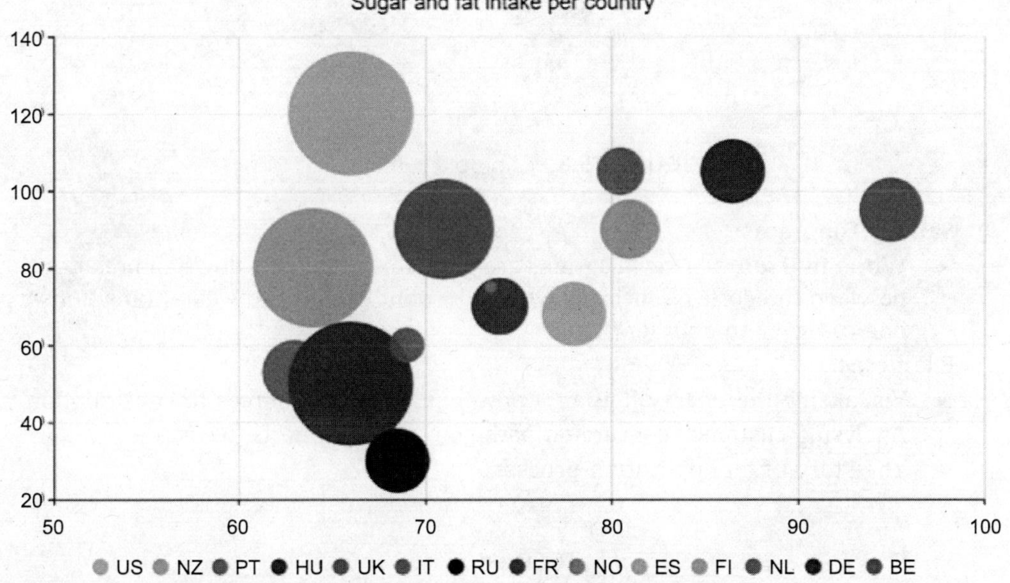

FIGURE 15.7 Bubble charts

8. **Choropleth Maps:**
   - **When to Use:** Choropleth maps are useful for visualizing spatial data by colouring regions or geographic areas based on a variable's value.

Examples:

- Showing the unemployment rate by state in a country.
- Displaying population density across different regions of a continent.

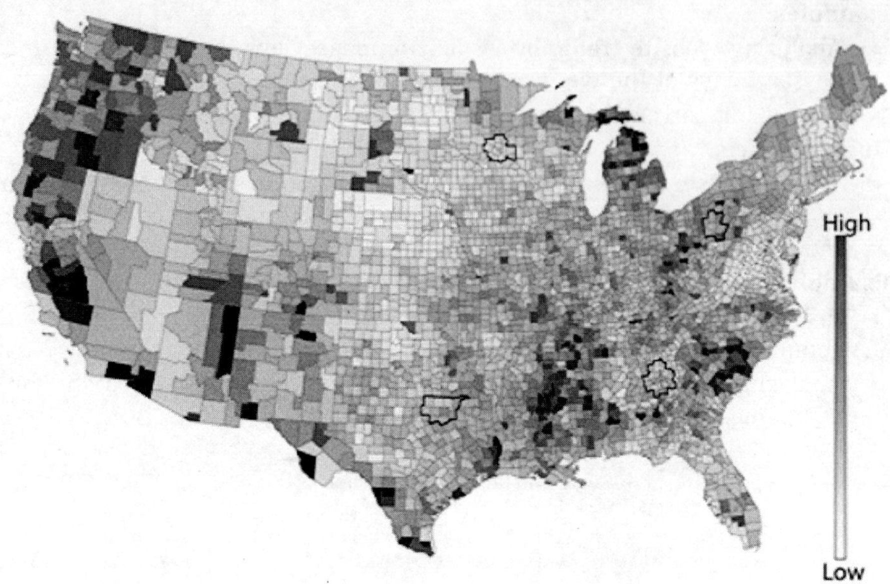

FIGURE 15.8 Choropleth maps.

9. **Sankey Diagrams:**
   - **When to Use:** Sankey diagrams are great for visualizing flows and relationships between categories, especially when you want to show how data transitions from one category to another.

   Examples:
   - Visualizing the energy flow in a power plant, from sources to consumption.
   - Analysing customer conversion paths on an e-commerce website.
   - The story of an application process

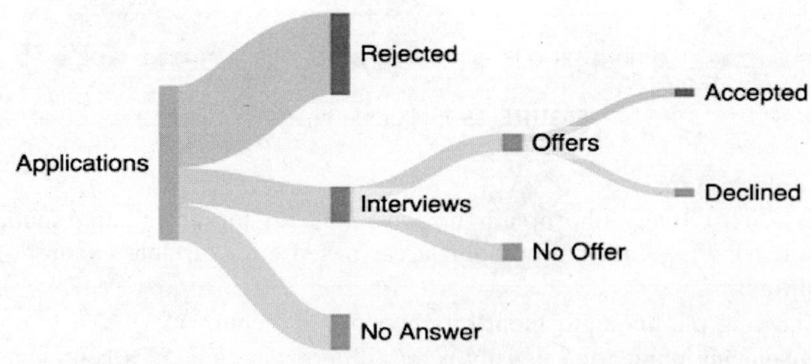

FIGURE 15.9 Sankey diagrams.

10. **Word Clouds:**
    - **When to Use:** Word clouds are used to highlight the frequency or importance of words or terms within a dataset, such as text data.

    Examples: Visualizing the most frequently mentioned words in customer reviews.
    - Displaying the key topics in a collection of news articles.

FIGURE 15.10 Word cloud.

COMMON DATA VISUALIZATION TOOLS

There are several popular data visualization tools available to help you create compelling visuals and reports. Below mentioned is an overview of some of these tools, their features, capabilities, and pricing and licensing considerations:

1. *Tableau*

In the past few years, Tableau has become very famous as a strong tool for business intelligence and data visualisation. It was created by Tableau Software and lets users connect, view, and share data in a very easy to use and engaging way. Tableau is a popular tool among workers in many fields because it is easy to use and can do a lot of analysis. We will talk about Tableau's most important features and uses, how it affects data-driven decision-making, and how it turns complicated information into insights that can be used.

Features and Capabilities:

- Tableau is a powerful data visualization and business intelligence tool known for its ease of use.
- It supports various data sources, including spreadsheets, databases, and cloud-based data.

- Features interactive dashboards, drag-and-drop functionality, and a wide range of visualization options.
- Provides robust data analytics and the ability to create calculated fields.
- Offers collaboration features for sharing and collaborating on visualizations.

Pricing and Licensing:

- Tableau offers several pricing tiers, including Tableau Desktop (for individual use), Tableau Creator (for teams and organizations), and Tableau Server and Tableau Online (for sharing and publishing dashboards).
- Pricing can vary depending on the edition, user type, and deployment method (cloud or on-premises).

2. *Power BI (Microsoft Power BI)*

Microsoft made Power BI, which stands for "Power BI." It is a powerful business intelligence (BI) tool. Users can connect to different data sources, change and display data, and share ideas with others through live dashboards and reports. A lot of companies and organisations use Power BI to make decisions based on data and learn more about how their processes work. Power BI is famous for having an easy-to-use interface that lets you make visually appealing and engaging reports quickly, without having to know a lot about code or technology. It's becoming more famous in many fields and is a useful tool for organisations to use for data analysis, reports, and making decisions.

Features and Capabilities:

- Power BI is a business analytics tool by Microsoft that integrates seamlessly with other Microsoft products.
- Offers data connectivity to various sources, data transformation capabilities, and data modelling.
- Provides a range of visualization options, including custom visuals and custom themes.
- Allows for natural language querying using Power BI Q&A.
- Enables collaboration and sharing through the Power BI service.

Pricing and Licensing:

- Power BI offers a free version called Power BI Desktop.
- For business use, Power BI Pro licenses are available on a monthly per-user basis.
- Power BI Premium offers dedicated cloud capacity and is suitable for larger organizations with higher scalability requirements.

3. *Microsoft Excel*

Excel is a spreadsheet programme made by Microsoft that is used by a lot of people and is essential in many business, school, and study settings. Excel is a powerful spreadsheet programme that lets you store, sort, and quickly do calculations on numbers. It helps people organise data by letting them put it in rows, tables, and cells, and it also does math for you automatically. Businesses have been using spreadsheets for a long time, mostly to keep track of expenses and do other math.

Features and Capabilities:

- Excel is a widely used spreadsheet software by Microsoft.
- It offers basic data visualization capabilities through charting and graphing tools.
- Excel supports data analysis through functions and pivot tables.
- It's commonly used for small-scale data visualization and analysis tasks.

Pricing and Licensing:

- Excel is available through Microsoft 365 subscription plans, which offer various editions and pricing tiers.

4. *Google Data Studio*

Google Data Studio is a free data visualization and reporting tool developed by Google. Using data from different sources, it lets users make dynamic and flexible dashboards and results. For people and companies, Google Data Studio is meant to help them turn data into interesting and useful visualisations without having to know a lot about coding or technology. Google Data Studio is a flexible tool that can be used for many various reporting and data visualisation tasks. Digital Studio is an easy-to-use tool for turning data into useful information, whether you're a marketer looking at how well a campaign is doing, a business analyst keeping an eye on key measures, or a data worker making dashboards for executives.

Features and Capabilities:

- Google Data Studio is a free web-based data visualization tool by Google.
- It integrates seamlessly with other Google products and third-party data sources.
- Offers a drag-and-drop interface for creating interactive reports and dashboards.
- Supports collaboration and real-time data updates.
- Users can create custom data connectors and visualizations.

Pricing and Licensing:

- Google Data Studio is free for individual use and small businesses.
- Enterprise-level users can explore additional features and support through Google Cloud Platform offerings.

5. *QlikView and Qlik Sense*

QlikView and Qlik Sense are two popular data visualization and business intelligence (BI) tools developed by Qlik, a software company known for its data analytics and visualization solutions. Some people who are good at programming and data modelling, like IT workers and power users, like to use QlikView for guided analytics. In contrast, Qlik Sense is made for self-service analytics and aims to make it easy for a wider range of people, including business customers, to understand and use.

Features and Capabilities:

- QlikView and Qlik Sense are business intelligence tools known for their associative data model.
- They offer data discovery and exploration capabilities.
- Provide interactive and self-service dashboards.
- Support various data sources and data transformation.
- Enable data storytelling through guided analytics.

Pricing and Licensing:

- Pricing for QlikView and Qlik Sense varies based on the edition, deployment model (cloud or on-premises), and user licenses.

6. *D3.js (Data-driven Documents)*

D3.js, which stands for Data-driven Documents, is a JavaScript library for creating interactive and dynamic data visualizations in web browsers. D3.js was created by Mike Bostock and is kept up to date as an open-source project. D3.js is widely used by developers, data scientists, and designers to transform data into engaging and informative visual representations.

Features and Capabilities:

- D3.js is a JavaScript library for creating custom data visualizations.
- It provides complete control over the visual design and interactivity of your visualizations.
- Suitable for developers and designers who want to build highly customized visuals.
- Supports a wide range of data formats and can be integrated into web applications.

Pricing and Licensing:

- D3.js is open-source and free to use. However, it requires web development skills to create and integrate visualizations.

CREATING INTERACTIVE DASHBOARDS

Interactive dashboards are dynamic data visualization tools that allow users to explore and interact with data in real-time. These dashboards are valuable for conveying insights, enabling users to make data-driven decisions, and providing a flexible, user-friendly interface for exploring complex datasets.

Interactive Dashboards

Interactive dashboards are user interfaces that display data in a visually appealing and interactive manner. They enable users to:

1. **Explore Data:** Users can drill down into data, filter, and slice it to gain a deeper understanding of specific aspects.
2. **Discover Insights:** Interactive elements like charts, graphs, and filters help users identify patterns, trends, and outliers.
3. **Monitor Performance:** Dashboards provide real-time updates, allowing users to track key performance indicators (KPIs) and respond to changes promptly.
4. **Make Decisions:** By providing an intuitive interface, interactive dashboards empower users to make data-driven decisions quickly and efficiently.

Process of Creating Interactive Dashboards

Creating interactive dashboards is an essential part of data visualization and reporting, as they allow users to explore and interact with data to gain insights. Various steps of the process for creating interactive dashboards are as follows:

1. **Define Your Goals and Objectives:** Start by clearly defining the purpose and objectives of your interactive dashboard. What questions should it answer? What insights do you want to provide to users?
2. **Gather and Prepare Data:** Collect and organize the data you need for your dashboard. Ensure that the data is clean, relevant, and in a format that can be easily visualized.
3. **Choose a Dashboarding Tool:** Select a suitable dashboarding tool that matches your requirements. Popular options include Tableau, Power BI, Google Data Studio, and others. Ensure that the tool supports interactivity.
4. **Connect to Data Sources:** Use your chosen dashboarding tool to connect to your data sources. Most tools allow you to connect to various data types, including databases, spreadsheets, web services, and more.
5. **Design the Dashboard Layout:** Plan the layout of your dashboard. Decide on the arrangement of charts, graphs, and other visual elements. Consider the order of information and how users will navigate through the dashboard.
6. **Create Visualizations:** Use the dashboarding tool to create interactive visualizations based on your data. Common types include charts, graphs, maps, and tables. Customize the visualizations to highlight key insights.
7. **Add Filters and Parameters:** To make the dashboard interactive, add filters, parameters, and controls. These elements allow users to slice and dice the data, change date ranges, select specific categories, and more.
8. **Implement Interactivity:** Set up interactions between different elements of the dashboard. For example, clicking on a chart can update related charts or tables dynamically. Ensure that users can explore data intuitively.
9. **Include Text and Annotations:** Provide context and explanations within the dashboard by adding text, titles, and annotations. Help users understand the significance of the data and the insights it offers.
10. **Test and Iterate:** Test the interactive dashboard thoroughly to ensure that all features and interactions work as intended. Gather feedback from potential users and stakeholders and make necessary improvements.
11. **Optimize for Performance:** Depending on the complexity of your dashboard and the size of your dataset, you may need to optimize it for performance. This may involve data aggregation, using extracts, or optimizing queries.
12. **Publish and Share:** Once your interactive dashboard is ready, publish it using the dashboarding tool. Determine who will have access to the dashboard and share it with your target audience.
13. **Train Users:** If necessary, provide training to users on how to use the interactive dashboard effectively. Ensure that they understand how to interact with filters, controls, and visualizations.
14. **Monitor and Maintain:** Continuously monitor the usage and performance of your dashboard. Update it as needed to reflect changes in data or user requirements. Regularly review and refine your dashboard to keep it relevant and valuable.
15. **Gather Feedback:** Encourage users to provide feedback and suggestions for improvement. Consider their input when making updates or enhancements to the dashboard.

Tools and Techniques for Building Interactive Dashboards

To create interactive dashboards, you can use a variety of tools and techniques, depending on your specific needs and skillset. Following are some common approaches:

1. **Business Intelligence (BI) Tools:** BI platforms like Tableau, Power BI, and QlikView offer user-friendly interfaces for designing interactive dashboards. They provide drag-and-drop functionality, pre-built visualization templates, and data connectivity to various sources.
2. **Programming Languages:** Using languages like JavaScript (with libraries such as D3.js or React), Python (with libraries like Plotly or Bokeh), or R (with Shiny), you can create custom interactive dashboards tailored to your requirements.
3. **Web Development Frameworks:** Web development frameworks like Angular, React, or Vue.js can be used to build fully customized dashboards with interactive features. These require programming skills but offer maximum flexibility.
4. **Data Visualization Libraries:** Many data visualization libraries, such as Chart.js or Plotly, provide interactive charting components that can be embedded in web applications or websites.
5. **API Integration:** Integrating with RESTful APIs or other data sources allows you to pull in real-time data, enabling dynamic updates in your dashboard.
6. **Dashboard Design Principles:** When designing interactive dashboards, consider user experience (UX) and user interface (UI) design principles. Ensure that elements like navigation, filtering, and tooltips are intuitive and user-friendly.

Examples of Interactive Dashboards for Various Use Cases

1. **Financial Performance Dashboard:** Users can explore financial data, compare revenue across regions, and drill down into specific time periods or product lines. Interactive elements include line charts, bar charts, and dynamic filters.
2. **Sales and Marketing Dashboard:** This dashboard allows users to track sales leads, conversion rates, and marketing campaign performance in real-time. Interactive features include funnel charts, heatmaps, and data filters.
3. **Healthcare Analytics Dashboard:** Healthcare professionals can monitor patient data, track disease outbreaks, and analyse treatment outcomes. Interactive elements include geographic maps, patient timelines, and data slicers.
4. **E-commerce Analytics Dashboard:** Retailers can analyse sales data, track inventory levels, and monitor website traffic. Interactive components include pie charts for product categories, dynamic price range sliders, and real-time updates.
5. **Project Management Dashboard:** Project managers can visualize project timelines, resource allocation, and task progress. Interactive features include Gantt charts, drag-and-drop task management, and resource allocation sliders.
6. **Social Media Analytics Dashboard:** Social media marketers can monitor engagement metrics, track follower growth, and analyse content performance. Interactive elements include real-time social media feeds, word clouds, and sentiment analysis.

7. **Energy Consumption Dashboard:** Utility companies and homeowners can track energy usage, set goals for conservation, and explore cost-saving opportunities. Interactive features include line charts, energy consumption gauges, and historical comparisons.

FIGURE 15.11 Sales and marketing dashboard.

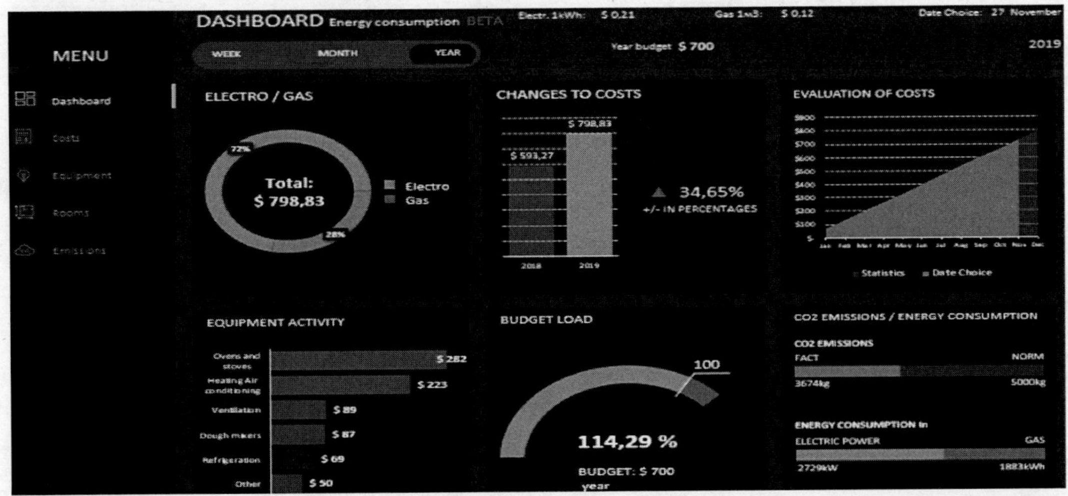

FIGURE 15.12 Energy consumption dashboard.

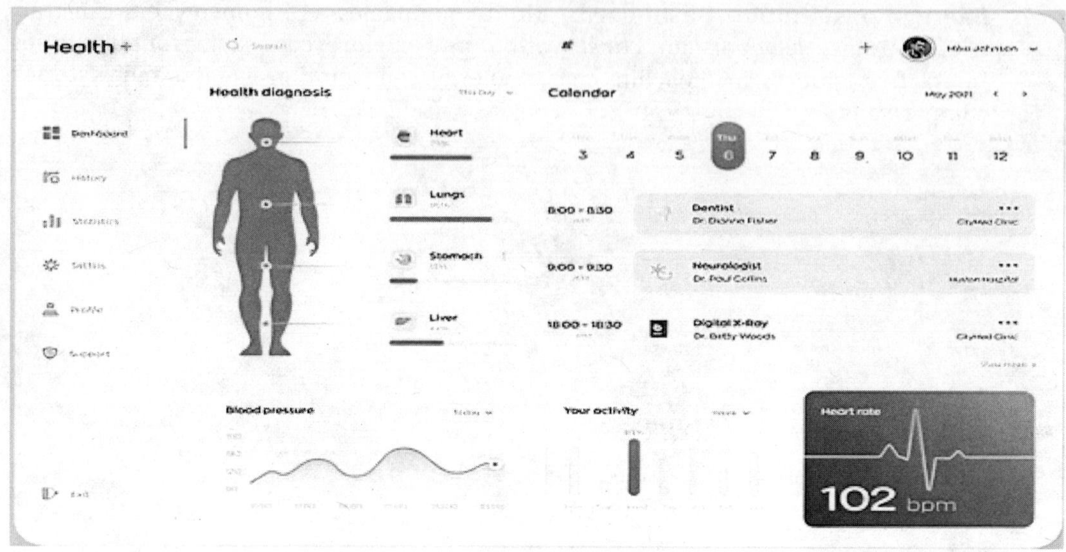

FIGURE 15.13 Healthcare analytics dashboard.

CREATING HR DASHBOARDS IN EXCEL

Creating HR dashboards in Excel involves several steps, including data preparation, designing the dashboard, using Excel functions, and storytelling to communicate the findings effectively.

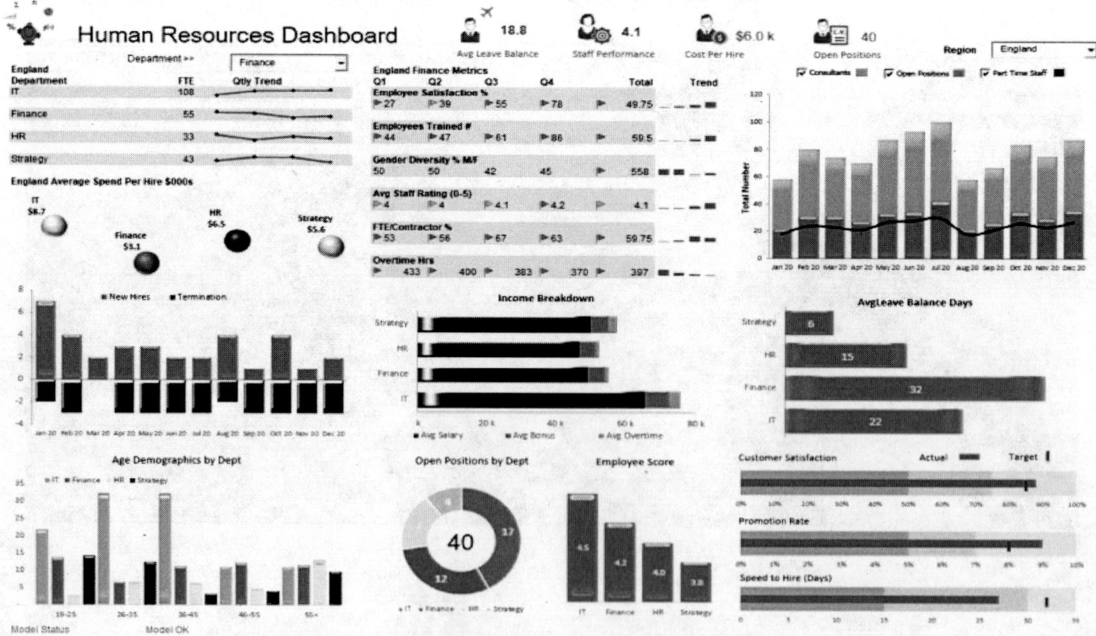

FIGURE 15.14 HR Dashboards.

Following are the steps to create HR dashboards:

1. *Data Preparation*

- Gather and organize your HR data. This may include information about employee demographics, performance, recruitment, turnover, etc.
- Ensure your data is clean and structured. Remove duplicates, handle missing values, and format data appropriately.

2. *Designing the Dashboard*

- Determine the key HR metrics and KPIs you want to track and display on the dashboard. Common HR metrics include turnover rate, employee engagement, recruitment metrics, and more.
- Decide on the layout and structure of your dashboard. Consider using separate sheets for data, charts, and summary.
- Create a visually appealing design. Use colour coding, fonts, and formatting to make the dashboard easy to read and understand.

3. *Excel Add-ins/Functions for Dashboards*

1. **Excel Add-ins:**
    - **Power Query**: Power Query is a powerful tool for data transformation and integration. It can help you import, clean, and shape your HR data from various sources.
    - **Power Pivot**: Power Pivot enables you to create data models and relationships, which can be useful when dealing with complex HR data sets.
    - **Power BI**: While not an Excel add-in, Power BI is a separate Microsoft tool that can connect to Excel and create interactive, visually appealing HR dashboards.
2. **Named Ranges:**
    - Use named ranges to make your formulas and data references more readable and maintainable. Define named ranges for key HR metrics, employee lists, and other relevant data.
3. **Developer Tab:**
    - The Developer tab allows you to add and customize form controls, which are useful for creating interactive elements like buttons, dropdown lists, and checkboxes on your dashboard.
4. **Form Controls:**
    - Form controls like combo boxes and radio buttons can be linked to Excel cells and used to filter or manipulate data on your HR dashboard dynamically.
5. **Important Excel Formulas:** Excel offers several powerful formulas for data analysis in HR dashboards:
    - **VLOOKUP:** Use to look up information from a table based on a unique identifier (e.g., employee ID).
    - **INDEX and MATCH:** Combine these functions for more advanced lookup and reference operations.
    - **SUMIF, AVERAGEIF, COUNTIF:** Calculate sums, averages, and counts based on specified criteria.

- **PivotTables:** Use PivotTables to summarize and analyse large datasets quickly.
- **IF and IFERROR:** Create conditional calculations and handle errors gracefully.
- **DATE and TIME functions:** Useful for date-based calculations, e.g., calculating employee tenure.

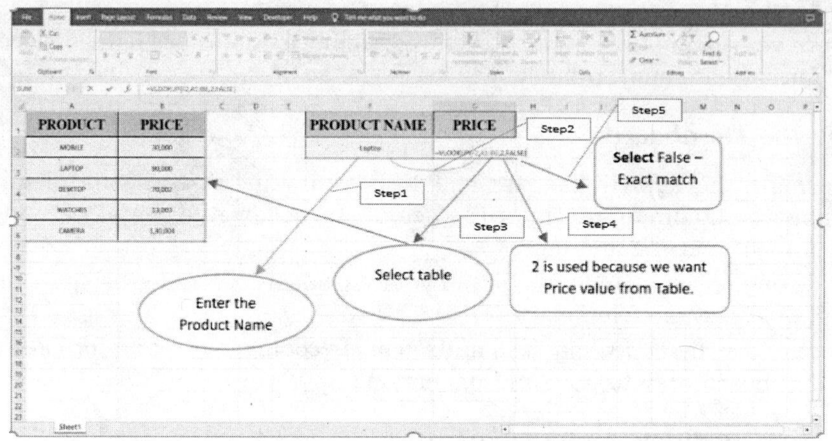

FIGURE 15.15 VLOOKUP application in excel.

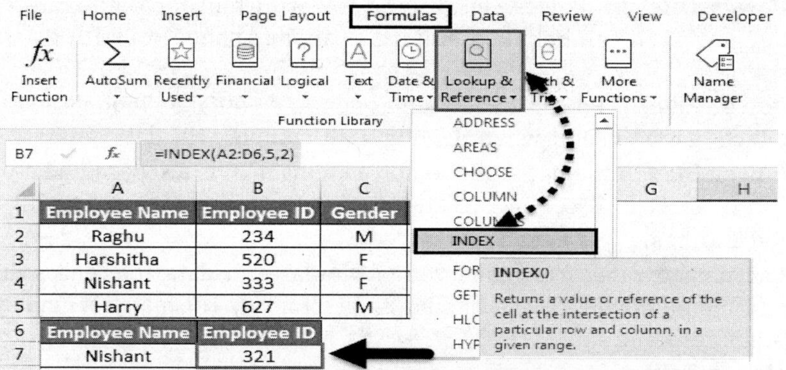

FIGURE 15.16 LOOKUP & INDEX application in excel.

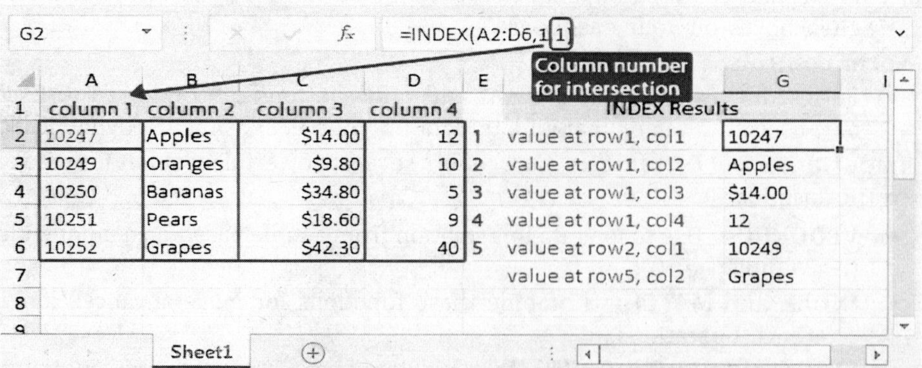

FIGURE 15.17 INDEX application in excel.

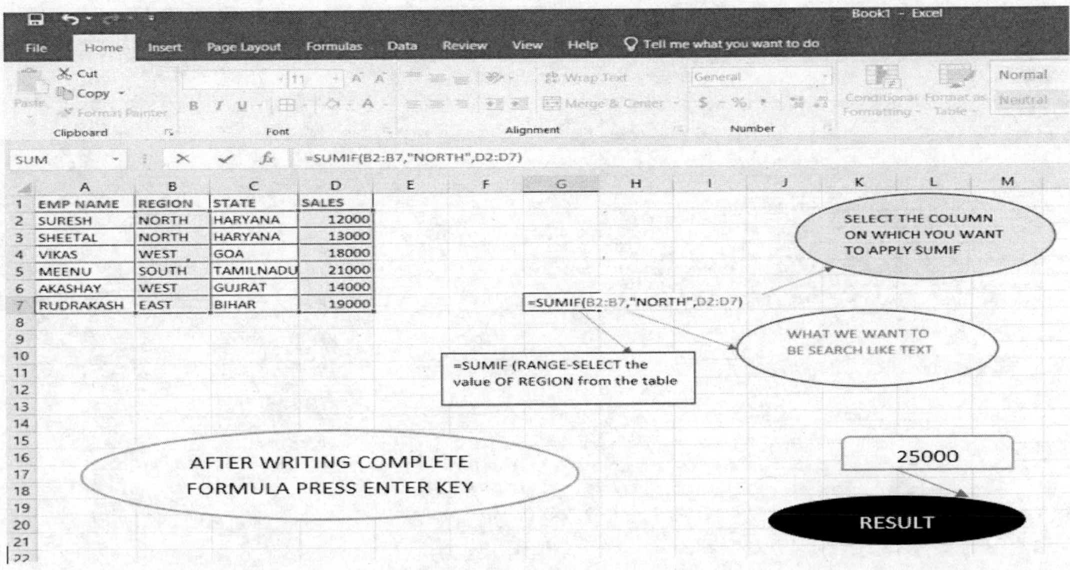

FIGURE 15.18 SUMIF application in excel.

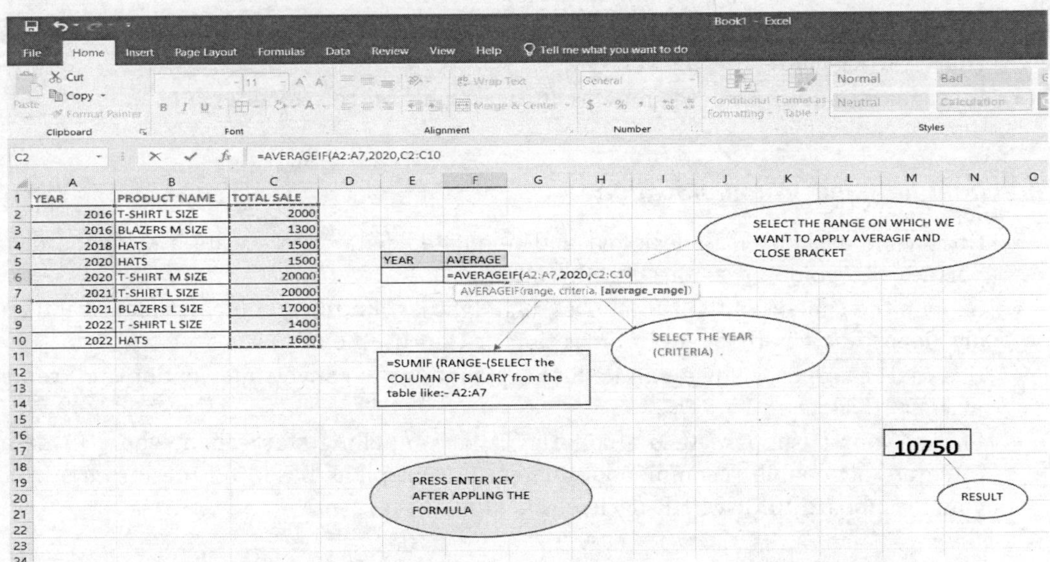

FIGURE 15.19 AVERAGEIF application in excel.

4. *Application of Excel Functions in HR Dashboards*

- Use VLOOKUP or INDEX/MATCH to fetch employee information based on criteria.
- Calculate turnover rates using COUNTIF and AVERAGEIF to filter data by specific conditions.
- Utilize PivotTables to create summaries and cross-tabulations of HR data.

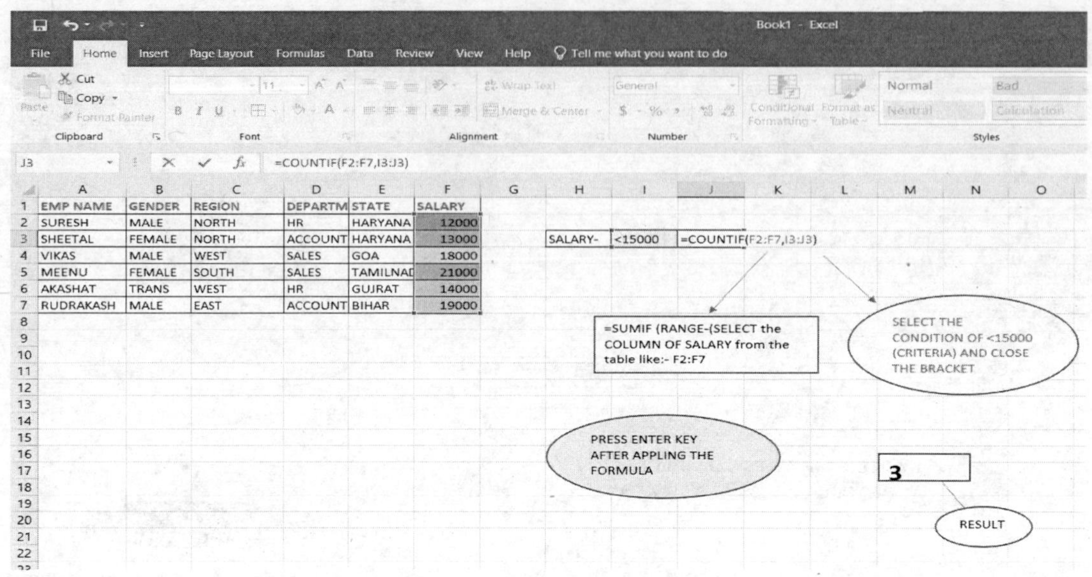

FIGURE 15.20 COUNTIF application in excel.

- Create dynamic charts using Excel's charting tools (e.g., bar charts, line charts, pie charts) to visualize HR metrics.
- Incorporate slicers and dropdowns using Form Controls to filter and interact with data dynamically.

5. *Storyboarding and Communication*

- Once your dashboard is designed and populated with data, create a storyboard or narrative to guide users through the findings.
- Explain the context of the HR metrics, highlight key findings, compare historical data, and identify areas that require attention or improvement.
- Use charts, graphs, visuals, and textual explanations to convey information and trends in your HR data.
- Ensure your dashboard tells a coherent and compelling story about your HR data. Integrate actionable recommendations and action plans based on the insights from your dashboard to drive HR decision-making.

STORYBOARDING: CONNECTING THE DOTS AND INTEGRATING THE FINDINGS

Storyboarding is a visual storytelling technique commonly used in various fields, including filmmaking, advertising, user experience design, and more. It involves creating a series of images or sketches arranged in a sequence to convey a narrative or convey information. When you're tasked with connecting the dots and integrating findings in a storyboard, you're essentially using visual storytelling to present a coherent and organized narrative that incorporates your research or data.

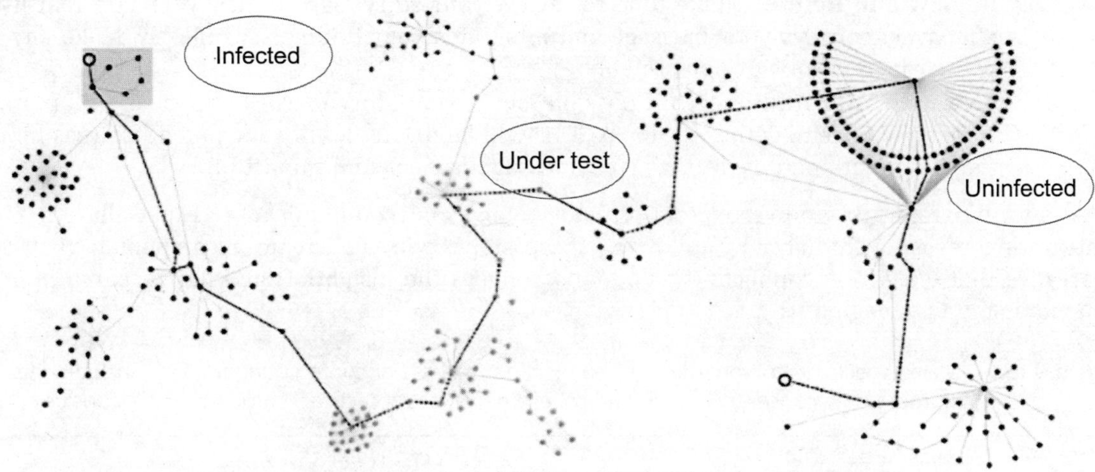

FIGURE 15.21 Storyboarding: Connecting the dots and integrating the findings.

Following are the steps to storyboard while connecting the dots and integrating your findings effectively:

1. **Define Your Objective:** Start by clarifying the purpose of your storyboard. What message or information do you want to convey? Who is your target audience? Understanding your objective is crucial to frame your storytelling.
2. **Gather Your Findings:** Collect all relevant research, data, or information that you intend to include in your storyboard. This could be statistics, customer feedback, survey results, or any other relevant data.
3. **Identify Key Points:** Determine the most critical findings or insights from your research that need to be included in your storyboard. These key points will serve as the foundation for your narrative.
4. **Create a Storyline:** Develop a clear and concise storyline that connects the dots between your findings. Think about how your data points relate to each other and how they contribute to your overall message.
5. **Sketch Your Storyboard:** Begin sketching or creating visual representations of your storyline. Each frame or panel in your storyboard should depict a specific scene or concept related to your findings. Use visuals like charts, graphs, icons, or illustrations to represent data or ideas.
6. **Maintain a Logical Flow:** Ensure that the sequence of frames in your storyboard follows a logical flow. Each frame should lead naturally to the next, allowing the viewer to easily grasp the connections between the findings.
7. **Annotate and Explain:** Include brief captions, notes, or annotations for each frame to provide context and explanations for the findings presented. Use concise language and make it easy for your audience to understand.
8. **Design and Aesthetics:** Pay attention to the visual design of your storyboard. Use consistent colours, fonts, and visual elements to maintain a cohesive look. Consider the overall aesthetics to make your storyboard engaging and visually appealing.

9. **Review and Refine:** Take time to review your storyboard critically. Ensure that it effectively conveys your message and integrates your findings seamlessly. Make any necessary revisions or adjustments.
10. **Test with Your Audience:** If possible, share your storyboard with a small group or target audience to gather feedback. This will help you identify any potential areas for improvement and ensure that your message is clear and impactful.

Storyboarding is a powerful tool for storytelling and communication, especially when integrating research findings. By following these steps, you can create a compelling visual narrative that effectively connects the dots and conveys the insights from your research in a memorable and engaging way.

TABLE 15.1 Main aspects of storyboarding for connecting the dots and integrating findings, including its purpose, key concepts, benefits, steps, examples, best practices, challenges, and conclusion

Topic	*Description*
Introduction	• Storyboarding as a visual communication technique • Purpose: Connecting and integrating findings • Importance in various fields
Key Concepts	• Storyboard components: frames, scenes, narration • Narrative flow and storytelling principles • Integration of research findings
Benefits	• Clarity in presenting complex information • Engagement and communication with stakeholders • Enhanced understanding and retention of data • Improved decision-making and problem-solving
Steps in Storyboarding	1. Define the purpose and scope 2. Gather and analyse research findings 3. Identify key insights and messages 4. Create a storyboard structure 5. Sketch frames and scenes 6. Add narration and annotations 7. Review and refine the storyboard
Examples	• Storyboard examples from different contexts • Demonstrations of effective integration
Best Practices	• Keep it simple and focused • Use visuals to support key points • Maintain a logical and coherent narrative • Consider the audience's perspective
Challenges	• Balancing detail with simplicity • Ensuring a smooth flow of the narrative • Adapting to different research types and subjects
Conclusion	• Storyboarding as a valuable integration tool • Enhancing communication and decision-making • Encouragement for its adoption in diverse fields

DATA VISUALIZATION AND REPORTING IN PYTHON

Python is a versatile programming language widely used for data visualization and reporting due to its rich ecosystem of libraries and tools.

Using Python Libraries for Data Visualization:

1. **Matplotlib:**
   - Matplotlib is a fundamental library for creating static, publication-quality visualizations in Python.
   - It provides a wide range of chart types, customization options, and support for various data formats.
   - Example usage:

```
Python
import matplotlib.pyplot as plt
plt.plot(x_data, y_data)
plt.xlabel("X-axis Label")
plt.ylabel("Y-axis Label")
plt.title("Title of the Plot")
plt.show()
```

2. **Seaborn:**
   - Seaborn is built on top of Matplotlib and offers a high-level interface for creating aesthetically pleasing statistical visualizations.
   - It simplifies complex visualizations and provides easy-to-use functions for creating advanced plots.
   - Example usage:

```
Python
import seaborn as sns
sns.scatterplot(data=df, x="x_column", y="y_column",
hue="category_column")
```

3. **Plotly:**
   - Plotly is a library for creating interactive and web-based visualizations with Python.
   - It supports a wide range of chart types, including scatter plots, bar charts, heatmaps, and more.
   - Example usage (scatter plot with Plotly Express):

```
Python
import plotly.express as px
fig = px.scatter(df, x="x_column", y="y_column",
color="category_column")
fig.show()
```

Generating Interactive Plots and Charts with Python

To generate interactive plots and charts in Python, you can use libraries like Plotly, Bokeh, and Dash. Following is an example using Plotly:

1. **Plotly (Interactive Scatter Plot):**

```
Python
import plotly.graph_objs as go

trace = go.Scatter(x=df['x_column'], y=df['y_column'], mode='markers')
layout = go.Layout(title="Interactive Scatter Plot", xaxis=dict(title="X-axis"), yaxis=dict(title="Y-axis"))
fig = go.Figure(data=[trace], layout=layout)
fig.show()
```

Integrating Python with Reporting Tools

Integrating Python with reporting tools allows you to generate dynamic and data-driven reports. Following are some steps to integrate Python with reporting tools:

1. **ReportLab:** ReportLab is a Python library for creating PDF reports. You can use it to generate PDFs programmatically and include Python-generated visuals and data.
2. **Jupyter Notebooks:** Jupyter Notebooks provide an interactive environment where you can create reports by combining Python code, data visualizations, and narrative text. You can export notebooks as HTML or PDF reports.
3. **Business Intelligence (BI) Tools:** Many BI tools, such as Tableau, Power BI, and QlikView, offer integrations with Python. You can embed Python scripts and visualizations into these tools' dashboards and reports.
4. **Web Frameworks:** If you are building web-based reports, Python web frameworks like Django and Flask can be used to create dynamic web pages with embedded visualizations and data tables.
5. **Automated Reporting Scripts:** Write Python scripts that fetch and process data, generate visualizations, and then use libraries like ReportLab or Jupyter to create automated reports that can be scheduled to run regularly.
6. **Dashboarding Tools:** Tools like Dash (by Plotly) allow you to build interactive web-based dashboards with Python. You can include visualizations, data tables, and interactivity within the dashboards.

DATA VISUALIZATION AND REPORTING IN R

R is a powerful programming language and environment for statistical computing and graphics.

Leveraging R Packages for Data Visualization

1. **ggplot2:**
   - ggplot2 is a popular R package for creating elegant and customizable data visualizations.
   - It follows a grammar of graphics approach, making it easy to build complex visualizations.
   - Example usage:

```
Python
library(ggplot2)
ggplot(data = df, aes(x = x_column, y = y_column)) +
  geom_point() +
  labs(title = "Scatter Plot", x = "X-axis Label", y = "Y-axis
Label")
```

2. **lattice:**
   - The lattice package in R is useful for creating conditioned plots, such as multiple panel charts.
   - It provides a powerful interface for creating trellis plots.
   - Example usage:

```
Python
library(lattice)
xyplot(y_column ~ x_column | category_column, data = df, type = "b")
```

3. **Highcharter (for interactive charts):**
   - The Highcharter package allows you to create interactive and dynamic JavaScript-based charts in R.
   - It is particularly useful for building web-based interactive dashboards.
   - Example usage:

```
Python
library(highcharter)
highchart() %>%
  hc_add_series(df, "scatter", hcaes(x = x_column, y =
y_column))
```

Creating Interactive Reports with R

1. **Shiny:**
   - Shiny is an R package for creating interactive web applications and dashboards directly from R scripts.
   - You can build interactive reports with input controls, reactive elements, and dynamic plots.

- Example usage:

```
Python
library(shiny)
ui <- fluidPage(
  titlePanel("Interactive Report"),
  sidebarLayout(
    sidebarPanel(
      # Input controls here
    ),
    mainPanel(
      # Output plots and tables here
    )
  )
)
server <- function(input, output) {
  # Define reactive expressions and render outputs here
}
shinyApp(ui = ui, server = server)
```

Combining R and Reporting Tools for Powerful Insights

1. **R Markdown:**
   - R Markdown is an R package that allows you to create dynamic reports that combine R code, text, and visualizations in a single document.
   - You can export R Markdown documents to various formats, including PDF, HTML, and Word.
   - Example usage:

````
Python
---
title: "Dynamic Report"
output: html_document
---

## Data Visualization

```{r}
library(ggplot2)
ggplot(data = df, aes(x = x_column, y = y_column)) +
  geom_point()
````

2. **knitr:**
   - knitr is an R package that integrates R code into various document formats, such as LaTeX, HTML, and Markdown.
````

- It allows for the creation of dynamic and reproducible reports by embedding R code chunks within documents.
- Example usage:

```
Python
```{r}
library(ggplot2)
ggplot(data = df, aes(x = x_column, y = y_column)) +
  geom_point()
```

3. **R with BI Tools:**
   - Some business intelligence (BI) tools like Tableau and Power BI allow you to use R scripts within their platforms.
   - You can leverage the power of R for advanced analytics and visualizations while benefiting from the user-friendly interfaces of these tools.

DATA VISUALIZATION AND REPORTING IN BUSINESS INTELLIGENCE (BI) PLATFORMS

Business Intelligence (BI) platforms are software solutions designed to help organizations collect, analyse, and visualize their data to make informed business decisions. They play a crucial role in data visualization and reporting by providing tools and features that streamline the process.

Understanding BI Platforms and Their Role

Business Intelligence platforms serve as a centralized hub for data management, analysis, and reporting. Their primary roles include:

1. **Data Integration:** BI platforms connect to various data sources, such as databases, spreadsheets, cloud storage, and web services, allowing organizations to aggregate data from multiple sources into a single repository.
2. **Data Transformation:** They offer tools for data cleaning, transformation, and preparation, ensuring data accuracy and consistency.
3. **Data Analysis:** BI platforms provide analytical capabilities to explore data, identify trends, perform calculations, and create interactive visualizations.
4. **Data Visualization:** They enable the creation of charts, graphs, dashboards, and reports to visually represent data insights.
5. **Reporting:** BI platforms allow for the creation of standardized and ad-hoc reports, which can be automated and distributed to stakeholders.
6. **Data Sharing:** Users can collaborate and share data, reports, and dashboards within the organization, ensuring that insights are accessible to decision-makers.
```

Examples of BI Platforms:

1. **Tableau:**
   - Tableau is a widely used BI platform known for its user-friendly interface and robust data visualization capabilities.
   - It supports a wide range of data sources, offers drag-and-drop functionality for creating dashboards, and provides interactive features for exploring data.
   - Tableau Desktop is used for authoring reports and dashboards, while Tableau Server and Tableau Online allow for sharing and collaboration.
2. **QlikView and Qlik Sense:**
   - QlikView and Qlik Sense are BI platforms that use associative data models to provide intuitive data exploration and discovery.
   - Users can create interactive dashboards and explore data relationships easily.
   - QlikView is known for its traditional, guided analytics, while Qlik Sense offers a more self-service approach.
3. **Looker:**
   - Looker is a modern BI platform that focuses on data exploration and collaboration.
   - It allows users to create and share data experiences, explore data using a modelling language called LookML, and build interactive dashboards.
4. **Power BI (Microsoft Power BI):**
   - Power BI is Microsoft's BI platform, tightly integrated with other Microsoft products.
   - It offers a user-friendly interface for data visualization and reporting, with features for natural language querying and integration with Azure services.
5. **SAP BusinessObjects:**
   - SAP BusinessObjects is an enterprise-level BI platform that provides tools for reporting, ad-hoc analysis, and dashboard creation.
   - It is known for its robust security and scalability, making it suitable for large organizations.

How BI Platforms Streamline Data Analysis and Reporting Processes

BI platforms streamline data analysis and reporting in several ways:

1. **Data Integration:** BI platforms consolidate data from multiple sources, reducing the need for manual data collection and integration.
2. **Data Preparation:** They offer data cleaning and transformation features, ensuring data accuracy and consistency.
3. **Visual Exploration:** Users can explore data visually, making it easier to identify patterns and insights.
4. **Interactivity:** BI platforms enable users to interact with data, drill down into details, and filter data to answer specific questions.
5. **Automation:** Reporting processes can be automated, reducing manual efforts and ensuring that reports are generated and distributed on time.
6. **Collaboration:** BI platforms facilitate collaboration by allowing users to share insights, dashboards, and reports with colleagues and stakeholders.

7. **Scalability:** BI platforms can scale to handle large datasets and accommodate growing user needs.

By using BI platforms, organizations can streamline their data analysis and reporting processes, democratize access to data, and empower decision-makers with timely and actionable insights. These platforms play a crucial role in driving data-driven decision-making across various industries.

DATA VISUALIZATION AND REPORTING FOR BIG DATA

Data visualization and reporting for big data present unique challenges due to the sheer volume, velocity, and variety of data involved. Traditional data visualization and reporting techniques may not be sufficient to handle large datasets effectively. Various guidelines to approach data visualization and reporting for big data:

1. **Data Preparation and Processing:**
   - **Data Aggregation:** Aggregating or summarizing data is often necessary when dealing with large datasets. Use tools or scripts to pre-process and aggregate the data before visualization to reduce the data's size and complexity.
   - **Data Sampling:** For initial exploration and analysis, consider working with a sample of the data rather than the entire dataset. Sampling can provide insights without overwhelming your tools and infrastructure.
   - **Data Cleaning:** Large datasets may contain errors, missing values, or outliers. Implement data cleaning and quality control processes to ensure data accuracy.
2. **Choose the Right Tools and Technologies:**
   - **Big Data Technologies:** Leverage big data technologies like Apache Hadoop, Spark, or cloud-based solutions (e.g., AWS, Azure, Google Cloud) for data storage and processing.
   - **Visualization Tools:** Use data visualization tools and libraries that can handle large datasets efficiently. Tools like Tableau, Power BI, Plotly, and D3.js have features for handling big data.
   - **Data Warehouses:** Consider using data warehouses and databases optimized for analytics, such as Amazon Redshift, Google BigQuery, or Snowflake, to store and query large datasets.
3. **Data Visualization Techniques for Big Data:**
   - **Sampling and Summarization:** Displaying a summary or a sample of the data can provide insights without overwhelming the viewer. For example, summary statistics, histograms, or random sampling can be used.
   - **Aggregations:** Visualizing aggregated data can help reveal trends and patterns. Bar charts, line charts, and heatmaps with aggregated values are effective for large datasets.
   - **Data Drilldown:** Allow users to drill down into specific areas of interest. Interactive dashboards with zoom-in and filtering capabilities can be helpful.
   - **Scalable Visualizations:** Consider using scalable visualization techniques like scatter plots with alpha blending or hexbin plots for dense data points.

4. **Distributed Data Processing:**
   - **Parallel Processing:** Utilize parallel processing frameworks like Apache Spark to distribute data visualization tasks across multiple nodes for faster rendering and scalability.
   - **Distributed Databases:** If your data is stored in distributed databases, ensure that your visualization tools can connect to and query these data sources efficiently.
5. **Performance Optimization:**
   - **Data Compression:** Use data compression techniques to reduce the size of data transferred to visualization tools, especially for real-time or remote data access.
   - **Data Indexing:** Optimize data indexing to speed up data retrieval for reporting and visualization.
6. **Real-time Data Streaming:** For big data that is generated in real-time or near real-time, consider using stream processing platforms like Apache Kafka or Apache Flink for data ingestion and processing.
7. **Monitoring and Alerting:** Implement monitoring and alerting systems to detect issues with data processing or visualization performance. This helps in maintaining the quality of your big data reports.
8. **User Training:** Train users and data analysts on the specific tools and techniques needed for working with big data. They should be aware of the limitations and best practices for handling large datasets.
9. **Collaboration and Sharing:** Use collaboration and sharing features of your visualization tools to ensure that insights from big data are accessible to stakeholders and decision-makers.
10. **Consider Data Storytelling:** Create data stories that guide the audience through the insights and narratives hidden within big data. Storytelling helps make sense of complex information.

Data visualization and reporting for big data require a combination of technology, tools, and best practices to effectively extract insights and communicate findings. By applying these strategies, organizations can harness the power of big data to make data-driven decisions and gain a competitive advantage.

DATA VISUALIZATION AND REPORTING FOR MACHINE LEARNING AND AI

Data visualization and reporting play a crucial role in understanding, interpreting, and communicating the results of machine learning (ML) and artificial intelligence (AI) models. Visualizations and reports help stakeholders, including data scientists, business analysts, and decision-makers, make informed decisions based on ML and AI insights.

1. **Model Evaluation and Performance:**
   - **Confusion Matrices:** Use confusion matrices and associated visualizations like heatmaps to assess classification model performance.

- **ROC Curves and AUC:** ROC curves and the area under the curve (AUC) provide insights into binary classification model performance. Visualize ROC curves to compare models.
- **Precision-Recall Curves:** Precision-recall curves are useful for evaluating models with imbalanced datasets.

2. **Model Explainability and Interpretability:**
   - **Feature Importance:** Visualize feature importance scores, such as those from tree-based models or feature selection techniques, to understand which features are most influential.
   - **Partial Dependence Plots (PDPs):** PDPs visualize the effect of one or two features on a model's predictions while holding other features constant.
   - **SHAP (SHapley Additive exPlanations):** SHAP values provide explanations for individual predictions. Visualize SHAP summary plots to understand how features contribute to model outputs.
3. **Data Pre-processing:**
   - **Data Distribution:** Visualize data distributions and identify outliers or skewed distributions that may require pre-processing.
   - **Correlation Matrix:** Plot correlation matrices to explore relationships between features and identify multicollinearity.
4. **Model Training and Validation:**
   - **Learning Curves:** Plot learning curves to assess model performance on training and validation datasets. These curves help identify overfitting or underfitting.
   - **Hyperparameter Tuning:** Visualize hyperparameter tuning results to identify the best set of hyperparameters for your models.
5. **Anomaly Detection:**
   - **Anomaly Heatmaps:** Use heatmaps to visualize anomalies in time series or spatial data.
   - **Dimensionality Reduction:** Visualize the results of dimensionality reduction techniques like t-SNE or PCA to detect clusters or outliers.
6. **Natural Language Processing (NLP):**
   - **Word Clouds:** Create word clouds to visualize frequently occurring words in text data.
   - **Topic Modelling:** Use topic modelling techniques like Latent Dirichlet Allocation (LDA) and visualize the topics and their distribution in a corpus.
7. **Time Series Analysis:**
   - **Time Series Plots:** Visualize time series data to identify trends, seasonality, and anomalies.
   - **Forecasting Plots:** Display model forecasts along with historical data for evaluation.
8. **Dashboarding and Reporting:**
   - **Dashboard Tools:** Create interactive dashboards using tools like Tableau, Power BI, or Python libraries like Dash or Streamlit to provide dynamic access to ML and AI insights.

- **Report Generation:** Automate report generation using R Markdown, Jupyter Notebooks, or reporting libraries to share model results, insights, and recommendations.

9. **Stakeholder Communication:**
   - **Data Storytelling:** Present ML and AI results in the form of a narrative, using visuals to guide stakeholders through the data, models, and insights.
   - **Explanatory Visualizations:** Create visualizations that simplify complex model outputs, making them understandable to non-technical audiences.
10. **Feedback Loop:**
    - **Interactive Feedback:** Implement interactive elements in dashboards to allow stakeholders to provide feedback and refine models or insights iteratively.

Effective data visualization and reporting for ML and AI involve a combination of domain knowledge, data expertise, and communication skills. These practices ensure that the insights generated by ML and AI models are actionable, interpretable, and valuable to the organization.

DATA SECURITY AND COMPLIANCE IN REPORTING

Ensuring data security and compliance with reporting tools is crucial to protect sensitive information and maintain legal and regulatory requirements. Following are some best practices for handling data security and compliance in reporting:

1. **Data Encryption:**
   - **Transport Encryption:** Use secure communication protocols (e.g., HTTPS) to encrypt data in transit when transferring data between users and reporting tools or data sources.
   - **Data-at-Rest Encryption:** Implement encryption for data stored in databases, storage systems, or cloud services to protect data at rest.
2. **Access Control:**
   - **Role-based Access Control (RBAC):** Implement RBAC to restrict access to reports and sensitive data based on user roles and responsibilities.
   - **Authentication:** Require strong authentication methods, such as multi-factor authentication (MFA), to ensure that only authorized users can access reports.
3. **Data Masking and Redaction:**
   - **Mask Sensitive Data:** Use data masking to hide sensitive information, such as personally identifiable information (PII), credit card numbers, or social security numbers, from users who do not need to see it.
   - **Dynamic Redaction:** Implement dynamic redaction that allows data to be revealed only to authorized users based on their permissions and role.
4. **Audit Trails:**
   - **Audit Logs:** Enable comprehensive audit logging to track who accesses reports, what changes are made, and when these actions occur.
   - **Monitoring:** Regularly monitor audit logs for suspicious activities or unauthorized access.

5. **Data Minimization:**
   - **Collect Only What's Necessary:** Limit the data collected and stored to what is necessary for reporting purposes. Avoid collecting excessive or unnecessary data.
6. **Compliance with Regulations:**
   - **GDPR (General Data Protection Regulation):** If handling European Union (EU) citizen data, ensure that your reporting practices comply with GDPR requirements, such as data subject rights, consent management, and data protection impact assessments.
   - **HIPAA (Health Insurance Portability and Accountability Act):** If handling healthcare data in the United States, ensure that reporting tools and processes comply with HIPAA regulations, including data encryption, secure access controls, and audit trails.
   - **Other Regulations:** Depending on your industry or geographical location, be aware of and comply with other relevant regulations, such as CCPA (California Consumer Privacy Act), FERPA (Family Educational Rights and Privacy Act), or industry-specific standards.
7. **Secure Data Integration:**
   - **API Security:** Ensure that APIs used for data integration with reporting tools are secure and follow authentication best practices.
   - **Data Masking During Integration:** Apply data masking or anonymization techniques when integrating data from different sources to prevent exposure of sensitive information.
8. **Regular Security Audits:** Conduct regular security audits and vulnerability assessments of your reporting tools, infrastructure, and processes to identify and remediate security weaknesses.
9. **Employee Training and Awareness:**
   - Train employees on data security best practices and the importance of compliance with data protection regulations.
   - Foster a culture of data security awareness and responsibility among your team.
10. **Data Retention and Deletion:** Define clear data retention policies, including the deletion of data that is no longer needed for reporting or legal purposes.

Questions for Discussion

Short Questions

1. What is the purpose of data visualization in HR Analytics?
2. What are the advantages of using specialized tools in HR data visualization?
3. What are some popular tools for data visualization in HR Analytics?
4. What is the purpose of an interactive dashboard in HR Analytics?
5. What tools are commonly used to build interactive dashboards in HR?
6. How does storyboarding aid in HR data visualization?

7. What makes Python suitable for HR data visualization and reporting?
8. How do BI platforms enhance HR data reporting?
9. What challenges does big data introduce in HR data visualization?
10. Why is data security important in HR analytics reporting?

Long Questions

1. Analyse the impact of data-driven decision-making in HR practices.
2. Evaluate the effectiveness of specialized data visualization tools in HR analytics.
3. Compare different types of data visualizations and their applicability in HR analytics.
4. Explain the importance of interactive dashboards in HR analytics. Describe the detailed process of creating interactive dashboards for HR analytics.
5. Analyse different use cases of interactive dashboards in HR and their impact on organizational decisions.
6. Explain the process and importance of using Excel functions for creating effective HR dashboards.
7. Discuss the role and process of storyboarding in enhancing HR data visualization.
8. Explore the use of Python in HR data visualization and reporting, including its advantages and limitations.
9. Delve into the applications and benefits of using R for data visualization and reporting in HR analytics.
10. Analyse the role of machine learning and AI in advancing HR data visualization and reporting.
11. Discuss the significance and challenges of data security and compliance in HR analytics reporting.

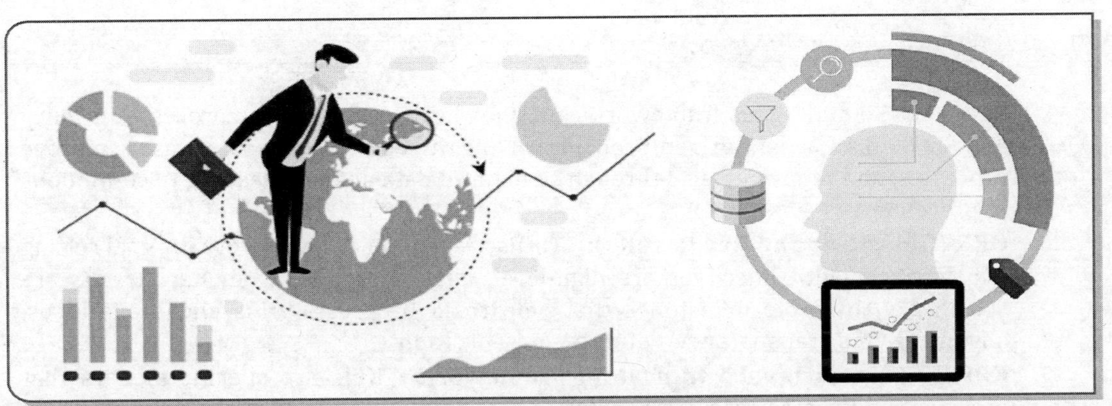

Annexure

ANALYTICS FRAMEWORKS

Analytics frameworks provide structured approaches to organize, analyse, and derive insights from data. These frameworks are essential in a variety of domains, from business and marketing to data science and decision-making. Given below are some commonly used analytics frameworks:

1. **CRISP-DM (Cross-Industry Standard Process for Data Mining):** CRISP-DM is a widely used framework for data mining and analytics. It consists of six phases: Business Understanding, Data Understanding, Data Preparation, Modelling, Evaluation, and Deployment. This framework guides data professionals through the entire process of extracting valuable knowledge from data.
2. **Business Intelligence Framework:** This framework is centered around the concept of business intelligence and focuses on delivering actionable insights for decision-making. It typically includes data collection, data storage, data analysis, and data presentation components. The goal is to provide key stakeholders with relevant information for strategic planning.
3. **SMART (Specific, Measurable, Achievable, Relevant, Time-Bound) Framework:** SMART is a framework used in goal-setting and performance measurement. It emphasizes setting specific, quantifiable, and realistic objectives with defined timelines. This framework is essential for assessing performance and making data-driven adjustments.
4. **Balanced Scorecard:** Originally introduced by Kaplan and Norton, the Balanced Scorecard framework provides a balanced view of an organization's performance by measuring financial, customer, internal process, and learning and growth aspects. It helps organizations align their strategies and operations with their objectives.

5. **LEAN Six Sigma:** This framework combines Lean principles for process efficiency and Six Sigma for data-driven problem-solving. It seeks to eliminate waste, improve processes, and reduce defects through structured data analysis, leading to continuous improvement.
6. **OKR (Objectives and Key Results):** OKRs are a popular framework for goal setting and management. Objectives are high-level, qualitative goals, and Key Results are specific, quantifiable milestones that help track progress. OKRs encourage focus, alignment, and transparency within an organization.
7. **KPI (Key Performance Indicator) Framework:** KPIs are specific metrics that organizations use to track performance and progress toward their goals. The KPI framework involves selecting, measuring, and analysing key metrics to assess the health of various aspects of a business or project.
8. **Big Data Analytics Frameworks:** In the context of big data, several frameworks are widely used, including the Hadoop ecosystem, Apache Spark, and Apache Flink. These frameworks enable the processing and analysis of vast and diverse data sets efficiently.
9. **A3 Problem-solving:** Derived from Toyota's problem-solving approach, the A3 framework simplifies complex problems onto a single sheet of paper. It encourages a structured analysis and a disciplined approach to addressing issues by defining the problem, analysing root causes, and proposing solutions.
10. **PDCA (Plan-Do-Check-Act) Cycle:** Often associated with continuous improvement, the PDCA framework is used to iteratively solve problems. It involves planning a change, implementing it, checking its results, and acting on those results by making necessary adjustments.
11. **SWOT Analysis (Strengths, Weaknesses, Opportunities, Threats):** This framework is used for strategic planning. It involves identifying an organization's internal strengths and weaknesses and external opportunities and threats to make informed decisions.
12. **Decision Analysis Framework:** Decision analysis involves identifying the problem, developing alternative solutions, assessing the risks and uncertainties, and making informed decisions based on data and analytical tools like decision trees or cost-benefit analysis.

These frameworks serve as valuable tools for different aspects of analytics, ranging from data preparation and processing to strategic decision-making. The choice of framework depends on the specific goals and challenges an organization or individual is facing, as well as the nature of the data and the complexity of the problem at hand.

PARAMETRIC AND NONPARAMETRIC TEST IN HR ANALYTICS

Parametric and nonparametric tests are two broad categories of statistical methods used in HR analytics to analyse data, test hypotheses, and draw conclusions. The choice between these types of tests depends on the nature of the data and the assumptions that can be made. Given below are the differences and common applications of parametric and nonparametric tests in HR analytics:

Parametric Tests

Parametric tests assume that data follows a specific probability distribution, typically the normal distribution, and that the data has equal variances (homoscedasticity). The data should be continuous and have interval or ratio scale properties.

Common Parametric Tests in HR Analytics

- **t-Test:** The t-test is used to compare the means of two groups, such as comparing the salaries of male and female employees in an organization.
- **Analysis of Variance (ANOVA):** ANOVA is used to compare the means of more than two groups, for example, comparing the performance scores of employees across different departments.
- **Linear Regression:** Linear regression is used to model and analyse the relationships between variables, such as predicting employee performance based on years of experience, education level, and training hours.
- **Multiple Regression:** Multiple regression extends linear regression to analyse multiple independent variables' impact on a dependent variable. For instance, it can be used to predict employee turnover based on factors like salary, job satisfaction, and work hours.

Nonparametric Tests

Nonparametric tests do not rely on specific distribution assumptions and are more robust in the presence of non-normally distributed data or when data scales are ordinal or nominal.

Common Nonparametric Tests in HR Analytics

- **Mann-Whitney U Test:** Used to compare two independent groups when the assumptions for the t-test are not met. For example, comparing the job satisfaction scores of two different teams.
- **Kruskal-Wallis Test:** A nonparametric alternative to ANOVA for comparing multiple independent groups.
- **Wilcoxon Signed-Rank Test:** Used to compare two related groups when the data is not normally distributed, such as comparing pre-training and post-training performance scores of the same employees.
- **Chi-Square Test:** Used to analyse the association between categorical variables, such as assessing whether there is a relationship between gender and promotion rates.

Choosing between Parametric and Nonparametric Tests

- **Data Distribution:** If your data is approximately normally distributed and meets other parametric assumptions, parametric tests are often more powerful and provide more precise results.
- **Data Type:** Parametric tests are suitable for continuous data with interval or ratio scales, while nonparametric tests are more appropriate for ordinal, nominal, or non-normally distributed data.
- **Sample Size:** Parametric tests tend to be more robust with larger sample sizes, while nonparametric tests can be useful with smaller sample sizes or skewed data.
- **Research Question:** The choice of test should align with your research question and the assumptions that you can reasonably make about your data.

In HR analytics, it's essential to select the appropriate test based on the characteristics of your data and the specific hypotheses or questions you want to address to ensure accurate and valid results.

MULTIVARIATE STATISTICS IN HR ANALYTICS

Multivariate statistics in HR analytics involve the analysis of multiple variables or factors simultaneously to gain insights into complex relationships and patterns within human resources data. This approach is useful for addressing various HR-related questions and challenges, such as employee retention, performance evaluation, diversity and inclusion, and more. Given below is a step-by-step guide on how to perform multivariate statistics in HR analytics:

1. **Define the Research Question:** Start by clearly defining the research question or problem you want to address with multivariate statistics. For example, you might want to understand the factors that influence employee turnover, assess the impact of training programs on performance, or analyse the relationships between various HR metrics.
2. **Data Collection and Preparation:** Gather relevant HR data from your organization, ensuring that it covers the variables needed to address your research question. Common data sources in HR analytics include employee records, survey responses, performance evaluations, and more. Clean, pre-process, and organize the data for analysis, addressing missing values and outliers as necessary.
3. **Choose the Right Multivariate Techniques:** There are several multivariate statistical techniques you can use in HR analytics, depending on your research question and data type. Some common techniques include:
    - **Multiple Regression Analysis:** To understand the relationship between a dependent variable (e.g., turnover) and multiple independent variables (e.g., salary, job satisfaction, work hours).
    - **Factor Analysis:** To identify underlying factors or dimensions within a set of related HR variables (e.g., employee engagement, job satisfaction, and work-life balance).
    - **Principal Component Analysis (PCA):** To reduce the dimensionality of HR data while retaining essential information.
    - **Discriminant Analysis:** To classify employees into different groups based on their characteristics.
    - **MANOVA (Multivariate Analysis of Variance):** To analyse the impact of categorical independent variables on multiple dependent variables.
4. **Conduct the Analysis:** Perform the chosen multivariate analysis technique using statistical software (e.g., R, Python, SPSS). Ensure you interpret the results in the context of your research question. Look for significant relationships, patterns, and insights within the data.
5. **Visualize the Results:** Create visualizations such as scatter plots, bar charts, heat maps, or correlation matrices to help convey the findings and make them more accessible to stakeholders.
6. **Interpret the Findings:** Interpret the results in the context of your research question. What do the relationships between variables reveal? Are there any actionable insights for HR decision-making?

7. **Report and Share Insights:** Document your findings in a clear and concise report or presentation. Share your insights with HR professionals and other relevant stakeholders, and discuss potential actions or strategies based on the results.
8. **Continuous Monitoring and Improvement:** HR analytics is an ongoing process. Keep collecting and analysing data, and adjust your strategies and models as needed to stay aligned with your organization's goals and objectives.

The Multivariate statistics in HR analytics should be used to support evidence-based decision-making, helping organizations make informed choices to improve HR practices, employee engagement, and overall performance.

ROOT CAUSE ANALYSIS IN HR ANALYTICS

Root cause analysis in HR analytics is a systematic process for identifying and addressing the underlying reasons behind HR-related issues or challenges. It helps HR professionals and organizations understand the causes of problems, such as high turnover, low employee engagement, or performance issues. Given below is a step-by-step guide on how to perform root cause analysis in HR analytics:

1. **Define the Problem:** Clearly define the HR problem or issue you want to analyse. Be specific about the symptoms, trends, or patterns you've observed, such as high turnover rates, low productivity, or a spike in absenteeism.
2. **Collect Relevant Data:** Gather HR data related to the problem. This may include employee records, surveys, performance evaluations, attendance records, exit interviews, or any other relevant information. Ensure the data is complete, accurate, and covers a sufficient time period for analysis.
3. **Identify Potential Causes**: Brainstorm and create a list of potential factors that could contribute to the problem. These factors can be categorized as organizational, environmental, or individual. For example, factors might include lack of career development opportunities, poor management, workplace stress, or personal factors affecting employees.
4. **Data Analysis**: Apply appropriate statistical and analytical techniques to the data to investigate the relationships between the potential causes and the problem. Common techniques include correlation analysis, regression analysis, and multivariate statistics, as mentioned in the previous response.
5. **Hypothesis Testing**: Formulate hypotheses about the potential causes and their impact on the problem. For example, you might hypothesize that low employee engagement is related to inadequate career development opportunities. Test these hypotheses using statistical methods to determine whether they are supported by the data.
6. **Root Cause Identification:** Based on the data analysis and hypothesis testing, identify the root causes that are most strongly associated with the problem. Look for statistically significant relationships and causal links.
7. **Validation:** Validate the identified root causes by consulting with subject matter experts in HR, conducting focus groups, or administering additional surveys or interviews. This helps ensure that the identified causes align with the experiences and perceptions of employees and stakeholders.
8. **Documentation and Reporting:** Document the results of the root cause analysis in a clear and organized manner. Present your findings, including the identified root causes, in a report or presentation that can be shared with HR professionals and organizational decision-makers.
9. **Action Planning:** Develop an action plan to address the identified root causes. This plan should include specific, measurable, achievable, relevant, and time-bound (SMART) goals and strategies for improving the HR situation.

10. **Monitor and Evaluate:** Implement the action plan and continuously monitor its effectiveness. Measure and evaluate key HR metrics to assess whether the changes are producing the desired results. Adjust the plan as needed based on ongoing data analysis.

Root cause analysis in HR analytics is an iterative process that helps organizations address underlying issues and make data-driven decisions to improve HR practices, employee satisfaction, and overall organizational performance.

DATA DRIVEN TEAMWORK IN HR ANALYTICS

Data-driven teamwork in HR analytics is about fostering collaboration among HR professionals, data analysts, and other relevant teams within an organization to leverage data and analytics to make informed decisions. Given below is a guide on how to perform data-driven teamwork in HR analytics:

1. **Define Clear Objectives:** Start by defining clear objectives for your data-driven HR analytics initiatives. What specific HR challenges or questions do you want to address? Be specific about the goals and expected outcomes.
2. **Build a Cross-Functional Team:** Create a cross-functional team that includes HR professionals, data analysts, IT experts, and any other relevant stakeholders. This team should have a mix of skills, knowledge, and expertise to effectively analyse and interpret HR data.
3. **Data Collection and Integration:** Collect and integrate relevant HR data from various sources, including HR systems, surveys, performance evaluations, and other relevant sources. Ensure data quality and consistency by cleaning and pre-processing the data.
4. **Data Analysis and Visualization:** Work collaboratively to perform data analysis using appropriate statistical and machine learning techniques. Create visualizations and dashboards that provide insights into HR-related metrics and trends. Tools like Power BI, Tableau, or custom Python/R scripts can be helpful for visualization.
5. **Establish Data Governance:** Implement data governance practices to ensure data accuracy, security, and compliance with privacy regulations, such as GDPR or HIPAA. Define data access controls and establish protocols for data sharing within the team.
6. **Regular Meetings and Communication:** Schedule regular meetings where team members can discuss findings, insights, and progress. Effective communication is key to ensure everyone is aligned and working towards common goals.
7. **Collaborative Decision-Making:** Use data-driven insights to inform HR decisions and strategies. Encourage collaboration among team members to discuss how the data can be used to make better HR-related decisions. Make sure that decisions are based on evidence rather than intuition.
8. **Continuous Learning and Skill Development:** Invest in the skill development of HR professionals and data analysts. Encourage team members to learn new data analysis techniques, tools, and methodologies that can improve their ability to derive insights from HR data.
9. **Feedback Loop:** Establish a feedback loop where the HR professionals can provide feedback on the effectiveness of data-driven insights in their decision-making process. Use this feedback to refine and improve HR analytics processes.
10. **Document Insights and Best Practices:** Document the insights derived from HR analytics and best practices for future reference. This documentation will help in creating a knowledge base for the team.

11. **Evaluate and Adjust:** Continuously assess the impact of data-driven HR initiatives on HR metrics, and be prepared to adjust strategies based on the results and evolving business needs.
12. **Share Success Stories:** Highlight success stories and demonstrate the value of data-driven HR decisions within the organization to garner support and enthusiasm for future analytics projects.

Data-driven teamwork in HR analytics is an ongoing process that requires a collaborative and iterative approach. It empowers HR professionals to make more informed decisions, optimize workforce management, and improve overall organizational performance.

HOW TO PERFORM FACTOR ANALYSIS PROBLEM IN HR ANALYTICS?

Factor analysis is a valuable multivariate statistical technique commonly used in HR analytics to explore underlying factors or dimensions within a set of related HR variables. Given below is a step-by-step guide on how to perform factor analysis in HR analytics:

1. **Define the Research Question:** Start by clearly defining the research question or problem you want to address with factor analysis in HR analytics. For example, you may want to identify underlying factors that influence employee satisfaction, engagement, or performance.
2. **Data Collection and Preparation:** Gather relevant HR data from your organization, ensuring it covers the variables you want to analyse. Common HR data sources include employee surveys, performance evaluations, and other relevant records. Clean, pre-process, and organize the data, addressing missing values and outliers as necessary.
3. **Choose the Variables:** Select the HR variables that you believe are related to the underlying factors you want to uncover. These variables should be theoretically or empirically related to each other.
4. **Assumption Check:** Before conducting factor analysis, it's essential to check for the assumptions of factor analysis, such as sample size adequacy, linearity, and the absence of multicollinearity.
5. **Select the Factor Analysis Method:** There are different methods for factor analysis, including principal component analysis (PCA) and common factor analysis. The choice depends on your research objectives and the nature of your data. PCA extracts linear combinations of variables, while common factor analysis extracts factors that are assumed to underlie the observed variables.
6. **Run the Factor Analysis:** Use statistical software (e.g., R, Python, SPSS) to perform the factor analysis. The software will provide you with factor loadings, eigenvalues, and other relevant output. Interpret the results based on the loadings of the variables on the factors.
7. **Evaluate the Results:**
   - **Factor Loadings:** Examine the factor loadings to understand the strength and direction of the relationship between variables and factors. High loadings indicate a strong association.
   - **Eigenvalues:** Look at the eigenvalues of each factor. Eigenvalues represent the amount of variance explained by each factor. Retain factors with eigenvalues greater than 1 or through the scree plot method.
   - **Rotation:** Consider rotating the factors to achieve a more interpretable solution. Common rotation methods include Varimax and Promax.
   - **Interpretation:** Assign meaningful labels or names to the factors based on the variables that load most strongly on them. Interpret the factors in the context of HR and your research question.

8. **Report and Share Insights:** Document your findings in a report or presentation. Share the insights with HR professionals and other stakeholders, and discuss how the identified factors may be used to improve HR practices or policies.
9. **Continuous Monitoring and Improvement:** HR analytics is an ongoing process. Continue to collect and analyse data, and adjust your factor analysis as needed to support HR decision-making.

Factor analysis can help organizations better understand the latent constructs underlying their HR data, leading to more informed and effective HR strategies and policies.

HOW TO PERFORM REGRESSION ANALYSIS IN HR ANALYTICS?

Regression analysis is a valuable statistical technique used in HR analytics to understand the relationships between one or more independent variables (predictors) and a dependent variable (the outcome or target) within a dataset. In the context of HR analytics, regression analysis can help you explore and quantify the impact of various HR-related factors on outcomes like employee performance, retention, or satisfaction. Given below is a step-by-step guide on how to perform regression analysis in HR analytics:

1. **Define Your Research Question:** Start by clearly defining the research question you want to answer. For example, you might want to determine how factors like salary, years of experience, and job satisfaction affect employee performance ratings.
2. **Data Collection and Preparation:** Gather the relevant HR data for your analysis. This data should include the dependent variable (e.g., performance ratings) and one or more independent variables (e.g., salary, years of experience, job satisfaction). Ensure that your data is clean, complete, and well-structured.
3. **Choose the Right Type of Regression:** Decide which type of regression analysis is most suitable for your research question. Common types of regression used in HR analytics include:
    - **Simple Linear Regression:** When you have one independent variable and one dependent variable.
    - **Multiple Linear Regression:** When you have multiple independent variables and one dependent variable.
    - **Logistic Regression:** Used when the dependent variable is binary (e.g., employee turnover—yes/no).
4. **Perform the Regression Analysis:** Use statistical software like R, Python (with libraries like scikit-learn, statsmodels), or specialized HR analytics tools to perform the regression analysis. Here's a simplified example of how to do this in Python using the statsmodels library:

Python

```
import statsmodels.api as sm

# Define your dependent variable (Y) and independent variables (X).
Y = df['performance_ratings']
X = df[['salary', 'years_of_experience', 'job_satisfaction']]

# Add a constant term for the intercept.
X = sm.add_constant(X)

# Fit the regression model.
model = sm.OLS(Y, X).fit()

# Get summary statistics.
print(model.summary ())
```

5. **Interpret the Results:** Review the regression output to interpret the results. Key aspects to consider include:
    - **Coefficients:** These indicate the direction and strength of the relationship between independent variables and the dependent variable.
    - **P-values:** Assess the significance of the coefficients. Lower values suggest stronger evidence of a relationship.
    - **R-squared (or adjusted R-squared):** Measure the goodness of fit, indicating how well the model explains the variation in the dependent variable.
    - **Residuals:** Examine the distribution of residuals to ensure the model assumptions are met.
6. **Evaluate Model Performance:** Assess the model's performance using techniques like cross-validation, mean squared error, or other relevant metrics to understand how well it predicts the dependent variable.
7. **Report and Share Insights:** Document your findings, draw meaningful insights, and communicate your results to HR professionals and other stakeholders. Discuss the practical implications and potential actions based on the analysis.
8. **Continuous Improvement:** HR analytics is an ongoing process. Periodically update your models and analyses with new data and continue to refine your understanding of the relationships between HR factors and outcomes.

Remember that regression analysis is a tool for hypothesis testing and predictive modelling. It can help HR professionals make data-driven decisions, design more effective HR policies, and identify factors that impact employee performance, satisfaction, and retention.

HOW TO PERFORM LINEAR REGRESSION IN HR ANALYTICS?

Performing linear regression in HR analytics can help you analyse and understand the relationships between variables. Linear regression is a statistical technique used to model the linear relationship between a dependent variable and one or more independent variables. Given below is a step-by-step guide on how to perform linear regression in HR analytics:

1. **Define Your Research Question**: Start by clearly defining the research question or problem you want to address using linear regression. For example, you might want to understand how years of experience (independent variable) affect an employee's salary (dependent variable), or how the number of training hours' influences job performance.
2. **Data Collection and Preparation:** Gather relevant HR data that includes both the dependent variable (the variable you want to predict or explain) and one or more independent variables (predictors). Ensure that your data is clean, complete, and well-structured. Common HR data sources include employee records, survey responses, performance metrics, and more.
3. **Data Exploration and Visualization:** Before running a linear regression, it's a good practice to explore and visualize the data. Use scatter plots, histograms, and summary statistics to understand the distribution and relationships between variables. This step can help you identify potential outliers or non-linearity in the data.
4. **Choose the Right Type of Linear Regression:** There are different types of linear regression, depending on the number of independent variables and the nature of the data:
   - **Simple Linear Regression:** When you have one dependent variable and one independent variable.
   - **Multiple Linear Regression:** When you have one dependent variable and two or more independent variables.
   - **Logistic Regression:** When the dependent variable is binary (e.g., turnover or retention) and you want to model the probability of an event occurring.
5. **Model Building:** If you're conducting simple linear regression, the model can be represented as:

$$QY = \beta_0 + \beta_1 X + \varepsilon$$

   - Y is the dependent variable (e.g., salary)
   - X is the independent variable (e.g., years of experience)
   - β_0 is the intercept (constant)
   - β_1 is the coefficient for the independent variable
   - ε is the error term

   For multiple linear regression, the model includes multiple independent variables:

$$Y = \beta_0 + \beta_1 X_1 + \beta_2 X_2 + \ldots + \beta_n X_n + \varepsilon$$

   Use statistical software (e.g., *R*, Python, or specialized HR analytics software) to perform the regression analysis and estimate the coefficients (β_0, β_1, β_2, etc.).

6. **Model Evaluation:** Evaluate the goodness of fit of the model using metrics such as R-squared, adjusted R-squared, p-values, and standard errors. These statistics help assess how well the model explains the variation in the dependent variable.
7. **Interpret the Results:** Analyse the coefficients of the independent variables to understand the strength and direction of their relationships with the dependent variable. Positive coefficients indicate a positive relationship, while negative coefficients indicate a negative relationship. Also, assess the p-values to determine the significance of the relationships.
8. **Predict and Validate:** Use the regression model to make predictions based on the relationships discovered. You can apply the model to new data to predict outcomes or understand the impact of changing independent variables.
9. **Report and Share Insights:** Document your findings in a clear and concise report or presentation. Share insights and actionable recommendations based on the regression analysis with HR professionals and relevant stakeholders.

Linear regression in HR analytics can help organizations make data-driven decisions regarding hiring, compensation, performance, and various HR-related factors. It's important to continuously monitor and update your models as new data becomes available to ensure their accuracy and relevance.

HOW TO PERFORM LEAST SQUARE MODEL IN HR ANALYTICS?

In HR analytics, as in many other fields, the least squares model is commonly used to analyse relationships between variables, make predictions, and estimate coefficients. The least squares method is often used for regression analysis, where you aim to understand the impact of one or more independent variables on a dependent variable. Here's how to build a least squares model in HR analytics:

1. **Define Your Research Question:** Start by clearly defining the research question or problem you want to address using the least squares model. For example, you might want to understand the relationship between employee performance (dependent variable) and variables like training hours, experience, and job satisfaction (independent variables).
2. **Data Collection and Preparation:** Gather the necessary HR data, ensuring that you have data on both the dependent and independent variables. This data might come from various sources such as employee records, surveys, performance evaluations, and more. Clean and pre-process the data, dealing with missing values and outliers as required.
3. **Choose the Right Type of Regression Model:** Determine the type of regression model that suits your research question. Common types include:
   - **Linear Regression:** Used when the relationship between the dependent and independent variables is linear.
   - **Multiple Regression:** Used when you have multiple independent variables.
   - **Logistic Regression:** Used when the dependent variable is binary (e.g., turnover or not turnover).

   Decide whether you want to perform simple linear regression (one independent variable) or multiple linear regression (more than one independent variable) based on the complexity of your research question. For example:

   Simple Linear Regression: $Y = \beta_0 + \beta_1 X$

   Multiple Linear Regression: $Y = \beta_0 + \beta_1 X_1 + \beta_2 X_2 + \ldots + \beta_k X_k$

   In these equations, Y represents the dependent variable, $X_1, X_2, \ldots, X_k$ represent independent variables, β_0 is the intercept, and $\beta_1, \beta_2, \ldots, \beta_k$ are the coefficients you will estimate.
4. **Model Building:** Build the regression model using statistical software such as *R*, Python (with libraries like scikit-learn or statsmodels), or specialized HR analytics tools. The software will estimate the coefficients ($\beta_0, \beta_1, \beta_2, \ldots$) that minimize the sum of squared differences between the predicted values and the actual values. Simple example using Python and the scikit-learn library for a linear regression model:

```python
from sklearn.linear_model import LinearRegression
from sklearn.model_selection import train_test_split

# Assuming X contains your independent variables and y contains the dependent variable
X_train, X_test, y_train, y_test = train_test_split(X, y, test_size=0.2, random_state=42)

model = LinearRegression()
model.fit(X_train, y_train)
```

5. **Model Evaluation:** Evaluate the model's performance to ensure that it provides meaningful insights. Common evaluation metrics include R-squared, mean squared error (MSE), and root mean squared error (RMSE).
6. **Interpret the Results:** Interpret the coefficients of the independent variables in the context of your research question. Coefficients represent the strength and direction of the relationship between the independent variables and the dependent variable.
7. **Make Predictions and Inferences:** Once your model is built and validated, you can use it to make predictions or inferences based on new or existing data. For example, you can predict employee performance for individuals based on their training hours, experience, and job satisfaction scores.
8. **Report and Share Insights:** Document your findings, insights, and model performance in a report or presentation. Share the results with HR professionals and other stakeholders to inform decision-making.
9. **Continuous Improvement:** HR analytics is an ongoing process. Monitor the performance of your model over time, update it as needed, and consider collecting more data to improve its accuracy and relevance.

Remember that building a least squares model in HR analytics requires a solid understanding of the statistical concepts involved and the ability to interpret the results in the context of HR-related questions and objectives. It can be a powerful tool for making data-driven decisions and optimizing HR practices.

EMPLOYEE ATTITUDE SURVEY FORM

Creating an effective employee attitude survey form is essential for gathering valuable feedback and insights from the employees. Below is a sample template for an employee attitude survey form. You can customize it to fit the specific needs and goals of the organization:

Employee Attitude Survey

Introduction: Thank you for taking the time to participate in our employee attitude survey. Your feedback is important to us, and it will help us understand how we can improve our workplace and your overall experience at the Company. Please be honest and candid in your responses. Your responses will be kept confidential.

Section 1: *Demographic Information (Optional)*

1.1 Employee ID (Optional): ____________ 1.2 Department: ____________________
1.3 Job Title: _________________________ 1.4 Years with the Company: __________

Section 2: *Job Satisfaction*

Please rate the following statements on a scale of 1 to 5, with 1 being "Strongly Disagree" and 5 being "Strongly Agree."

2.1 I am satisfied with my current job.
- 1 (Strongly Disagree)
- 2 (Disagree)
- 3 (Neutral)
- 4 (Agree)
- 5 (Strongly Agree)

2.2 I find my job challenging and engaging.
- 1 (Strongly Disagree)
- 2 (Disagree)
- 3 (Neutral)
- 4 (Agree)
- 5 (Strongly Agree)

2.3 My workload is manageable.
- 1 (Strongly Disagree)
- 2 (Disagree)
- 3 (Neutral)
- 4 (Agree)
- 5 (Strongly Agree)

Section 3: *Work Environment*

3.1 The work environment at [Company Name] is conducive to productivity.
- 1 (Strongly Disagree)
- 2 (Disagree)
- 3 (Neutral)
- 4 (Agree)
- 5 (Strongly Agree)

3.2 I feel safe and comfortable at work.
- 1 (Strongly Disagree)
- 2 (Disagree)
- 3 {Neutral)

- 4 (Agree)
- 5 {Strongly Agree)

3.3 Communication within the company is effective.
- 1 {Strongly Disagree)
- 2 (Disagree)
- 3 {Neutral)
- 4 (Agree)
- 5 {Strongly Agree)

Section 4: *Management and Leadership*

4.1 I have a good relationship with my immediate supervisor.
- 1 {Strongly Disagree)
- 2 (Disagree)
- 3 {Neutral)
- 4 (Agree)
- 5 {Strongly Agree)

4.2 Our company's leadership inspires confidence.
- 1 {Strongly Disagree)
- 2 (Disagree)
- 3 {Neutral)
- 4 (Agree)
- 5 {Strongly Agree)

Section 5: *Additional Comments*

Please provide any additional comments or suggestions for improving the work environment, company culture, or any other aspect of your experience at the Company:

Section 6: *Conclusion*

Thank you for completing our employee attitude survey. Your feedback is invaluable, and it will help us make the Company a better place to work. Your responses will be kept confidential, and we appreciate your honesty. If you have any further concerns or suggestions, please feel free to contact the HR department.

[*You can design this survey form using your preferred software or survey tool. Additionally, ensure that the survey is distributed to employees and that their responses are collected and analysed to make meaningful improvements in your organization.*]

PERCEIVED STRESS SCALE (PSS)

The Perceived Stress Scale (PSS) is a widely used psychological instrument for measuring the perception of stress in an individual's life. It was developed by Sheldon Cohen, Tom Kamarck, and Robin Mermelstein in 1983 and has since become a standard tool for assessing an individual's level of stress and their ability to cope with it.

The PSS is a self-report questionnaire that consists of a series of statements related to a person's thoughts and feelings about their daily life and experiences. The respondent is asked to rate how often they have experienced these thoughts and feelings over the past month. Typically, the scale uses a 5-point Likert-type scale, ranging from "0" (Never) to "4" (Very Often). The higher the total score, the higher the perceived stress.

The following is an example of some statements that might be included in the PSS:

1. In the last month, how often have you felt that you were unable to control the important things in your life?
2. In the last month, how often have you felt confident about your ability to handle personal problems?
3. In the last month, how often have you felt that things were going your way?

The PSS is designed to assess the degree to which situations in one's life are appraised as stressful, rather than measuring the objective presence of stressors. It is a valuable tool for researchers, clinicians, and organizations to understand how individuals perceive and respond to stress, which can have a significant impact on their physical and mental well-being.

Scoring the PSS involves adding up the responses to all the items. The total score can range from 0 to 40, with higher scores indicating higher levels of perceived stress. Researchers and professionals often use established cut-off points to categorize individuals into low, moderate, or high stress groups based on their scores.

The PSS is widely used in various fields, including psychology, medicine, and occupational health, to assess stress levels and to evaluate the effectiveness of stress management interventions or well-being programs. It can help identify individuals who may need additional support to manage and reduce stress in their lives.

WHO-5 WELL-BEING INDEX

The WHO-5 Well-being Index is a self-reported questionnaire designed to assess an individual's overall well-being and mental health. It was developed by the World Health Organization (WHO) as a brief and simple tool for measuring well-being. The WHO-5 is widely used in healthcare, research, and clinical settings to screen for depressive symptoms and to monitor changes in well-being over time.

The WHO-5 consists of five positively worded statements that address various aspects of emotional well-being and mental health. Respondents are asked to rate the frequency with which they have experienced each statement over the past two weeks on a 6-point Likert-type scale, with response options ranging from "0" (At no time) to "5" (All of the time).

The following are the five statements typically included in the WHO-5 Well-being Index:

1. I have felt cheerful and in good spirits.
2. I have felt calm and relaxed.
3. I have felt active and vigorous.
4. I woke up feeling fresh and rested.
5. My daily life has been filled with things that interest me.

To calculate an individual's WHO-5 well-being score, sum the scores for each of the five items, with total scores ranging from 0 to 25. Higher scores are indicative of better well-being, while lower scores may suggest poorer mental health or depression.

The WHO-5 is often used as a screening tool for depressive symptoms. A total score below a certain threshold (e.g., a score of 13 or less) is sometimes used to identify individuals who may be at risk for depression. It can be a valuable tool for healthcare professionals to quickly assess a person's mental well-being and identify those who might benefit from further evaluation or intervention.

The brevity and simplicity of the WHO-5 make it a practical tool for routine assessment in clinical practice and research. It can also be used to monitor changes in well-being over time and to evaluate the impact of interventions designed to improve mental health and overall well-being.

EMPLOYEE ENGAGEMENT SURVEY

An employee engagement survey is a valuable tool for assessing the level of engagement and satisfaction among your employees. It helps organizations understand how employees feel about their work, their relationship with their supervisors, and their overall experience in the company. The following are an example of some key elements to consider when creating an employee engagement survey:

1. **Survey Objectives:** Clearly define the objectives of your survey. What specific aspects of employee engagement are you trying to measure? Common objectives include assessing job satisfaction, work relationships, organizational culture, and overall well-being.
2. **Survey Design:** Create a well-structured survey with a mix of closed-ended and open-ended questions. Closed-ended questions can include Likert scale ratings (e.g., 1–5 or 1–7) to measure agreement or satisfaction. Open-ended questions allow employees to provide qualitative feedback.
3. **Anonymity and Confidentiality:** Assure employees that their responses will be anonymous and confidential. This encourages them to provide honest and candid feedback.
4. **Survey Length:** Keep the survey reasonably short. Long surveys can discourage participation. Aim for a duration of 10–15 minutes.
5. **Questions to Include:** Common questions in an employee engagement survey may cover topics like job satisfaction, relationship with supervisors, teamwork, career growth opportunities, work-life balance, and overall well-being. Here are some sample questions:
    - On a scale of 1–5, how satisfied are you with your current role?
    - Do you feel valued and appreciated at work?
    - How well does your supervisor support your professional growth and development?
    - How satisfied are you with the work-life balance in your current role?
    - Do you feel a sense of belonging and connection with your colleagues?
    - How would you rate the company's commitment to employee well-being?
6. **Pilot Test:** Before administering the survey to all employees, conduct a pilot test with a small group to identify any issues with the questions or survey process.
7. **Survey Distribution:** Choose a platform for survey distribution, such as email, online survey tools, or paper forms. Ensure clear instructions for participation.
8. **Timing:** Consider the timing of the survey. Avoid administering it during high-stress periods or busy seasons.
9. **Data Analysis:** After collecting responses, analyse the data to identify trends, strengths, and areas for improvement. Consider both quantitative (numeric) and qualitative (textual) feedback.
10. **Action Planning:** Share the survey results with the management team and develop an action plan to address any areas of concern. Communicate the results and action plan to employees to show that their feedback is valued.

11. **Follow-up Surveys:** Conduct follow-up surveys at regular intervals (e.g., annually) to track changes in employee engagement and measure the effectiveness of implemented improvements.

Employee engagement surveys can help organizations identify areas where they can enhance the working environment, boost morale, and retain talent. Regular communication and action based on survey findings are essential to maintain and improve employee engagement over time.

WORK-LIFE BALANCE SURVEY

A work-life balance survey is a valuable tool for assessing how well employees in your organization are managing their work responsibilities and personal lives. This type of survey helps identify areas where improvements can be made to support employee well-being and job satisfaction. The following is an example of a sample work-life balance survey with potential questions you can use or adapt to your specific needs:

Work-Life Balance Survey

Introduction: Thank you for taking the time to participate in this work-life balance survey. Your feedback is important to us and will help us better understand how we can support your well-being. Please answer the following questions honestly and to the best of your ability. Your responses are completely confidential.

Section 1: *General Information*

1.1 Employee ID (optional):
- This question can help you link responses to specific individuals while maintaining anonymity.

1.2 Department/Team:
- Identify the department or team to which the employee belongs.

1.3 How long have you been with the organization?
- Less than 1 year
- 1–2 years
- 3–5 years
- More than 5 years

Section 2: *Work-Related Questions*

2.1 On average, how many hours do you work per week?
- Less than 40 hours
- 40–50 hours
- 51–60 hours
- More than 60 hours

2.2 Do you regularly work overtime or bring work home?
- Yes
- No

2.3 Do you feel that your workload is manageable?
- Very manageable
- Manageable
- Somewhat manageable
- Unmanageable

2.4 Are you satisfied with your current job responsibilities and workload?
- Very satisfied
- Satisfied
- Neutral
- Dissatisfied
- Very dissatisfied

Section 3: *Work-Life Balance Questions*

3.1 How often do you feel that work interferes with your personal life (e.g., family, hobbies, leisure activities)?
- Rarely or never
- Occasionally
- Often
- Always

3.2 Are you able to disconnect from work during your time off (e.g., evenings, weekends, vacations)?
- Yes, I can easily disconnect
- Yes, but it's challenging
- No, I often think about work during my time off

3.3 How satisfied are you with your current work-life balance?
- Very satisfied
- Satisfied
- Neutral
- Dissatisfied
- Very dissatisfied

3.4 Have you ever had to make personal sacrifices (e.g., missing important events or family time) due to work commitments?
- Yes
- No

Section 4: *Suggestions and Comments*

4.1 Do you have any suggestions or comments on how we can improve work-life balance in the organization?

Conclusion: Thank you for completing this survey. Your input is invaluable in helping us create a better work environment for our employees. Your responses are confidential, and your honesty is appreciated.

Remember to analyse the results of the survey to identify trends, pain points, and areas for improvement. Use the feedback to make necessary changes to support your employees' work-life balance and overall well-being.

MENTAL HEALTH ASSESSMENT QUESTIONNAIRE

A Mental Health Assessment Questionnaire is a tool designed to evaluate an individual's mental health and well-being. It can be used in various settings, including clinical assessments, workplace well-being programs, and general health check-ups. The questionnaire typically consists of a series of questions that cover a range of mental health-related issues. The following is an example of sample set of questions that you can use as a starting point for creating your own questionnaire. You can modify and expand upon these questions to tailor them to your specific needs and objectives:

1. **General Mental Health:**
   - On a scale of 1 to 10, how would you rate your overall mental health and well-being?
2. **Stress and Coping:**
   - How often do you feel overwhelmed by stress?
   - What strategies or techniques do you use to cope with stress?
3. **Anxiety:**
   - Do you frequently experience feelings of anxiety or nervousness?
   - Are there specific situations or triggers that make you feel anxious?
4. **Depression:**
   - Have you experienced persistent feelings of sadness, hopelessness, or a lack of interest in activities you used to enjoy?
5. **Sleep Quality:**
   - How would you describe the quality of your sleep?
   - Do you have trouble falling asleep or staying asleep?
6. **Work-Life Balance:**
   - How well do you feel you are managing your work-life balance?
   - Do you often find it challenging to disconnect from work-related responsibilities?
7. **Social Support:**
   - Do you feel you have a strong support system in your personal and professional life?
   - Are you satisfied with your current social relationships?
8. **Substance Use:**
   - Do you use alcohol, tobacco, or other substances to cope with stress or emotions?
9. **Physical Health:**
   - How would you rate your physical health and its impact on your mental well-being?
10. **Suicidal Thoughts:**
    - Have you ever had thoughts of self-harm or suicide?
11. **Access to Mental Health Resources:**
    - Are you aware of and have access to mental health resources or counselling services?

12. **Self-Care Practices:**
    - What self-care practices do you engage in to maintain your mental well-being?
13. **Mental Health History:**
    - Have you ever been diagnosed with a mental health condition or sought professional help for mental health issues?

It's important to emphasize the importance of honest and confidential responses when administering this questionnaire. Use a scale or open-ended questions to capture the individual's experiences and feelings. Additionally, consider offering resources and support for those who may indicate a need for assistance in the questionnaire.

When using a Mental Health Assessment Questionnaire in a workplace context, ensure that responses are kept confidential and that there is a clear plan for addressing and supporting employees who may be struggling with mental health issues.

WELL-BEING PROGRAM EVALUATION PLAN TEMPLATE

Creating a Well-being Program Evaluation Plan is crucial for assessing the effectiveness of your program and making informed decisions for improvement. The following is an example of template to help you structure your evaluation plan:

Well-being Program Evaluation Plan Template

I. Introduction

- **Program Overview:** Provide a brief description of the well-being program, its objectives, and its target audience.
- **Purpose of the Evaluation:** Explain why you are conducting this evaluation and what you aim to achieve.

II. Evaluation Goals and Objectives

- **Goal 1:** State the primary goal of the evaluation.
  - **Objective 1.1:** Specify the first measurable objective.
  - **Objective 1.2:** Specify the second measurable objective.
- **Goal 2:** State any additional goals and objectives.

III. Evaluation Methods

- **Data Sources:** Describe where you will gather data (e.g., surveys, focus groups, usage metrics).
- **Data Collection Instruments:** Specify the tools you will use (e.g., surveys, questionnaires).
- **Data Collection Schedule:** Provide a timeline for data collection.

IV. Evaluation Metrics and Indicators

- **Key Performance Indicators (KPIs):** List the specific metrics you will track (e.g., engagement rates, stress reduction, program utilization).
- **Baseline Data:** Include any relevant data from before the program's implementation.
- **Target Outcomes:** Define the desired outcomes for each metric.

V. Data Collection and Analysis

- **Survey/Questionnaire Administration:** Explain how and when surveys or questionnaires will be distributed.
- **Data Analysis:** Describe the data analysis methods you will use (e.g., statistical analysis, qualitative coding).
- **Reporting Schedule:** Indicate when and how the results will be reported.

VI. Stakeholder Involvement

- **Identify Stakeholders:** List the key individuals or groups involved in or affected by the program.
- **Stakeholder Engagement:** Describe how stakeholders will be engaged in the evaluation process.

VII. Ethical Considerations

- **Confidentiality:** Explain how participant data will be protected.
- **Informed Consent:** Detail the informed consent process for participants.
- **Privacy:** Address how participant privacy will be maintained.

VIII. Budget and Resources

- **Resource Allocation:** Outline the budget, personnel, and other resources required for the evaluation.
- **Resource Responsibility:** Identify who will be responsible for each aspect of the evaluation.

IX. Reporting and Dissemination

- **Report Audience:** Specify who will receive the evaluation report.
- **Report Format:** Describe the format of the evaluation report.
- **Recommendations:** Provide a space for making recommendations based on the evaluation findings.

X. Action Plan

- **Actionable Steps:** Outline specific steps to be taken based on the evaluation results.
- **Responsible Parties:** Assign responsibility for each action step.

XI. Timeline

- Create a timeline that includes milestones for data collection, analysis, reporting, and implementation of action steps.

XII. Appendices

- Include any additional documents, questionnaires, or supporting materials.

This template serves as a starting point for your Well-being Program Evaluation Plan. Customize it to fit the specific needs and goals of your well-being program and organization. Regularly review and update the plan to ensure it remains aligned with the program's objectives and changing circumstances.

KEY PERFORMANCE INDICATOR (KPI) DASHBOARD

A Key Performance Indicator (KPI) dashboard is a visual tool that displays a set of key metrics or performance indicators relevant to your organization's objectives. It provides a quick, at-a-glance overview of how your well-being program is performing. The following is an example of template for creating a KPI dashboard for your well-being program:

Well-being Program KPI Dashboard Template

I. Dashboard Title

- [Your Organization Name] Well-being Program KPI Dashboard
- [Date]

II. Overview Section

- **Program Summary:** A brief description of your well-being program's goals and purpose.
- **Time Period:** Specify the time frame covered by the dashboard (e.g., monthly, quarterly, annually).

III. Key Performance Indicators: For each KPI, provide the following information:

- **KPI Title:** The name of the specific metric.
- **KPI Definition:** A brief description of what the KPI measures.
- **Target:** The desired goal or benchmark for the KPI.
- **Current Value:** The most recent data point for the KPI.
- **Trend:** An arrow or indicator showing whether the KPI is trending up, down, or stable.
- **Graph/Chart:** A visual representation of the KPI's historical data (e.g., line chart, bar chart).

IV. KPI Metrics

1. **Employee Engagement**
   - KPI Title: Employee Engagement
   - KPI Definition: The percentage of employees actively participating in the well-being program.
   - Target: 80%
   - Current Value: 75%
   - Trend: ▲ (Upward trend)
   - Chart: [Insert Engagement Rate Chart]
2. **Stress Reduction**
   - KPI Title: Stress Reduction
   - KPI Definition: The average reported reduction in stress levels among program participants.
   - Target: 20% reduction
   - Current Value: 15%
   - Trend: ▼ (Downward trend)
   - Chart: [Insert Stress Reduction Chart]

3. **Program Utilization**
    - KPI Title: Program Utilization
    - KPI Definition: The percentage of employees accessing program resources.
    - Target: 70%
    - Current Value: 65%
    - Trend: ▲ (Upward trend)
    - Chart: [Insert Utilization Rate Chart]
4. **Well-being Survey Results**
    - KPI Title: Well-being Survey Results
    - KPI Definition: The average score on well-being surveys administered to employees.
    - Target: 75 (on a 100-point scale)
    - Current Value: 70
    - Trend: ▲ (Upward trend)
    - Chart: [Insert Survey Results Trend Chart]
5. **Insights and Recommendations**
    - Based on the KPI data, provide insights and recommendations for improving the well-being program.
    - Summarize key findings and suggest actions to address any performance gaps.
6. **Additional Information**
    - Include any additional notes, relevant context, or acknowledgments.
7. **Data Sources**
    - List the sources of data for each KPI and where to find more detailed information.
8. **Dashboard Owner and Contact Information**
    - Name and contact details of the person responsible for maintaining and updating the KPI dashboard.

Customize this template to include the specific KPIs that are most relevant to your well-being program and organization. Regularly update the dashboard with fresh data and use it as a powerful tool for monitoring and improving the performance of your well-being program.

EMPLOYEE FEEDBACK FORM

Creating an Employee Feedback Form is a valuable tool for gathering input and insights from your employees regarding your well-being program, workplace environment, and other relevant topics. The following is an example of template for an Employee Feedback Form that you can adapt to your organization's needs:

Employee Feedback Form Template:

Title: [Your Organization's Name] Employee Feedback Form

Instructions: This form is intended to collect honest and anonymous feedback from employees. Your input is important to us, and it will be used to improve our well-being program and workplace environment.

Section 1: Employee Information (Optional)

- Name: [Optional—Employees can choose to provide their names if they wish]
- Department/Team: [Optional—Employees can mention their department or team]

Section 2: Feedback on the Well-being Program

1. How would you rate the overall effectiveness of our well-being program?
   - Excellent
   - Very Good
   - Good
   - Fair
   - Poor
2. Which specific components or aspects of the well-being program do you find most valuable, and why?

   [Open text response]
3. Are there any aspects of the well-being program that you feel could be improved? If so, please provide suggestions.

   [Open text response]
4. Have you encountered any challenges or obstacles in participating in the well-being program?

   [Open text response]

Section 3: General Workplace Feedback

5. On a scale of 1 to 10, how satisfied are you with your overall work environment and conditions?
   - (1) Extremely Dissatisfied
   - (10) Extremely Satisfied
6. Do you have any concerns or suggestions related to your work environment or workplace culture that you would like to share?

   [Open text response]

Section 4: Suggestions and Comments

7. Is there anything else you would like to share with us, whether related to the well-being program, workplace, or any other topic?

   [Open text response]

Section 5: Contact Information (Optional)

- Email Address: [Optional – Employees can choose to provide their email for follow-up if they wish]

Section 6: Declaration

I understand that my feedback is confidential, and I have the option to remain anonymous. I am providing this feedback voluntarily.

- [Checkbox] I wish to remain anonymous.

Submit Button: [Include a button for employees to submit their feedback]

This template is a starting point, and you can modify it to fit your organization's specific needs and culture. It's essential to ensure that the feedback process is confidential and that employees feel comfortable sharing their thoughts and concerns. After collecting the feedback, analyse the data, identify common themes, and use the insights to make improvements to your well-being program and workplace environment.

PRE- AND POST-PROGRAM SURVEYS

Pre- and Post-Program Surveys are essential tools for assessing the impact of your well-being program on employees. These surveys help you collect data before and after the program implementation to measure changes in attitudes, behaviours, and well-being. The following are the examples of templates for both pre-program and post-program surveys:

Pre-Program Survey Template:

Title: [Your Organization's Name] Well-being Program Pre-Program Survey

Instructions: This survey is designed to understand your current well-being and gather information before the program begins. Your responses will remain confidential.

Section 1: Demographic Information (Optional)

- Name: [Optional]
- Department/Team: [Optional]
- Job Title: [Optional]
- Years of Service: [Optional]

Section 2: Current Well-being

1. On a scale of 1 to 10, how would you rate your overall well-being?
   - (1) Very Poor
   - (10) Excellent
2. How often do you experience stress at work or in your personal life?
   - Rarely
   - Occasionally
   - Frequently
   - Very Frequently

Section 3: Well-being Behaviours and Practices

3. Which well-being practices do you currently engage in? (Select all that apply)
   - Regular exercise
   - Healthy eating habits
   - Adequate sleep
   - Mindfulness or meditation
   - Social activities
   - Stress management techniques
   - None of the above
4. Do you have any specific well-being goals or areas you'd like to improve on? If so, please describe.

   [Open text response]

Section 4: Expectations from the Well-being Program

5. What are your expectations for the well-being program?

   [Open text response]

Post-Program Survey Template

Title: [Your Organization's Name] Well-being Program Post-Program Survey

Instructions: This survey is intended to gather feedback on your experience with the well-being program and to assess any changes in your well-being. Your responses will remain confidential.

Section 1: Demographic Information (Optional)

- Name: [Optional]
- Department/Team: [Optional]
- Job Title: [Optional]
- Years of Service: [Optional]

Section 2: Program Experience

1. How would you rate your overall experience with the well-being program?
   - Excellent
   - Very Good
   - Good
   - Fair
   - Poor
2. Did you actively participate in the well-being program?
   - Yes
   - No

Section 3: Changes in Well-being

3. On a scale of 1 to 10, how would you rate your current overall well-being compared to before the program?
   - (1) Worse
   - (10) Better
4. Have you noticed any changes in your well-being as a result of the program? If so, please describe.

   [Open text response]

Section 4: Program Impact

5. Which specific components of the program do you believe had the most significant impact on your well-being?

   [Open text response]

6. What additional well-being resources or initiatives would you like to see in the future?

   [Open text response]

Use these survey templates as a starting point, and customize them to fit the specific goals and content of your well-being program. Administer the pre-program survey before the program begins, and the post-program survey after its completion. Analyse the responses to assess the program's impact and gather valuable feedback for continuous improvement.

Index